Non-Governmental Organizations (NGOs) and Sustainable Development in Sub-Saharan Africa

Advance Praise for *Non-Governmental Organizations (NGOs) and Sustainable Development in Sub-Saharan Africa*

"Professor Robert A. Dibie is an expert on public management of NGOs. He has assembled a group of African scholars who have a great deal of knowledge in the field of NGOs operations in Africa. The text makes a great overview of the management of NGOs in Africa." —**Kayode Makinde**, vice chancellor, Babcock University Nigeria

"This book is a magnificent collection of African minds and cases on collective approaches to sustainable development in the continent. Every African, especially political leaders or aspirants, should take a retreat with this book and reassess why we lack conscience and keep our people characterized as underdeveloped." —**Emmanuel Otu**, associate professor of chemistry, Indiana University Southeast

"This book is an intelligent discussion of an important international phenomenon. It is a frank, honest, and balanced examination with special appeal to practitioners and administrators. The study's examination of challenges and opportunities facing NGOs in sub-Saharan Africa is both intriguing and provocative." —**Samory Rashid**, associate professor of political science, Indiana State University

Non-Governmental Organizations (NGOs) and Sustainable Development in Sub-Saharan Africa

EDITED BY
ROBERT A. DIBIE

LEXINGTON BOOKS

A division of
ROWMAN & LITTLEFIELD PUBLISHERS, INC.
Lanham • Boulder • New York • Toronto • Plymouth, UK

LEXINGTON BOOKS

A division of Rowman & Littlefield Publishers, Inc.
A wholly owned subsidiary of The Rowman & Littlefield Publishing Group, Inc.
4501 Forbes Boulevard, Suite 200
Lanham, MD 20706

Estover Road
Plymouth PL6 7PY
United Kingdom

British Library Cataloguing in Publication Information Available

Library of Congress Cataloging-in-Publication Data

Non-governmental organizations (NGOs) and sustainable development in sub-Saharan Africa / edited by Robert A. Dibie.
p. cm.
Includes index.
ISBN-13: 978-0-7391-1653-1 (cloth : alk. paper)
ISBN-10: 0-7391-1653-3 (cloth : alk. paper)
1. Sustainable development—Africa, Sub-Saharan. 2. Non-governmental organizations—Africa, Sub-Saharan. 3. Sustainable development—Africa, Sub-Saharan—Case studies. 4. Economic development projects—Africa, Sub-Saharan—Case studies. I. Dibie, Robert A., 1956–
HC800.Z9E55652 2008
338.967'07—dc22 2007033254

Printed in the United States of America

The paper used in this publication meets the minimum requirements of American National Standard for Information Sciences—Permanence of Paper for Printed Library Materials, ANSI/NISO Z39.48–1992.

This book is dedicated to two special women in my life, my mother Mrs. Sarah Eloh Dibie and my beautiful wife Josephine Dibie.
Josephine thanks for being extremely patient throughout yet another book project.

Contents

List of Figures ix

List of Tables xi

List of Abbreviations xiii

Preface xv

Acknowledgements xviii

Chapter 1
Introduction: NGOs and Human Development in Africa: Theory and Model for Collaboration
Robert A. Dibie 1

Chapter 2
NGOs and Development Administration in Africa
Ogwo Jombo Umeh 27

Chapter 3
NGOs, Public Bureaucracy, and Sustainable Development in Africa
Robert A. Dibie 47

Chapter 4
The Perception of NGOs Performance in Anglophone Africa
Akpovire Oduaran 65

Chapter 5
NGOs and Community Based Environmental Projects in Botswana and Ethiopia
Saliwe Kawewe 85

Chapter 6
NGOs and Development in Botswana and Nigeria
Robert A. Dibie and Saliwe Kawewe 107

Chapter 7
Motivation and Volunteerism in NGOs in Ghana and Nigeria
Josephine Dibie and Robert A. Dibie 121

Chapter 8
NGOs and Development in Cameroon
Wilfred Gabsa 139

Chapter 9
NGOs and Religion in Zimbabwean Uncertain Times
Johnston Akuma-Kalu Njoku 157

Chapter 10
NGOs and Development in the Democratic Republic of Congo
Francois N. Muyumba 173

Chapter 11
Strategic Repositioning of NGOs for Sustainable Development in Africa
Felix Moses Edoho 203

Chapter 12
Current and Future Roles of NGOs in the Empowerment of Women in Africa
Josephine Dibie and Robert A. Dibie 229

Chapter 13
Public Administration and Sustainability in Africa
Robert A. Dibie and Ogwo Jombo Umeh 253

Index 275

About the Contributors 281

List of Figures

Figure 1.1: Model on How NGOs and National Governments Could Foster Partnership in Achicving Sustainable Development 16

Figure 5.1 Model for NGOs and Community Based Development Policy 100

Figure 7.1 Relationship Between Met Expectations and Perceived Organizational Support 133

Figure 10.1 Partnership Model 180

Figure 11.1 The Structural Role of NGOs in Society 209

Figure 11.2 Strategic Management Model 217

List of Tables

Table 3.1 NGOs and Their Activities in Some African Nations 56

Table 3.2 Predicament Facing NGOs in Africa 57

Table 5. 1 Climate and Ecology of Botswana 90

Table 5.2 Africa Population Growth Rate (1980-1997) 97

Table 6.1 Perception of the Citizens of Botswana and Nigeria of the Role of NGOs 111

Table 6.2 Types of Collaborations 114

Table 7. 1 Names of NGOs that Participated in the Study 128

Table 7.2 Profile of NGO Staff and Volunteers that Responded 129

Table 7.3A Motivational Factors and Expectations of NGO Staff and Volunteers 130

Table 7.3B Motivational Factors and Expectations of NGO Staff and Volunteers 131

Table 7.4 Levels of NGO Employees Expectations and Attitudes 132

Table 8.1 NGOs in the Domain of Economic Development 145

Table 8.2 An Indication of Feminist Associations 146

Table 8.3 The Evolution of AIDS Infection from 1990-1998 148

Table 11.1 Descriptive Understanding of NGOs 206

Table 11.2 NGOs Activities in Kenya 212

Table 12.1 Policies for Women's Empowerment 238

List of Abbreviations

ADF	African Development Fund
BBC	British Broadcasting Corporation
BONGO	Business Organization Non-Governmental Organization
CADEC	Catholic Development Commission
CEDAW	Communique for the Eradication of all Discrimination Against Women
CBO	Community-based Organizations
CIDA	Canadian International Development Agency
CIG	Common Initiative Group
COWAN	Country Women's Association of Nigeria
DRC	Democratic Republic of Congo
EEC	European Economic Community
FONGO	Funder Organization Non-Governmental Organization
FWCW	Fourth World Conference on Women
GEF	Global Environmental Facility
GONGO	Government Organized Non-Governmental Organization
GRO	Grassroots Organizations
GSO	Grassroots Support Organizations
HRWWR	Human Right Watch World Report
IITA	International Institute of Tropical Agriculture
IMF	International Monetary Fund
INGO	International Non-Government Organization
KANGO	Kenya HIV/AID NGOs Consortium
MSO	Membership Support Organizations
NANGO	National Association of Non-Governmental Organizations
NFGO	Non for Gain Organization
NGO	Non-Governmental Organizations
NORAD	Norwegian For Development
ODA	Official Development Assistance
OAU	Organization of African Unity
PONGO	Political Non-Governmental Organization
QUANGO	Quasi Autonomous Non-Governmental Organizations
SAP	Structural Adjustment Program
SIDA	Swedish International Development Agency
TANGO	Tanzania Association of Non-Government Organization

UN	United Nations
UNEP	United Nations Environmental Program
UNEU	United Nations Emergencies Unit for Ethiopia
USAID	United States International Development Agency
WFP	World Food Program
ZCBC	Zimbabwe Catholic Bishop's Conference

Preface

NGOs and Sustainable Development in Sub-Saharan Africa

Robert A. Dibie

National governments, non-governmental organizations (NGOs), the private sector and civil society throughout Sub-Saharan Africa have been exploring various opportunities to improve the social and economic base of their people. These institutions have, however, failed to effectively collaborate in the coordination of their development goals. Over the past five decades the African continent has been undergoing a process of structural transformation in the areas of governance, economic, cultural, technological and institutional growth, however, the citizens of several African nations have not shared in these new dimensions. This shortcoming is related to the crisis of political legitimacy that is characterized by increasing distance between citizens and their institutions of governance across sub-Saharan Africa.

In addition, the critical issues that are also worrisome to the African people and have spilled over to the political problems and inefficient institutions of governance are the crisis of efficiency, lack of legitimacy, the crisis of identity and the crisis of equity. Due to these four crises and the inability of national governments in Africa to effectively deal with them, NGOs have become the new institution that has been defending the needs, interests and values of the people in the past four decades.

As a result of this predicament in the continent of Africa several international non-governmental organizations (INGOs), community based organizations and civil society organizations are beginning to attempt to fill the current gap of governance and legitimacy policy making dilemma that several nations face. During the period (1960-present) when several sub-Saharan African nations have been finding it difficult to confront the issues central to their governance, NGOs have emerged as the most trusted institutions. The new active role of NGOs has also created a new set of problems in several African nations. In this respect, national and regional governments have been undermined in responding to the social and economic development needs of their people. In some African countries, this lack of regards for the powers of the national government has made some regimes to crack down on the activities of NGOs.

In the past two decades the concept of globalization has been affecting several African nations in a different dimension. One of the instruments of globalization is the global civil society which is made of NGOs and other form of organizes popular expression and representation. These global civil society institutions have been positively influencing the day-to day operations of governments of several African nations, NGOs development projects and human rights policies. In practice, however, community based organizations in Africa continue to seek the dissolution of the centralized powers of their national governments. They seem to prefer its replacement with local governments, NGOs and grassroots organizations at all levels of the society.

This book examines the role of NGOs in the sustainable development processes being explored in the African continent. In the past three decades several students, scholars and practitioners who have been interested in examining NGOs activities pertaining to Sub-Saharan African countries and processes of achieving sustainable development have had a difficult time finding a comprehensive book on the subject. Consequently, such readers often become disappointed, frustrated and discouraged.

This book explores the intriguing challenges that NGOs face in the developing processes of the African people. It is intended to provide guidance for civil society organizations and their client groups who are engaged in the struggle on how to find viable means to collaborate with NGOs, the private and the public sectors in the development of social and economic base of their nation. While the involvement of civil societies in the achievement of sustainable development is an extremely complex process, this book argues that it requires increased knowledge and cooperation on the part of government officials, NGOs staff, the private sector, unions, professional leaders, and community groups. Therefore, community based organizations and public servants must carefully consider whether they possess the necessary institutional resources as well as economic development opportunities before they embark on any activity.

Sustainable development activities might not be useful or reasonable for every rural community in Africa. However, communities, irrespective of their size or location must consider their economic destiny as a major component of their political agenda. One thing is very clear; the forces of globalization or sustainable development do not respect national, regional, rural, or community boundaries. This book clearly states that for African nations to succeed they must find ways other than the centralized powers of the national government. In addition, the transformation of several sub-Saharan African nations in the twenty-first century will be a function of many factors. African nations must disengage themselves from the notion that good public and political leaders are born, not made. African states should put greater emphasis on the development of political and managerial skills through formal education, industrial training, and seminars. Developing nations in Africa should embrace the assistance of NGOs and other civil societies in seeking this transformation. This book stresses that unless African nations transform their political and managerial talents the continent will not be able to achieve sustainable development.

The primary audiences for this book are students and administrators who are planning to work in nonprofit organizations or NGOs in Africa or other developing nations. The book will also be very useful for professional practitioners of local economic development agencies at the regional, city or rural governments. It is hoped that it will be a reference for professional practitioners and economic development or planning specialists as they carry out their responsibilities. In addition, the book is intended to provide guidance for community based organizations and donor NGOs clients who are engaged in the struggle to find viable means to develop the economic base of their communities. Policymakers at either the national and regional governments or the community level will find the book useful in exploring the role that NGOs, the private sector, unions, community groups, and other civil society institutions can play in local economic and employment development activities.

This book is a text full with many practical experiences. At the same time it is also a statement about how to understand the crucial need for national and regional governments to collaborate with NGOs, the private sector and community based organizations in the development process of a nation. It is a book of concepts, instruction, and cases. I hope this arrangement of materials will provide a process and a set of values for most of the intended readers.

Robert A. Dibie

Acknowledgments

I am most grateful to the NGOs staff and public servants in several African countries who responded to my survey and assisted me during my field research. This book also bears marks of positive influence of many scholars of the Third World Studies conference in the United States. The list of my debtors is long and the mere mention of their names hardly repays my debt to them. The following professors reviewed the manuscript and provided thoughtful and serious evaluation before it was sent to the press: Jombo Umeh, California State University Hayward; Saliwe Kawewe, Southern Illinois University; Johnston Akuma-Kalu Njoku, Western Kentucky University; Akpovire Oduaran, University of Botswana; Felix Edoho, Lincoln University Missouri; and Professor Toyin Falola, University of Texas Austin. I also want to express my gratitude to the scholars who contributed to this book.

The book has also profited from many of the graduate students who have taken non-profit organizations management and NGOs courses from me. These students have challenged me to give them the most and the best that I can. I hope this book goes some distance to meeting their challenge. Authors of the various chapters accept full responsibility for the content of their work, and they invite comments. The country case studies included in this book are based on field research and composites of several experts experience on NGOs and rural economic development in Africa.

Dr. Willie Clarke-Okah, of the commonwealth of learning Vancouver, Canada has graciously read some of the chapters on NGOs and sustainable development with a critical eye. He has also generously shared with me his extensive knowledge of western donors and NGOs operations in Africa and his perspectives generally. His influence has definitely improved the chapters on administration and sustainability.

I am grateful to my wife and best friend Josephine Dibie who kept my eye on writing not only a successful book but a book of quality. Only her deep devotion to both quality and success could have encouraged, inspired, guided, nudged, and tolerated a husband possessed with a mercurial temperament.

Robert A. Dibie

Chapter 1

Introduction: NGOs and Human Development in Africa: Theory and Model for Collaboration

Robert A. Dibie

Post independence governments in several African nations have experienced the emergence of non-governmental organizations (NGOs). The increasing participation of NGOs in the funding of projects in the African continent has reflected a shift in western industrialized nations' donor assistance programs formally channeled through regional and national governments. While the activities of NGOs have mostly been positive in some countries, in other nations they have been accused of intruding into the domestic affairs of the indigenous government. This view is somewhat worrisome because most nations in Africa depend mostly on international non-governmental organizations (INGOs) for a significant aspect of their welfare, social, education, religious and health programs. There is a growing appreciation of the role that NGOs are beginning to play in meeting aid and development goals in most African nations (Patel and Wilson 2004). NGOs have been commended for being a progressive instrument that has formed some integration between the development agenda and the interests of poor people. NGOs programs in Africa have also helped in the liberation of women, poverty alleviation, increase in civil society organizations participation in governance and human development in general (Obiyan 2005). To help us understand the dynamics of NGOs operations in several African nations, this chapter will attempt to address two questions. First, what are the conditions in African nations that seem to attract NGOs? Second, are NGOs really interested in human development in the African continent nations or are their interests more consistent with the needs of external funding agencies or donors?

The conditions in most African countries that seem to attract NGOs are numerous. Julius Ihonvbere (2004) pointed out that political and economic instability, infrastructural and institutional decay, poverty, hunger, disease, bureaucratic inefficiency, and the near collapse of educational and research institutions are some of the reasons why sustainable development has been very slow in Africa. These problems often galvanized NGOs to intervene in nations that are plague with devastating conditions. NGOs general believe in helping to alleviate the poor and increase the welfare of deprived groups in several African nations. Thus, it is the failure of the respective national governments of most African nations, their institutions and structure in addressing the problems of the welfare, poverty and human development that has led to the emergence of NGOs in most African nations. Phillip Huxtable (1998) and Eghosa Osaghae (2005) contend that public leaders use their positions in most African nations to extract wealth for self-enrichment while the majority of the population in their nation is left to fend for itself or dependent on INGOs for their daily health, nutrition, social and human development. He further exerts that in most Africa countries, service in the military or police force is a license to steal. Officers who have benefited from the corrupt systems now parade themselves as millionaires and co-opted to contest for political position. Elections are easily rigged by these ex-military officers as in the case of Nigeria, Rwanda, Cote d' Ivoire, Ghana, Uganda and Sierra Leone. The aftermath of these practices is that these African nations are often left with few resources with which to pursuit its sustainable development goals.

The lack of trust of national and regional governments in most African countries is one of the reasons why donor agencies from western industrialized nations prefer to channel their funding through INGOs. The distrust resulted from the level of corruption that prevails among public officials of some African countries. The instability and institutional decay that are enormous in the public sector of African nations also make international donors to feel that leaders from such nations lack the insight to better understand how quality public management, strategic planning and accountability can effectively help to ensure gains in productivity, mission readiness, efficiency and the ability achieve sustainable development.

NGOs as used in this text refers to different types of charities, volunteer groups, religious and cultural groups, people, cooperatives, community associations, and grassroots organizations who are non-profit seeking private organizations. NGOs are regional, national and international groups, and communities that tend to bring people together for the purpose of providing services and solving community problems. Their major goals are to provide welfare, economic growth to human development around the world, observe religious beliefs, promoting social and cultural beliefs as well as communicating ideas around the world. Generally, NGOs are less bureaucratic in their structure and are committed to poverty alleviation and human development. Unlike government who tend to use an urban-rural approach in the implementation of public policy, NGOs prefer to use grassroots tactical strategies in executing their projects in several African nations. They adapt to changing environmental conditions and manage changes effectively, constantly transitioning to new strategies, turning as necessary in new directions to achieve their goals or missions of human development.

INGOs operating in the African continent have been both a messy reality and a vision. As a messy reality, INGOs includes the various associations, groups, NGOs, movements that are engaged in negotiations at global level (Kaldor 2005). INGOs include the American evangelical churches, the American Enterprise Institute, the Muslim Brotherhood, as well as the "nice" progressive" civic groups like Ammesty International and the World Social Forum. As a vision Mary Kaldor (2005) pointed out that INGOs could be associated with a global constitutional order, where different visions of the future, including global America, global poverty, global Christianity and global Islam are debated, argued and shaped. In the past five decades the role of NGOs has increased in African countries because of two reasons. In the first place, the prescription of the structural adjustment policies (SAP) by the World Bank and the International Monetary Fund (IMF) to salvage the failing economy of many African nations (Onimode 2004; Patel and Wilson 2004). The introduction of SAP has caused more problems than anticipated. The consequences of SAP in many African nations have been that of increased poverty and underdevelopment. Further, the instrument of globalization and privatization that was included in the SAP created a devastating trend of poverty and tremendous underdevelopment gap between the Northern and Southern nations (Onimode 2004). These gaps became very difficult for governments in the African continent to handle. As a result of looking for alternative organizations that would salvage the devastating rate of poverty and underdevelopment, NGOs became recognized as a prominent institution in the development process in most African nations. During the era of SAP, NGOs have become important instruments for providing credit and other resources, promoting economic development, reducing poverty as well as managing the negative impact of SAP.

The second reason for the emergence of NGOs is associated with the deliberate attempts by the United Nations, the World Bank and the IMF to delegate aid programs to NGOs (Grant and Keohane 2005). These international institutions preferred NGOs to fill the gap that both government and the private sectors could not effectively manage in several African nations. NGOs were a better choice to national and regional governments in many African countries because of their commitment to social welfare, human development and change. Deborah Eade (2000) pointed out that the rise of neoliberalism has generated a powerful international ideology about what constitutes good governance, democratization and the proper roles of the state and civil society in development. From this perspective NGOs became a convenient instrument through which nonprofit organizations could promote social liberalism and political pluralism. Hulme and Edward (1997: 21) and Manuel Castells (2005) contends that the notion of "new world order" and "global civil society" that were introduced in the 1980s and 1990s brought with it new functions for NGOs to play. This new world order concept also exposed the limitation of the national government and its institutions in meeting the challenges of most African countries that were very poor.

The fact that social, health, education, economic and infrastructural development problems have increasingly transcend the powers of most national governments in Africa, INGOs has been attracted to the continent to take action. Such global awareness of the problems facing African nations does not have pan-religious elements; rather it is to be argued to taken a secular humanitarian approach which is rooted in the growing awareness of the daily life of the African people. This approach has also galvanized more globalize flow of resources and processes to the continent. Bruce Mazlish (2005) contends that as a result this multi-factored process of globalization, existing governments in Africa are less and less able to shape the current world around their respective nations. This process has also created a vacuum in which national decisions are often on the wrong scale for problems that are not only international but global in dimension.

The public and private sectors of most African countries have been unable to generate enough economic resources to meet the needs of their citizens, leaving the affected nations to be dependent on foreign aid and INGOs. Further, the lack of vigorous proactive programs in meeting the public needs and the inability to sustain excellence by national governments of poor countries created underdevelopment. Corruption and mismanagement have also led to debt burden as well as opened up a new dimension for NGOs as the only organization that could truly help reduce poverty and increase human development. In several African nations, NGOs are now being favored by donors in western developed nations because they are perceived as being self-renewing organizations that can create and sustain a transformational environment in leadership, human and resource development and management.

Another question that this text attempt to address is: the extent to which NGOs are interested in poverty alleviation and human development in African countries. Are NGOs interests more consistent with the needs of external funding agencies or donors? Stephen Ndegwa (1996) and Deborah Eade (2000) contends that several NGOs in Africa tend to support or introduce projects that are consistent with the interest of organizations in the western industrial countries that fund them. These western organizations tend to support the promotion of democracy as a condition for receiving funding and other aids from the west. In order to continue to receive funding, NGOs consciously take directives from donors in their nation of origin. This practice according to Stephen Ndegwa has help to promote and galvanized programs that enhance western economic and political interests in the African continent.

Kelechi Kalu (2004) and Andrew Ewoh (2004) pointed out that the United States, Canada, France and Great Britain has consistently been very influential in the ways government in most African nations run their affairs. The influence of these four western industrialized nations is further promoted by their NGOs who operate in Angola, Kenya, Nigeria, Ghana, Cameroon, Ethiopia, Guinea, Botswana, Zambia, Zimbabwe and South Africa. If African nations do not succumb to the desires of these western progressive economic and political states, there are often the tendencies for projects implemented by NGOs from such states to fold up. Shelly Feldman (2003: 22) exerts that NGOs act as brokers speaking on behalf of their members rather than mobilizing people to speak on their behalf. Further, she argued that NGOs serve as buffers between citizens and states, militating against rather than encouraging people to struggle on their own together with others who share their interests. Pearce's (2000: 53) contend that while NGOs have succeeded in influencing official donors and governments in African nations on individual projects, and even on some programs themes, they have failed to bring about more fundamental changes in attitudes and ideology, on which real progress ultimately depends.

Phillip Huxtable (1998) exerts that the resources of international financial institutions (IFIs), INGOs, domestic political actors and wealthier nations from Europe and North America tend to influence politics of African countries. The large American and European donations that support the United Nations (UN) and several INGOs has prompt claims that NGOs are tools of these western nations. The fact that Arab, African and Latin American nations give less aid to poor countries around the world means they have to rely on western donations (Ewoh 2004). Further, most of the income from the relatively few profitable enterprises goes to transnational corporation (TNCs) operating in Africa and little is used to promote economic development within the nation. These transnational corporations, as in the case of Nigeria, Botswana, South Africa, Zimbabwe and the Democratic Republic of Congo have often caused devastating environmental problem for the indigenous people. Their influence, however, on the national government actors has made it impossible for them to be punished or accountable to the indigenous people.

Ruth Grant and Robert Keohane (2005) pointed out that lack of adequate accountability by NGOs has heightened concerns about the way they use and abuse power around the world. They stressed that INGOs are not legitimated by ties to defined public. As a result most INGOs operating in the African continent do not have well-defined procedures for accountability to anyone other than financial contributors and quite a small set of people who are their senior members in Europe and North America. This does not come as a surprise because NGOs are formed on the basis of entrepreneurial initiatives and not a process of delegation. Thus, holding NGOs accountable will only be relevant when authority were delegated to their managers operating in the African continent.

Some scholars have argued that INGOs have not been able to eradicate poverty in developing nations because of the geo-political motivation behind aid-giving (Eade 2000; van Diesen and Walker 1999). This ambivalence is further clouded by the misunderstanding between bilateral and multinational aid agencies and donors on how to make significant contribution to poverty eradication in the African continent. Most African nations are confronted with this dilemma because their burden put constraints on the government's ability to invest in sustainable development programs in education, health and technology transfer. Therefore, donors should not only micromanage NGOs funding, they should also consider speedier and extensive debt relief to African nations. This is crucial if poverty in African will ever be eradicated. The fact that NGOs presence in most African nations have contribute immensely to human and material development, financial resources, administrative know-how and other infrastructures that have spillover to far reaching cultural, social, economic and political transformation in the African continent makes scholars to view their intension as positive (Castells 2005; Ewoh 2004; Onimode 2004).

In the past two decades research findings relative to the intriguing question of whether or not the proliferation of NGOs has resulted in political change and economic development in the African continent. Some scholars indicated that it is impossible to prove a relationship between the withering of the authoritarian state in Africa and the rise of NGOs and grassroots social movements that (Hirschman 1987:98). On the other hand, scholars such as Sanyal (1994:40) and Williams (2003) contend that the political impact of bottom-up [NGO] projects has been less striking than their economic impact in most parts of the African continent. William (2003) in particular noted that if NGOs do not contribute to political change, it is because NGOs may have voice, but not vote.

In another study conducted by Welch (2003:325), he found that: "African human rights NGOs ameliorate rather than transform situations. According to him NGOs monitor and analyze, rather than achieve rapid, blanket changes. NGOs take incremental steps rather than massive leaps. Welch, (2003) and Chazan (1994:276) however, contended that NGOs seem to have played a vital role in the process of political change in Africa, where they have also been instrumental in pluralizing the institutional environment by encouraging political participation. NGOs dependence on funding from western industrial countries has somewhat emasculated their ability to serve as catalysts for the poor in several African countries (Edwards and Hulme 1995:20).

NGOs acclaimed humanitarian sympathy has also not been positively acknowledge by African intellectuals. Most African scholars and political leaders view foreign NGOs with reservation, and skepticism. These African leaders see foreign NGOs' operations in Africa through the prism of their colonial antecedents (Waiguchu 1999; Manji and O'Coill 2002; Welch 2003). Generally their perception about the role of foreign NGOs in African development is that they represents a continuity of the work of their precursors, the missionaries and voluntary organizations that cooperated in Europe's colonization and control of Africa. According to (Welch 2003: 317) missionaries operation in the African continent during and after the colonial era could be summarized as: First they had the Bible and we had the land. Then we had the Bible and they had the land. Welch (2003) contend that this behavior of missionaries during the colonial period can still be perceived the way foreign NGOs now operate through out the African continent.

Although NGOs that are funded by western industrial countries tend to seek economic and political reforms in several African nations, such reforms should not be imposed. Appropriate reforms in the African continent should be mutually agreed upon. Imposing reforms is another way of being authoritarian and dose defuses democratic tendencies that the western industrialized nations seem to be promoting in Africa countries. Development in African nations and other developing countries cannot be successful without a sustaining objective, political will, and an effective organization for the mobilization of popular support. African nations will have to come up with a government structure that encourages responsible political action and facilitates the involvement of a wide cross section of the citizens in the development process. African governments will have to form partnership with the private sector, NGOs and grassroots organizations in the process. Sustainable development policies capable of bringing about substantial improvement of conditions such as poverty alleviation, human development and basic infrastructure would require the elimination of special privileges for the few, the dismemberment of large land holdings, and the creation of greater social responsibilities on the part of the private sector.

NGOs Operations in African Nations

To what extent are NGOs playing increasing role in the sustainable development process in Africa countries? In order to answer this question, this book will provide an overview of NGOs operations in many African nations. NGOs general has been noted for selecting the poorer groups or targeted groups communities needed to be saved from devastating human conditions. NGOs play very important roles in choosing appropriate programs or activities that are concerned with alleviation of poverty and its impact on welfare of workers and disadvantaged sections of the society. The appropriate needs are then added to projects in such a way that they meet the immediate needs and requirements for the sustainable development process of a particular country. These NGOs strategic plan has also helped enormously in improving the living standards of several poor people and in the long rum encourage grassroots organization's participation in the developing process (Obiyan 2005; Patel and Wilson 2004). All these grassroots mobilization activities engineered by NGOs have contributed to human welfare, democracy and economic development around the African continent.

The modernization theory argues that since foreign investment and NGOs intervention and activities in the African continent has promoted growth and development, such practice could be considered as contributing positively towards human and social progress. Further, globalization has into question existing governance system and the role of nations in Africa in determining their own destiny. The introduction of new markets, technological innovations such as the internet, new actors and networks have given rise to opportunities for addressing poverty and fostering global solidarity, the exchange of ideas, knowledge, and shared communities to achieve human development (Patel and Wilson 2004). The opportunities to promote social and democratic development in Africa have also increased the era of globalization with the proliferation and growth of domestic, transnational and international civil society organizations in Africa. Shelley Feldman (2003) contends that NGOs interests are often complemented by state initiatives to enhance the services and training available to rural dwellers, especially women. NGOs also focus on reducing women's fertility and increase their income, access to credit, and opportunities for literacy training. They also tend to seek transformation of women's condition that often breeds gender inequality in developing countries. NGOs generally believe that the delivery of resources to rural dwellers could increase democratic representation and lead to more equitable access to other public and private institutions.

As in the case of Ghana, Rwanda, Botswana and South Africa NGOs have embraced modernization efforts introduced by regional and national governments for market base inequality. At the same time NGOs have supported the notion of civil society as the arena of democratic alternative in Botswana. This approach has led to the debate on social mobilization of marginalized individuals in the operating nation. The current trend of social mobilization has galvanized the notion of empowerment. Governments in Kenya, Zimbabwe, Nigeria, and South Africa have now introduced programs for women empowerment in line with projects that NGOs have been promoting.

In Botswana and Ethiopia the goals of some NGOs operating there have been to restructure responsibility from the national and regional governments to family and communities. This NGOs initiative has help to promote the view that privatization policy is an appropriate tool to achieve sustainable development. Hulme and Edward (1997) and Feldman (2003) exert that such NGOs initiative has help to legitimize the abrogation of state accountability in providing for common good, reinforcing individual responsibility and creating social relations which are fully compatible with the sustainable and human development goals.

NGOs have shown increase interests in promoting democracy and human rights in Kenya and many West African nations. Ndegwa (1996) and Fisher (1998) pointed that the GERDESS network in the sub region of West Africa includes election monitoring. Other NGOs such as the African Partners of IRED (development Innovation and Networks located in Geneva) have been very active in promoting democracy in Africa. The IRED also hold conferences regularly in Burkina Faso to enhance the democratic process in that nation.

Many INGOs poured in aids to help famine victims in Ethiopia, Sudan, Zimbabwe, and Botswana. NGOs have donated 13.4 million United States dollars to help resolve the environmental problems in Botswana (Eade 2000; Welch 2003). The funding of this project was provided by the United Nation Environmental Program (UNEP) and the Global Environmental Facility (GEF). The funding was made available to help rural communities restore local plants, improve depleted soil and create new jobs opportunities.

The 1980s marked the period when several INGOs flock to North and East Africa to help famine victims. In spite of the aids NGOs provided for Sudan, Ethiopia, Zimbabwe and Chad the people in the rural communities of these nations has been faced with devastating environmental conditions. Some African scholars have argued that foreign NGOs and the national governments were not doing enough to help solve the severe environmental problems in these sub-Saharan African nations (Asefa 2003; Dibie 2001; James 1993).

The inability of NGOs and their aids to understand the dynamics of implementing a coevolution agricultural system is one of the reasons why after over three decades of NGOs assistance the indigenous people of Botswana and Ethiopia are still dependant on foreign aids rather than growing their own food.

In Ethiopia NGOs such as the World Food Program (WFP) has introduced the largest food-for-work program in Africa. Over the past three decades, peasants constructed more than one million kilometers of soil and stone bonds on agricultural land and built almost one-half million kilometers of hillside terrace. They also closed off more than 80,000 hectares of hillsides land to most forms of use to foster the regeneration of naturally occurring plant species, and planted 300,000 hectares of trees, much of it community woodcuts (Dibie 2001; Hoben 1995). The World Bank and the European Community have been very active in promoting development programs in various sectors of several African nations. The World Bank through its Sector Investment Program (SIP) has established a leading broad sector approach to investment lending which many poor African and Asia countries have benefited from immensely. World Bank programs around the African continent have encouraged capacity building initiatives as condition for governments to receive aid from foreign donors and the International Monetary fund (IMF). The SIP requires government from poor nations to accept aid under specific conducive conditions.

Most governments and the people in several African countries will not be able to achieve human development and poverty alleviation without the help of NGOs such as World Vision, Red Cross, Catholic Relief Services, and Oxford Committee for Famine Relief, Cooperatives of American Relief Everywhere, and various religious ministries. Network of churches and local organizations with links to foreign benefactors have also help in securing funding for emergency relief, health and education projects in many African countries.

The ability of INGOs to influence public policies in most African countries also determines the dimension of resources or aid that such nations might get from foreign donors (Ewoh 2004; Leather and Eade 2005; Patel and Wilson 2004). When this relationship is positive there is the tendency for NGOs to gain access to national government officials. Phillip Huxtable (1998) pointed out that INGOs tend to pressure African governments more directly. For example, in the Democratic Republic of Congo, Sierra Leone, Liberia, Ethiopia, Angola, Burundi and Rwanda INGOs and domestic NGOs with international funding have become the principal suppliers of many social services once provided by the government (Obiyan 2005). In most cases the indigenous government role in Africa has been reduced to that of coordination and regulation of INGOs projects. Patel and Wilson (2004) contend that INGOs has played a significant role in supporting African development through donor aid and in initiation and support of a wide range of civic service programs such as volunteering, community development, and community service program. They exerted that thirty six percent of the total number of social welfare and community service programs in countries such as Botswana, Malawi, Ghana, Lesotho, Tanzania, South Africa, Zimbabwe, Zambia, Mozambique and Swaziland are linked to INGOs.

As in the case of President Mobotu's regime in the Democratic Republic of Congo, NGOs play a very important role in the political process of most African nations by supporting opposition movement within the nation. Further, Domestic NGOs that are involved in religious, democratic, human rights, and women's rights groups, benefits immensely from their association with wider international NGOs connection (Huxtable 1998). Nyangoro and Shaw (1989) noted that INGO in Africa provided financial support, material resources, training; skilled personnel that help rural and grassroots organizations pressure the government and build capacity among the population. Further example of such INGOs support includes the role of International women's group in organizing part of Kenya's women's rights movement (Nzomo 1998). In Senegal several Islamic groups tend to attract resources from INGOs in other Islamic nations to the country (Villalon and Kane 1998).

In the twenty-first century sustainable economic development in many African countries would require poor nations in the continent to set economic, social and environmental goals that they can achieve with little or no help from foreign donors. African nations' governments should also be willing to establishing binding partnership with the private sector, NGOs and grassroots organizations to promote poverty alleviation, social and human development goals. The surplus that might be gained from the above productive partnership should be used in the underdeveloped areas within a country to provide human capital, basic infrastructure, and modern industries.

Impediment to Development in Africa

The impediments to development in Africa are numerous. The most obvious impediments to sustainable development in the continent are corruption, external debt, ethnic conflicts, poor governance environment, maladministration, poor leadership, inadequate rule of law and lack of accountability and transparency. Governance is used in this text to refer to the exercise of political power in managing the affairs of a nation. Politics is defined in this text as, what people do to get what they want from government. Ladipo Adamolekum (1999) and the World Bank (1994) contend that politics in most African countries are personalized and patronage appointments have become a very important instrument of maintaining power. In order for some African leaders to pragmatically maintain power, they assume broad discretionary authority in such a way that they at times lose legitimacy. The problem is further compounded by the mismanagement and maladministration of the wealth that is produced by the respective African nations. As currently practiced, several African leaders crave or lost for power, have made them control information and the media, co-opt NGOs and end up creating an environment that is not conducive for a dynamics economy.

The problem of development in Africa is not the unavailability of resources but the misuse of it thereof. Most Africans are suffering today while their greedy leaders don't seem to care. Several African leaders do not show a sense of social responsibility as indicated by their non-efforts to contribute to the well being of their citizens. Quite a number of African leaders do not show a sense of social justice, respect the law of their nation, and the rights of their people. While some dubious rich leaders have gotten richer, building empires and traveling around the world, the poor in their respective nations suffer and die (Obiyan 2005). Most political leaders and senior public managers at the apex of government hierarchy use their position to extract wealth for self-enrichment while the bulk of the population is left to fend for itself or in some cases dependent on NGOs to receive little amount of health and nutrition (Ayittey 2005; Vilallon and Huxtable 1998). Thus, most African leaders seek prosperity at the expense of their people.

The lack of a good judiciary system and an effective rule of law is another problem militating against development in Africa. Several Africa leaders tend to be above the law. Many present and former presidents of some African nations often ignore with disrepute the summons of the court. When this happens they seldom go unpunished by the government. This practice makes it difficult for the government to enforce accountability in the governance of a nation. Further, several African countries are characterized with the practice whereby political executives undermine the independence of the judiciary system through patronage appointments. In addition to these problem is the fact that judiciary administration of most African nations are confronted with a shortage of professional staff, inadequate funding, poor physical infrastructure, corruption and weak enforcement. The police department of many African nations is now known as the most corrupt institution.

Another impediment to development in several African nations is the duality of constitutional legalism versus actions that are partly or fully anchored in unconstitutional state power and action (Booysen 2004; Obiyan 2005). These constitutional shortcomings after independence limited or constraints the people of many African nations in seeking human rights, national self-determination and the right to practice democratic self-governance. Immediately after independence citizens of many African nations realized the need for an indigenous constitution. The need emerge because of citizens concern about presidential usurpation of power. Consequently the need led to constitutional amendment or call for political reform by local NGOs and civil society organizations in several African countries. These NGOs, community based organizations and civil society groups felt that the constitution that they inherited from their formal colonial regimes did not adequately advocate the peoples' political bill of rights and the assurance of legitimacy for their struggle for self-determination and shared governance.

William Tordoff (1997) and Susan Booysen (2004) pointed out that the major problems that African nations faced were not only those of economic development, in addition their primarily threat were non-acceptance and illegitimacy of the independence constitutions. They indicated that: (1) the preceding colonial African administration did not rule in terms of the principles of constitutionalism and that the European model of constitutionalism was seen to be foreign to Africa; and (2) African leaders did not know how to handle the concept of individual rights or the separation of powers between the head of state and the head of government. Therefore the combination of constitutional and legal concentration of powers in the president has caused a lot of political instability throughout the African continent.

The imminence of post independence politics in several African countries often led to the demands of ethnic groups and communities that lacked confidence in the impartiality of the new national government. The concern about partiality of the national government and brutal state powers also led ethnic, religious and civil society groups in Africa to try to maximize their position, constitutionally or otherwise. In most cases African leaders use the constitutional and legal provisions to effectively constrain opposition challenges. Despite the concern of INGOs and civil society organizations, the president of several African nations continues to enjoy a range of powers that allow them to exercise control over the electoral process. Such powers often allow them to make any statutory instrument as they consider necessary to ensure that elections are properly and efficiently conducted as well as deal with situations connected or resulting from elections. This provision makes the president to become the sole ruler of the electoral process. This is one of the reasons while incumbent presidents in several African nations are never defeated through the electoral process.

Thus, there is plenty of evidence around the African continent to substantiate the fact that sectional groups are merely interest groups competing for scarce economic resources and political leaders often invoke traditional sentiments to reinforce their appeal. Economic development in several African nations has been constrained by the complex combination of constitutional legalism in the conducting of elections and the excessive abuse of government powers. The great dilemma facing many African nations in the twenty-first century is to decide whether there are circumstances in which the manifestation of collective and social groups' rights should be promoted over adherence to unconstitutional and illegal procedure and injustice.

The lack of electoral legitimacy in several African countries constitutes one of the reasons while the political environment is not conducive for a dynamic economy. The history of many African nations also reveals that most of their political leaders do not like to relinquish their position or power to other person. If they do at all, it had to be a hand picked successor. This practice has made most African leaders to leave office unceremoniously because they are either forced out or they are unable to rig elections (Adamolekun 1999; Vilallon and Huxtable 1998). Further, many African countries do not have periodic, open, competitive, free and fair elections. As a result, rigged elections do not provide political executives the mandate to govern, rather it encourage them to be less accountable and transparent to the citizens. Adamolekun (1999) and Patel and Wilson (2004) contend that the absence of peace during election period without question, constitute a major explanation for the phenomenon of collapsing nation states in Africa. African nations such as Angola, Burundi, Democratic Republic of Congo, Liberia, Nigeria, Rwanda, Sierra Leone, Somalia, and Sudan have been characterized by persistent civil war and political crisis. These political crises, ethnic conflicts and civil strife also constitute a major reason why several African countries have not been able to achieve sustainable development.

Another problem affecting Africa's development is their desire to import most of their capita and consumer goods from western industrialized nations. This practice has made nearly all of them to accumulate external debt and balance of payment deficit. As a matter of fact, the debt and export ratio of several African nations has become unmanageable in the past twenty-five years (Ayittey 2005). The enormous debt crisis that most African nations face has also slow down their development process. The debt burden has also made them to be more dependent on the World Bank, the International Monetary Fund, the London and Paris clubs to help them finance their balance of payment predicament. The dependency on these international financial institutions carries the consequences of the imposition of the structural adjustment programs (SAP) on several African nations by these institutions. Payment of these debts has made it difficult for several African states to accumulate extra revenue to invest in the development of basic infrastructure.

The consequences of lack of accountability and transparency are corruption, abuse of public office for private again by political leaders and public administrators in several African nations. Adamolekun (1999) and Ayittey (2005) pointed out that persistent lack of development in Africa is due largely to leaders who are not committed to the economic development of their societies and who lack the legitimacy, skills, honesty and commitment to democracy. Onimode (2004) argued for instance that the problem of development in Nigeria is poor leadership. Being an officer in the military or police force in Nigeria and the Democratic Republic of Congo has been a license to steal from the public in the past three decades.

Although African countries were able to win the battle for independence for the continent, they lost the war on decolonizing their minds and have remained mired in uncertainty about their place in world development. Several African countries inherited the notion of the national government as the main agent of development from their former colonial administrators. The aftermath of this practice is the domination of the national economy by the government. While the improve performance of a nations' public management is often linked to reduced role of the government, the overextended role of the African state could be argued to be one of reasons for its poor performance. Peter Haruna (2004) pointed out that although several African states have introduced reforms in their civil service, such reforms have been based on Anglo-American ideas, that do not adapts well in a culture based on a different kind of localism. As a result there has been a mismatch between the lived experiences of the African people and their government operations. For instance, the African culture requires political leaders and public administrators to help relatives and protect ethnic and regional interests in issues of national policy. Under such circumstances a civil service reform issue should be how to balance such a strong feeling of ethnicity with the objectivity and neutral competence required of public managers and leaders. The inability of the government to understand this mismatch and effectively correct it often leads to inefficiency and underdevelopment.

The economic development of the western industrialized nations contributed to the underdevelopment of African countries (Frank 1969; Nafziger 1997). In the process of seeking globalization, western European countries colonized African nations and used them as their economic satellites. Therefore it can be argued that development in the African continent is not self generating nor autonomous but ancillary. The process of globalization has lead to brain drain of Africa's best scholars and scientists. Brain drain as used in this text refers to the flight of highly qualified Africans to other nations outside the continent due to low salary, inadequate infrastructure and lack of security. These African experts have become inventors of high technology, trade and business entrepreneurs, and educators in several western developed countries. Robert Dibie (2003) and Eghosa Osaghae (2005) exert that pre and post independence globalization processes have shaped the future in much the same way it had shaped Africa's underdevelopment. The absence of these African experts has result in a vacuum of development in the continent. The tragedy facing Africa today could, therefore, be traced to the uneven effects of the 'two-way street' that is associated with globalization.

Several scholars have pointed out that accountability and transparency, the rule of law, electoral legitimacy, freedom of expression and association, and development oriented leadership are the crucial factors in achieving genuine governance in Africa (Ayittey 2005; Onimode 2004; Villalon and Huxtable 1998). This text adopts the perspective that if more public leaders are trained to be development oriented managers, there is the possibility that accountability and performance monitoring would improve considerably in several African nations. Exposing leaders to the skills of implementing growth-oriented and market-friendly economic policies would enhance the quality of life of all their citizens. Such pragmatic policies would also correct the problem of maladministration and corruption in the public sector. Other methods that could help to improve developments in the African continent include the effective rule of law, change in social behavior (e.g., leaders' not seeking prosperity at the expense of their people), work ethics and the commitment to social responsibility by leaders.

According to Adamolekun (1999) and Eghosa Osaghae (2005) future African nations' government reorientation programs should include: (a) a reduction in the role of the state in national economic management; (b) an enhanced role for sub-national government; (c) a new partnership between the public, private sectors, community based organizations and NGOs in the production and provision of goods and services (see figure 1:1 for an illustration of this partnership); and (d) efforts aimed at achieving improved performance in the public management. African state governments would have to adopt a pragmatic and dynamic effort to implement these government reorientation factors effectively in order to achieve sustainable development in the twenty-first century.

The primary concerns of the African people today are national poverty mitigation, safety improvement and the provision of basic infrastructure. African leaders must learn to be accountable to the people at all times. Africans countries need leaders that they can respect, admire, and lean on for results. African need leaders that would be skillful enough to take the following actions:

1. Leaders that would be able to effectively address the issue of ethnic and religious killing of citizens in certain parts of their nation.

2. Leaders that would put a stop to corruption and be able to bring back the gift of hope and encouragement to the masses.
3. Leaders that would be transparent and accountable to the people, as well as putting the public interest above personal greed.
4. Leaders that would truly make their respective nations proud again through the provision of safety and basic infrastructure.
5. Eminent and practical leaders with the conscience and the vision to strengthen the judiciary institution and effectively enforce the rule of law as a priority task.
6. Leaders that would have the ability to empathize with the needs of the citizens.
7. Leaders that would have an understanding of the experiences of the down trodden, the weak and weary, and the unemployed.
8. Leaders that have the knowledge and skills on how to create favorable political environment, promote patriotism among citizens and attract development to their respective country in general.
9. Leaders that would be able to mobilize the public, private sectors, community based organizations and NGOs in the development process.

The impediments to development in Africa reflects the lost of government control. This predicament could also be associated with the loss of adequate guarantees to protect the public interests in several African countries. The bone of contention, therefore, is that Africa's nations need to find an appropriate partnership between the public, private sectors, community base organizations and NGOs in their sustainable development efforts in order to avoid falling into the trap of all-or-none government. National governments in the African continent need to promote community-based development to largely meet the practical needs and demands of their civil service and people.

Figure 1.1 shows the dynamics of achieving sustainable development as well as the interrelation between NGOs, national and regional governments, the private sector and grassroots organizations in the process. When a nation wants to achieve sustainable development, there are three goals that must be set. The goals are (1) economic goals; (2) social goals; and (3) environmental goals. In order to effectively achieve sustainable development certain level of each of these goals must be attained. Achieving one or two of these goals might not lead to sustainable development. The commitment, conviction and dedication of NGOs, national and regional governments, the private sector and grassroots organizations to the goals is the foundation of achieving sustainable development in particular country. There is also the need for such a county to establish the will and motivation to achieve the set economic, social and environmental goals.

The economic goals should be designed to increase productivity capital. This goal should address measures on how to increase financial resources, infrastructure, equipment, and other productive resources. The economic goals towards attaining sustainable development require the development of partnerships between the public sector, private sector, NGOs and grassroots

Figure 1.1: Model on How NGOs and National Governments Could Foster Partnership in Achieving Sustainable Development

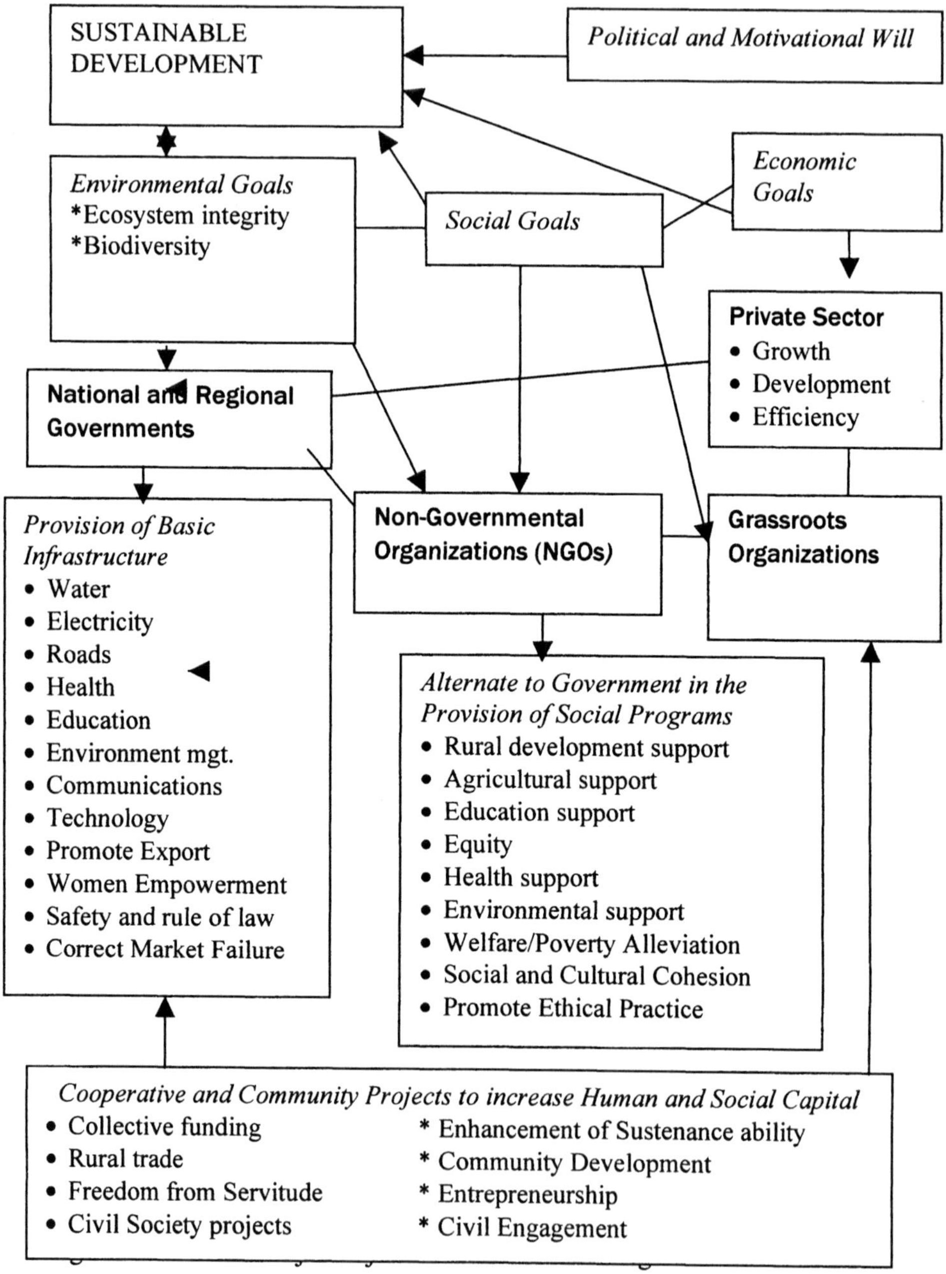

organizations. The major objective of the national government here is to improve its operating efficiency, encourage sustainable growth and development. The private sector should also aim at promoting growth, development, private ownership of enterprises and efficiency. The NGOs would support the government in the provision of services in education, health, welfare, social, agricultural and ethical values.

The social goal of the government of a nation that is seeking sustainable development is to increase human and social capita. The goal includes investing in health, nutrition of individuals and education. It should cover investing in formal and informal social institutions. The government should encourage its partners (NGOs, Grassroots Organizations and the Private sector) in the development process to provide quality educational opportunities, build social and cultural integration programs as well as address poverty and the general well-being of the local community. NGOs could do a lot in helping a country to achieve its social goals. They could encourage workplace diversity and volunteering, establish training and human development, support ethical and philanthropy practice. The private sector could also seek some initiative in the sustainable development process.

The environmental goals are closely related to how to preserve the ecological system of a nation for its future generation. Generally such environmental goals should involved increasing the natural capital and assets. The Government of a nation should crease and implement policies that would help to enhance the capacity and biodiversity integrity of its environment. The government policy should include the creation of parks; car pooling, green spaces, planting trees, waste management, purchasing recycled product, and office recycle products. NGOs should support the government in environmental preservation, training of environmental experts, forestry, soil management projects and rural irrigation projects, promotion of sustained farming practice and cooperative farming techniques.

It is important not note that achieving sustainable development depends on three sustainable practices. According to Keith Seel (2001) these practices includes content, context and process. (1) The content practice emphasis the negative and positive impact of private or public organizations activities on the economy; (2) the context practice address public and private organizations support or resistant to change. Such changes could be structure, planning, ethics, political culture or governance in nature. The changes could also include demographic, competitive or cooperative actions of others; and (3) process dimension postulates the ways in which values and ideas enter the operations of the private or public organizations who are involved. Collaboration among NGOs, the public and private sectors as well as community based organization is an important value that could stimulate accountability in the processes of sustainable development in the African continent. This also includes the complex interactions and interrelationships between individuals and organizations that are working toward achieving the sustainable development objectives of a nation. Participation of these institutions and civil societies would put accountability on the African development agenda and of course the global governance debate. NGOs operating in the African continent need to be increasingly transparent in order to be perceived as credible by both the government and people in their respective location.

Overview of Chapters

NGOs and Sustainable development in Sub-Saharan Africa is divided into three sections. The first section is made up of chapters that examine general theoretical and analytical issues in debate on partnership in the sustainable development processes in Africa. The second section is devoted to chapters on specific country case study and analysis of NGOs projects in Africa. The third section focus mainly on chapters dealing with the administration of sustainability in the African continent in the twenty-first century.

The emphasis in section 1 is on theoretical explanation and model of development that might help African governments to form partnership with NGOs, civil society organizations and the private sector. In Chapter 1, Robert Dibie examined two questions. First, what are the conditions in African nations that seem to attract NGOs? Second, are NGOs really interested in human development in the African continent or are their interests more consistent with the needs of external funding agencies or donors? He argued that political and economic instability, infrastructural and institutional decay, poverty, hunger, disease, bureaucratic inefficiency, and the near collapse of educational and research institutions are some of the reasons why sustainable development has been very slow in many nations in Africa. According to the authors these problems have attracted NGOs to intervene in nations that are plagued with devastating conditions. Dibie contends that the failure of the national governments of most African nations in addressing the problems of welfare, poverty and human development has led to the emergence of NGOs in most African nations. Further, he stressed that the second reason for the emergence of NGOs is associated with the deliberate attempts by the United Nations, the World Bank and the IMF to delegate aid programs through NGOs. Dibie exerts that the notions of "new world order" and "global civil society" that were introduced in the 1980s and 1990s brought with them new functions for NGOs. These new globalization concepts also exposed the limitation of the national governments of several African nations in meeting the challenges of their people. The author provided a model that would help the national and regional governments, NGOs, civil societies, the private sector and community based organizations to collaborate in the process of seeking sustainable development in the African continent.

In chapter 2, Robert Dibie and Ogwo Jombo Umeh described some of the development administration intensions and the role played by NGOs. They stressed that NGOs operations in the African continent truly stand for what is expected of them as modernization agents. It is Dibie and Umeh's contention that given the amount of power and influence known to be held by NGO's in the cultural, social, economic, and political sphere of the African people, they would also be a significant force in fostering the course of administration and development of the African people.

In chapter 3, Robert Dibie explores the extent to which NGOs serve as alternative to the development processes in most African nations. He made attempts to determine the predicaments INGOs face in the implementation of their projects and development plans in some Africa countries. Dibie argues that NGOs ability to succeed in helping Africa to develop will depend on the positive relationship between them (NGOs), the respective African governments, civil society groups and the private sector. He contends that the national government of most African nations would have to create an enabling environment for NGOs to rationalize their operations locally. Transparency, simple coordination and accountability policies will be helpful in fostering the partnership between the government, NGOs, the private sector and community based organizations in the development process. Dibie also examines the level of education and health projects funded by NGOs in several African nations.

In chapter 4, Akpovire Oduaran advances the argument that a total reliance on NGOs by an African nation for development is a poor and impractical approach to achieving sustainable development. He argued that because of the major changes posed by globalization, rather than depending on foreign aid and NGOs, local communities can pursue development policies that compliment their national economic objectives. Oduaran suggests that the national government in many English speaking African nations must support regional and local economic development policies in order to bring about more equitable distribution of development in their respective nations. He contends that the nature of diversity that exists within the Anglophone African sub-continent makes it difficult for anyone to attempt a detailed discussion of the performance of NGOs within the limits allowed in this chapter. Even at that, it is possible for one to take a sample of views about African NGOs performance with the intent of proposing a preliminary agenda for training geared towards high-impact performance. Oduaran concludes that NGOs training in Anglophone Africa must begin first of all with the conceptualization of the term NGOs. It is only then that scholars can explore the resurgence in the movement, to assess NGOs performance, and be in a better position to suggest needs and issues that NGOs training must address.

In section 2, chapter 5, Saliwe Kawewe examines how community based environmental policies can be best implemented to achieve success in Botswana and Ethiopia. She argued that community based environmental policy will enable indigenous organizations and communities to discover and learn from the implementation experiences of other successful programs around the world. Kawewe also addresses the need for government, NGOs, and community based organizations to form partnership in order to achieve both environmental and economic growth in Botswana and Ethiopia. She provides some policy recommendation for the governments of Botswana and Ethiopia in the twenty-first century.

In chapter 6, Robert Dibie and Saliwe Kawewe argues that post independence NGOs in Botswana and Nigeria are concerned with poverty alleviation, education, health, the environment, legal rights for women and human rights protection in general in the rural areas of both countries than regional governments. They stress that while most NGOs began as relief and welfare organizations as their original mission, their operations in both nations have spilled over into development projects. They contend that local and international NGOs have moved beyond the mere design of development policies to the strategy of involving grass-root organizations in elevating the life of citizens, fighting inequality and poverty in the society. They exerts that the grass-root approach, sometimes fall short in meeting the needs of women, the poor and the general empowerment of the average citizens. Dibie and Kawewe conclude that in the past two decades NGOs in Botswana and Nigeria have spread their activities into the areas of fostering democracy in both nations. NGOs have also initiated direct and indirect interventions in the provision of technical assistance and funding to indigenous Community based organizations (CBOs).

In chapter 7, Robert Dibie and Josephine Dibie examines some of the human resources problems that NGOs confront in Ghana and Nigeria. They explored what motivates the behavior of paid staff and volunteers in several NGOs in both nations. Dibie argues that the existence of a psychological contract combined with well-known difficulties in mandating volunteer behavior might cause volunteers to perceive breach of such contract seriously. Consequently, such perceived breach would affect the level of participation and withdrawal in the activities of the organization. The authors attempt to find the extent to which volunteers enter their working relationship with specific expectations and to what extent NGOs in Ghana and Nigeria fulfill these expectations. The major question addressed in the chapter is: In what ways can the psychological contract and extrinsic as well as intrinsic motivational factors be used to understand the behavior and performance of volunteers in NGOs operating in Ghana and Nigeria? The findings of this chapter reveal that the level of volunteer participation and withdrawal is dependent on their perception and the ability of NGOs to provide support and fulfill their expectations.

In chapter 8, Wilfred Gabsa contends that the proliferation of NGOs is just one of those ripple effects of the wind of democracy in Cameroon. Gabsa addresses such questions as: can NGOs replace the government in the management of the affairs in Cameroon? What responsibilities do they have and how are these responsibilities separated from those of the State? How do NGOs compare to institutions of the government? Is it possible for these organizations to play the role of the government? Do they stand a good chance of serving the people better than the government does?

In chapter 9, Johnston Njoku examines the role of religious NGOs in Zimbabwe. He argued that the autonomy of the citizens of Zimbabwe depends on the strength of its public and civil society consciousness. Further Njoku identified the types and nature of civil societies in Zimbabwe and the links they have with their communities. He describes the contemporary problems facing NGOs in the nation. Njoku discusses the sustainability of religious NGOs activities in the development process of the nation and provided some recommendations.

In chapter 10 Francois Muyumba provides some insights into the operations of NGOs in the Democratic Republic of Congo. He discusses the social and economic consequences of the current ethnic conflicts and suggested the role NGOs could play in resolving the conflict. Muyumba argues that the resolution, peace building and reconstruction of the Democratic Republic of Congo will depend on the ability of the national government, NGOs and domestic civil society groups to work together. According to Muyumba, there is no substitute for the creation and use of capable NGOs and local civil society groups for conflict resolution training, research, distribution of good and services, and education throughout the nation. He concludes by challenging the citizens of the Democratic Republic of Congo not to equate sustainable development process with ethnocentrism, and to work towards creating a peaceful political and social environment in the nation.

In section 3, chapter 11, Felix Edoho uses a strategic management approach to examine the deplorable development situation in several African nations. He stresses that governments in Africa need moral and upstanding public servants and NGOs staff that can be trusted and held responsible in order to alleviate the African people from the vicious circle of poverty. Edoho contends that public servants cannot be trusted to be independently responsible for development projects in Africa. He calls for strict laws to govern administrative behavior of political leaders and senior public administrators as well as NGOs field staff. He also advocated correction and punishment for those who deviate from legislated standards. Edoho argued that public administrators must genuinely use strategic management tools such as planning, marketing mix, cost-benefit analysis, forecasting, research and development to care for their citizens. According to Edoho, the key to Africa's development is leadership notably, purposeful, citizen-oriented and entrepreneurial leadership.

In chapter 12, Josephine Dibie and Robert Dibie address the current and future roles of NGOs in the empowerment of women in Africa. They explore the factors that militate against the integration of women into senior administrative and political leadership positions in the continent. It contends that if women are under represented in Africa because of open or indirect mechanism of exclusion and discrimination, then educating women and girls is not enough, and may even result in little change if the public and private sectors institutions are not changed simultaneously. Further Dibie and Dibie stressed that the public, private sectors and NGOs in Africa need to introduce diversity management programs as a policy at the national and regional governments in order to engage talented women in its process of seeking sustainable development. The authors also argued that in offering women the opportunity to access economic resources as well as to disentangle their identities from those of their families they will contribute immensely in the sustainable development process of Africa. If the problem is not women's lack of resources, but lack of acknowledgement of those resources and experiences that women actually bring with them into the public and private sectors, then there is no need to wait for women to be more educated or experienced. They contend that no development process will be totally beneficial to a nation if it does not involve women.

In chapter 13, Robert Dibie and Ogwo Jombo Umeh examines why post independence public administration in Africa have not helped in the transformation of the continent into a broad-based sustainable development and user friendly institutions. Dibie and Umeh argue that the failure of African governments to adopt development administration after independence has detracted their ability to achieve sustainable development in the twenty-first century. They discusses how NGOs have adequately transform themselves for tasks and performance in the post-independence period against the backdrop of political, social, and cultural conflicts, environmental impediments and debt crisis in the African continent. Dibie and Umeh also argue that the mismatch between current public administration practices and the needs of the civil society has impaired the capacity of several national governments in Africa to function effectively. In conclusion, they discusses some factors that would help national governments in the continent to establish broad-based development administration dynamics that would promote collaboration among the government, NGOs, multinational corporations, the private sector and community based organizations in the sustainable development process of the African continent.

Conclusion

The chapter has examined the role of NGOs in the social, economic and human development of the African people over the past five decades. It argued that domestic, transnational and international NGOs initiatives has been relevant and appropriate in addressing human development in several African countries during their post independence era. It advocates the there is an urgent need for a better understanding of the role of NGOs and civil society groups in the ongoing search for social, economic, political and technological transformation for several African nations. This understanding is very important in the process of Africa nations seeking sustainable development.

Examples from several African nations demonstrate that domestic civil society and foreign NGOs continues to be major providers for the poorest and least developed nations in Africa. Their focus has often been that of potential services as a social and economic development intervention that might produce a wide range of positive impact on the people. INGOs have been very active in building peace, democratic governance, and improve human development in several African nations. Although INGOs have been very active in providing community services in African, one of the major impediments to poverty elevation in the continent has been its political elites. Political leaders in most nations in the continent have dominated the social and economic policy making and institutions that protect human rights and advance human development. The lack of vision, limited implementation capacity, dysfunctional economics, inadequate policies, poor quality of leadership, poor governance, mismanagement of public resources and corruption have failed the majority of the people in the African continent.

Further, a unique feature of the NGOs in the continent is that there are has been a tremendous growth in both domestic and INGOS. Although this is a good thing, we advocate in this paper that social welfare and community service programs need to integrate both indigenous approaches and appropriately address local needs. Several well though programs have failed in the past due to lack of indigenous understanding of an imposed foreign model.

Since national and regional governments in African cannot achieve sustainable development alone, the ideal approach for them would be to create or form an effective and complimentary partnership with local, informal community based organizations, the private sector and both transnational international NGOs. This partnership should be mobilized to engage in providing services to the citizens with compromising cultural diversity, ethnicity, social solidarity and human rights. The outcomes of such partnership could range from peace, domestic and international understanding, to improved job skills, health and education, to sustained civic engagement of all stakeholders in the continent.

Finally, while NGOs have graciously funded several communities service programs in Africa. The source of their funding has been foreign donors. Another set of problem might arise if a nation continues to be too dependent on foreign donors. The irony is that although foreign donors means well, they often have their own perspective of what kind of social and economic development projects is needed in the African continent. In most cases these foreign initiatives might not be appropriate for Africa and its people.

References

Adamolekun, Oladipo, ed. *Public Administration in Africa.* Boulder, CO: Westview Press, 1999.

Asefa, Sisya. "Perspective on Reforming the Current Constitution for a Better Future in Ethiopia." *Addis Ababa Tribune*, 5 May 2003, 3(N).

Ayittey, George. *Africa Unchained: The Blueprint for Africa's Future.* New York: Palgrave Macmillan, 2005.

Booysen, Susan. "The Dualities of Contemporary Zimbabwean Politics: Constitutionalism versus the Law of Power and the land 1999-2002." *African Studies Quarterly* 7, no. 2 and 3 (2004): 21-43.

Castells, Manuel. "Global Governance and Global Politics." *American Political Science Review* 38, no. 1 (2005): 9-16.

Chazan, Naomi. "Engaging the State: Associational Life in Sub-Saharan Africa." In *State Power and Social Forces: Domination and Transformation in the Third World,* edited by J. Migdal, A. Kohl, and V. Shue. Cambridge: Cambridge University Press, 1994, 255-289.

Dibie, Robert. *Public Management and Sustainable Development in Nigeria.* Aldershot, England: Ashgate Press, 2003.

Dibie, Robert. "Indigenous Participation in the Environmental Policy of Ethiopia and Botswana." *Journal of Sustainable Development in Africa* 2 (Winter/Spring 2001): 1-10.

Dibie, Robert, and Saliwe Kawewe. "Education Policy and the Future of Sustainable Development in Zimbabwe and Nigeria." *Social Development Issues* 21, no. 3 (1999): 22-29.

Eade, Deborah, ed. *Development, NGOs and Civil Society.* Bloomfield, CT: Kumarian Press, 2000.

Edwards, M., and D. Hulme, eds. *NGOs, Performance and Accountability: Beyond the Magic Bullet.* London: Earthscan, 1996.

Feldman, Shelley. "Paradoxes of Institutionalization: The Depoliticization of Bangladeshi NGOs." *Development in Practice* 13, no. 3 (2003): 5-26.

Frank, Gunder Andre. *Latin America: Underdevelopment or Revolution?* New York: Monthly Review Press, 1969.

Grant, Ruth, and Robert Keohane. "Accountability and Abuses of Power in World Politics." *American Political Science Review* 99, no.1 (2005): 29-43.

Hansmann, H. "Economic Theories of Nonprofit Organizations." In *The Nonprofit Sector: A Research Handbook*, edited by W. W. Powell. New Haven, CT: Yale University Press, 1987.

Haruna, Peter. "Reforming Ghana's Public Service: Issues and Experiences in Comparative Perspective." In *Annual Editions: Public Administration*, edited by Howard Balanoff. Guilford, CT: McGraw-Hill, 2004.

Hoben, Allan. "Paradigms and Politics: The Cultural Construction of Environmental Policy in Ethiopia." *World Development* 23, no. 6 (1999): 1007-1021.

Hulme, D., and M. Edward, eds. *NGOs, State and Donors: Too Close for Comfort.* London: Macmillan, 1997.

Huxtable, Phillip. "The African State toward the Twenty-First Century: Legacies of the Critical Juncture." In *The African State at a Critical Juncture*, edited by Leonardo Villalon and Phillip Huxtable. Boulder, CO: Lynne Rienner, 1998, 297-293.

Ihonvbere, Julius. "Reconstructing the State: Constitutionalism as Public Policy in Africa." In *Agenda Setting and Public Policy in Africa*, edited by Kelechi Kalu. Aldershot, England: Ashgate Press, 2004.

James, Valentine. *Africa's Ecology: Sustaining the Biological and Environmental Diversity of a Continent.* Jefferson, NC: Mcfarland and Company Publishers, 1993.

Kaldor, Mary. "The Hi-jacking of Global Society." *Journal of Civil Society* 1, no.1 (2005): 23-24.

Leather, Alan, and Deborah Eade, eds. *Development, NGOs and Trade Unions.* Bloomfield, CT: Kumarian Press, 2005.

Manji, Firoze, and Carl O'Coill. "The Missionary Position: NGOs and Development in Africa." *International Affairs* 78, no. 3 (2002): 567-583.

Mazlish, Bruce. "The Hi-jacking of Global Society: An Essay." *Journal of Civil Society* 1, no.1 (2005): 5-17.

Nafziger, Wayne. *The Economics of Developing Countries.* Upper Saddle River, NJ: Prentice Hall, 1997.

Ndegwa, Stephen. *The Two Faces of Civil Society: NGOs and Politics in Africa.* West Hartford, CT: Kumarian Press, 1996, 111-115.

Nyangoro, Julius,and Timothy Shaw. *Corporatism in Africa: Comparative Analysis and Practice.* Boulder, CO: Westview, 1989.

Nzomo, Maria. 1998. "The Women's Movement and Democratic Change." In *The African State at A Critical Juncture*, edited by Leonardo Villalon and Phillip Huxtable. Boulder, CO: Lynne Rienner, 1998, 297-293.

Obiyan, Sat. "A Critical Examination of the State versus Non-Governmental Organizations (NGOs) in Public Sphere in the Global South: Will the State Die as the NGOs thrive in Sub-Saharan Africa and Asia." *African and Asian Studies* 2, no. 2 (2005): 301-325.

Onimode, Bade, ed. *Africa Development and Governance Strategies in the 21st Century*. New York: Palgrave Macmillan, 2004.
Osaghae, Eghosa. "State, Constitutionalism, and the Management of Ethnicity in Africa." *Africa and Asian Studies* 4, no. 1-2 (2005): 83-105.
Osaghae, O. *Between State and Civil Society in Africa: A Summary of the Research Findings*. Dakar: CODESRIA, 1994.
Patel, Leila, and Theresa Wilson. "Civic Service in Sub-Saharan Africa." *Nonprofit and Voluntary Sector Quarterly* 33, no.4 (2004): .22-38.
Pearce, J. "Development, NGOs, and Civil Society: The Debate and its Future." In *Development, NGOs and Civil Society*, edited by Debora Eade. Oxford: Oxfam Press, 2000.
Riddell, J. B. "Things Fall Apart Again: Structural Adjustment Programs in Sub. Saharan Africa." In *The Political Economy of Development and Underdevelopment*, edited by K. P. Jameson and C. K. Wilber. New York: McCraw-Hill, 1996.
Sanyal, B. *Cooperative Autonomy: The Dialectic of State-NGOs Relationship in Developing Countries*. Research Series *100*. Geneva: ILO, 1994.
Seel, Keith. "A Hundred-Year Horizon: Considering Sustainable Development in the Nonprofit Sector." In *The Nonprofit Handbook Management*, 3rd ed., edited by Tracy Daniel Connors. New York: John Wiley and Son, Inc, 2001.
Tordoff, William. *Government and Politics in Africa*. Bloomington: Indiana University Press, 1997.
Van Diesen, Arthur, and Karen Walker. *The Changing Face of Aid to Ethiopia: Past Experience and Emerging Issues in British and EC Aid*. Christian Aid Report 1999.
Villalon, L., and P. Huxtable, eds. *The African State at a Critical Juncture*. Boulder, CO: Lynne Rienner, 1998.
Villalon, L., and O. Kane. "Senegal: The Crisis of Democracy and the Emergence of the Islamic Opposition." In *The African State at A Critical Juncture*, edited by Leonardo Villalon and Phillip Huxtable. Boulder, CO: Lynne Rienner, 1998, 143-166.
Waiguchu, J. Muruku. "Rethinking and Managing Nonprofit Organizations in Africa." In *Management of Organizations in Africa: A Handbook and Reference*, edited by J. M. Waiguchu, E. Tiagha, and M. Mwaura. Westport, CT: Quorum Books, 1999.
Welch, C. "Human Rights NGOs and the Rule of Law in Africa." *Journal of Human Rights* 2, no. 3 (2003): 315-327. http://www.tandf.co.uk/journal.
Williams, Michael. "Global Civil Society: Expectations, Capacities and the Accountability of International NGOs. 21st Century Trust." 2003. http://www.21stcenturytrust.org/williams2.html (accessed May 3, 2005).
World Bank. *Governance: The World Bank's Experience*. Washington, DC: World Bank, 1994.

Chapter 2

NGOs and Development Administration in Africa

Ogwo Jombo Umeh

The conduct of civil servants in several African nations constitutes the greatest impediment to attaining sustainable development in the continent. Ethics have totally disappeared from the public administration system of most African countries. The pervasive ambience of present day public administration and the African society could be described as one of corruption, malpractices, dishonesty, lack of integrity, absence of moral values and ethical conduct. The differences in values, beliefs, religion and culture have led to different forms of administrative and accountability styles. The collapsing state of the public sector in most African nations is due largely to leaders who are not committed to the development of their societies and who lack honesty and commitment to shared governance. While the government of a nation is expected to render social stability, regulate the market, make laws, determine the tax structure, create infrastructure, dominate key industrial sectors and deliver goods and services to its citizens, the situation is, however, not so in many African nations.

It has become very difficult for the government of several African nations to depend on its public administration and agencies to achieve development goals. Balogun et al. (1999) and Adamolekun (1999) contend that public administration in many Africa countries is confronted with problems such as (1) irregular payment of civil servants, (2) lack of office supply and equipment to effectively function, (3) rapid turnover of governments and political systems, (4) incompatible socio-cultural practices, (5) volatile economic performance, (6) too rapid change in the nature, size and complexity of task, (7) high rates of population growth and rapid urbanization, (8) govern functions are often dispersed among an excessive number of ministries, authorities and agencies, and this result in inadequate leadership within the government for policy formulation, planning, and implementation, and (9) various public administrators and agencies do not have the sufficient competence to develop solid plans and projects for the citizens. Given the preponderance of the liberal democratic model inherited from past colonial regimes political reforms and relationship between politicians and civil servants has been allowed to degenerate in several African nations.

Kiggundu (1989) argues that African countries lack organizations in the true sense of it. Their organizations, he suggests, are pre-scientific, and as such are not capable of bringing about development. While government and its public administration institutions directly and indirectly affects the life of every citizens, civil society organizations have not been given the opportunity to fully participate in the governance and development processes of their respective nations. Civil society as used in this chapter refers to all institutions that are not identified with the government. This range from NGOs such as chambers of commerce to voluntary organizations, community based organizations and religions groups.

With the introduction of Structural adjustment programs to several African nations in the past three decades by the World Bank and International Monetary Fund (IMF) newer collaborations are being formed between NGOs and African governments. The debt crisis that several African nations face has also made them to realize the tremendous potentials of NGOs as alternative instrument of providing social services to citizens. NGOs in African have been recognized for mediating clientele and donor needs in a way that accommodate the interests of poor African citizens and the donor organizations. For over eighty years NGOs have built long term capacity as service providers to communities in the rural areas of Africa. They have often built close relationships with those who use their services. Unlike the current system of public administration in several African nations, NGOs process of bureaucratization has not interfered with the donors goals of assistance in the distribution of resources to the disenfranchised in rural communities. In mist of government institutions in Africa, NGOs have frequently been credited with providing resources and services that transform the daily lives of poor rural communities (Eade 2000; Thin 2002). In several African nations, NGOs are noted for fostering dynamic forms of economic dependence as well as ignoring the structural inequality of the marketplace. NGOs have also promoted new forms of gender equality and more pragmatic forms of women liberation than those associated with government policies of most nations in the continent.

The African economy, multiple perspectives on aid dependence and the role of NGOs as an alternative for economic change and social justice in the continent has insinuated the need for development administration in Africa. Post independence African states inherited a public administration system that constitutes a mismatch between the civil service and what its society requires. As a result of this mismatch public administration system across the African continent has almost collapsed or has been ineffective. The small number of African nations that have survived some transformation have remained relatively insulated from the development process, elitist in orientation, and have continue to operate to satisfy the needs of very few members of their society. According to Adamolekum (1999) such public administration system have failed to serve the needs of a rapidly changing society in the twenty-first century and to effectively discharge the traditional functions of government in a developing nation. The distinction between current public administration practices and development administration is mainly in the notion of inclusiveness of NGOs, market-regulated, privately controlled and voluntarily organized civil society organizations in the development process of the African continent (Leather and Eade 2005). Thus, African nations need development administration systems that would promote collaboration between government and civil society, as well as encourage shared governance and accountability. Development administration would foster and represent the varied interests of their constituents and encourage efforts to mobilize for political change.

This chapter examines why post independence public administration in Africa have not help transform the continent towards developmental, civil society oriented or user friendly institutions. It argues the failure of African governments to adopt development administration after independence has cost the continent sustainable development. It also discussed how NGOs have adequately transform themselves for tasks and performance in the post-independence period against the backdrop of political, social, and cultural conflicts, environmental impediments and debt crisis in the African continent. The chapter also presents an argument that the mismatch between current public administration practice and the needs of the civil society has impaired the capacity of several national governments in Africa to function effectively. The concluding section provide some suggestions on the need to establish development administration mechanism that would promote collaboration between the government, NGOs, multinational corporations, the private sector and community based organizations in the sustainable development process of the African continent.

Elements of Development Public Administration

The public sector of most African nations is engulfed in unethical activities, corruption and moral disarray. The strategy to improve performance in these low developing African nations is often linked to the reduced role of the government in the delivery of goods and services. Heinz Eulau (1977) called the development administration field an "intellectual wasteland," even among public administration professionals, comparative public administration's lot has been that of a minority. Other problems include that of language and cultural barriers; lack of adequate or reliable data; suspicion of the unknown foreigner by native indigenes; paucity of publication outlets; the negative impact of too frequent change of regimes in African countries. A first step in this process is to articulate some of the salient definitions of development administration. Development administration, like other sub-fields in the social sciences of the development genre, has become established and recognized as a distinct enterprise of academic study and practice.

A rapidly growing literature and several specialized journals, for example, *African Administrative Studies*; *Indian Journal of Public Administration*;

Administration; *Public Administration and Development*; *Quarterly Journal of Administration and Third World Planning Review*. Journals which feature items of interest to development administration specialists include, *Administration and Change*; *Africa Development*; *Asian Development Review*; *Canadian Journal of Development Studies; Development and Change*; *Development Policy Review*; *International Organization*; *Journal of Developing Areas*; *Journal of Development Studies*; *Latin American Perspectives*; *Middle Eastern Journal; Public Administration Review*; *Third World Quarterly*; *World Development*; and *World Politics*, attest to the accumulation of knowledge and experience within the subject and symbolize its transition from a "putative" to an increasingly "secure" status. According to David Luke:

> a number of appointments of development administration specialists during the past 25 years by universities, research institutions, training establishments, international, regional and national development agencies have created a 'development administration community with an entrenched interest in fostering exclusivity of expertise in the interpretation of the management and administration of development, and in the mediation of the relationship between the subject and related branches of the social and environmental sciences (Luke, 1986: 73; Esman, 1988: 125-134).

The development administration field can be said to have exerted a great influence on development thinking and practice, hence, the World Bank devoted a number of its annual *World Development Report* series to an examination and, exposure of contemporary issues in the field (World Bank 1983). Its admonishments, however, have quite properly become a focus of controversy (Murray 1983). Evidence suggests that the issues presented by the World Bank's Report, including the voluminous literature which, form diverse perspectives, chronicles lessons learned, emerging trends, and paths to follow in the future. These evidences suggest pragmatic consensus within the development community. However, persistent trends running through the evolution of the field include a concern with the creation, maintenance, and strengthening of organizational and administrative capacity as an instrumentality of the development process which includes, for instance, to facilitate efficiency of service delivery, responsiveness to citizens, accountability to the people, and equity in the distribution of resources. This common concern is reflected in some of the most notable works to have appeared in the field from which the specialization has emerged (Chambers, 1974; Gould, 1980; Hyden, 1983; Leonard, 1977; Lele, 1979; Riggs, 1964; Jun, 1976). Textbook definitions abound on the definition of development administration.

The field of development administration has undergone tremendous amount of change since being established under the aegis of the Comparative Administration Group (Riggs, 1976; Jun, 1976; Savage, 1976; Siffin, 1977; Bryant and White, 1982). In the theoretically confused field of development administration, one assumption that can be found throughout the extensive literature is that modern administration can be used as a primary tool for promoting and implementing change in underdeveloped nations (Bryant and White, 1982: 23). Martin Landau suggests that:

> Development administration is to be seen as a directive and directional process which is intended to make things happen in a certain way over intervals of time. It is a 'causal factor or independent variable (1970: 75).

Although there have been numerous attempts to define development administration, Esman's definition seems to capture the thrust of such efforts:

> Development administration refers to those activities of government that foster economic growth, strengthen human and organizational capabilities and promote equality in the distribution of opportunities, income and power. These activities inevitably involve deliberate attempts at social and behavioral changes (1974: 3).

However, this statement of activities and goals of development administration seems to raise more questions than it settles. According to Riggs:

> The ultimate problem for development administration may be how to implement decisions that express discretionary social decisions, not only through programs that effectively bring about environmental transformations, but also by means which minimize the costs felt by those involved to be a loss of agency, and also by further increasing their discretionary powers (1970: 72).

Hope's definition of development administration is quite instructive. He suggests that:

> Development administration in contextual and operational terms implies efficient organization and management of development activities of a nation to attain the goals of development . . . the conscious study of the conditions of public administration in the least-developed countries . . . the study of what is expected of public administration in the LDCs (1984: 65).

Thus, development administration involves a process that explains and justify through the giving of information what has be done, what is currently being done and what is planned. These administrative activities may be based on inter alia economic, political, social, personal, and legal reasons. What is clear, however, is that there has to be at least two parties involved in the accountability process. In the African context of development administration, accountability is driven to some extent by cultural factors which include not only economic but also legal, social, cultural and political elements. In practice, these elements enables the role played by culture in public administration in Africa to be illuminated, amplified and misunderstood for the personal interests of public leaders. There remains then the final question of the character of the administrative instruments needed for the overall surveillance and coordination of sustainable development in Africa.

Development Administration as a Process of Theorizing

What are some of the serious issues that tend to dominate scholarship in the field of comparative and development administration? Jon suggests that at a basic level, theorizing involves a concern with the conceptual issues in a given field. He goes on to point out that better understanding of these conceptual issues will not only contribute to theoretical progress but will also improve the foundations of knowledge and the understanding of our institutions and problems that involve human values (Jun, 1993: 46-47).

In a recent retrospective essay, Ferrel Heady raises two issues. The first pertains to educational preparation and methodological preferences, including research agendas in comparative public administration. According to Heady:

> The comparativists were eager to find a framework for analysis that would permit comparisons on a global basis. They had a special interest in the administrative problems of newly independent developing countries and confidence that these problems could be dealt with by transfer of administrative technologies from more advanced countries. But they were unable to agree on a paradigm for the field or a consensus as to how "scientific" their studies could claim to be (1998: 33).

Secondly, Heady raises other common concerns for the field that include the following questions: (1) what is the best framework (or what are acceptable optimal frameworks) for the comparative study of national systems of public administration? (2) What are the current and prospective probabilities for achieving "scientific" knowledge about improvement in administrative capabilities in each of the above settings? (3) What are the major trends and prospects for development in less developed nations? (4) How can a competent civil service operating in an adequate administrative structure be achieved in international organizations and NGOs, given the context of a global nation-state system? (5) And, what are the implications for comparative and international administration of possible future system transformation? (Heady, 1989: 503). Again, while these represent crucial theoretical preoccupations of the field and so deserve attention, they are not, however, the key questions of this chapter.

Several theories and approaches have been advanced to depict ways of philosophizing in the study of development public administration (Riggs, 1964; Chilcote, 1974; Rostow, 1957; Huntington, 1968; Galtung, 1971; Wallerstein, 1975; Valenzuela and Valenzuela, Deutsch, 1961; dos Santos, 1970; and Frank, 1966). All of these scholarly contributions throughout the history of development public administration have lead to the philosophical analysis of the field of development administration. Of these perspectives, the modernization and dependency theories seem to have played a very dominant role in guiding intellectual development in this field.

Modernization theory was a philosophy that grew out of a perception that government can contribute positively toward social progress (Appleby, 19945). For example, government mitigated the Great Depression of the 1930s; successfully mobilized and managed the war economy of the1940s; financed and supervised the Marshall Plan partnership that restored the shattered economies of Western Europe; and guided the unprecedented and sustained economic growth of the 1950s, and early 1960s (Galbraith, 1957). These examples demonstrate that big government can be regarded as the beneficent instrument of an expanding economy and increasingly just society. It was also the thought that only through proactive government do what came to be known as African countries redeemed from poverty and ignorance.

There were two themes in modernization that reinforced the notion of big government and the salience of development administration as a moral and intellectual vocation. The first was the universality and inevitability of the spread of Western values and practices such as instrumental rationality, secularism, individualism, and science-based enlightenment to all areas and peoples of the world (Black, 1966; Riggs, 1957). The hope was that modernization would convey to the late "developers" (that is, African countries) the same benefits, just as inevitably as it already had in Europe and North America. In effect, development administration was to represent a complex of insights, skills, and practices that could facilitate modernization and thereby help to vindicate and universalize America's moral responsibility to share its technical achievements with less fortunate peoples.

The second theme of the modernization paradigm derived from the "elitist" bias. The agents of modernization would be an enlightened minority who have acquired Western education and are committed to transforming their societies along Western lines. This transforming minority will work out of urban centers, and collaborating with the government, they would rationalize economic life, expand the modern centers, help improve the quality of life, and gradually penetrate the traditional institutions of the rural periphery through the state bureaucracy. Overall, public administration would be the principal instrumentality by which the modernizing elites would bring about change (Esman, 1988). What follows is a discussion of other dimensions of modernization theory.

The modernization theory has also been conceptualized as an attempt to explain underdevelopment in the developing world. In a large scale study entitled *Becoming Modern*, which goal was to explore the psycho-cultural factors influencing development, Alex Inkeles and David Smith concluded that underdevelopment is a state of mind. Based on an "overall measure of modernization" or "OM Scale," devised by these scholars as part of their study, they determined the extent to which participants of their study exhibited characteristics of the modern man. The authors concluded by discussing the implications of the presence or absence of such modern men in a given society and went on to argue that modern attitudes produce modern behaviors that are essential to development. And, that without modern men, modern institutions are bound to fail (Inkeles and Smith, 1974).

Furthermore, the modernization theory suggests that culture, traditional attitudes and institutions stemming from the colonial experience have proved to be a serious and fatal stumbling block to any indigenous efforts for the developing countries to develop economically, socially, and politically. That is, values, institutions, and patterns of action of traditional society are an "expression" and "cause" of underdevelopment and are obstacles to modernization (McClelland, 1963). In his book, *No Shortcuts to Progress,* Goran Hyden argues that to achieve development, Third World countries must first develop the institutional capacity for bringing it about (Hyden, 1982; Huntington, 1967).

The dependency theory is equally an attempt to explain underdevelopment in African nations. In general terms, this school of thought argues that a number of factors account for the underdevelopment status of African countries. These factors include colonial experience, terms of trade, financial markets, military assistance, development assistance, and foreign aid, just to mention some. It rejects the modernization view that the unit of analysis in studying underdevelopment is the nation-state. For example, it argues that the cultural and institutional features of a country are not the key factors explaining its backwardness, and underdevelopment, but are rather intervening variables only.

Theotonio dos Santos identifies three basic forms of dependency, colonialism, financial-industrial, and multinationals. The latter form arises out of the power of large multinational corporations that maintain operations in African countries. He sees this as limiting the developmental potential of newly industrial nations. He goes on to suggest that this new form of dependence restricts the size of the local markets and this contributes to income inequality in African countries (dos Santos, 1970; Umeh, 1992; and Korten, 1995). According to Valenzuela and Valenzuela, the dependency perspective assumes that the development of a national or regional unit can only be understood in connection with its historical insertion into the worldwide political-economic system which emerged with the wave of European colonization of the world. This global system is thought to be characterized by the unequal but combined development of its different components (1978: 543-557). As Sunkel and Pedro pointed out that:

> Both underdevelopment and development are aspects of the same phenomenon, both are basically simultaneous, both are linked functionally and, they interact and condition each other mutually. This result . . . in the division of the world between industrial, advanced, or "central" countries, and underdeveloped, backward or "peripheral" countries (Sunkel and Pedro, 1970).

In sum, they suggest that the center (that is, the developed nations) is viewed as capable of dynamic development responsive to internal needs, and as the main beneficiary of the global links. On the other hand, the periphery (that is, African countries) are seen as having a reflex type of development, one which is both constrained by its incorporation into the global system and which results from its adaptation to the requirements of the expansion of the center. Again, dos Santos indicates that:

> Dependency is a situation in which a certain number of countries have their economy conditioned by the development and expansion of another . . . placing the dependent countries in a backward position exploited by the dominant countries (dos Santos, 1970).

Immanuel Wallerstein reinforces the position articulated by dos Santos and others. Considered as the driving force behind the "world-system" school of thought, his best articulation of this thought was done in his book, *The Modern World-System: Capitalist Agriculture and the Origins of the European World-Economy in the Sixteenth Century.* Wallerstein sees dependency as a sub-set of his broader world system perspective. Overall, he attempts to explain the existence of the gap between rich and poor countries by arguing that all states form part of a capitalist world economy in which the existence of differences in wealth is not an anomaly but rather a natural outcome of the fundamental processes driving that economy. In his view, the gap between rich and poor ultimately will disappear, but only when the capitalist world system that has been in place since the sixteenth century itself disappears (Wallerstein, 1975).

In an attempt to shed light on how the process by which development can be fostered in African countries, W.W. Rostow saw the process of change as a series of stages through which each national unit has to go through (otherwise known as the Stage Theory of Development). According to Rostow, Great Britain was the crucial example since it was defined as being the first state to embark on the evolutionary path of the modern industrialized world, the inference being that this path was a model, to be copied by other states. In specific, Rostow's theory lays out five stages that should lead to development, (1) the traditional society (where agriculture is the basis of power); (2) the preconditions for takeoff (a transition stage where land is no longer the basis of power, there is infusion of technology that is supported by resources raised from land); (3) the take off (when a new class of entrepreneurs emerge, technology expands into agriculture and commerce, profit is reinvested, and quality of life rises because production is now expanded; (4) the drive to maturity (there is sustainability—output outstrips population growth, and more sophisticated industries are established; and (5) the age of high mass consumption (increased resources are allocated to social welfare/security, and the welfare state is developed) (Rostow, cited in Seligson, 1984: 120-121).

Rostow's stage theory has been criticized as being terribly misguided at least because development is greatly influenced by time. For example, when the now developed nations were going through the process, they had a secure political, administrative, social, economic and cultural base. The experience of African nations is totally different since they do not have their basic institutions in place; their entrepreneurial and administrative capacities are weak to nonexistent. Overall, Rostow's model is considered to be too deterministic as a practical guide for development (Esman, 1974: 3-26; Huntington, 1968).

There is the functionalist approach, which emphasizes the need to adopt the elements of a modern bureaucracy. This approach has been a prevalent mode of philosophizing comparative and development administration since the 1960s. Adoption of this approach might also have been a consequence of its parent field, public administration (Wilson, 1887). It precedes from the assumption that organizational efficiency and productivity can be achieved through the application of scientific method and a set of management principles that place heavy emphasis on hierarchical command and strict adherence to work rules (Bryant and White, 1982: 33); budget control, planning, systems analysis, efficient allocation of human resources, and recently total quality management. The functionalists put their emphasis on the structural and functional coordination among administrative units and also on the organizational adaptation to its environment. Also, the functional way of philosophizing assumes that because people are by nature rational and self-interested, human motivations and behaviors are predictable and can be empirically explained by testing a set of hypotheses and examining causal relationships. It assumes that social reality is already created by external forces and, that rational explanations can be given. Based on this approach, all that needs to be done is to measure and uncover the truth by determining causal relationships that exist in objective reality. Finally, it adopts a deductive approach to change, seeing it as a set of principles to induce and guide action (Jun, 1993: 47-48).

Finally, there is the prismatic theory of Fred W. Riggs, which has also provided an approach for philosophizing comparative and development public administration. Riggs theorized that in the process of development, the nature of public administration undergoes a transformation similar to that experienced by a ray of white light passing through a prism. He outlined the theory of the prismatic society in his *Ecology of Public Administration* (1967) and developed it in greater detail in his *Administration in Developing Countries* (1967). The main inspiration for this theory came from Talcott Parson's social systems theory. This theory states that every society can be understood holistically as consisting of numerous interrelated and complementary subsystems, and any aspect can by grasp only in relation to the other subsystems and their characteristics. Then, following Max Weber, Parsons also developed two extreme ideal types of the traditional and modern society with pairs of opposite characteristics (Subramanian, 1990: 8).

Riggs focused on the intermediate society that he thought was characteristic of African countries or developing nations. He described institutions or subsystems as "fused" because each system performed several related or even unrelated functions. In his view modern society was diffracted (like white light which has passed through a prism in separate colors), with each subsystem or institution having a clearly defined function. African societies were seen as light within the prism halfway between fused and diffracted, that is, prismatic, with no clear institutional division of function, some performing several functions together (Riggs, 1967; Khanna, 1974: 103-125).

Oladikpo Adamolekun (1999: 14) captures the revitalization of public administration in Africa with the concept of "new public management." According him, this concept seeks to apply market principles to public administration and might be appropriate for African nations. The new public management concept explores the principles of competition, contracting to the private sector, customer orientation, merit based recruitment and promotion as well as increased autonomy for managers. In order for these principles to be effective in African nations, there is the need for respective national governments to incorporate performance measure in the way goods and services are delivered to citizens.

Themes of Development Administration in Africa

The lack of administrative responsibility is the most crucial impediment to development in sub-Saharan Africa (Adamolekun, 1999; World Bank, 2005 2003). According to Frederick Mosher (1968) and Terry Copper (2006) administrative responsibility is the most important variable for the achievement of any public sector goals. If African public administrators could be made to be responsible for complying with laws under which their government operates the level of their contribution to their society and nations would be higher than what it is today. Therefore a responsible administrator's reorientation is what most African nations need in the attempt to respond to the needs for a systematic treatment of administrative ethics that is grounded in both the realities of honest practice, justice, equity and fairness. Thus responsible public administrators must be oriented toward being able to account for their conduct to professional practices such as their supervisors, elected officials, the courts, and the citizenry, which means being able to explain and justify why specific actions they took resulted in particular consequences (Copper, 2006). African leaders need both foreign NGOs and vigorous ethics training to instill the values that will require them to be able to act in ways that are consistent with their inner convictions as professional guardians of public goods of their respective nations.

Although the concept of sustainable development has been promoted by several African nations the improvement in human conditions in the continent, reduction of poverty, ignorance and diseases is just one aspect of the problem that has not been adequately addressed. The other aspect of the development administration problems involves lack of societal transformation, political instability and social, cultural as well as economic practices that are unethical. Further to the foregoing problems, some common themes to be discussed in this part of the chapter include control of bureaucratic abuse, ethical leadership, government and NGOs partnership, consolidating administrative and societal pluralism, and development-oriented administrative capacity. According to David Fashole Luke, these variables or persistent trends, as he refers to them, constitute a continuing challenge to the efficacy of African countries caught in the management of the development process (Luke, 1986: 75).

Control of Bureaucratic Abuse:

NGOs could help the government of most African nations to monitor the abuses associated with bureaucratic corruptions, negligence, and arbitrary behavior. These practices tend to victimize the public or citizens that the bureaucrats are suppose to serve (Rondinelli, 1983; White, 1987). Bureaucrats in several African nations must be taught and reminded that they have been entrusted with the public good and trust and should not use their position as a forum for personal, religious and ethnic interests. In most cases corruption involves the selling of public services or preferential access to public services that should be awarded according to objective criteria, free of what economist call rents (Esman, 1991). Rather than being unfair and partial one of the goals of African bureaucrats must be to achieve greater responsiveness to their diverse publics, to constrain the dominant theme of accountability upward with the necessity of responsiveness downward. Foreign NGOs should be mobilized to help train African bureaucrats the concept of nonprofit management and the theme of dual accountability as well as optimal responsiveness. These concepts involve a beneficial change in emphasis in the direction of functional efficiency and public satisfaction. The concepts further set the preconditions for the realization of co-production (Umeh and Andranovich, 2005). In the twenty-first century public administrators is Africa need to be taught the concept of optimal responsiveness that is appropriate to their environment. This means greater responsiveness than is now been practice or permitted in most African nations today. It is paramount however, to introduce responsiveness that is limited by the legitimate requirements of nationwide principles of justice equality for all, fairness and no harm to the least advantage or minority.

Ethical leadership:

African leaders should be trained or oriented to facilitate problem solving by helping their citizens get information, by identifying points of agreement and disagreement, and by encouraging people to find integrative solutions to conflicts (Bryant and White, 1982; Yukl 2006). Just as NGOs managers are able to effectively mobilize volunteers; African leaders should regard themselves as servant leaders who must empower their citizens' instead of using power to dominate them. Trust should be established by being completely honest and open, keeping actions consistent with values and showing trust in citizens and professional public administrators. Development administration scholars believed that citizens and subjects of a leader that practice such principles in African are likely to be inspired to become servant leaders themselves (Dibie and Gadzekpo, 2003; Montgomery and Esman, 1971: 359; Yukl, 2006).

Ethical leadership leader is what African nations need in the twenty-first century. Such leaders must practice the concept of integrity. Consistency between actions and immoral principles does not quality for someone to be an ethical leader. Therefore, a political leader or public administrator that believes it is morally acceptable to steal from the government would not be classified as high in integrity. Ethical leadership behaviors that could be regarded as morally justifiable include following the same rules and standards applied to others, being honest and candid when providing information or answering questions, keeping promises and commitments, and acknowledging responsibility for mistakes while seeking to correct them (Yukl, 2006). It is often very shameful to note that several African leaders usually use kindness to gain trust of people during election years, but as soon as they are elected they turn around to exploit the same citizens that have trusted them for years. According to Terry Copper (2006) and Dibie and Gadzekpo (2003) in order for a leader to be regarded as ethical he or she must intend no harm and respect the rights of all affected parties.

Government and NGOs Partnership:

The achievement of sustainable development in Africa and the capacity to provide goods and services efficiently is not confined to government or NGOs or private profit seeking organizations alone (Esman, 1991; Michie, 1989). The ability of NGOs to encourage or stimulate purposeful, efficient, and sustained collective action is a practice that governments in African nations should emulate in the twenty-first century (Rondinelli, Nellis, and Cheema, 1984). Government, the private profit seeking organizations and NGOs in Africa need to form an inclination to associate and pursue common objectives by voluntarily actions. This partnership could be independent of government and without the expectations of economic profit as a motive. The result of such partnership could lead to a heterogeneous set of activities that may be assisted by foreign religious NGOs, secular bodies, and even some international government donors. The management of such operations should however, be based on the principles of nonprofit and they must fiercely be independent of government.

Partnership that can facilitate the management and maintenance of services for which governments are responsible, such as health centers, community forest, neighborhood sanitation, and irrigation should be encouraged in several African nations. In the past most of these projects were the results of local initiatives by NGOs or individuals or CBOs responding to community needs and opportunities for collective action independently of government (Esman, 1991; Dibie and Gadzekpo, 2003). Overall, what characterizes NGOs or CBOs association apart from the variety of functions they perform is their autonomy, self-management, and accountability to their members. They have been able to create an impressive record of converting the resources available to them into goods and services that benefit their individual members as well as their communities. This is a concept that African governments must learn from NGOs in the twenty-first century.

Consolidating Administrative and Societal Pluralism:

Instead of attempting to operate the economy as well as monopolize public services, African governments should capitalize on pluralism inherent in their respective nations (Esman, 1991; Uphoff et al., 1979). The de-monopolizing practice should involve stimulating, cultivating, and tapping every resource of initiative that can produce commodities and services of value to the nation. The notion of embracing pluralism means some sharing of power with organizations outside of the government as well as decentralizing management within the national and regional government administrative structure. Milton Esman (1991) and Adamolekun (1999) contend that the relaxation of government control in several African nations and the dispersion of economic initiatives and management responsibility are more likely to enhance their sustainable development efforts, robustness, economic, social, political, religious, and cultural problem-solving performance.

Administrative pluralism practices that promote the diffusion of management capabilities and skills should also be encouraged by African nations' governments. The principles of administrative pluralism should be enhance by government incentives and sanctions that reward public administrators who use resources efficiently, responsibly, and ethically. African governments should sponsor their middle and upper level bureaucrats to seek management skills in better formal educational settings. As part of their responsibility for education, African governments should provide facilities for further management training and career development al all levels. This should not be limited to public administrators; it should also be open to local NGOs staff and the private sector. Management training at the academic and practical levels is highly favored by foreign donors such as the USAID and CIDA. These international organizations are often prepared both to provide facilities and to train trainers and management researchers.

Development-oriented Administrative Capacity:

Generally African nations suffer from lack of development-oriented administrative capacity and honest and dedicated political leadership (Balogun and Mutahaba, 1999; Dibie and Gadzekpo, 2003). Unfortunately, the cultural and ethnic diversities as well as inter-group tensions and animosities in several African nations have prevented the emergence of a broadly-based political consensus or clearly perceived national sustainable goal. Balogun and Mutahaba (1999) and Adamolekun (1999) argued that the perennial problem of overlapping jurisdictions and conflicting sets of responsibilities among public administrators and their various ministries or agencies concerned with planned development also reflects the dilemma of ensuring inter-jurisdictional or intergovernmental coordination. In the twenty-first century, African governments should rigorously reevaluate the adequacy of their respective public sector machinery. A recent review of several African nations' government structure and capacity by the World Bank (2005) reveals that administrative development and institutional reforms should be initiated immediately to set a new framework for economic and social development. Such sustainable development goals of every African nation must be revised as necessary in response to changing needs and circumstances. Sustainable development goals must also be appropriate for the environment in the respective African nations.

Conclusion

This chapter has examined the pervasive ambience of present day public administration in the African continent. It argued that post independence public administration in the African continent has been characterized as being one of corruption, malpractices, dishonesty, lack of integrity, absence of moral values and ethical conduct. The panacea for all these public administrative problems is moral education and the effective enforcement of the rule of law. It further contend that a nation's public administration environment that is characterized by strong social values, belief, accountability practices and processes in formal organizations are likely to be heavily influence by values and beliefs that would lead to sustainable development. The mechanism of development administration is however, the major instrument for achieving sustainable development in Africa in the twenty-first century. The concept of development administration also explores the principles of competition, contracting to the private sector, customer orientation, merit based recruitment and promotion as well as increased autonomy for managers. Development administration principles also call for the establishment of genuine partnership between government, NGOs, civil society organizations and the private sector in the process of policy formulation and implementation as well as in the delivery of goods and services.

Today, many activities conducted by various African governments, business organizations, and academic institutions are global in scope; involving interactions, and sometimes collaborations among multiple countries and international organizations, yet the public administration system in place is ill-equipped to fulfill the national objectives and the aspirations of the common people. Furthermore, NGOs projects to alleviate poverty in African countries have continued to be inclusive and involve the participation of civil society organizations, small private entities and volunteer organizations (Eade, 2002; Korten, 1990). Overall, national and local governments, multinational corporations, nongovernmental organizations, and international organizations, including educational institutions should all contribute to defining and solving civil society problems and underdevelopment issues.

The goals of development administration that can support the objectives of sustainable development, good governance, and shared governance are clear. African nations need a development administration system that is responsive, transparent, efficient, and inclusive. African governments must realize that its people are the owners of their government, as such public leaders should not lord over the citizens. Rather public leaders should respond to their concerns and needs with dispatch and dedication. African nations' government leaders should be compassionate, accountable and transparent. Honesty and the ability of public leaders to decide between the right and wrong actions are qualities that would promote a professional and competent development administration. African nations' government should be willing to form partnership with NGOs in efficiently delivery of goods and services.

Finally, since several African nations are full of people who are victims of poverty and neglect, it is very important that governments operating under such political environment adopt a development administration system that has a heart that feels for the poor and a mind that cares for their needs. The distinctive role of NGOs and civil society organizations provides the transformation that African nations' government need in the twenty-first century and perhaps offers development administration as a new framework for intervening in national development policy.

References

Adamolekun, L. *Public Administration in Africa*. Boulder, CO: Westview Press, 1999.

Adamolekun, L., and L. Rowlands, eds. *The New Local Government System in Nigeria: Problems and Prospects for Implementation*. Ibadan: Heinman, 1979.

Appleby, P. *Big Government*. New York: Knopf, 1945.

Asia, Scandinavian Institute of African Studies. Uppsala, 1995.

Balogun, Jide, and Gelase Mutahaba. "Redynamizing the African Civil Service for the Twenty-first Century: Prospects for a Non-Bureaucratic Structure." In *Bureaucracy and the Alternatives in World Perpective*, edited by Keith Henderson, P. Dwivedi. New York: St. Martin Press, 1999, 190-195.

Black, C. E. *The Dynamics of Modernization*. Boulder, CO: Westview Press, 1966.

Brandt, W. *North-South: a Program for Survival: The Report of the Independent Commission on Inernational Development Issues*. London: Penguin, 1990.

Bryant, Coralie, and Louise White. *Managing Development in the Third World*. New York: St. Martin, 1982.

Chambers, R. "Managing Rural Development: Ideas and Experience from the East." In *A Centennial History of the U.S.*, edited by Ralph Chandler. New York: Free Press, 1974.

Chilcote, Ronald H. "Dependency: A Critical Synthesis of the Literature." In *Commission on International Development Issues*. Penguin: London, 1974.

Copper, Terry. *The Responsible Administrator*. San Francisco: Jossey-Bass, 2006.

Deutsch, Karl W. "Social Mobilization and Political Development." *APSR* 55 (1961): 493-514.

Dibie, Robert, and Leonard Gadzekpo. "Managing Public Serice Ethics in Ghana and Nigeria." *Politics Administration and Change* 39 (2003): 1-24.

Dimock, Marshall. *Philosophy of Administration*. New York: New York University Press, 1957.

dos Santos, Theotonio. "The Structure of Dependence." *The American Economic Review* 60 (May 1970): 231-236.

Eade, Deborah, eds. *Development, NGOs and Civil Society*. Bloomfield, CT: Kumarian Press, 2000.

Eade, Deborah, eds. *Development and Culture*. Bloomfield, CT: Kumarian Press, 2002.

Esman, Milton. *Management Dimensions of Development*. Bloomfield, CT: Kumarian Press, 1991.

Esman, Milton. "Administrative Doctrine and Developmental Needs." In *Administration of Change in Africa*, edited by E. Philip Morgan. New York: Dunellen, 1974, 3-26.

Esman, Milton J. "The Maturing of Development Administration." *Public Administration and Development* 8 (1988): 125-134.

Frank, Andre Gunder. "The Development of Underdevelopment." *Monthly Review* 18 (September, 1966): 17-31.

Galtung, Johan. "A Structural Theory of Imperialism." *Journal of Peace Research* 2 (1971): 81-116.

Gould, D. J. *Bureaucratic Corruption and Underdevelopment in the Third World: The Case of Zaire*. New York: Pergamon, 1980.

Heady, Ferrel. "Comparative Public Administration in the U.S." In I *Centennial History of the U.S.*, edited by Ralph Chandler. New York: Free Press, 1987, 477-508.
Heady, Ferrel. "Issues in Comparative and International Administration." In *Handbook of Public Administration*, edited by Jack Rabin, W. Bartley Hildreth, and Gerald J. Miller. New York: Marcel Dekker, 1989, 499-521.
Heady, Ferrel. "Comparative and International Public Administration: Building Intellectual Bridges." *PAR* 58, no. 1 (Jan/Feb 1998): 32-39.
Hicks, V. K. *Development from Below: Local Government and Finance in Developing Countries of the Commonwealth*. Oxford: Oxford University Press, 1961.
Hope, K. R. *The Dynamics of Development and Development Administration*. Westport, CT: Greenwood Press, 1984.
Huntington, Samuel P. *Political Order in Changing Societies*. New Haven, CT: Yale University Press, 1968.
Hyden, Goran. *No Short Cuts to Progress: African Development Management in Perspective*. Berkeley: University of California Press, 1983.
Inkeles, Alex, and David H. Smith. "Becoming Modern." In *Becoming Modern: Individual Change in Six Developing Countries*, edited by Alex Inkeles and David Smith. Cambridge, MA: Harvard University Press, 1974.
Jun, Jong S. "Renewing the Study of Comparative Administration: Some Reflections on Current Possibilities." *PAR* 40 (1993): 480-451.
Jun, Jong S. "What is Philosophy of Administration?" *Administrative Theory and Praxis*, 15, no. 1 (1993): 46-51.
Jun, Jong S., and Deil S. Wright. *Globalization and Decentralization: An Overview*. Boulder, CO: Westview Press, 1993.
Khanna, Kishan. "Contemporary Models of Public Administration: An Assessment of their Utility and Exposition of Inherent Fallacies." *Philippine Journal of Public Administration* 18, no. 2 (1974): 103-125.
Kiggundu, Moses. *Managing Organizations in Developing Countries: An Operational and Strategic Approach*. West Hartford, CT: Kumarian Press, 1989.
Korten, David. *Getting to the 21st Century: Voluntary Action and the Global Agenda*. West Hartford, CT: Kumarian, 1990.
Landau, Martin. "Development Administration and Decision Theory." In *Development Administration in Asia*, edited by Edward Weidner. Durham, NC. Duke University Press, 1970, 73-103.
Leather, A., and D. Eade, eds. *Development NGOs and Trade Unions*. Bloomfield, CT: Kumarian Press, 2005.
Lele, Uma. *The Design of Rural Development: Lessons from Africa*. World Bank/Johns Hopkins University Press, 1974.
Leonard, D. K. *Reaching the Peasant Farmer: Organization Theory and Practice in Kenya*. Chicago: University of Chicago Press, 1977.
Luke, David F. "Trends in Development Administration: The Continuing Challenge to the Efficacy of the Post-Colonial State in *Third World*." *Public Administration and Development* 6, no. 1 (1986): 73-85.
Lundquist, Lennart. "From Order to Chaos: Recent Trends in the Study of Public Administration." In *State and Market*, edited by Jan-Erik Lane. London: Sage, 1985.
McClelland, David. "The Achievement Motive in Economic Growth." In *Industrialization and Society*, edited by Bert Hoselitz and Wilbert E. Moore. Paris: UNESCO, 1963, 74-95.
Michie, Aruna M. "Decentralization and Public Welfare in Rural India." Paper Prepared for the Annual Western Social Science Association Meeting, Albuquerque, New Mexico, April 26-29, 1989.

Montgomery, John D. *Technology and Civic Life*. Cambridge, MA: MIT Press, 1974.
Montgomery, John D., and Milton Esman. "Popular Participation in Development Administration." *Journal of Comparative Administration* (November, 1971): 359-383.
Mossher, Fredrick. *Democracy and the Public Service*. New York: Oxford University Press, 1968.
Murray, D. J. "The World Bank's Perspective on How to Improve Administration." *PAR* 3 (October –December 1983): 123-147.
Peters, Guy B. *Public Bureaucracy in Comparative Perspective*. Alabama: University of Alabama Press, 1988.
Riggs, Fred. "Agraria and Industria: Toward a Typology of Public Administration." In *Toward a Comparative Study of Public Administration*, edited by W. J. Siffin. Bloomington: Indiana University Press, 1957.
Riggs, Fred. *Administration in Developing Countries: The Theory of Prismatic Society*. Boston: Houghton Mifflin, 1964.
Riggs, Fred. *The Ecology of Administration*. New York: Asia Publishing House, 1967.
Riggs, Fred. "The Idea of Development Administration." In *Development Administration in Asia*, edited by Edward Weidner. Durham, NC: Duke University Press, 1970, 25-72.
Riggs, Fred W. "The American Tradition in Public Administration." Paper Presented at the National Conference of the ASPA 1976.
Riggs, Fred W. "Public Administration in America: Why Our Uniqueness is Exceptional and Important." *PAR* 58, no. 1 (Jan/Feb 1998): 1-20.
Rondinelli, Dennis A. *Development Projects as Policy Experiments*. New York: Methuen, 1983.
Rondinelli, Dennis, John Nellis, Shabbir Cheema. "Decentralization in Developing Countries." World Bank Staff Working Paper no. 581, Washington, DC: World Bank 1984.
Rostow, W. W. *The Stages of Economic Growth*. Boulder, CO: Lynne Reinner, 1955.
Savage, Peter. "Optimism and Pessimism in Comparative Administration." *PAR* 36 (1976): 415-423.
Siffin, William. "Two Decades of Public Administration in Developing Countries." *PAR* 36 (1977): 61-71.
Subramanian, V., ed. *Public Administration in the Third World: An International Handbook*. New York: Greenwood Press, 1990.
Sunkel, Osvaldo, and Pedro Paz. *El Subdesarrollo Latinamericano y la Teoria del Desarrollo*. Mexico 1970, 6.
Thin, Neil. *Social Progress and Sustainable Development*. Bloomfield, CT: Kumarian Press, 2002.
Tummala, Krishna. "Comparative Study and the Section on Comparative and International Administration (SICA)." Silver Jubilee Issue. *PAR* (1988): 1-2.
Umeh, O. J. "Determinants of Administrative Development in Seven African Countries." *Indian Journal of Public Administration* 30, no. 1 (1991): 47-61.
Umeh, O. J., and Greg Andranovich. *Culture, Development and Public Administration in Africa*. Bloomfield, CT: Kumarian Press, 2005.
Umeh, O. J., and Greg Andranovich. "Capacity Building and Development Administration in Southern African Countries." *International Review of Administrative Sciences* 8, no. 1 (1992): 57-70.
United Nations. *Report on Interregional Seminar on Decentralisation for Development, Khartoum*. New York: United Nations, September 1981.

Valenzuela, Samuel J., and Arturo Valenzuela. 1978. "Modernization and Dependency: Alternative Perspectives in the Study of Latin American Underdevelopment." *Comparative Politics* 10 (July, 1978): 543-557.

Wallerstein, Immanuel. "The Present State of the Debate on World Inequality." In *World Inequality: Origins and Perspectives on the World System*, edited by Immanuel Wallerstein. Montreal: Black Rose Books, 1975, 12-28.

Weaver, James M. Rock, and K. Kusterer. *Achieving Broad-Based Sustainable Development.* Bloomfield, CT: Kumarian Press, 1996.

White, Louise G. *Creating Opportunities for Change.* Boulder, CO: Lynne Reinner, 1987.

Wilson, Woodrow. "The Study of Administration." *Political Science Quarterly* 2 (June 1887). Reprinted from *Quarterly December* 1941d (1887): 481-506.

World Bank. *World Development Report 1983.* Washington, DC: Oxford University Press, 1984.

World Bank. *World Development Report 2005.* Washington, DC: Oxford University Press, 2006.

Yukl, Gary. *Leadership in Organizations.* Upper Sadlle River, NJ: Prentice Hall, 2006.

Chapter 3
NGOs, Public Bureaucracy, and Sustainable Development in Africa

Robert A. Dibie

The development process in Africa in the past six decades has been very slow. The World Bank annual human development index of 2004 reported that the average growth rate for many African states is between the ranges of two or three percent in the fast four decades. Post independent governments in the continent have been confronted with ethnic and religious conflicts, corruption, mismanagement of public resources and political instability. Development could not take place under hostile environment. In an attempt to enhance economic development several Africa countries adopted the structural adjustment program (SAP) in the 1980s and 1990s. The SAP economic policies were prescribed by the World Bank and the International Monetary Fund. The consequences of the SAP policies were such that most African nations became poorer.

In several African nations only a very few public servants follow the basic principles of integrity, respect for the rule of law, respect to the rights of other citizens and punctuality to work. Many African nations are not poor because they lack natural resources or because nature was cruel to them. Such African countries are poor because they lack positive attitude towards work. Several African countries seem to be poor because they lack the will to comply with and teach the functional principles of integrity, social responsibility, accountability, respect for the rule of law, work loving, respect for other citizens, strive for saving and investment and punctuality to work. The observation of INGOs staff is that the difference in the attitude of public servants towards providing goods and services to the citizens was derived from year's educational background and culture.

While various nations in the African continent have received some $540 billion in loans and paid back some $550 billion in principal and interest between 1970 and 2002, there is no substantial development to show for it (UN

Conference on Trade and Development Report 2004). Mark Engler (2005) contends that nations in Africa are stock with a debt of almost $295 billion. This dependency trap continue to make nations in sub-Saharan Africa to pay more in debt service to advance capitalist countries than countries in the continent actually receive from the western industrialized nations in aid. Thus, the continuation of exploitative interest payments constitutes a reverse transfer of resources from poor to wealthy industrial nations in Europe and North America. In the process of creating awareness for the debt issue many NGOs and civil society organizations have campaigned and expressed concerned that the G8 (8

wealthy industrialized nations of the world) make some initiatives to cancel the debts of poor African nations.

Many NGOs have emerged during the pre and post independence history of African countries. The goals of these NGOs are geared toward helping and monitoring states in their role as protectors of human rights and the alleviation of poverty. The predicament that has faced many African states, however, especially after independence has made it very difficult for them to effectively accept the role of protectors of their citizens. The political instability and non-conducive environment is further galvanized by the fear of assuming an open-ended responsibility in the time of inadequate national security. Most African nations tend to argue that while formal colonial government created some of their problems, during post-colonial times they have created policies such as the SAP that further restricted access to western countries. At the same time, European and North American countries are reducing the amount to support that they are willing to give to poor states in the African continent.

Kelechi Kalu (2004) contend that if SAP was a viable macroeconomic policy option for nation suffering from external debt, poverty and underdevelopment, why is the policy set specifically by Western governments and institutions to correct these problems in Africa and not in the Western nations? Why have the World Bank and IMF not been able to compel adjustment on the United States, Britain, Japan and France as these Western nations have also suffered economic decline, recession, and external debts, bureaucratic and corporate corruption? The argument of whether the World Bank and the IMF are agents of Western industrialized nations is another debate that is beyond this chapter. What is significant here; however, is the poor conditions in Africa that has attracted NGOs to the continent. Alan Leather and Deborah Eade (2005) and Peter Sollis (2002) argued that one of the problems facing government and NGOs in Africa countries is the lack of distinction between development assistance and disaster relief as well as the lack of collaboration in the pursuit of social justice and human rights. As a result the policies and programs put in place for the ramification of existing relief development continuum are less clear cut and have constituted the failure of SAP.

The failure of SAP and the notion of sustainable development which emerged in the 1980s and 1990s encouraged African states to embark on decentralization as a primary solution to the development problems. The extent to which decentralization of government authority and responsibility has promoted local development is tested by the role which NGOs continue to play in many African nations. Decentralization as used in this study refers to a cordial partnership between the national government of an African state, NGOs, Community Base Organization (CBOs) and the private sector.

During the past four decades several NGOs and donor nations have played substantial role in the sustainable development processes in Africa. This period has witnessed the establishment of genuine cooperation between African governments, local communities and international non-governmental organizations (INGOs). In many cases, the relationship has fostered efficiency, effectiveness and encouraged increased productivity of agricultural products in some rural communities in Ethiopia, Botswana, Zimbabwe, Nigeria, Uganda, Democratic Republic of Congo, Tanzania, and Cameroon. George Ayittey (2005) pointed out that lack of development vision, effective planning, budgeting, personnel and administrative management by the government of some African states has made it difficult for them to effectively mobilize INGOs operations to their advantage.

In addition INGOs, Civil Society Organizations (CSO) or CBOs have contributed immensely to the sustainable development processes in many African countries. Community based organizations in the form of social, religious or kinship groups are not new in the African continent. These traditional groups have increasingly played complimentary role to the functions of regional and national governments in several sub-Saharan African nations. Their major goal has been to support members of their voluntary organization during hardship. Community based organizations have also complimented the role of missionary organizations and regional governments in rural areas. Most missionary organizations in Africa tend to pursue health, education, peace-building and other humanitarian agenda.

While during disaster INGOs activities were limited to relief and rehabilitation, they often will spillover their operations to development projects such as road construction, schools and hospital building during normal times. In most cases, however, political instability and lack of an open door policy by indigenous government often put constraints on INGOs projects within a nation. The impacts of these constraints have galvanized a new partnership between INGOs, local NGOs and community based organizations. In the future, there is certainly a great potential for extensive partnership between CBOs, INGOs and NGOs, however, African nations would have to provide a favorable environment for these integration to take place.

This chapter explores the extent to which NGOs serve as alternative to the development processes in most African nations. The study also attempts to determine the predicaments INGOs face in the implementation of the projects and development plans in some Africa countries. It argued that NGOs ability to succeed in helping Africa to develop will depend on the positive relationship between them (NGOs) and respective African governments. The national government of most African nations would have to create an enabling environment for NGOs to rationalize their operations locally. On analyzing the behavior of the public bureaucrats in several African nations, it was discovered that the great majority of civil servants in the continent do not follow the principles of ethics, integrity, and respect for the rule of law, respect for the rights of other citizens, strive for saving and investment, punctuality and work loving. The chapter contends that transparency and accountability, simple coordination, change in attitude towards work, respect for the rule of law and anti-corruption policies will be helpful in fostering the partnership between the government, NGOs, the private sector and community based organizations in the development process. The study examined the level of education and health projects that NGOS funded in several African nations. Interview and the administration of questionnaire were used to determine the role of NGOs in Africa's development. NGOs staff, government officials, academics, project staff, and stakeholders of community based organizations were interviewed. The research also included review of literature and documents on foreign aids to Africa.

INGOs, Donors, and Humanitarian Projects in Africa

More than 15,000 INGOs operate in the African continent alone. According to Waiguchu (1999:374) about 600,000-800,000 NGOs has operations in the Africa continent. This figure encompasses all organizations that exhibit characteristics of nonprofit or voluntary organizations as well as domestic and foreign NGOs. Over one-half of the NGOs operating in Africa are religious-based, while the rest represent nonsectarian nonprofit variety (Waiguchu, 1999:374).

Western media often portray image of the governments of several Africa nations as having poor leadership, mismanagement, and official corruption. This western image of Africa has made the continent to be viewed synonymously with poverty, political instability, social unrest, and genocidal civil wars. Thus, the Africa continent is correlated with poverty (O'Connor, 1991:1). The increase of NGOs in African continent needs to be understood in this context. As humanitarian agencies, NGOs are perceived as efficacious institutional mechanisms to help change this Afro-pessimistic environment. This is one of the reasons one can find the best and the worst examples of NGOs operations in the African continent. The notion that INGOs might take advantage of the venerability of poverty in the African continent has galvanized concern about the emerging trend toward on controlled NGOs operations in the several nations (Hearn, 2002:35).

Majority of the NGOs in Africa could be found in nations such as Nigeria, Kenya, Egypt, South Africa, Ethiopia, Ghana, Cote d'Ivoire, Zimbabwe, Uganda, Tanzania, Zambia, and Senegal (World Resources Institute, 2003; Waiguchu, 1999). Research show that Nigeria and Kenya are homes to larger numbers of NGOs in the Africa continent (Waiguchu, 1999:374). Data reported by Salih (2002) indicated that between 1980 and 2000, NGOs in 17 African countries increased from 1,854 to 5,896. In Nigeria, for example NGOs increased from 1,350 to 4,028. During the period, Islamic NGOs also increased from 138 to 891 (Salih, 2002). Similar number of NGOs also have projects is

Latin American and Asian countries. The United States Agency for International Development (USAID) started its operations in Africa as an agent for economic development. In recent times, however, it has engaged itself with the promotion of governance and democratization projects in Africa and several Latin American countries. Adedeji (1993) and Onimode (2004) contend that in the past three decades international aid from INGOs has been directed to the African continent. Official Development Assistance (ODA) and NGOs activities continue to support indigenous government operations in the area of health, education, agriculture, religion, environment, rural development, women development, democratic movement and so no. Farouk Mawlawi (1993) and Paul Nugent (2004) pointed out that NGOs also play an effective role in mediation, humanitarian assistance and peace-building in many African nations.

Many sub-Saharan nations seem to continuously appeal to INGOs and Western donors such as the United States International Development Agency, Swedish International Development Agency (SIDA), Norwegian for Development (NORAD), Canadian International Development Agency (CIDA), World Food Program (WFP), the European Economic Community (EEC), and Global Environmental Facility (GEF). These International donors and the United Nations (UN) have been responsible for providing humanitarian and social development to several African nations in the form of health services, education, environmental revitalization, supply food to famine victims, road construction, and the development of new governance system (Ndegwa, 2002; Ayittey, 2005). During the famine in Zimbabwe, Ethiopia, Botswana, Sudan and Somalia these INGOs were instrumental to the establishment of progressive food-for-work programs. Van Diesen Arthur and Karen Walker (1999) pointed that the largest multilateral donor to Ethiopia is the African Development Bank group that donated US$92.3 million to Ethiopia in 1996. The European community donated US$68.2 million, while the International Development Association disbursed US$53.3 million (Human Right Watch World Report, 2003). The external donation to Ethiopia by INGOs such as Care and World Vision, Development Cooperation for Emerging Countries, Catholic Relief Services and Western government were used for emergency and relief, development construction, health, education, agriculture, road construction, human resources development, development administration and environmental management programs. Severe debt burden continue to make it difficult for the Ethiopia government to invest in quality health and education as well as poverty alleviation of its citizens living in the rural areas of the nation. More NGOs help is required to move Ethiopia toward sustainable development.

The ethnic civil wars in Rwanda, Sudan and the Democratic Republic of Congo have also attracted a lot of INGOs into these nations. These foreign humanitarian organizations have been responsible for emergency relief of refugees as well as the provision of health services and resettlement plan. In addition to INGOs activities in the above nations, it was reported that foreign donors gave aid worth over US$13.4 million to address some of the environmental problems in Botswana (Human Right Watch World Report, 2003). The United Nation Environmental Program (UNEP) and the Global Environmental Facility (GEF) provided most of the aids for the Botswana environmental projects. These gestures from UNEP and GEF have also attracted co-funding from the Swedish International Development Agency and the Norwegian Development. These INGOs funding is now the bases of a program called the community natural resources management. The goal of the community natural resources management program is to help rural communities restore local plant life, improve depleted soil and create new jobs opportunities.

Following the genocide that took place in Rwanda in the mid 1990s, several INGOs and Western nations have been pouring in aid to help the nation to develop a solid political, legal, social and economic system of governance. Human Right Watch World Report (2002) noted that the International Monetary Fund (IMF) donated US$12 million to help reduce poverty in the country. In another development the IMF, the World Bank, the International Fund for Agriculture and the African Development Fund collaborated to forgive Rwanda US$25 million of its foreign debt (HRW, 2003). The same report stated that Germany granted Rwanda US$16.8 million aid in various development projects. China also provided a grant of US$3.8 million and another US$16 million as cancelled debt. The United Kingdom has equally been very generous to the Rwandan government; it has provided over US$70 million in general budget support. The United Kingdom in 2002 gave US$50 to support civil society, gacaca research and press freedom in Rwanda. In 2003 the United States government provided development assistance of more than $14 million and another set of $1.5 million under the Great lake Justice initiatives (HRW, 2003). In addition to what the United States government donated to the Rwandan government, the USAID gave US$32 million as assistance in the same year. The European Community provided aid of more than US$155 million to Rwanda. This fund was used to promote the European Initiatives for Democracy and Human Right in the nation. The European Union also gave NGOs operating in Rwanda another $4 million. It gave another one million dollar for the rebuilding of the Rwanda Supreme Court (Leather and Eade, 2005)

Technical support was also provided by the Netherlands government to Rwanda. The technical aid was approximately US$19 million in 2002 (Human Right Watch World Report, 2003). Some of this fund was used to promote decentralization and significant financial support to local human rights organizations and press. The Belgium government donated US$21.75 million to the Rwandan government and some NGOs to tackle the gacaca problem. It also coordinated several diplomatic initiatives in addressing the gacaca problem (Eade, 2000).

Edward and Hulme (1995) estimated that during 1980-1993, the total spending by NGOs in the OECD countries surged from US$2.8 billion to US$5.7 billion in current prices. It was reported 1994 that CARE, the largest NGO in the world had a budget of US$400 million, Catholic Relief Services, US$300 million, and World Vision, US$300 million (InterAction, cited in Hearn, 2002:44). Currently, NGOs in Africa manages about US$3.5 billion in foreign aid (New York Times August 20, 2005).

Stephen Ndegwa, (2002) contend that NGOs provide Kenya 30-40 percent of its total development expenditure, as well as over 40 percent of the overall health care and family planning services. In an effort to strengthening the role of women in civil society and the political process in Nigeria and Kenya, USAID has provided funding to galvanize the process of women empowerment. The women empowerment program in some African countries tend to focus on women's fundamental human right, civil responsibilities and democratic participation. NGOs coordinating the projects contend that enabling women's participation in national, regional, community, and rural governance will increase the chances of issues concerning women to be adequately addressed. The issues include access to health care, clean water, education and creation and enforcement of gender balanced laws. The United Nations Report (2003) pointed that if women are allowed to participate equally as men in the democratic process; they will be able to achieve more equitable representation in government and could advocate their causes in the sustainable development processes of the African continent. The funding from USAID has stimulated the formation of several local women NGOs in Nigeria and Kenya. Some of such NGOs are the Nigeria Association of Women Journalist, Women, Law and Development Center and the Gender and Development Action. These women NGOs have continue to be involved in community mobilization to improve the well being of women status around the country.

The inability for African states to recognize the differences between poverty and vulnerability has created a lot of development programs in the continent. Neil Thin (2002) and Peter Sollis (2002) argued that policy makers in African nations tend to be engulfed in stereotypes that buttress poor people's lives as simple monotonous and predictable. Thus, the government and NGOs notion of how the poor act under adversity do not conform to their actual behavior. This is because that behavior is largely determined by past experience and could stimulate severe conflict. For sustainable development to be achieved government, INGOs, CBOs and the private sector would have to find a framework that might help to deal with the hidden scars of warfare and past experiences through policies and programs that could support the reconstitution of the family, kinship ties, social and cultural institutions within a given African state.

The grassroots development approach captures what Neil Thin (2002) and Peter Sollis (2002) tried to explain. It argues that the livelihood of peasants and small farmers will be better served by organizing communities and building small scale enterprises to manage the resources and products of a nation. NGOs are considered central to the process of managing the resources and products of nations in Africa. NGOs could form partnership with governments, the private sector and community base organizations (CBOs) in establishing an inclusive policy making process. The approach would further, encourage the participation of different social groups to perceive communities as a vehicle for self determination and sustainable development.

Methodology

The goal of this study is to examine the extent to which INGOs assistance in Africa nations has promoted development of the continent. The second goal of the study is to determine the predicaments that INGOs face in the implementation of the projects and development plans in some Africa counties. The study argues that the magnitude of partnership between INGOs and local governments will determine the level of success of the NGOs program in Africa. Thus the enhancement of local institutions capacity affects the long-run development of a society in Africa. There is the tendency that this partnership would spill-over to increase the effectiveness of achieving sustainable development in rural and urban communities in the continent.

The data for this study were collected in 2004 and 2005 by contacting INGOs that have operations in the African continent. Questionnaires were administered in several African nations. Data collection also consisted of interviews, documents and observations. Semi structured interviews were conducted in several Africa countries. The INGOs were selected randomly from the World Directory of Development Organizations and Programs on the basis that they have projects in Africa and their programs were geared towards sustainable development. The INGOs contacted were asked to provide detailed information about their projects in Africa. Questionnaires were sent to thirty-five INGOs that have established operations in Africa. Twenty-seven out of the thirty-five INGOs that were contacted responded. A total of 600 questionnaires were administered to the staffs of twenty-seven INGOs operating across Africa. Four hundred and seventy-three INGOs staff responded. Detailed budgetary information was requested, but some INGOs were very reluctant to provide such information for various reasons. Being in the research site allowed me to collect data through observation and informal discussions as well as cross checking documentary evidence which were made available to and obtained by the author. The choice of this methodology was based on the belief that it would provide wider and more insightful framework for studying NGOs role in Africa's development. The major goal of this study is to examine the level of development assistance that INGOs provided to African states.

The following specific research questions provided the basis of this study.

1. Does your organization have any project in Africa? If yes, what is the nature of your program in the continent?
2. What are the impediments your INGOs face in implementing your program in Africa?
3. What kind of partnership do your INGOs have with local governments or Community Base Organizations (CBOs) in the African nation where your project exist?
4. What model of cooperation can deliver social and economic justice in Africa and what does this mean for NGOs in the future?

Data Analysis and Discussion

Table 3.1 shows the INGOs that responded. The table provides a variety of projects that various INGOs under take in the African continent. The table identifies INGOs, the location of their operations in Africa and type of projects. The dimension of INGOs activities reflected their mission and objectives as well as the dynamics of sustainable development that they belief in. Some INGOs provide relief assistance, agricultural assistance, health assistance and others provided education support, environmental support and various construction projects. Only very few of the INGOs operating in Africa provide technical/technology support or assistance.

Table 3.2 shows some of the predicaments INGOs staff has identified as militating against their projects in the African continent. Eighty-two percent of the respondent stated that political instability, war and frequent ethnic conflict have immensely affected their operations in countries such as Sudan, Ethiopia, Rwanda, and the Democratic Republic of Congo. While thirty-five percent of INGOs staff indicated that most governments are not in favor of their projects, fifty percent disagree and contend that most African states have welcomed their operations.

There was a general consensus among the respondent (sixty-five percent) that citizens of most African nation were in favor of their projects. seventy percent of the respondents also indicated that the type of bilateral relation between the donor nations and the African state in most cases indicate the level of funding that their INGOs would get. When there is a favorable relationship the level of funding often increases, however, whenever the relationship is weak funding from donors often dry up. Eighty-four percent of the respondent contend that small budget often affect their ability to complete several projects in Africa.

One other problem that has been militating against INGOs in Africa is the level of expert staff that they have coordinating projects. Eighty-four percent of the respondent indicated that one of the predicaments that they often had was in availability of qualified staff in the field.

Corruption and lack of support from public officials from most African state was indicated as a major predicament affecting INGOs operation in several African states. Eighty percent of the INGOs staff who responded complained that whenever they wanted some clearance from government institutions. Senior public managers often demand gift in return for any services they provided. The respondents wonder why such practice should be part of the culture of the African bureaucracy. Illness and accidents while in Africa was view not to be a major problem, however, sixty-five percent of the respondents indicated that whenever any of their staff fall sick while they were working in a rural area without hospitals or doctors that could become a major problem.

Several of the respondents indicated that lack of strategic women needs in many African states constitute a major problem in the implementation of some of their programs. Strategic women needs are those want that female associate with their subordinate position in society. These needs include legal rights and protection under the law from abuse by men, equal wages and land rights. Sustainable development will not be achieved in the African continent unless national governments are willing to formulate and effectively implement policies that would help women change their existing roles and attain greater equality.

Table 3.1
NGOs and Their Activities in Some African Nations

NGOs	Nations	Type of Activities
Amnesty International	Many African Nations	Human Rights
Save the Children	Many African Nations	Immunization, Support United Nations led peace enforcement
The International Committee of Red Cross	Many African Nations	Humanitarian mission to protect lives; Disaster Relief, Food, and Clothing
United States Agency for International Development	Many African Nations	Poverty Reduction, promotion of governance and democratization projects; women empowerment programs
The International Famine Center	DR of Congo, Rwanda, Zimbabwe, Sudan etc	Emergency Relief, Agriculture, Forestry and Environmental Projects
Christian Relief and Development Association (CRDA)	Ethiopia, Mozambique, Sudan, Niger, Chad, etc.	Coordinate local and INGOs activities; Health; Health and Education projects
Catholic Relief Services (CRS)	Zambia, Kenya, Mozambique, Rwanda, DR of Congo, etc.	Emergency Relief, Health, Food, HIV/AID, Clothing
Development Cooperation for Emergency Countries (DCEC Italy)	Ethiopia, Zambia, Rwanda, etc.	Disbursement for Agriculture, Forestry, Fishing and Environmental Development
Care and World Vision	Ethiopia, Liberia, Botswana, Kenya, Somalia, Sudan, etc.	Environmental, Health, Roads and Education Projects
Swedish International Development SIDA (Sweden)	Ethiopia	Education and Health Projects
Norwegian Agency for International Development NORAD (Norway)	Ethiopia, Somalia	Famine Relief, Agriculture, Health and Education
African Development Bank	Many African Nations	Education, Rehabilitation and Health Projects
World Bank	Many African Nations	Economic Development Projects, HIV/AID and SAP
United Nations Environmental Program (UNEP)	Ethiopia, Botswana, Kenya, Zambia, South Africa	Integrated Moral, Rural Development, Environmental Development
Ford Foundation	Nigeria	IITA; Agriculture
UNICEF	Many African Nations	Children Health, HIV/AID and Medical Research

Source: Derived from survey data 2004

Table 3.2
Predicament Facing NGOs in Africa

Statements about Barriers to NGOs Operations in Africa	Check your responses below				
	Strongly Agree %	Agree Somewhat %	Don't Know %	Disagree Somewhat %	Strongly Disagree %
The environment in the country is not good for development	82	5	0	10	3
The government is not in favor of INGOs working in the nation	25	10	15	2	48
The citizens are not in Favor of INGOs operations in some nations	35	0	0	0	65
Conflict, war and similar problems affect INGOs operations in some nations	78	0	0	2	20
There is bilateral relations between the nation and INGOs donor countries	65	5	25	5	0
INGOs do not have enough staff in rural areas of the Nation.	74	10	13	3	0
Corruption and lack of Support from public service officials	65	15	0	15	5
Illness and accidents while Africa	47	18	6	21	8
INGOs budget in the nation is too small	64	20	6	10	0

Source: Derived from survey data 2004

INGOs, Government and CBOs Partnership

One of the major questions that this study attempt to explore is the kind of partnerships INGOs in Africa has been able to establish with local governments or Community Base Organizations (CBOs). It argued that the success of INGOs operations in the African continent will greatly depend on their ability to maintain a cordial relationship with local governments and CBOs. A favorable relationship would enhance the process of sustainable development in Africa.

The findings from Botswana indicated that INGOs such as Global Environment Facility (GEF), Swedish International Development (SIDA), Norwegian for Development (NORAD), United Nations Environmental Program (UNEP) have closely worked with the national governments of many African nations and several CBOs to establish a successful community natural resources management program. This group jointly formulated the national environmental policies and is actively involved in the implementation of the policies in Botswana.

The Tanzania Association of non-governmental organizations (TANGO) is made of about five hundred NGOs. This association collaborates with thirty districts and six regional community based organizations. In the past two decades TANGO has been very active in promoting people-centered development programs in Tanzania. The goal of the people centered program is to seek justice, peace, good governance, human rights, gender equality and equity, and sustainable development in the nation. TANGO has also served as a resource hub for information and skills exchange with the national and local governments.

Kenya HIV/AID NGOs consortium (KANCO) was established in 1990. This association is made of about 680 international and domestic NGOs. The association effort is geared towards complimenting the government of Kenya response to HIV/AID (Ongo'ombe, 2004). Respondents from the association indicated that KANCO have established and facilitated a networking system to provide forum for sharing resources and enhancing collaborative efforts both at national and district levels. Generally, NGOs, community base organizations and several religious organizations in HIV/AID and Sexually Transmitted Infection field continue to provide over 60 percent of these services at the grassroots in Kenya. Thus, INGOs, CBOs, the private and Christian health sectors continue to incremental provide health services over and above what the government of Kenya has been able to provide to its citizens. KANCO has also been able to attract funding from the United States Agency for International Development, the Department for International Development of the United Kingdom and several other donors from the Western Industrialized nations. KANCO has been able to build strong ties with Kenya's national government agencies that are involved in policy formulation and health programs.

The partnership between the government of Zimbabwe and INGOs has not been conducive. The President of Zimbabwe, Robert Mugabe, has continuously accused NGOs of promoting foreign interests and supporting the national government opposition party (Movement for Democratic Change). The government further stressed that "some NGOs and churches are causing confusion in the country because they are converting their humanitarian program into politics."(UN Integrated Regional Information Networks, 2004). The government of President Mugabe in September 2002 ordered NGOs to register with one of its agencies under the Private Voluntary Organizations Act of 2002. During a parliament speech on July 20, 2004, President Mugabe stated that he was going to introduce a Bill repealing the Private Voluntary Organizations Act and replacing it with a new law that will create a NGOs Council that would micromanage the affairs of NGOs in Zimbabwe. It will be recalled that NGOs have been working in Zimbabwe since the nation gained independence from Britain in 1980. It is therefore very troubling for respondents to note that President Mugabe has not acknowledge the fact that NGOs have often stepped into the shoes of the national government by providing services that ought to be provided by the government. The government also failed to address the enormous difficulties that the ordinary people of Zimbabwe would suffer if NGOs operations were closed in the nation. The break down in the partnership between NGOs and the national government is further galvanized by the failure to acknowledge that NGOs have sought to complement the delivery of humanitarian services that are either non-existent or on the verge of collapse. The aftermath of this strange relationship will nevertheless affect the process of sustainable development in Zimbabwe.

INGOs respondents about their operations in Ethiopia were quite positive. They indicated that INGOs and CBOs have maintained significant partnership in the provision of health and education in Ethiopia as well as formulating dialogue between donors, the government and NGOs. Respondents indicated that the national government of Ethiopia seems to have realized that in light of the tremendous development challenges facing the nation, a harmonious and mutually reinforcing partnership between NGOs, the government, donors and civil society is crucial for the country to attain sustainable development. Partnership between the Ethiopian national government, civil society, CBOs and NGOs continues to be the basis for increasing service delivery to its citizens living in the rural areas of the nation. The number of NGOs and CBOs has increased since the overthrow of the nation's military regime in 1991. Constraints within the policy environment in which NGOs and CBOs operate has somewhat continue to hamper their operations in the nation.

More than 90 percent of the INGOs respondent indicated that their operations in the African continent have been adversely affected by the fact that most government functions are dispersed among an excessive number of ministries, authorities, and agencies. This has resulted in a diffusion of responsibility, authority, and inadequate leadership within the government for policy formulation, planning, and implementation of programs. In some cases the government ministries and agencies in several African countries do not have sufficient competence to develop solid plans and projects for their public and private sectors. Many African nations have also found it difficult to implement projects on schedule or within the cost estimates. They also complained that government partnership with INGOs were generally vague. Most African governments do not respect schedule and often would not make specific provision for manpower, equipment, and materials required. Financial arrangements are often not fully worked out and join projects with INGOs are not evaluated to ascertain if they meet the administrative standard or economic viability. Whenever some African governments experience the above problems they often will abandon the project for INGOs to solely implement.

The attainment of economic and social development in Africa is dependent on effective statesmanship and partnership between the governments, the private sector, CBOs and NGOs. This consortium would only be effective within a favorable political environment. Development will not be successful without a sustaining philosophy of collective ownership, political action of a dramatic order, and the involvement of a wide cross section of the citizens in the process. By providing resources for poverty alleviation and helping the national and regional governments to provide infrastructure, many NGOs will be able to improve the living standards of the African people. INGOs utilizing the grassroots approach have had major impact on the people in need. Such efforts have contributed to the capacity-building efforts and the rejuvenation of community-based partnership with other local NGOs. These partnerships could spill over to the restructuring of a given society in Africa. On the one hand, a cordial relationship between the local people, CBOs, private sector, INGOs and the national and regional government is crucial for the sustainable development processes of African nations. On the other hand, policies and an effective rule of law system that are sensitive and appropriate to the local needs might constitute as viable instruments for achieving development.

Conclusion

This chapter has examined alternate strategies that African nations could utilize to achieve sustainable development. It identifies NGOs as an alternative instrument for achieving poverty alleviation, social and human development goals in African countries. It argue that in order to move urban and rural dwellers out of poverty national and regional governments, NGOs and the private sector would have to form a partnership. While the national government should play a major role in economic development, they should also solicit the help of NGOs and the private sector in the processes of modernization, diversification and expansion of their national economies. While such partnership in development is crucial, participants need to better integrate their activities more effectively within a clearly defined and understood conceptual framework.

It is evident that INGOs operating in Africa will prefer to work directly with the local people rather than public bureaucrats. This finding is very worrisome because on analyzing the behavior of the public bureaucrats in several African nations, it was discovered that the great majority of civil servants in the continent do not follow the principles of ethics, integrity, and respect for the rule of law, respect for the rights of other citizens, not willing to support positive government action to eradicate corruption, strive for saving and investment, punctuality and work loving. The chapter contends that transparency and accountability, simple coordination, change in attitude towards work, respect for the rule of law and anti-corruption policies will be helpful in fostering the partnership between the government, NGOs, the private sector and community based organizations in the development process. As one of the INGOs director stated, sustainable development requires more local people to have the opportunities to take responsibility for financial resources, improve their management skills, and enhance their leadership through participation in NGOs projects. INGOs, government and CBOs partnership that promotes local community capacity, local people participation in the decision-making processes of their projects would be an effective and efficient strategy to enhance sustainable development in Africa. Several INGOs staff indicated that most African nations are poor today because they lack the will to comply with and teach the principles of social responsibility, respect for the rights of other citizens, respect for the rule of law, ethics and integrity, punctuality to work and work loving. According to them, these principles make the major differences between rich western industrialized countries and poor African nations.

In many African nations policies designed to combat poverty through economic growth are in most cases different from laws seeking to reduce vulnerability of the poor within the nations. In the twenty-first century there should be a shift towards humanitarian assistance that promotes the priorities of the poor by increasing their participation in program formulation and implementation challenges. Since women and children are often the victims of refugee and displace population it would be better if special attention is paid to their needs.

Although the provision of basic infrastructure and the expansion of the agricultural sector by the national and regional government might have a spillover effect on the economy, the public sector or national government alone cannot generate the employment and growth needed by a poor African nation. Such a country will have to collaborate with both the NGOs CBOs and the private sector to achieve its economic, social and environmental goals. Example from the western industrialized countries shows that their private sectors in most cases are bigger than the public sector.

Scholars who criticize the structural adjustment programs, the IMF, the London Club, the Paris Club, the World Bank and INGOs should leave these agencies alone. These scholars might even argue very soon that these agencies should tell African leaders to stop their citizens from eating or breathing. Africa's destiny and development are in her hands and the leadership owes their citizens the responsibility to deliver or stay away from government.

Finally, sustainable development goals could be achieve in many African states if national and regional governments would introduce policies and programs that support the reconstitution of the family and kinship and the social and cultural institutions that are critical to aiding recovery. It is very important that foreign donor and the international communities who provide humanitarian relief and development assistance in Africa should seriously consider the empowerment of gender in the continent. INGOs, local NGOs, CBOs, the private and public sectors need to pay special attention to factors influencing the demand for education for girls and rural women. African women need to be provided with access to the types of resources that would help them contribute to long-term stability. Expanding non-formal education system to rural communities may prove useful in the sustainable development processes that most African nations tend to be pursuing in the twenty-first century.

References

Adedeji, Adebayo, ed. *Africa within the World: Beyond Disposition.* 2nd ed. London: Zed Books, 1993.

Ayittey, George. *Africa Unchained: The Blueprint for Africa's Future.* London: Palgrave Macmillan, 2005.

Drabek, Anne Gordon. "Development Alternatives: The Challenge for NGOs." Supplement, *World Development* 15 (Autumn, 1987).

Eade, Deborah, ed. *Development, NGOs and Civil Society*. Bloomfield, CT: Kumarian Press, 2005.

Engler, Mark. "Debt Cancellation: Historic Victories, New Challenges." Special Report, *Foreign Policy in Focus* (May 17, 2005).

Fisher, Julie. *NGOs and the Political Development of the Third World*. Bloomfield, CT: Kumarian Press, 1998.

Fonjong, Lotsmart. "Fostering Women's Participation in Development through Non-governmental efforts in Cameroon." *Royal Geographical Society* 167, no. 3 (2001): 223-239.

Ihonvbere, Julius. "Reconstructing the State: Constitutionalism as Public Policy in Africa." In *Agenda Setting and Public Policy in Africa*, edited by Kelechi Kalu. Aldershot, England: Ashgate Press, 2004.

INTRAC. "Institutional Co-operation between African NGOs and External Partners: Current Constraints and Ways Ahead." Background Paper for the International Symposium on Building the Capacity and Resources of African Non-Governmental Organizations held in African Union Conference Centre. Addis Ababa, Ethiopia: December 2004, 5-7.

Kalu, Kelechi. "The Role of Ideas, Theory and Models of Public Policy Processes in Africa." In *Agenda Setting and Public Policy in Africa*, edited by Kelechi Kalu. Aldershot, England: Ashgate Press, 2004.

Hearn, Julia. "The 'Invisible' NGOs: U.S. Evangelical Missions in Kenya." *Journal of Religion in Africa* 32, no. 1 (2002): 32-60.

Hoben, Allan. "Paradigms and Politics: The Cultural Construction of Environmental Policy in Ethiopia." *World Development* 23, no. 6 (1995): 1007-1021.

Human Right Watch (HRW). "Continued Confidence in the Rwanda Domestic Political and Economic situation among Donors 2002-2003." *HRW World Report* (December 31, 2003).

Leather, Allan, and Deborah Eade, eds. *Development NGOs and Trade Unions*. Bloomfield, CT: Kumarian Press, 2005.

Mawlawi, Farouk. "New Conflict, New Challenges: The Evolving Role for Non-governmental Actors." *Journal of International Affairs* 46, no.2 (1993): 39-53.

Ndegwa, Stephen. "Civil Society and Political Change in Africa: The Case of Non-Governmental Organizations in Kenya." *International Journal of Comparative Sociology* 35, no. 1-2 (2002): 19-40.

New York Times. "NGOs Show their Growing Power" (January 20, 2006). http://www.globalpolicy.org/ngos/role/globdem/credib/2002/0322/power.htm (accessed Jan. 20, 2006).

Nugent Paul. *African since Independence: A Comparative History*. London: Palgrave Macmillan, 2004.

O'Connor, A. *Poverty in Africa: A Geographical Approach*. London: Belhaven Press, 1991.

Ongo'ombe, Maureen. "Kenya AID NGOs Consortium as an HIV/AIDs Networking Organization." *Kenya Journal of Social and Religious Concern* 1 (2004): 1-9.

Onimode, Bade. *African Development and Governance Strategies in the 21st Century*. London: Palgrave Macmillan, 2004.

Redcliff, M., and D. Goodman, eds. *Environment and Development in Latin America: The Politics of Sustainability*. Manchester: Manchester University Press, 1991.

Salih, M. A. Mohammed. "Islamic NGOs in Africa: The Promise and Peril of Islamic Voluntarism." Occasional Paper, Center of African Studies, University of Copenhagen, 2002.

Sollis, Peter. "The Relief-Development Continuum: Some Notes on Rethinking Assistance for Civilian Victims of Conflict." *Journal of International Affairs* 47, no. 2 (2002): 451-471.

Thin, Neil. *Social Progress and Sustainable Development*. Bloomfield, CT: Kumarian Press, 2002.

United Nations. *Conference on Trade and Development Report on Africa*. United Nations Integration Regional Information Networks, htt://allAfrica.com (2004).

United Nations Integrated Regional Information Networks. "Zimbabwe: NGOs Slam Moves to Introduce Tighter Control" (July 19, 2004): 1.

United Nations. "More Aid is needed says government." UN Integration Regional Information Networks, htt://allAfrica.com (2003).

Van Diesen, Arthur, and Karen Walker. "The Changing Face of aid to Ethiopia—Past Experience and Emerging Issues in Britain and EC Aid." *Christian Aid Report* (1999).

Waiguchu, J. Muruku. "Rethinking and Managing Nonprofit Organizations in Africa." In *Management of Organizations in Africa: A Handbook and Reference*, edited by J. M. Waiguchu, Edward Tiagha, and M. Mwaura. Westport, CT: Quorum Books, 1999.

Wallace, Don. "The Role of Multi-Lateral Institutions in African Development." *Law and Policy in International Business* 30, no.4 (2002): 697-711.

World Bank. *Development and the Environment.* New York: Oxford University Press, 1992.

World Bank. *Human Development Index Report*. New York: Oxford University Press, 2004.

World Resources Institute. *World Resources 2002-2004: Decisions for the Earth: Balance, Voice, and Power*. UNDP/UNEP/World Bank/IMF, 2003.

Zewdu, Medhin. "Government Initiated Community Based Natural Resources Management." A Paper Presented at a Workshop on Community Based Natural Resources Management, 2000.

Zewdu, Medhin. "Sustainable Development in Ethiopia." Addis Ababa, Ethiopia: Heinrich Boell Foundation and Institute of Biodiversity Conservation and Research, 2002.

Chapter 4

The Perception of NGOs Performance in Anglophone Africa

Akpovire Oduaran

Anglophone Africa consists of all English speaking African countries that were previously colonized by Britain with the exception, perhaps, of Namibia that was a German colony. The administration of Namibia (formerly known as South West Africa) was later transferred to apartheid South Africa. At independence, Namibia decided to adopt English as its official language. Anglophone African countries are located in Western, Eastern, and Southern Africa sub-continents. The political systems vary from one nation to another until the latest move towards democratization. Some of the countries, for example, Nigeria, Ghana, Liberia, and Uganda had been under military rule at different points in time in their post independence history. A few English speaking African nations have also been under one party rule since independence even though there are claims to the existence of democracy. Such countries include Zimbabwe under Robert Mugabe, Malawi under Kamuzu Banda, and Kenya under Jomo Kenyantta. Their economies also differ greatly, varying from almost mono-commodity nations like Botswana, Lesotho, Namibia, Swaziland, Ghana, and Sierra-Leone to multi-commodity countries such as South Africa, Zimbabwe, Mauritius and Nigeria.

The increase of non-governmental organizations (NGOs) activities in many African nations has galvanized a suspect relationship between public leaders and NGOs. Stephen Ndegwa (1994) pointed out that the greater the activities of NGOs toward development in some African nations the more they have displaced the national government as the sole development agent. This sudden NGOs role in the development process has made some African state governments to introduce measures to control their activities so that non-public stakeholders do not use them as fora to challenge the policies of the national government. The governments of Zimbabwe, Ethiopia, Sudan, South Africa,

Tanzania and Uganda are examples of African states that have attempted to control NGOs and their resources in the name of preserving national sovereignty (Olowu and Sako 2003; Collins 2000). Despite the restriction placed on NGOs activities in a number of African nations, they have become key partners with the United Nations in development assistance, providing over US$5 billion annually to African countries (Mawlawi 1993; Wallace 2002). Further, the United States Agency for International Development UASID and several of its European and Canadian counterparts have been very active in supporting the private sector and local NGOs in Africa for their economic growth to be broad-based and somewhat sustainable. These international NGOs contend that African states need to play a larger role in their development process. These foreign NGOs have also focused their efforts in capacity building, organizational development, technical assistance, policy and regulatory analysis, program support and marketing information as well as humanitarian support (Williamson and D'Alessandro 1999).

Several English speaking African nations have not effectively benefited from the resources provided by NGOs. A large percentage of their population continues to live below the poverty line. The World Bank Report (2000) indicated that over forty-three percent of Africans live on less than one dollar a day.

The argument advance in this chapter is that a total reliance on NGOs by an African nation for development is a poor and impractical approach to achieving sustainable development. The chapter further argued that because of the major changes posed by globalization, rather than depending on foreign aid and NGOs, local communities can pursue development policies that compliment their national economic objectives. It suggest that national government in many English specking African nations must support regional and local economic development policies in order to bring about more equitable distribution of development in their respective nations. The nature of diversity that exists within the Anglophone African sub-continents makes it difficult for anyone to attempt a detailed discussion of the performance of NGOs within the limits allowed in this chapter. Even at that, it is possible for one to take a sample of views about African NGOs performance with the intent of proposing a preliminary agenda for training geared towards high-impact performance. The chapter further suggests that NGOs training in Anglophone Africa must begin first of all with the conceptualization of the term NGOs. It is only then that scholars can explore the resurgence in the movement, assess NGOs performance, and be in a better position to suggest needs and issues that NGO training must address.

Conceptual Clarification

The term NGO has been used in this chapter to refer to organizations that are independent from direct control by any government, and provide different kinds of services to the civil society while they remain non-political, non-profit-making, non-violent and non-criminal in nature (Willetts, 2004, 6-7). According to Farouk Mawlawi (1993) NGOs are private, voluntary, non-profit organizations whose members combine their skills, means and energies in the service of shared ideals and objectives. NGOs have been creating enormous opportunities for development practitioners, academics, donors and policy makers in several African nations. Their activities have contributed to raising public awareness about human rights, the environmental policy, poverty alleviation, democratization process, economic development and health issues in the continent (Ott 2001; Wilbur 2000). NGOs have also promoted peace building and mediation as a means to foster conflict resolution in the African continent.

In contradistinction, the term "NGO" has not been used to refer to the more locally-based groups known as grassroots organizations or community based organizations (CBOs). These civil society organizations are also equally active at local, national, or global level. The point of congruence between NGOs and CBOs come in the fact they both refer to social movements' classification and are therefore part and parcel of civil society, a concept that embraces all social activity by individuals, groups and movements (Willetts, 2004, 5). For any civil organization to qualify to be classified truly as an NGO, it must be independent and non-partisan.

Sustainable development is a term used to describe the process of natural resources preservation in a wise manner. It encourages the popular participation of the citizens of a nation in the effort to eliminate poverty and the general improvement of the livelihood of the people of a nation. Robert Dibie (2004, 154) exert that sustainable development is the desire for a nation to meet the development needs of the present without compromising the ability of future generations to meet their own needs. This process involves economical, security, social, cultural and popular participation of the citizens of a nation in decision making. Generally, sustainable development encompasses the management of natural resources, capacity building of human resources, policy instruments governing investment activities, conflict resolution, peace and democratization (Weaver et al.1996).

Robert Wilbur (2000) contends that the cooperation of NGOs and major stakeholders in an economy is absolutely very important for the attainment of sustainable development. This partnership is also very essential for the success of an aggressive economic development policy of any nation. A major stakeholder is any person or institution who directly or indirectly controls resources or possesses the expertise needed to make things happen. Major stakeholders will often include political or public officials or institutions, NGOs, private sector entrepreneurs, industrialists, labor leaders, public administrators and so on.

One factor that is missing in several African nations is the fact that communities are not developing their own industrial policies. A nation's industrial policy will mean a little unless there is a related policy at the local or community level to take advantage of the federal and state or regional government resources as they are available. The failure of state or communities to adopt some policy regarding their economic development future has caused extreme disaster in several African countries (Eade, 2002). It is often after such a disaster that foreign NGOs are attracted to such areas. The impact of this existing approach is bewildering and sometimes counterproductive in moving an African nation toward achieving sustainable development.

Felix Edoho and Robert Dibie (2001) pointed that development policies of many African nations might have a spatial dimension on a human face. They contend that (1) national development policies are needed to increase social control over the economic changes of corporate investment; (2) communities and civil societies need a greater role in controlling their economic stability and quality of life; (3) citizens and their representatives should have increased control and certainty over their livelihood. This means that sustainable development can only be achieved in the African continent if appropriate partnership are formed among the national government, NGOs, the private sector and community based organizations. It is paramount for such collaboration to provide assistance to the communities in their economic development planning process. Therefore, an appropriate approach to aid and development should seek to foster dynamic organizational and related capacities of the national and regional governments of an African country. It is very crucial for NGOs and the private sector to collaborate with the government in creating conditions that are more favorable to poverty reduction and sustainable development in the African continent.

Assessment of NGOs Performance in Anglophone Africa

The British Broadcasting Service (hereinafter, BBC) initiated in February of 2004 a highly important and revealing discussion program christened "African NGOs: Achievers or Deceivers?" The opinions expressed by the respondents on the topic were quite informative, and these provide reasonable background on which this chapter is based. However, before exploring the outcomes of the BBC discussion, it might be rewarding to observe that after the end of the Cold War, African development had begun to be influenced by the waves of economic, social and political liberations that had become predominant in the relationships between the continent and the Northern States of Europe, Canada and the United States of America. Along with the waves also came rejuvenated and reinvigorated NGOs movements.

The resurgence of the NGOs movement in Africa had begun to attract donor interest. Sooner than later, more NGOs began to emerge in the continent. Among the documented aims, African NGOs sought to achieve were networking for the provision of relief services especially in the war-torn and drought-stricken nation states. NGOs in Africa also provided services for seriously deprived and disadvantaged women and youth, environmental conservation, and contribution to development projects. The challenging movements emerged in Anglophone Africa that sought to combat governments over human rights issues and, more recently, tackling the HIV/AIDS pandemic that has afflicted over 28.1 million Africans. The people infected with HIV/AIDS in Africa constitute more than half of a global figure of forty million (World Bank, 2004).

To date, the assessment of NGOs performance in Anglophone Africa has been more subjective than objective, and there are hardly any hard core quantitative data and published research information to draw from. Some of the assessments have been encouragingly ebullient whilst others have been scathing. This discussion seeks to utilize such preliminary assessments, whatever the value they might have, to make a case for NGOs training in Anglophone Africa.

A cursory exploration of the literature on the subject did indicate that Anglophone African NGOs have made an impact at advocacy and policy levels. Indeed, Aloo (2004, 58; Kaplan 1999) have drawn attention to the fact that apart from thriving very well since the Cold War, the NGOs movement in Africa had achieved such professional development levels to the extent that regional networks like the *Association of African Women for Research and Development* (AAWORD based in (Senegal), and the Development Alternatives with Women for a New Era (DAWN based in Nigeria/Senegal), amongst others, have come to strengthen the movements. There are many more positive comments on the achievements of the NGOs movement. At the same time, however, there have been numerous negative assessments of NGOs performance in Anglophone Africa.

Anglophone African nations are increasingly accessible to foreign NGOs. Several NGOs from western industrialized nations continue to explore humanitarian programs in sub-Saharan Africa. They sponsor trade shows, conferences, environmental management projects, women liberation movement, and education and HIV/AIDS and religious programs and so on. Advocacy NGOs groups are also involved in promoting research towards common humanitarian goals as well as the free delivery of goods and services to people in need in rural communities across several Anglophone African nations.

The BBC discussion already alluded to above did hint that: While some governments welcome NGOs, others find them a nuisance or even a threat to their interests (BBC, 2004, 1). When it comes to assessing the impacts NGOs in Africa have made, the above summary and reflective statement coming from the BBC can provide a guiding light. In other words, NGOs operating in the African continent are described as a blessing, a nuisance or a threat.

Are NGOs in Africa a Blessing?

In an expository review of NGOs movements in Africa, Omolewa (2003, 1) made it be known that NGOs have actually promoted African values of community development, spirituality, devotion to the family, relaxed attitude towards time and the readiness to forgive and move ahead towards achieving great things for the civil society. That could be true, but NGOs operations in Anglophone African have also been looked at both in negative and positive ways.

In an attempt to find the views of people about the above question, 35 people were randomly selected from around the world. Below are their opinions about NGOs activities in Africa. Their views are followed by comments by the author. Positive comments about the African NGO performance could be

gleaned from the first thirteen respondents interviewed (BBC News, 2004, 1-25). The respondents' opinions are expressed as follows:
Opinion Number 1:

"NGOs are the rapid response unit of humanitarian disasters all over the world. Members of these unique organizations put their lives on the line to operate in volatile areas during conflicts, and providing unconditional services to poverty stricken people . . . Their successes out-make their deficiencies. They are more accountable than government agencies . . . corrupt governments get jittery when NGOs are operating because accountability is the key to the new world order, which these governments lack." (Michael Bobby Bull, Liberian in Atlanta, Georgia, USA).

Comment: This opinion squarely pitches NGOs performance against that of governments in many countries in Africa. The experience of Michael Bobby Bull must have influenced his opinion in concluding that African NGOs are to a large extent a blessing, it does not matter whatever deficiencies they have.

Opinion Number 2:

"Some NGOs are doing a wonderful job. In Bayelsa State of Nigeria, UNICEF virtually runs the Primary Health Care System. The government cannot even provide immunization twice a year, so NGOs keep up the good work." (Anonymous, Nigeria)

Comment: Although this commentator may not have fully conceptualized NGOs, she equally reviews NGOs performance against the background of government involvement in health care delivery. She concluded that some NGOs are doing a "wonderful" job. This brings out the reality that when it comes to assessing NGOs performance in Africa, we cannot actually generalize too much. The fact remains that NGOs vary in performance from one country to another.

Opinion Number 3:

"There is no doubt that here in Angola it is the NGOs that are feeding and healing the population. It is the NGOs that are clearing the minefields and it is the NGOs that are providing counsel and support to a population ravished by decades of war. In countries where governments are either unable or unwilling to assist, NGOs provide an essential lifeline to millions of people and their contribution should be recognized despite their short-comings." (Jez, Angola)
Comment: This is a further confirmation of the many good sides of NGOs performance in Africa. But the opinion equally acknowledges the fact that the NGOs have a lot of short-comings.

Opinion Number 4:

"Many submissions make reference to profligacy on such items as land-rovers and expert costs, and yet in contrast to much bilateral aid agencies most NGOs are much more careful with their money since they have rather less of it. With smaller NGOs you run the risk, just as you do with small charities in the UK, of selfish directors creaming off most of the funds for their own benefit, but my impression is that overheads rapidly increase with the size of the organization. Moreover, small NGOs are often tightly focused on specific issues and often more able to achieve clear results than over-ambitious larger projects. Small is beautiful except when it's ugly." (Steve Ball, UK)

Comment: In the opinion of Steve Ball, most NGOs are better than many bilateral aid agencies in terms of careful spending of funds. It could be that the allegations of financial mismanagement often leveled against NGOs must be carefully investigated.

Opinion Number 5:

"If there were no NGOs, what do you think would have happened to the 12 million people who were starving in Ethiopia or the millions displaced in Sudan? They would have died in silence without a witness. At least the NGOs are serving as witnesses to crimes African regimes commit against their subjects. That is important. Other than being a witness, there is nothing much NGO can do in Africa. Because the systems of governance do not allow change, and African states know the best means of controlling the population is to keep them destitute" (Yusuf Mohammed, USA).

Comment: Yusuf Mohammed appreciates the important role of NGOs in meeting the needs of millions of starving Ethiopians. Beyond that, NGOs, in his opinion, have been "witnesses to crimes African regimes commit against their subjects." It must be that African NGOs double in their activities as watchdogs of human right abuses, many of which may be unreported and/or under-investigated and prosecuted.

Opinion Number 6:

"I have worked for two international NGOs and the United Nations, in Africa, Europe and Asia. I was clearing landmines and unexploded ordinance and training national staff to do the same thing. Bearing in mind the huge number of explosive devices that I and the people my NGO have trained have destroyed, how can this be a bad thing? When the mines are cleared, the fields can be replanted and the houses and infrastructure rebuilt. Most people do not realize the very positive impact NGOs have on developing countries because NGOs tend to focus on what they are doing, rather than self-promotion." (Sean, Moorhouse, USA)

Comment: Sean Moorhouse placed immense value on the risk-taking commitment of NGOs, and that, in his view, should make less serious the negative allegations being leveled against NGOs. It might be deduced from this opinion that NGOs have safeguarded lives and made hitherto heavily mined farmlands cultivatable for the benefit of the masses of our people.

Opinion Number 7:

"NGOs have consistently stepped up the pace to expose corrupt leaders, tyrants, counter powerful multi-national corporations, advocate for the poor, and stand up to powerful Western governments. Most NGOs are now the sole bread winners for millions of Africa's poor." (Eyiinahn Glay, Zahgounla, Liberia)

Comment: NGOs have taken on board the rather intricate and high-risk activity of exposing Africa's corrupt leaders. They may have gone much further to counter leaderships that are tyrannical and multi-national corporations whose activities are largely anti-people in terms of neglecting to safeguard lives and the sustainable livelihoods of people. Many of the NGOs may have gradually transformed into becoming "bastions" of hope for the hopeless.

Opinion Number 8:

"It is not fair to discredit the entire NGOs operations in some African countries because of a few bad apples. There's a lady in Somaliland who happens to be a NGO worker and she always goes out of her way in helping Somali Landers. Her web log the taste of Africa, my journey to a nation unknown to the world says it all. As far as I'm concerned this particular lady is a Saint." (Osman Qaal, Canada)

Comment: Osman Qaal acknowledges the fact that there have been allegations of poor performance on the part of some NGOs. In his opinion, however, the few bad apples must not be allowed to soil the numerous others that are doing equally excellent jobs in the African continent in terms of providing humanitarian and economic development assistance.

Opinion Number 9:

"Being a citizen of Matabeleland, I know what it is to be denied any form of development. I know what it is like to be denied food even that which is donated by outsiders. I fully support the existence of NGOs, even when they are interpreted to be interfering with governance. These organizations have had some of their staff risking their lives for the sake of my people in Matabeleland. The truth be told, Matabeleland has existed since 1986 because of NGOs. The Government's aim was and remains, to exterminate us." (E. K. Maseko, USA)

Comment: In Maseko's opinion, NGOs have continued to be a major source of community development and renewal by the way they have helped the people to come together to share ideas and resources to help alleviate poverty in several African nations.

Opinion Number 10:

"NGOs are made up of people that decide to go to another country, usually very distant from where they live. They go to these places only because they have a dream that is make a better world. And if a person decides to dedicate his life for a country where he wasn't born, is not because he want to become rich with the money destined for the poorest people, but only what they promised to do with it. Truly, there will be no great need for proliferation of NGOs if our leaders (government) in Africa would imbibe the spirit of 'being your brother's keeper' instead of been self centered, ego centric, greedy and covetous." (Lanre Rasaq Araba, United States of America)

Comment: This respondent pitches his argument against African governments that largely fail to deliver on their promises for good governance. In other words, the way we may reduce the activities of NGOs, if that is actually feasible since they constitute an important segment of the civil society, is for the governments to perform satisfactorily in terms of meeting the needs of the people in Africa.

Opinion Number 11:

"The NGO philosophy is not new in Africa's development. In Ghana we call them Nkosuo Kuo and among the Yoruba's in Nigeria, NGOs are called Agbe Idagbasoke. However, the 1990s wave of globalization which introduced a new concept of multi discipline participation in development recognized the formation and involvement of NGOs in the development process. This, in some way, has led to miss-conception that an NGO is another way of creating jobs and amassing wealth." (Bayo, Ghana)

Comment: To Bayo, NGOs remain as valid as viable instruments providing support where public service seems to have failed. The NGOs remain valid even though the adoption of a multi-disciplinary approach seems to have generated some misunderstanding among different people.

Opinion Number 12:

"One of the most common complaints seems to be the use of 4 x 4 vehicles used by NGOs. This is laughable. Is Africa swamped by these vehicles? Of course it isn't. NGO workers often have to travel long distances over terrible roads and in dangerous environments. If they didn't have these vehicles, they would spend more time fixing the engines than helping people. People who own jeeps in countries like the US and UK are wasting their money, for many NGOs it is a necessity. Of course some NGOs are bad and some are good. However, the people who could really tell you who is bad and who is good can't. They don't have internet access. Ask them who they think is doing more NGOs or their government. (Richard, UK and East Africa)

Comment: The most valid assessment of NGOs performance ought to come from the direct beneficiaries of NGOs services. Unfortunately, the recipients of NGOs services are often neglected in debates and comments on NGOs performance. But Richard's comments seem to imply that NGOs are serving very purposes in Africa.

Opinion Number 13:

"It is my belief that much more would be achieved by NGOs if they concentrate on providing development assistance to the poor man in the village rather than wasting time arguing with governments. Most NGOs are based in town and make noise on civil and political rights. My view is that the typical African does not need freedom of expression. These people need to be helped how to realize their social and economic rights. Most NGOs are not accountable either. They are more or less like briefcase organizations. On the other hand most African governments treat NGOs as the unofficial opposition. I believe NGOs and government can work hand in hand for the benefit of our people." (Pacharo Kiyara, Malawi)

Comment: Kiyara recognizes the importance of the role of NGOs services but remain worried that NGOs are engaging more and more in confronting governments instead of concentrating on their primary responsibility. It is not clear if Kiyara is aware that there are NGOs that are functioning in the area of human rights violations and must necessarily appear to be confrontational when in fact they may be doing exactly what their instrument of establishment expects them to do.

While it may not be possible to make comments on every opinion expressed, it is valuable to appreciate numerous other comments as these have influenced the benchmarking that should guide the development of NGOs training programs that are urgently needed for high-impact performance in Anglophone Africa, in general. Leanne Black (2003) has pointed out the result-oriented, bureaucratic imperatives of many African governments. He further contends that NGOs and donor agencies have effectively nullify the long-term, participatory, and process-oriented approach to capacity building and humanitarian programs in the continent.

Most opinions indicated above would rather have us appreciate NGOs in Africa as having positively impacted their communities, no matter the shortcomings that others might want to point out. One important lesson we have learnt in Africa is that leaders are advised to look out for the dark cloud in every silver lining. That means that, African leaders do not have to look only for "praise singers." Every word of appreciation needs to be taken a bit more carefully before the leader runs into the danger of living in self-delusions. It is in line with that age-long African value that we must also consider opinions that are not so positive. Indeed, some of these opinions are scathing but they could raise serious issues for NGO training in Anglophone Africa in the twenty-first century or future generation.

Are NGOs in Africa a Nuisance or Threat?

Whatever the goals of foreign NGOs in Africa, establishing a project in the continent takes a great deal of efforts, time and resources. It also involves maneuvering around major obstacles not normally encountered in their nation of origin. For some NGOs, however, establishing projects in Africa is integral to their humanitarian mission. The desire to establish programs in the African continent is not only associated with NGOs sponsored or financed by USAID, CIDA and their counterparts from Europe, the International Red Cross or the Doctors without borders. Other NGOs are notably Advocacy groups whose missions require humanitarian activities around the world to supplement their domestic projects are also very active in several African nations.

Below are twenty-four more excerpts from the BBC February 2004 discussion program. Thirteen out of the twenty-four respondents indicated that NGOs are not a nuisance in Africa. The remaining eleven respondents stated that foreign NGOs operating in the African continent are established to benefit their expatriate staff, upper class Africans and senior public leaders and administrators. Some of these foreign NGOs had established projects in many countries for over a decade without any meaningful difference in the lives of the poor living in and around the project sites. The following are their opinions about NGOs operation in Africa:

Opinion Number A:

"Most NGOs do not have exit strategies. Projects have to be generated continually to keep them in business. They have no respect for African cultures and do not understand them. The Western governments they come from are to blame in most causes of poverty. Look at Iraq." (Lois, Kenya)

Comment: Lois was clearly angered by some of the NGOs that, in his opinion, have over-stayed their welcome. He was also of the view that Western governments are in the first place responsible for poverty. People like Lois do not seem to pay equal attention to African governments and leaders that have failed to live up to their promises in delivering services to their people.

Opinion Number B:

"I worked for a NGO in North Wollo, Ethiopia where a vast number of the population are exposed to starvation even during the good rainy season and harvest. This organization was hiding in the mountains of North Wollo for almost a decade without making a meaningful difference on the lives of the poor. In fact, the NGOs projects in North Wolo have only benefited the upper class, some district officials, its expatriates, few literate and economically well-to-do male farmers and its national staff. This program has been recently phased out and its staff members have left the area to find better jobs in similar nonprofit organizations while local poor are still suffering greatly from hunger and disease." (Jote Chemeda, Ethiopia, USA)

Comment: Jote was here lamenting the failure of NGOs to build elements of sustainability into what they are doing. The departure of the NGO has in some cases visited untold hardship on the people that they had served.

Opinion Number C:

"I have seen quite a lot of NGOs in Nigeria and Cotonou that have strived to better the lives of the down trodden particularly in remote villages where they give out food, shelter and clothing. I have also heard of some NGOs collecting money from Western donors for their selfish motives rather than because they wants to help."(Filippo, Italy)

Comment: Filippo had mixed feelings about the work of NGOs. He did not provide sufficient and valid evidence of the allegations he was making, but the fact remains that a lot of people may really have doubts as regards the value of having NGOs that are not honoring their promises to the people on whose behalf they solicit for and obtain funds.

Opinion Number D:

"There is no denying the fact that NGOs have made a tremendous contribution to the development of Africa over the past two decades, especially in the area of democratization, human rights and the rule of law. The question has always been asked whom do they represent and where do they get their mandate from? It is a difficult question to answer if you open the closet of today's NGOs. Not only have they abandoned the lofty ideals of fighting injustices, impunity, corruption, etc, but they are themselves party to these vices. There is not talk of democracy, let alone human rights and the rule of law in most NGOs plans. It is time they put their act together." (Robert Wundeh Eno, Cameroonian in the Gambia)

Coment: Here is another case of a respondent that is worried that NGOs are abandoning their mandates in spite of the good work many of them may be doing in Africa.

The other comments below clearly reflect the dilemma that NGOs are facing in Anglophone Africa. Be that as it may, the comments serve the purpose of the analysis we shall attempt at the end of the remaining comments.

Opinion Number E:

"To a great extent the NGOs who come to mind are businesses. Yes, they may answer to shareholders" "investors or the concerned but terms such as accountable and democratic are deliberately used to blur the fact that the aid industry is just that an industry. How many governments are truly holding agencies accountable? It is interesting to note how development courses have mushroomed in the universities in the United Kingdom (UK). What is wrong with administration, business and all the other courses we see people take in the UK so they can contribute to the greater good of society? Once more, agencies are very good at using those words and stock phrases such as sustainable, participation and poverty alleviation to try and differentiate themselves from businesses or administrations trying to deliver services or create wealth within a setting. What entitles me to make such sweeping statements? Fourteen years working in the aid industry as a volunteer, a member of a number of very reputable NGOs, at times with the United Nations and as a donor and the desire to create the debate you have opened to be brought to ever greater attention of those who drop money into collection tins believing the pennies WILL cause lasting change." (Paul Crook)

Opinion Number F:

"The problem of bogus NGOs is a worryingly under-researched area. Not only do they tarnish the image of genuine NGOs but may also lead to an over-estimation of the developmental capacity of certain regions. It is not improbable that bogus NGOs fraudulently appropriate tens of millions of dollars of donor funding and charitable contributions every year. On a more normative level, it is indeed time for them to be rounded up. (William Greene, UK)

Opinion Number G:

"I recently traveled throughout West Africa, covering many miles on foot, via bush-taxi, by rail, by donkey and on top of an occasional horse, when I was lucky. My trip was in the fashion and company of local people. At three o'clock in the morning, while stuck near the Senegal/Gambia border for several hours, I got a much needed lift from an NGO representative in the latest edition of a Land Rover." (Anonymous)

Opinion Number H:

"There is a wide array of NGOs operating in Africa. Some are mobilizing people to tackle poverty, but other are more interested in mobilizing funding to ensure their organization's own survival. Many seem to be struggling to adapt to their governments working closely with donors around the development of Poverty Reduction Strategies; the new aid modality in which it is envisaged that civil society (and NGOs) will help hold their government for fear of the financial and political repercussions." (Haze Plunkett, Tanzania covering East Africa)

Opinion Number I:

"NGOs are an indispensable partner for development. That said it is important that they remain impartial players. In Zimbabwe, some of them have become an unofficial opposition to the government. They should leave the politics to the politicians." (Memezi Nyoni, Zimbabwe)

Opinion Number J:

"Some NGOs in Africa mean well by attacking and cutting through government incompetence and bureaucracy to solve problems affecting our people. However, most of them are just money and leisure spinning entities that buy expensive 4 x 4 Land Cruisers and hold numerous unproductive seminars day in day out. A US$10, 000 budget to a foreign donor may not mean much to them, but it is substantial in a society where most people are poor. And some NGOs thrive on this factor exploiting it as much as they can." (Chileshe Mutale, Zambia)

Opinion Number K:

"NGOs are probably well intentioned outfits who undertake a lot of humanitarian activities. However all systematic improvement to African people have come from better governance, fiscal discipline and economic reforms. The output of NGOs has been sentimental and patronizing TV programs for Western consumption that provide a feel good factor. NGOs are an industry sector in their own right increasing imports (especially of 4 x 4s). Other than this any sustained benefits from NGO activities are yet to be seen." (Anirudh Ganguly, UK)

Opinion Number L:

"NGOs to a large extent are helping people here. Those in the rural areas are benefiting from food aid and conservation programs while we in urban areas are now more educated about human rights were it not for these NGOs, many of us would not know that our rights are being violated daily. Disturbing though, is the lavish spending by these NGOs on employees (believe you me, its must excessive!). If you can get a job with an NGO, especially the AIDS and sustainable development ones, then your life will change overnight. This is clearly widening disparities in society and creating serious rifts in classes of the haves and have-nots. So what really is the mission of NGOs. (Marie Chimuti, Harare, Zimbabwe)

Opinion Number M:

"NGOs are crucial for delivery of social services where the state is unwilling or unable to do so. However, their role is to supplement the government not to replace it. Anything else is simply unsustainable." (TD, South Africa)

Opinion Number N:

"NGOs are more and more becoming part of the problem instead of being part of the solution." (Carlos Dominguez, Spain).

Opinion Number O:

"NGOs are as diverse as the African continent itself. Of course there are some agencies that are making a difference, and some are causing more harm than good. But at least there is a choice. If one NGO isn't democratic or accountable, donors can always look for another one that meets those criteria. However, if development funds are channeled solely through national governments, when problems with corruptions and accountability arise, you can't "shop around" for a difference." (Anonymous)

Opinion Number P:

"If you want to know, take a keen look at the stark example of Kenya. For the past decade plus, the NGO sector has boomed, taking all the donor money the former government could not get. Today, what do they have to show for it? Poverty levels instead ballooned by over 20 percentage points. To me, majority of NGOs in Africa are just deceivers." (Hezekiah Agwara, Kenya)

Opinion Number Q:

"True, many NGOs in Africa are not established in the best interests of the targets they claim to serve. Only a few are genuine, and even so, they are spread thinly everywhere and make no impact at all. Many are money minting factories by their directors; others serve the interests of their sponsors abroad. Its high time NGOs that are fueling poverty were wound up." (Malinda Harrahs, Kenyan in Germany)

Opinion Number R:

"Whilst much good work is done many NGOs are extraordinarily naïve when dealing with government ministries. I would also suggest it is time that NGOs occasionally got out of their expensive Land Cruisers and walked, as this gives them the opportunity to meet or hear of those in greatest need." (Mark T Jones, Jordan)

Opinion Number S:

"Frankly speaking NGOs in Africa are potential job markets for expatriates who come from the funding countries and agencies. We can't however, dispute the work that they are doing but at the same time, the merits are more pronounced to the expatriates than the actual beneficiaries on the ground." (Yitatek Yitbarek, Ethiopian/South Africa)

Opinion Number T:

"As an NGO worker in Africa, I can say there are many NGOs contributing to the problems instead of solving them. More accountability and monitoring are necessary." (Sam Sanders, US)

Opinion Number U:

"Many NGOs operating in Africa today are what can only be described as Good Sent or Saviors. These organizations have and are saving thousands of lives that had no hope of a second chance to life. There are equally hundreds of other so called NGOs that I would rather call suckers. These NGOs are in fact, using the suffering of hopeless people to achieve other goals." (Joseph Harris, Liberian in U.S.)

Opinion Number W:

"Ideally, NGOs are expected to help Africans overcome many ills in the continent. But, unfortunately, in a poverty-stricken continent, where accountability counts less, ninety percent of NGOs in Africa are corrupt business outfits. They deceive their Western donors and contribute nothing to the society." (Jude Odinkonigbo, Enugu, Nigeria)

The twenty-two respondents' opinions expressed in this section mostly perceive African NGOs as a nuisance. Quite a few see them as a threat, and corrupt. It is very important to note that the BBC discussion program may not have been conducted in line with the usual procedures in quantitative and qualitative research methodologies. Therefore, most academics may want to "castigate" whatever opinions that might have been expressed as spurious and non-significant in the usual language of a social science research. Even at that the positive and negative opinions expressed about NGOs performance in Africa could provide some good basis for articulating NGO training needs in the future.

Possible Needs/Issues in NGO Training

Although it might be inadequate to rely on the opinions expressed in a single exercise to come to a valid conclusion as to what we need to do in order to have high-impact performing NGOs in Africa, the opinions expressed in the BBC World News discussion program reported in February 2004 as well as the 2002 SADCC Region NGOs Needs Assessment Survey conducted in a number of universities in Africa collectively may help us in identifying major NGO training needs that must be met in the twenty first century. The training needs includes: (1) Communication (including computer literacy); (2) NGO policy formulation and analysis; (3) Fund raising and financial management; (4) Capacity building and sustainability; (5) Organizational development; (6)

Community project planning and management; (7) Integrated extension; (8) Integrated skills project; and (9) Human resource management and development.

The need to establish training in African universities that would foster research in environmental analysis for sustainable development, information systems, science and technology for development, environmental impact assessment of policies, programs and projects evaluation, fund raising techniques and financial management, human resources development and environmental awareness programs. The modes of learning and training to adopt in this case are dictated by the very nature of the work of the professionals as well as their geographical area in the African continent.

Obviously, African nations cannot afford the luxury of individual countries entirely deciding on "what" and "how" of NGOs training. In fact, the very similar nature of problems facing the people would suggest the need for a regional training program that is based on a careful need assessment as has been done by some universities in Southern Africa. An effective benchmarking of NGOs training implies that African nations come up with a commonly agreed and approved curriculum. Such a curriculum should clearly articulate the philosophy, goals, and target audience, mode of delivery and program structure of the kind of training intended. It should also articulate the entry requirements, duration of training, staffing, courses, course synopsis and modes of evaluation.

Some African leaders already have doubts about the quality of work that our NGOs are doing. Therefore, any program that is introduced must be such that it would be recognized and accredited. This implies that designers of programs need to pay attention to the monitoring and evaluation of the programs as well as internal and external assessments of learners to determine their levels of achievement.

Furthermore, benchmarking NGO management and training programs would imply that designers need to consider affiliating the training to relevant, existing universities in the region. That should further add credibility to the provision. This could prevent the danger of further scathing criticisms of what African NGOs stand for.

Most of the ideas raised under benchmarking point to the fact that the first challenge African nations have to tackle are that of credibility of programs. Many things go into making programs credible. Apart from what have been suggested above, the effort being made must receive assurance of financial support for a certain length of time. In that case, all stakeholders who provide financial support for NGOs need to be aware of the need for the training.

Beyond funding, there is the question of the development of standard learning materials that come through the inputs of renowned experts. The materials must go through the process of content and copy editing with provisions for trial runs of such materials. In most cases, the intended NGOs training programs need to rely on qualified and, sometimes, highly experienced staff. Experienced and qualified staffing is actually a standard and basic prerequisite for the running of academic and research programs. If such staffing is unavailable, learners run the risk of "double" frustrations that usually accompany learning from a distance.

Finally, another important challenge that needs to be addressed is that of digital capability of Anglophone African countries. It is true that some efforts have been made thus far to make Internet connectivity a reality in several African nations. The adequate installation of computers with access to internet capability is another "kettle of fish" altogether. Added to that challenge is the computer literacy capability of the learners. These and other challenges would have to be addressed in deciding on the best modes of NGOs training delivery to be adopted.

Conclusion

This chapter has examined the perception of NGOs operations in English speaking African nations. It also explored the issues in NGO management and training for high-impact performance in Anglophone Africa. It proposed a benchmarking approach that could be based on the needs and issues raised about NGOs performance in Africa from a discussion program conducted by the BBC in 2004. Although the program may have been unscientifically conducted, it provided profound insights that informed the propositions made. This, of course, should be first step towards achieving standardized NGO training program for Anglophone African nations in general. The chapter also argued that collaboration among government, NGOs, the private sector and civil society organizations is the critical element toward attaining any meaningful development in Africa. It contends that foreign NGOs should work closely with host African nations and community groups or organizations. It is believed that NGOs would significantly strengthen their operations in Africa if national governments in the continent provide an appropriate political and administrative atmosphere for them to provide their humanitarian and development goods and services.

In the twenty first century, sustainable development is essentially a process by which government, NGOs, the private sector and community based groups manage their existing resources and enter into a new form of partnership arrangement among each other. This partnership should encourage the protection of the environment, create new jobs and stimulate economic activities in nations across the African continent.

The chapter also stressed the importance of locally oriented and economic based development. This orientation would foster the development of local initiatives in the growth process as well as the preservation of the environment for future generation of the African continent. There is also the goal for this collaboration to increase citizen participation in governance, create new employment and stimulate various economic activities. Generally, the sustainable development process that should be introduced need to involve the formulation of new public and private institutions, the development of alternative industries, the improvement in the capacity of existing employers to produce better products, the identification of new markets, the transfer of knowledge and the nurturing of new firms and enterprises. These tasks are obviously beyond what NGOs could handle in a particular African nation, hence there is the call for appropriate partnership among all stakeholders to be involved the sustainable development process.

African political leaders must be committed to the strengthening of the capacities of their people and national resources to cerate an economy that do not tolerate poverty and injustice. Further, NGOs and community development practitioners should contribute to this cause by stepping away from their own ideology and operations to examine whether they are actually fostering or constraining the sustainable development process in the African continent. The need to train professional public and private administrators, as well as NGOs staff is also very crucial for African countries to move toward achieving sustainable development. There is, therefore, an urgent call for universities in Africa to introduce appropriate curriculum to address these sustainable development and globalization issues into their degree programs.

References

Aloo, F. M. "The Non-governmental (NGOs) Movement in Africa." http://eurpoeeu.int/comm/development/body/publications/courier/81en/en-058-ni.pdf (accessed March 8, 2006).

Black, Leanne. "Critical Review of the Capacity-Building Literature and Discourse." *Development in Practice* 13, no. 1 (2003): 116-120.

British Broadcasting Corporation. "NGOs: Achievers or Deceivers?" *BBC News World Edition*. http://news.bbc.co.uk/2/hi/africa/3502733.stm (7 January2006).

Blakely, Edward. *Planning Local Economic Development: Theory and Practice*. London, England: Sage 1989.

Dibie, Robert. "Implication of Globalization in the Teaching of Public Administration in Africa: The Case of Nigeria." *International Journal of Public Administration* 23, no. 3 and 4 (2004): 151-169.

Dichter, Thomas. "Globalization and Its Effects on NGOs." In *Understanding Non-profit Organizations; Governance, Leadership and Management*, edited by Steven Ott. Westview Press, 2001.

Eade, Deborah, ed. *Development, NGOs and Civil Society*. Bloomfield, CT: Kumarian Press, 2000.

Edoho, Felix, and Robert Dibie. "Executing Environmental Policy and Waste Management in Ghana and Nigeria." *Journal of Sustainable Development in Africa* 2 (Winter/Spring 2001):1-10.

Fisher, Julie. *Non-Governments, NGOs and the Political Development of the Third World*. Bloomfield, CT: Kumarian Press, 1997.

Fisher, Julie. *The Road from Rio: Sustainable Development and Nongovernmental Movement in Third World*. Westview, CT: Praeger, 1993.

Kaplan, Allan. *The Development of Capacity*. Geneva: UN-NGLS, 1999.

Mawlawi, Farouk. "New Conflicts, New Challenges: The evolving Role for NGOs Actors." *Journal of International Affairs* 46, no. 2 (1993): 39-53.

Mutahaba Gelase, Reweikiza Balogun, and Mohamed Halfani. *Vitalizing African Public Administration for Recovery and Development*. Bloomfield, CT: Kumarian Press, 1993.

Ndegwa, Stephen. *The Two Faces of Civil Society, NGOs and Politics in Africa*. Bloomfield, CT: Kumarian Press, 1996.

Ndegwa, Stephen. "Civil Society and Political Change in Africa: The Case of NGOs in Kenya." *International Journal of Comparative Sociology* 35, no. 1-2 (1994): 19-41.

Olowu, Dele, and Soumana Sako, eds. *Better Governance and Public Policy: Capacity Building for Democratic Renewal in Africa.* Bloomfield, CT: Kumarian Press, 2003.
Omolewa, M. "On the concerns about African NGOs and the way forward." Unpublished Position Paper, Nigeria Permanent Delegation to UNESCO, Paris, 2003.
Ott, Steven, ed. *Understanding Non-profit Organizations: Governance, Leadership and Management.* Westview Press, 2001.
Thin, Neil. *Social Progress and Sustainable Development.* Bloomfield, CT: Kumarian Press, 2002.
United Nations *Development Program (UNDP), Human Development Report 2002.* New York: Oxford University Press, 2002.
Wallace Jr., Don. "The Role of Multi-lateral Institutions in African Development." *Journal of Law and Policy in International Business* 30, no. 4 (2002): 697.
Weaver, J., Michael Rock, and Kenneth Kusterer. *Achieving Broad-Based Sustainable Development: Governance, Environment and Growth with Equity.* Bloomfield, CT: Kumarian Press, 1996.
Wilber, Robert, ed. *The Complete Guide to Non-Profit Management.* New York: John Wiley & Son, 2000.
Willetts, P. "What Is a Non-Governmental Organizations (NGOs)?" http://www.staff.city.ac.uk/p.willetts/cs-ntwks/NGO-ART (5 February 1006).
Williamson, Irving, and Stephen D'Alessandro. "New Prospects for Private Sector led Trade, Investment and Economic Development in Sub-Saharan Africa." *Journal of Law and Policy in International Business* 30, no. 4 (1996): 637.
World Bank. *Attacking Poverty: World Development Report 2000-2001.* Washington, DC: World Bank, 2002.
World Bank. *World Development Report 2003.* Washington, DC: World Bank, 2004.

Chapter 5

NGOs and Community-Based Environmental Projects in Botswana and Ethiopia

Saliwe Kawewe

In the 1980s Ethiopia became very popular for its famine and drought disaster relief programs. Several international non-governmental organizations (NGOs) poured in aids to help famine victims in the nation. During the past two decades, it has also been reported that productive land in Botswana has been shrinking daily. As usual NGOs have donated 13.4 million United States dollars to help resolve the environmental problems in Botswana (Zewdu 2002). The funding of this project was provided by the United Nation Environmental Program (UNEP) and the Global Environmental Facility (GEF). The objective of the project is to help rural communities restore local plant life, improve depleted soil and create new jobs opportunities.

While Ethiopia has more severe environmental problems than Botswana, it was not listed as one of the recipients of the recently awarded UNEP fund. Instead, Mali, Kenya and Botswana where named. Despite the environmental aids that have been poured into Ethiopia since the 1980s, the government of the nation recently implemented its voluntary resettlement programs in drought-hit part of some regions. The United Nations OCHA integrated Regional Information Network of January 2003 reported that the people in Oromiya and Amhara regions of Ethiopia have been suffering from severe environmental conditions. It was also reported that over eleven million people in Ethiopia are now facing starvation due to drought. The United Nations Emergencies Unit (EUE) for Ethiopia contends early 2003 that resettlement programs initiated in the nation could cause more devastating environmental problems as well as threatened indigenous people.

The history of environmental problems in Botswana and Ethiopia point to the fact that attempts to resettle people or providing possible solutions to famine victims in both nations have often ended in failure. This shows that governments and NGOs that have been involved in the environmental struggle in Botswana and Ethiopia must have been using the wrong approaches in trying to solve the problem. Current attempts in Botswana and Ethiopia at formulating environmental policy that are exclusive to the indigenous people have led to comprehensive confusion rather than clarity. Sustainable development to Botswana and Ethiopia means finding alternative ways to the development techniques that are currently depleting their natural resources. The broad sentiment associated with the term is greater sensitivity to nature and natural resources. However, beyond this general association, formulation of more rigorous environmental policies in Botswana and Ethiopia has ignored the input of indigenous people who are supposed to help implement all the environmental policies in their rural land. Thus, environmental problems of these nations fall broadly into two categories - the problems arising out of poverty or the inadequacy of development itself, and the problems that arise out of the very process of development.

This chapter examines how community-based environmental policies can be best implemented to achieve success in Botswana and Ethiopia. It argues that community based environmental policy will enable indigenous organizations and communities to discover and learn from the implementation experiences of other successful programs around the world. The paper addresses the need for government, NGOs, and community partnership to achieve both environmental and economic growth in Botswana and Ethiopia. The analysis of environmental policies and programs in Botswana and Ethiopia reveals that poorly conceived, inadequately planned, insufficiently financed and lack of indigenous people's participation in the implementation of ecological policies have led to the failure of such policies in both nations.

The chapter recommends some policy options for the governments of Botswana and Ethiopia in the twenty-first century. It contends that the choice of community base approach and related options for the generation and utilization of benefits should be situation specific.

Famine and Environmental Protection Issues

The 1980s have been marked as the beginning of severe famine in Ethiopia and Botswana. The 1980s also marked the period when several international environmental NGOs flock to North and East Africa to help famine victims. Despite the aids the NGOs provided in the 1980s the people of Ethiopia and Botswana have continuously been faced with an expression of fundamental change in their environmental conditions. A new ecological view of the role of the people of Ethiopia and Botswana has been emerging, one that departs from the traditional perception of human dominion over nature and moves toward a more realistic appreciation of humanity's inter-relationship with their environment. This new view has led to action in which Africa scholars have questioned the knowledge, experiences, and ethical judgments of NGOs staffs operating in Ethiopia and Botswana. These African scholars have argued that foreign NGOs staffs were not doing enough to help solve the severe environmental problems in these sub-Saharan African nations (Asefa 2003; Dibie 2001; James 1993; Kraft 2003).

The need for community based organizations and indigenous people in Botswana and Ethiopia to receive solid training in environmental management cannot be emphasized enough. Moses Kiggundu (1989) makes the point very clear that the gift of environmental management knowledge also has far more lasting effects and is far more closely relevant to the concept of development. "Give a man a fish, as the saying goes, and you are helping him a little but for a very short while; teach him the art of fishing and he can help himself all his life. On a higher level, supply him with a fishing tackle; this will cost you a good deal of money, and the result remains doubtful; but even if fruitful, the man's continuing livelihood will still be dependent upon you for replacements. But teach him to make his own fishing tackle and you have helped him to become not only self-supporting, but also self reliant and independent. Robert Dibie (2001) contends that the first step toward choosing environmental training needs is for the government to decide where the communities and indigenous organizational are in the rural agricultural areas, and where they want to be in the near future. Further, the appropriate mixture of government and NGOs expertise as well as traditional methods and technical skills necessary to achieve the desired environmental goals should be determined. It is only through this kind of pragmatic approach that environmental policies can achieve its mission and objectives in Botswana and Ethiopia.

Before the 1980s environmental and famine issues were seen as local or regional concerns. After the 1980s, however, environmental issues assumed a global dimension, and began to be seen as intrinsic to economic growth or decline (Matthews 1991; De Waal 1997; Kraft 2003). International interest in these issues has been spurred by three major factors. First the biodiversity of tropical lands together with the high potential of the virgin tropical forests in preserving the world's environmental heritage. Second the role of deforestation in global weather change, most especially its contribution to the greenhouse effect. Third is the loss of valuable natural habitats, wild plants and animal species (James 1993; Kraft 2003; World Bank 1990; Pearce et al. 1990; Barbier 1989). NGOs have also been influenced by insights flowing from a new field of research known as earth systems science or global change. The system science studies composed of geology, ecology, oceanography, chemistry, paleobiology, meteorology, and earth system science.

Radcliff and Goodman (1991), Van Den Breemer et al. (1995), and Omar Norman (1996) introduced the concept of co-evolution. Co-evolutionary concept suggests that, in order to be successful, development policy should ensure either that the extension of agricultural practices foreign to specific socio-cultural settings is accompanied by appropriate indigenous knowledge and organizational structures. This is necessary to sustain the practices, monitor and react to the environment's responses to the new technology, introduce by foreign NGOs in Africa. This approach will also allow new techniques to develop out of local knowledge and experience in Botswana and Ethiopia. The concept helps us to understand the dynamics of community based relationship between nature and society, and the sustainability of specific livelihood in both nations. Robert Dibie (2001) used agricultural co evolution to describe the process whereby the manipulative actions of human beings on local ecosystems result in environmental responses in Botswana and Ethiopia. The inability of NGOs and their aids to understand this dynamics is one of the reasons why after over twenty years the indigenous people of Botswana and Ethiopia are still dependant on foreign aids rather than growing their own food.

The general effort to stimulate interest in environmental protection in Botswana and Ethiopia has focused on foreign aid from NGOs rather than the need to introduce sustainable development policies in both nations. Although Botswana have instituted a community based natural resources management in Chobe District, the context of the project is quite different from the situation in other parts of the nation, and its success else where depends on the prevailing natural resources, livelihood, culture, history, level of material well-being and education. The situation facing community base natural resources management in Botswana is not encouraging because on one hand, the nations have to find alternatives too many of the development techniques that are currently depleting their natural resources. On the other hand, the Botswana government has to reduce consumption of natural resources without adequately educating the rural communities on how to do so with modern techniques. Its implications for economic policy are at best vague because over the past two decades attempts at formulating environmental policy as opposed to selectively addressing particular problems such as protecting an endangered species, have led to comprehensive confusion rather than clarity (Millar 1995; Norman 1996). The benefit of economic growth in the world, however, comes at great cost in terms of resource depletion and pollution. But these costs and benefits are not shared equally among the world's peoples. Although sub-Saharan African countries have limited access to these benefits, they pay a disproportionate share of the costs.

Dependency theorists see the development and wealth of Botswana, Ethiopia and several other African nations as functions of the developing world. Thus, environmental destruction in Botswana and Ethiopia may be rooted in western imperialism and natural causes. Patterns of resource exploitation emerged that enabled the western imperialism to accumulate capital and assume political hegemony over the subordinate sub-Saharan African nations like Botswana and Ethiopia, leading to a pattern in which the nations resources were used in a manner incongruent with local needs. At the same time, these patterns of resource exploitation incorporated new products and technologies from other areas of the globe. Botswana especially became very dependent on both export and import trade, and decolonization did not end this pattern.

Ascher and Healy, (1990) contend that bad economic performance increases poverty, which accelerates environmental degradation. Thus, their environmental study posits a strong relationship between economic development, poverty and environmental quality. The need for citizen community based participation was subsequently added to these criteria (Weaver and O'Keefe, 1991). The inadequate involvement of NGOs employees and indigenous organizations and personnel in the implementation of community base natural resources management problem constitute one of the reasons why NGOs environmental programs have been less successful in Botswana and Ethiopia.

Environmental Policy in Botswana

A review of Botswana's environmental policies in the fast two decades reveal that the nation is in a transition period in which environmental resources management has become a priority but the government has not been able to fully and effectively implement its various policies. Botswana's climate is sub-tropical, ranging from continental to semi-arid with the wettest months (December and January) coming in the summer in years of normal rainfall. Winters are dry (with July and August normally the driest months) and there is occasionally frost around June. Average rainfall is less than 475 mini-meters annually, raging from 250 mini-meters in the desert region of the southwest to over 650 mini-meters in the northeast. Vegetation reflects rainfall and soil patterns in the east and southeast. The country is prone to periods of severe drought extending over a number of years. The 1981-1987 droughts were the most severe this century, but since 1988 a more normal rainfall pattern has prevailed (De Waal 1997). Since 2001 some regions in Botswana have gradually suffered from drought.

Table 5.1 shows the climate and ecology of Botswana. The vegetation across Botswana varies from acacia dominant savannah in the south and central region to mapane, silver leaf and Zimbaweean teak in the north. There are also marula and baobab on the salt plans. The nation has two main rivers. One is the Okavango and the other is the Chobe River. The Okavango River spread slowly across the delta area creating a unique wilderness of channels, islands and lagoons in the midst of the dry Kalahari Desert degradation (Abucar and Molutsi, 1993; Ringrose et al., 1996).

The climate and soil in Botswana are most suited to large scale ranching, which was the country's predominant economic activity until the development of the mining sector in the early 1970s. But, due to lack of water, stock can only be grazed on 20 percent of the land area. In the 1970s the rapid expansion of the national herd led to overgrazing. Like other governments in this region Botswana is reorganizing its ranching methods in a bid to limit overgrazing through a major program establishing fenced leasehold the Tribal Grazing Land Policy (TGLP) which was introduced in 1975. Communal areas are reserved under the program for small-scale farmers, although development of ranches has proceeded slowly and the TGLP also aims to improve conservation and farming techniques (Botswana National Conservation Strategy 1990). The government now aims to maintain a high but sustainable level of cattle production through improved livestock management and husbandry techniques, land conservation and a more efficient land tenure system (Abucar and Molutsi, 1993; Ringrose et al., 1996).

The United Nations Environmental Program entered into partnership with the Botswana government in the mid 1980s to help it prepare a National Conservation Strategy. This need have galvanized close cooperation between the government of Botswana and the United Nation Environmental Programs (UNEP) in preparing the clearinghouse mission report. That report reflected the importance attached to identifying policies and other measures, which would ensure the sustainability of all future development.

Some United Nations Development Programs have been implemented in

Botswana. The goals of the UNDP in the area of environment is to help the nation adopt an integrated model of the management of natural resources in order to improve the livestock of Botswana's people. The Botswana National Development Plan 8 and Vision 2016 reveal that the government of Botswana attaches great importance to the wide range of natural resources and features which exist throughout the nation, and especially in protected areas: national parks, game reserves, forest reserves and designated wildlife management areas. Apart from the interest of the government of Botswana in Environmental issues, the UNDP is assisting the nation in three priority areas: (1) the sustainable use of natural resources; (2) the implementation of the National Policy on Natural Resources Conservation and Development and; (3) the fulfillment of Botswana's commitment under environmental conventions to which it is a party.

Table 5. 1
Climate and Ecology of Botswana

Ecological Regions	Meters Above Sea Level	Rainfall in (MM)	Average Temperature (0C)
Hardveld	850-1489	400-500	20.6 (Gaborone)
Sandveld	800-1200	250-690	22.4 (Maun)
Okavango Delta	990-1030	400-500	22.0 (Shakawe)
Makgadikgadi	905-930	400-450	22.0 (Rakops)

Source: Ringrose et al. "Environmental Change in the Mid-Boteti Area of North Central Botswana: Biophysical Processes and Human Perceptions." *Environmental Management* 20, no. 30 (1996): 397-410.

Botswana's resources include fresh air, clean water, vegetation, and livestock. Botswana has a diversity of wildlife, soil, and human culture, visual, archaeological and other related features. It is upon these resources that many people depend directly for a livelihood. Some of the resources are appreciated internationally for their univalves: The Okavango Delta and the central Kalahari game reserves, for example have experienced (a) the depletion of fuel wood resources, groundwater resources, wildlife species and indigenous veiled products resources, (b) land erosion, (c) urban and rural pollution, and (e) rangeland degradation (Abucar and Molutsi, 1993; Ringrose et al., 1996). The government of Botswana has also been committed to sustainable development. However, achievement of sustainable development calls for comprehensive evaluation of environmental and economic implications before major new developments are undertaken. Consistent with this, the natural conservation strategy is specifically geared toward environmental protection and conservation.

The nation's environmental policy emphasizes effective utilization of land and livestock needs. It attempts to create instruments that are intended to solve the problems of livestock development and land use, in order to improve the cash income of the livestock industry. The primary government policy with regard to conservation is in connection with development goals which call for balanced development, more employment opportunities with the diversification of the rural economy, better utilization of resources, improved education and community participation in natural resources management.

Despite Botswana environmental policy goals, the social and cultural impact of the environment on the people of Botswana are left outside of the domain of environmental policy. Apparently, as the environment's potential of Botswana declines, the impoverished people continue to practice their traditional modes of utilization without realizing that changes are required and that the government had enacted new environmental policies. Depletion of wood resources both in commercial harvest of forests and as the main source of domestic fuel in most settlements continues in the nation. As a matter of fact, wood harvesting has been largely undertaken in an unrestricted manner. The people of Botswana have paid little or no attention to ensuring that yields are economically sustainable. There has also been an overuse and exploitation of some mineral products such as diamond, copper-nickel and coals, together with small amounts of gold and natural soda.

Minerals have provided the basis for Botswana's recent economic growth. However, large-scale mineral exploitation by the De Beer Botswana Company has also caused a lot of environmental pollution (Mpotokwane 1992). This has damaged the mineral capacities to provide for both subsistence and commercial needs. Pollution of air, water, soil and vegetation resources have also continued. As a result of human struggle to support life in both urban and rural areas of Botswana, the nation's environmental policy has been greatly ignored (Abucar and Molutsi 1993). Further large number of livestock, crops and people need to use the same land which was previously needed to support only a few. In Botswana poverty is increasing. This increases the number of live trees being destroyed. New trees are not being planted fast enough to rebuild lost woodlands. As a result, productive land is shrinking day by day.

The formation of a national conservative strategy for Botswana, recent studies have identified continuing sources of environmental problems, such as inadequate waste disposal, lack of public toilets in urban areas, inadequate industrial and mining waste disposal system, declining wood and other natural resources (Abucar and Molutsi 1993). Treated water has declined and most people and animals are increasingly dependent on ground water. This inadequate human resource development and financial commitment on the part of the government creates constraints in the implementation of environmental policy.

NGOs, community based organizations and various environmental activist groups concerned with a more comprehensive policy have not yet developed the ability to influence the government to implement stated goals. For example, the Kalahari Conservative Society is more interested in the conservation of wildlife and natural resources than in environmental problems that affect public health (Abucar and Molutsi 1993). The Ecological setting of Botswana society has experienced change brought about by population growth, rural-urban migration, economic changes and market opportunities. People move out of their villages to the cities in search of better opportunity to meet their basic needs and this result in transplanting rural culture into urban areas.

Although most of the traditional land methods practiced in the past have not yielded good results, environmental change could be achieved through innovative cultural change. What is required in the twenty-first century is pragmatic and innovative cultural practice, for example, the use of controlled crop rotation and fertilizers, which combines compatible indigenous and modern methods. Although some farmers employ fertilizers, little control is undertaken by the government to see that its use does not exceed limits laid down by environmentalists. New mechanized farming methods could also be adopted. Co evolution theory teaches one that the introduction of alternative cultural practices in farming requires cooperation between government, NGOs and community base farming organizations in the rural areas. It is imperative that measures, which promote community based participation and innovative cultural input, are adopted to replace the traditional practice in Botswana.

The unwillingness of the national government to decentralized and encourage the integration of urban and rural development as well as the concentration of population in major towns and cities in Botswana have increased public environmental problems due to lack of social infrastructure. The government has not paid more attention to the provision of public toilet service. This oversight of government has resulted in the use of uninhabited spots for toilet in Gabonrone the nation's, capital city. This practice in most urban areas in Botswana constitutes pollution and serious health hazard. The dumping of consumer waste along the main streets and roads of major cities and villages also constitutes health hazard. A comprehensive waste disposal system should be introduced in the nation. This is necessary for Botswana's environmental policy to succeed. It is also imperative to develop a long-term comprehensive co evolution and community based policies that will encourage the development of an environmental awareness and education programs. These programs should include environmental curriculum in schools and advertisements in radio and televisions.

The nations environmental policies in the past three decades which tends to emphasize technical solutions to environmental problems and issues, current events in the nation has demonstrated that technical solutions alone cannot solve the nation's environmental problems. The government of Botswana needs to form partnership with NGOs, and civil society and rural social organization in order to bring about co evolution and cultural changes in addressing its environmental problem. Through a policy of education for social development the current environmental policy could establish sustainable and adequate conditions for reducing the problems of environmental depletion in Botswana (Dibie and Kawewe 1999).

The new approach in the twenty-first should not only focus on increased education of and participation by NGOs, community based organizations in improving the environment and management of natural resources, it should also foster partnership between the public and private sectors. There is the need for the introduction of an environmental policy which address issue of indigenous cultural change and the need to improve the social economic conditions of the majority of the people of Botswana. It is now apparent that the government alone cannot solve the environmental problems of Botswana, the need form partnership with NGOs and other sectors become very crucial in addressing the problem.

Famine and its Environmental Premise in Ethiopia

Most people associate Ethiopia with famine. The problems of famine in Ethiopia have cost the nation over 500,000 lives (Asefa 2003). The problem of famine made President Mengistu's to introduce the policy of absolute intolerance for dissidence or opposition in the 1980s. The lack of tolerance for dissidence policy earned the Ethiopian leader many enemies domestically and among nations that surrounded Ethiopia. Within Ethiopia ethnic groups such as Tigray built resistance to Mengistu's regime and it neighbor Eritrea aggressively demand independence (Haile, 1986; Country Watch 2003). During this period Ethiopia's neighbor to the south, Somalia clashed frequently with Ethiopia. Toward the end of the 1980s, these resistance, chaos and civil war that pervaded the government of Ethiopia galvanized Mengistu to loosen up his regimes socialist reform policies. The aftermath of these political problems is that they spillover to environmental issues. Asefa (2003) contend that policies implemented by Mengistu's regime prevented the private sector to own land. His administration abolishes private ownership of land in favor of privatization in order for farmers and entrepreneurs to use the land as collateral in receiving loans that could be used in developing and solving environmental problems in the nation.

Due to the severe famine of the 1980s and 19990s almost all the forest in the nation has been destroyed. According to Shibiru Tedla (2000) less than three percent of Ethiopia's landscape is now covered with trees. The implication of fewer trees growing in the nation might prompt environmental disaster. Although Ethiopia has been suffering from drought, its government policies, citizen's interference and economic reasons are the most important reasons for the fast depletion and serious degradation of natural resources in the nation. Medhin Zewdu (2002) pointed out that government and the people especially those living in the rural areas have not been able to give appropriate attention to efficient protection to its natural forest resources. In recent times Ethiopia's natural resources, has faced a variety of environmental crises including drought since the 1980s and in 2001-2003. The temperature of the nation has already increased because of the lack of trees placing a greater burden on the fragile environment and the communities living in the rural areas. Erosion problems in some rural areas are now so severe that many foreign non-governmental organizations have been funding projects to terrace the terrain.

The climate of the nation has also affected the landscape in the northern part of Ethiopia. The topography of the nation reflects a dissected and sloping terrain, fragile soil and is subject to high erosion during rainstorms and the wet agricultural season. Low in organic matter and with little natural tree cover, Ethiopia is subject to severe soil erosion (Hoben 1995). The majority of the forest in Ethiopia now lies in the southwest region of the nation. Foreign NGOs are now encouraging indigenous Ethiopians to plant trees. Despite the tree planting projects more than 64 million people in Ethiopia still depend on wood for cooking (Zewdu 2002). Thus the problem of drought, bush fire, overstocking, uncontrolled population growth and increasing demand for firewood and building materials have caused most of the environmental damage in the nation. Failure by the government of Ethiopia to address these issues has led to the degradation of land spontaneous small-farmers, migration. The government of Ethiopia has not been very successful in coordinating resettlement programs, expanding commercial and state farms. Several private and public officials tend to exploit of the small forests in the nation. The problem of soil erosion appears to be less severe than in the north because of availability of trees and tall grass (Hoben 1995; Mulvihill 1988).

Before the 1974 revolution in Ethiopia, the Northern Ethiopians had long managed their landscapes and practiced some forms of conservation. The farming techniques mostly used in the rural areas is plow-based mixed farming system and this contributes to soil erosion through fine tilling, mono-cropping and a lack of vegetation covering the soil during the heavy raining seasons. Historically, however, political, institutional and economic conditions neither gives land rights to neither elites nor peasants. The strong incentives to invest in agricultural improvement and labor intensive conservation measures are just to provide food for the nation and prevent the depletion of its natural resources.

The northern culture of the nation encourages a strong relationship between the indigenous farmers and nature. Indigenous southern Ethiopian farming systems were more sustainable before the present century, but this was altered after many farming practices were changed as a result of the northern conquest (Herweg 1994). In the wake of the 1985 famine, the Ethiopian government launched an ambitious program of environmental reclamation supported by international donors and several (NGOs) and backed by the largest food-for-work program in Africa. Over the preceding five years, peasants constructed more than one million kilometers of soil and stone bonds on agricultural land and built almost one-half million kilometers of hillside terrace. They also closed off more than 80,000 hectares of hillsides to most forms of use to foster the regeneration of naturally occurring plant species, and planted 300,000 hectares of trees, much of it community woodcuts (Dibie 2001; Hoben 1995).

As part of the solution provided by both the government and NGOs in the past three decades measures have been taken to construct terraces, soil bunds, and check dams, diversion drains and the planting of trees on hillsides and in catchments areas. The Ethiopian government also instituted a reclamation policy and has also appealed to a variety of Western donors the World Food Program (WFP), the European Economic Community (EEC), and The United States. These foreign NGOs not only supplied food to the Ethiopian people, they also introduced massive food-for-work programs on the grounds and as such they were addressing the long-term, underlying cause of famine, rather than mere alleviating its sympathy. This enabled the foreign NGOs to defend the criticism that they were only keeping people alive so that they could die in large numbers the next time the rains failed. The foreign NGOs were also able to counter the argument that the food aid in the form of handouts would make people lazy. In addition, foreign NGOs spread high levels of food supply after the famine was over not only to the people in the north, that were actually affected by the famine, but, also delivered food to areas that had not been affected by the drought or famine (Hoben 1989; Roe 1991). The extent to which the food-for-work approach has helped the people affected by drought in both nations is questionable.

As a result of famine in the mid-1980s and 2001- 2003, existing government reclamation programs were greatly expanded. Activities on peasant lands were organized by the Community Forestry and Soil Conservation Development Department of the Ministry of Agriculture that was responsible for all food-for-work programs. The World Food Program's Project 2488, the European Economic Committee (EEC), and United States donations of grain and edible oils supported the effort. Other donors provided technical equipment and tools. Non-governmental Organizations (NGOs) played a major role in implementation, each being assigned to a particular geographic location. During 1985-1990 when Mengistu announced far reaching reforms and moved away from socialist agriculture, the reclamation program encountered a number of difficulties and was increasingly criticized by members of the NGO Community and Bureaucrats of the Ethiopian Ministry of Agriculture. Many critics complained about the top-down nature in which the program had been implemented. Some found fault that with the exclusion of peasant participation while preferential treatment was given to international donors who imposed their environmental values on the Ethiopian indigenous people. As the Ethiopian regime began to loosen its grip and crumble, this top-down approach to environmental programs was publicly criticized. Participants at an NGO-sponsored workshop on community forestry held in October 1990 noted that many of the programs apparently had technical problems that were in reality not related to the rehabilitation programs. Reliance on government-imposed institutions and their leaders was another set of problems. They pointed out that small farmers generally were not involved in identifying their needs and problems, establishing priorities, evaluating alternative solution or planning the implementation processes. As a result, indigenous farming systems technical knowledge, and common property institutions were ignored and thwarting farmer incentives for participation in community forestry projects.

Logistics as been one of the major problems facing the nation's national and regional governments in addressing the regional and local assessment needs. Collaboration of peasant into the process of rejuvenating the environment has been nominal at best. There has been very little discussion of indigenous techniques of soil amendment. Neither has there been any substantial discussion or acknowledgment of indigenous terracing of run-off pond, and irrigation. Study conducted by NGOs indicated that densely settled areas in the southwest were at environmental risk because of population pressure with no investigation into the distinctive farming system that appeared until recently, to have sustained such densities for centuries (Asefa 2003; Herweg 1994).

While foreign NGOs have played a major role in helping Ethiopia to resolve its environmental problems, the ecological knowledge of its indigenous communities, civil societies and economic institutions has not been fully tapped. Recent National Conservation Strategy (NCS) survey in Ethiopia reveal that indigenous farmers were able to use the color, texture and appearance of their crops to distinguish between poor and fertile soils; they know local climate characteristics and when to prepare their farms for the rains or to prevent too much soil moisture using simple farm implements such as the hoe, axe, and cutlass, which minimize exposure of the subsoil to the tropical climate (Herweg 1994). Similarly, the indigenous hunter has expert knowledge of the location of certain animals' plants waterbeds, forests and other laments of the local environment. There is therefore the need for the government of Ethiopia to form a partnership between these indigenous groups, the private sector, NGOs and community base organizations in rejuvenating an appropriate environmental think-tank that would help reduce the nation's dependency on foreign donors and models. Ethiopia definitely needs a new approach to addressing its environmental problems in the twenty-first century.

Cross National Analysis

Both nations have experienced growth in population over the past three decades. The growth in population has also spill over as a major problem for land use and the quality of the environment in Botswana and Ethiopia. The population increase in these nations translates into a need for more land for agricultural production.

The environmental situation is such that the savannahs and forests in Botswana and Ethiopia are exposed to human conversion as people aggressively try to farm the land. Thus, the lands in both nations are gradually changing from forest to savannah and then semi-arid vegetation. Botswana and Ethiopia are countries where the majority of the people (up to sixty-five percent) are farmers and land is of great importance to agriculture. But as the number of people who cultivate the land increase, the environmental degradation problem also expand. Slash and burn agriculture and rotational agriculture require large acreage of land and over the years the number of cultivators has been on the rise. The increase in poverty in most both countries has led to the increase in the number of people who have turned to the land as a source of sustenance (Zewdu 2002).

In Botswana and Ethiopia NGOs have tend to aggressively attempt to increase agricultural output through the community based natural resources management programs. These programs, however, have not been able to effectively improve traditional practices and help rural communities to benefit from the tourism that is drawn to forest areas. Coordinated environmental and forest policies that are well policed and has the full backing of the rural communities, indigenous organizations and the government is necessary for adequate solutions to be achieved.

Table 5.2 shows the trend in population growth in Africa, with attention to Botswana and Ethiopia. The increasing population trend and its impact on agriculture are more severe than it used to be seventy years ago. The intensification of agriculture through the establishment of planting programs in Botswana and Ethiopia faces competition from other land use activities. The concept of community based natural resource management programs becomes paramount in sustaining the societies in both nations.

Only five decades ago Botswana and Ethiopia's food production could adequately meet the needs of its population. At the beginning of the twenty-first century, both nations now rely heavily on imports for food, and starvation and health related diseases are at a crisis level. Adequate food supplies are the fundamental human needs. A history of colonialism, rising population growth and poverty, and political mismanagement, are just a few of the factors that have led to unsustainable environmental development practices in Botswana and Ethiopia.

It is readily apparent that the underlying elements creating the food problem in Botswana and Ethiopia are not only great, but complex. Agricultural, cultural, economic, and environmental issues cannot be separately analyzed without setting a goal for sustainable development.

The massive rural to urban migration in Botswana and Ethiopia and the subsequent disruption of community and regional cultures are some of the environmental problems these nations have been facing. The respective governments have dramatically altered their natural environment by urban and demographic growth, toxic output from industry, relentless deforestation, drought, desiccation of their lakes and rivers, exploitation of natural resources and materials for construction, among other factors. The social and cultural impact of the population on environment is left outside of the domain of environmental policy. Government environmental policies in Botswana and Ethiopia have not been able to ensure that environmental protection agencies are molded into effective vehicles for representation of both their interest and those of their local citizens.

Table 5.2
Africa Population Growth Rate (1980-1997)
(Population in Million and Average Annual Percentage Growth Rate)

Nations	1988	1990	1992	1994	1995	1996	1997	Ave Growth Rate
Libya	4.18	4.43	4.68	4.92	5.04	5.17	5.29	3.5
Tunisia	7.86	8.16	8.53	8.85	8.99	9.13	9.28	2.5
Morocco	23.07	24.01	25.03	26.02	26.52	27.02	27.51	2.2
Senegal	6.93	7.33	7.69	8.10	8.31	8.53	8.77	2.6
Somalia	8.38	8.62	8.30	9.01	9.49	9.81	10.13	2.5
Niger	7.22	7.67	8.16	8.73	9.03	9.34	9.66	3.3
Ethiopia	**47.64**	**51.18**	**54.79**	**54.89**	**56.40**	**58.23**	**60.12**	**2.8**
Djibouti	0.47	0.52	0.55	0.58	0.60	0.62	0.64	6.1
Guinea	5.43	5.76	6.10	6.42	6.59	6.76	6.93	2.7
Egypt	50.07	52.44	54.78	57.06	58.18	59.27	60.35	2.5
Mali	8.0	8.46	8.95	9.45	9.71	10.00	10.30	2.7
Sudan	23.04	24.06	25.10	26.16	26.71	27.27	27.86	2.4
Algeria	23.78	25.01	26.25	27.47	28.11	28.73	29.34	2.8
South Africa	32.70	33.96	35.18	36.37	36.96	37.64	38.30	2.1
Nigeria	90.87	96.20	101.88	108.01	111.27	114.57	117.90	3.0
Chad	5.40	5.68	5.98	6.29	6.45	6.61	6.78	2.5
Botswana	**0.90**	**1.24**	**1.32**	**1.39**	**1.42**	**1.45**	**1.48**	**1.51**
Burkina Faso	8.53	9.02	9.53	10.09	10.38	10.66	1.95	2.7
North Africa	108.97	114.09	119.26	124.32	126.84	129.32	131.77	2.5
Sub-Saharan Africa	480.17	508.31	536.97	563.84	579.83	613.71	613.71	2.7
All Africa	589.13	622.40	656.23	688.16	706.67	725.61	745.48	2.8

Source: http://www/worldbank.org/data/countrydata/adi/adi1-2.pdf (accessed 2/7/2006).

The goals of environmental policies in these nations have in most cases relied on the western values and the "Willingness to pay" principles, despite the differences in national contexture and culture. Such a stance has led to the creation of values and access to subsistence which is linked to sacrificing environmental quality for short-term economic gain. Appropriate environmental policies for Botswana and Ethiopia in the twenty-first century should entail a partnership between the government, NGOs, private sector and community base organizations.

Such collaboration should attempt to incorporate both indigenous and foreign knowledge of the environment. The environmental policies should also tackle changes in culture in the conservation of the forests in both nations.

Rejuvenating Community Based Environmental Policy

Sustainable environmental policies in Botswana and Ethiopia in the twenty-first century should not advocate the abandonment of technology and scientific farming for community based policy or verse versa. Indeed, it seeks an integration of community based approach to the synthesis of scientific ecology, technology, and traditional conservation techniques. It require government, (NGOs) to institutionalize an innovative community based natural resources management practice. Medhin Zewdu (2002) pointed out that in the past external intervention have been particularly disruptive with regard to local resources management institutions. Traditional institutions have often been replaced by state imposed committees and agencies, as state perceived local resources management to be inadequate. In the twenty-first century state interventions that undermined the customary land tenure in Botswana and Ethiopia seriously increase land tenure uncertainties for local farmers with negative effects on indigenous soil, forest and water conservation investment.

Figure 5.1 shows how the government of Botswana and Ethiopia can find the link between long-term global, regional and local sustainability of culture, economy, and ecology. The processes of finding the link between rural and regional context involves understanding the larger political, cultural, economic, and environmental nature of the people of both nations. It also shows details of local production systems. There should also be an understanding of the strategic roles of the society and communities based organizations. Decision-making and action among the community members occurs at different levels including individual, grassroots support organizations (GSOs), membership support organizations (MSOs), NGOs and local non-profit organizations.

Community level decisions should be made through democratic forums such as discussions and consensus development. Local community environmental and agricultural based operations should decentralize responsibilities and strengthen the role of rural communities and their institutions. Both the United Nations Development Programs and the Sustainable Development Information Service projects in Botswana and Ethiopia have not been able to achieve their respective goals. This is because these programs initially ignored the important role of community based organizations in policy making and implementation. It is therefore paramount that future environmental policies should institutionalize rural communities who are more capable of exercising proper local management and control of agricultural and cultural diversity. Rural communities may even be able to effectively channel to the state a proportion of their resources to help the government achieve its goals. These functions make rural communities based organizations and their members to be the daily managers of the environment.

According to Barbara Thomas-Slayter and Dianne Rocheleau (1995) and Robert Dibie (2001) managing local resources is not a matter of solving technical problems but an instrument of looking for sustainable solutions. There are many technical solutions. The critical issues in Botswana and Ethiopia are the political and motivational will of both the government and the people. One key approach to resolve these environmental problems lies with the regional and rural communities. In fact, much of what happens in Botswana and Ethiopia will depend on the choices and activities of thousands of farming households and rural communities' organizations.

In the twenty-first century, Botswana and Ethiopia should respond to soil erosion, loss of fertility, groundwater, soil pollution, pesticide contamination of both crops and workers, loss of forest, poverty of farmers, huge international debts by first developing the political will and seriously integrate community base organizations in the management of its affairs. This model has been called by a number of different names: organic, alternative, renewable, low input, ecological, or regenerative agriculture. The term gaining greatest acceptance seems to be "sustainable agriculture" (Jardins 1997; Zewdu 2002). Environmental resources are the heart of Botswana and Ethiopia's rural people's food production problems and ultimately need to be managed by local, small-scale collaborative efforts linked to large-scale planning and regulatory functions. If the Botswana and Ethiopian governments want to achieve its sustainable development goals, there must be a fit of ecological objectives with regional and rural communities' concern of how to manage their forest and farm land.

The governments of Botswana and Ethiopia as well as international organizations have played a dominant role in the design and implementation of most development projects in the two countries under discussion. At the same time, many of the more or less top-down projects have failed to meet local socio-cultural and environmental requirements. The regional governments are as significant as the national governments. But as the settings for environmental politics, local level of action is often obscured by the greater emphasis on national politics and the universal context of science and technology.

The challenge, however, is how to incorporate indigenous institutions and their ecological knowledge and humane environmental management practices in environmental assessment. Jardins (1997) and Mulvihill (1988) argue that it would be inappropriate to attempt a complete integration of the two systems without considering the context of devolution. Ushers (1981) sees devolution taking two forms: the movement of authority and responsibility from a higher to a lower level within an established and intact framework or actual transfer of authority and responsibility from one system to another. A similar strategy was used under the

Figure 5.1
Model for NGOs and Community Based Development Policy.

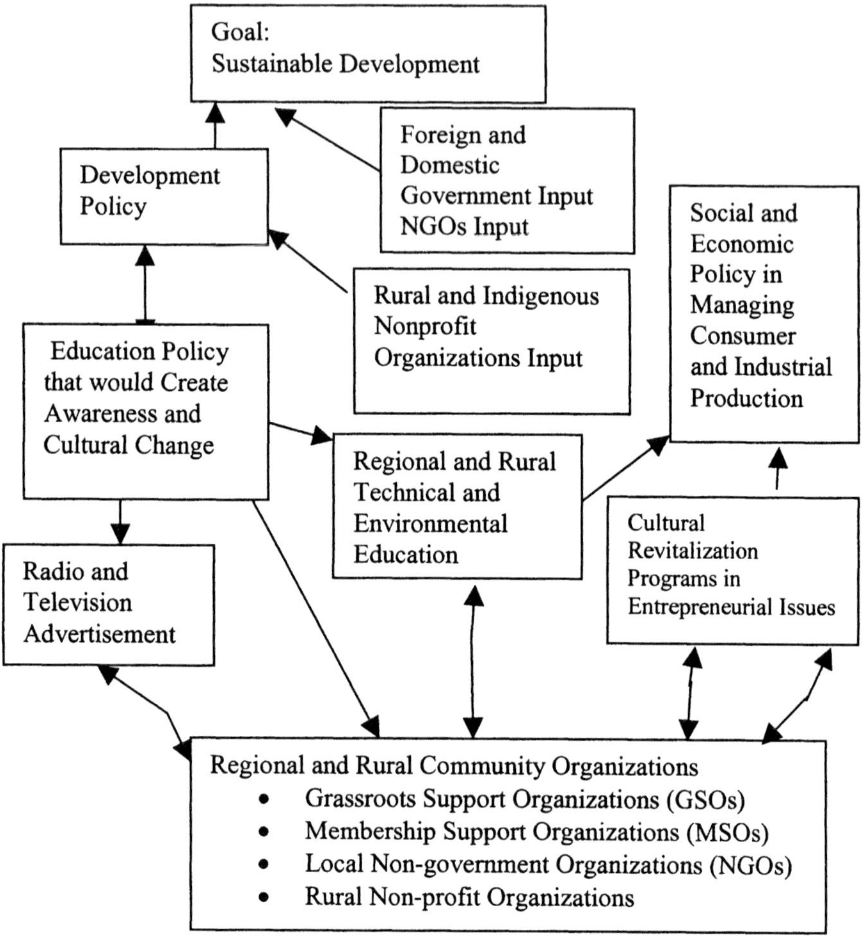

colonial British system of indirect rule in Botswana, which not only relied on indigenous institutions as agents sometimes puppets for local government administration but sometimes assisted them to develop on their own lines (Appiah-Opoku 1994; Crowder 1976; Jardins 1997).

In the twenty-first century, Botswana and Ethiopia should move away from the custom of regarding the national government as the only source of innovation in environmental matters and the states as laggards. But the growth of citizen environmental action at the local and state levels, and federal programs should help to build state administrative capacities which will also tend to foster new state environmental activities. Botswana and Ethiopia have an independent source of potential initiative and the complexity of the influences leading to such action varies with each state, the results might vary.

Another possible approach is the establishment of cooperative management regimes at the community level. A cooperative management regime is an institutional arrangement in which formal government agencies with jurisdiction over resources and user groups enter into agreement covering a specific geographic region and spell out a system of rights and obligations for those interested in the resources. Such cooperative institutions will formulate a collection of rules indicating actions that subjects are expected to take under various circumstances. The procedures for making collective decisions affecting the interests of government actors, user organizations, rural communities and individual users should be made through democratic processes. This could take shape in the form of sound networks that are connected to all levels of the society (Dibie and Kawewe 1999). This may improve communication, learning, and understanding between indigenous institutions and formal environmental management agencies.

Most of these policy and program instruments have to be implemented by government agencies such as National Environmental Agency and NGOs as well. It should be recognized that global economic situations and international environmental concerns also influence relevant policy instruments.

In the interaction between national and regional governments, communities and NGOs, the starting point should be the local community. Environmental policies developed at the national level should be adapted to the conditions of the rural population if they are to be effective. Of course, effective policies may, and are even intended to modify these conditions, which in turn may necessitate the formulation of new policies. The overall system of interactions between different actors and their respective responsibilities will essentially define the institutional environment needed to accomplish the goal of development policies that focus on the sustainable use and management of natural resources at local levels around Botswana and Ethiopia.

These environmental management systems proposed for the twenty-first century should be operationalized through a number of principles. The most important being the responsibility to every member of the community in the form of orientation towards conservative use. Others are judicious use of available resources in view of the need for self- sufficiency and independence from outside support; a minimal degree of specialization among community members and thus a widespread knowledge of the environment and its management; and also the recognition of psychological and spiritual values. Such involvement demands as propriety, some upgrading of environmental awareness in school curriculum. There is the need to look beyond the exploitation of environmental resources for immediate short-term against a more careful protection of resources for long-term sustainable economic returns. This would require incorporating training programs in environmental science into the nations' education system. National and regional governments should provide educational and public relations awareness programs in environmental matters through radio and television. This should be part of the school curriculum. Through education and public relations campaigns indigenous people and communities should be oriented towards conservative use. The recycling of waste product, utilization of refuses organic fertilizers; biomass and so on should be encouraged. These have great potential as raw materials, but are currently not well utilized in the two nations. A very conscious and deliberate action is also needed to improve the efficiency with which natural resources are transformed into end products. Greater efficiency not only has economic advantages, but also makes it possible to save resources in order to reduce environmental deterioration in the extraction as well as processing phases. The application of pesticides in farm estates and plantations is increasing annually as a result of infestation by pests. Environment policy should include pesticides control so as to prevent the indiscriminate use of chemicals and the pollution of the atmosphere, as well as the poisoning of the soil from wrong use of fertilizer.

Finally, environmental policies in the twenty-first century should be concerned with the problems arising out of poverty and those that arise out of the very process of development. The remedial approaches to these problems are closely interwoven with policies for sustainable development. These policies should embrace wider dimensions than the growth of gross national product alone, and must include some of the major environmental problems that arise in the context of urban and rural poverty. The problems of poor water supplies, inadequate sewerage, sickness, nutritional deficiency, and bad housing need to be dealt with in the process of planning and policy making. Goals and objectives in these areas should be incorporated into development plans as much as targets for the growth of output. Many environmental problems in Botswana and Ethiopia cannot be effectively addressed with western-based traditional regulatory tools alone, but citizen participation, incentives and educational efforts may be useful supplements.

Conclusion

Botswana and Ethiopia's history are remarkable. Over the course of four decades both nations have endured much environmental hardship. Botswana and Ethiopia have been plagued by grave poverty, chronic drought and famine. Without doubt both nations will have to undergo numerous changes and face several obstacles in their process of sustainable development. In this study we examined two approaches to ecological and environmental issues in Botswana and Ethiopia, called coevolution and community based natural resources management. Although coevolution and community based natural resources management have some differences, these approaches share some important similarities that make it appropriate for us to examine them in this study. The perspective linking economic equity, peace and environmental protection is potentially becoming very political in Botswana and Ethiopia. As the coevolutionary and Community based natural resources management models suggest, the maintenance of nature/society and intra-societal linkages is imperative to the sustainability of all agricultural production systems. An attempt was made in this study to stress that the extent to which Botswana and Ethiopia pursue a style of development that is more responsive to social and environmental goals must be determined by the resources available to them which include the indigenous human capital.

Modification to environmental policy in the twenty-first century in Botswana and Ethiopia must promote development of community based natural environmental management and involve fully participatory arrangement between NGOs, government and local people if the policy is to succeed. Promotion of this concept should permeate the rhetoric of the national conservation strategies throughout the governments of sub-Saharan Africa. Understanding why participation is so important in large-scale efforts to develop the environment is the key to identifying the adjustments and changes necessary so that policy directions are accompanied by field action. If a reasonable number of villagers from an area can be organized into a management cooperative, they can work with their other peers and the village authorities in brokering the understandings and consensus necessary to ensure that the environmental management plan, particularly the protection activities, can be effectively implemented. Local people must fully comprehend the objectives of management and the policy determinations behind them. They will also need to understand and accept their roles and responsibilities for achieving management objectives and how they in turn will participate in the benefits stream. These are all elements of the policy framework, which must permeate indigenous people's level. Moreover, the incorporation of indigenous institutions and their ecological knowledge in environmental assessment is tantamount to harnessing available human resources within communities at the grassroots level. This may reduce total dependence on outside ideas, goals, technology, and supervision in environmental management. It may also reduce expense in terms of the galaxy of outside experts in all fields needed to conduct environmental assessment and the lack of commitment to goals and aspirations of host communities.

Notwithstanding this problem, it seems worthwhile to collaborate with grassroots support organization, membership support organization, NGOs, and local Non profit organizations in the future, in an attempt to achieve sustainable economic development and environmental protection.

References

Abucer, Mohamed, and Patrick Molutsi. "Environment Policy in Botswana: A Critique." *Africa Today*, 1st Quarter (1993): 61-73

Appiah-Opoku, S. "Theoretical Orientation of Environmental Assessment in Canada: Application to the Third World." *Environments* 22, no. 3 (1994):103-110.

Arnstein, S. "Eight Rungs on the Ladder of Citizen Participation." In *Citizen Participation: Effecting Community Change*, edited by Caln and P. A. Barry. New York: Praeger, 1971, 69-91.

Ascher, W., and R. Healy. *Natural Resource PolicyMaking: A Framework for Developing Countrie*. Washington, DC: Durham, 1990.

Asefa, Sisya. "Perspective on Reforming the Current Constitution for a Better Future in Ethiopia." *Addis Ababa Tribune*, 16 May 2003, 3.

Barbier, E. B. "The Economic Value of Ecosystems." In *Tropical Wetlands. Gatekeeper Series*, no. 89-102. London: Environmental Economics Center, 1989, 1-12.

Botswana National Conservative Strategy. *National Policy on Natural Resources Conservation and Development*, no. 1. Gaborone, Botswana: Government Printer, 1990.

Breemer, Van Dem, C. A. Drijver, and L. B. Venema. *Local Resource Management in*

Africa. New York: Wiley & Sons Publishers, 1995.
Brokensha, D. "Local Management Systems and Sustainability." Paper Prepared for the Annual Meeting of the Society for Economic Anthropology, Riverside, California, April 1986, 3-4.
Crowder, M. *West Africa under Colonial Rule.* Toronto: Hutchinson and Company, 1976.
Darkoh, Michael K. "Desertification and Environmental Management in Botswana." In *Environmental Planning, Policies and Politics in Eastern and Southern Africa*, edited by Mohamed Salih and Shibru Tedla. New York: St. Martin's Press, 1999.
Davies, J. Clerence. "Environmental Institutions and the Reagan Administration." In *Environmental Policy in the 1980s*, edited by Norman Vig and Michael Kraft. Washington, DC: Congressional Quarterly Press, 1984.
De Waal, Alex. *Famine Crimes: Politics and the Disaster Relief Industry in Africa.* Bloomington: Indiana University Press, 1997.
Dibie, Robert. "Indigenous Participation in the Environmental Policy of Ethiopia and Botswana." *Journal of Sustainable Development in Africa* 2 (Winter/Spring 2001): 1-10.
Dibie, Robert, and Saliwe Kawewe. "Education Policy and the Future of Sustainable Development in Zimbabwe and Nigeria." *Social Development Issues* 21 (1999): 22-29.
Erocal, Denizhan. *Environmental Management in Developing Countries. Development Center of the Organization for Economic Co-operation and Development* (OECD), 1991.
Goulet, D. The Cruel Choice: *A New Concept in the Theory of Development.* New York: Atheneum, 1975.
Herweg, Karl. "Problems of Acceptance and Adaption of Soil Conservation in Ethiopia." Unpublished Paper. Addis Ababa, Ethiopia: Soil Conservation Research Project, 1994.
Hoben, Allan. *Land, Tenure among the Amhara of Ethiopia.* Chicago: University of Chicago Press, 1972.
Hoben, Allan. "Paradigms and Politics: The Cultural Construction of Environmental Policy in Ethiopia." *World Development* 23, no. 6 (1995): 1007-1021.
James, Valentine. *Africa's Ecology: Sustaining the Biological and Environmental Diversity of a Continent.* Jefferson, NC: Mcfarland and Company Publishers, 1993.
Jardins, Joseph. *Environmental Ethics: An Introduction to Environmental Philosophy.* Boston: Wadsworth Publishing Company, 1997.
Kiggundu, Moses. *Managing Organization in Developing Countries: An Operational and Strategic Approach.* West Harford, CT: Kumarian Press, 1989.
Kopp, R., and M. Hazilla. "Social Cost of Environmental Quality Regulations: A General Equilibrum Analysis." *Journal of Political Economy* 98 (1990): 853-73.
Kraft, Michael. *Environmental Policy and Politics.* New York: Harper Collins College Publishers, 2003.
Mathews, Jessica. *Preserving the Global Environment.* New York: Norton and Company, 1991.
Millar, Marian. *The Third World in Global Environmental Politics.* Boulder, CO: Lynne Rienner Publishers, 1995.
Mpotokwane, M. A. "Pollution Risks in Botswana." Unpublished Research Paper, 1992, 3-5.
Mulvihill, P. "Integration of the State and Indigenous Systems Wildlife management: Problems and Possibilities." Unpublished Paper, School of Urban and Regional Planning, Faculty of Environmental Studies, University of Waterloo, 1988.
Norman, Omar. *Economic Development and Environmental Policy.* New York: Kegan Paul International, 1996.
Pearce, D. W., A. Markanda, and B. Barbier. *Sustainable Development: Economics and Environment in the Third World.* London: Earthscan Publication, 1990.
Redcliff, M., and D. Goodman, eds. *Environment and Development in Latin America: The*

Politics of Sustainability. Manchester: Machester University Press, 1991.

Republic of Botswana. "Botswana's National Report for the United Nations Conference on Environment and Development." *Department of Town and Regional Planning, Ministry of Local Government and Lands Annual Report*. Gaborone, Botswana: Government Printers, 1992.

Republic of Botswana. "National Settlement Policy." *Final Draft Report, Department of Towns and regional Planning, Ministry of Local Government, Lands, and Housing Annual Report*. Gaborone, Botswana: Government Printers, 1996.

Ringrose, S., R. Chanda, N. Musisi, and F. Sefe. "Environmental Change in the Mid-Boteti Area of North-Central Botswana: Biophysical Process and Human Perceptions." *Environmental Management* 20, no. 3 (1996): 397-410.

Roe, Emery. "Development Narratives or Making the Best of Blueprint Development." *World Development* 19, no. 4 (1991): 287-300.

Sadler, B., and J. Bothroyd. *Traditional Knowledge and Environment Assessment*. A Manuscript report prepared for the Canadian Environmental Assessment Research Council, Ottawa, Canada, March 1993.

Schwab, R. M. "Environmental Federalism." *Resources* 92. Washington, DC: Resources for the Future, 1988, 27.

Shibiru, Tedla. "Community Based Natural Resources Management in Ethiopia. An Overview." Unpublished Report, 2002.

Switzer, Jacquiline. *Environmental Politics: Domestic and Global Dimensions*. New York: St. Martin's, 1994.

Thomas-Slayter, B., and Dianne Rocheleau. *Gender, Environment and Development in Kenya*. Boulder, CO: Lynne Rienner Publishers, 1995.

United Nations. "Dialogue on Border Issues Unthinkable Says Eritrea." *UN Integration Regional Information Network*. htt://allAfrica.com (accessed 2 March 2006).

United Nations. "More Aid Is Needed Says Government." *UN Integration Regional Information Networks*. htt://allAfrica.com (accessed 2 March 2006).

Usher, P. J. "Sustenance or Recreation: The Future of Native Wildlife Harvesting in North Canada." In *Proceedings: First International Symposium on renewable Resources and the Economy of the North*, edited by M. M. Freeman. Ottawa: Association of Canadian Universities for Northern Studies, 1981, 56-71.

Vig, Norman J. "Presidential Leadership: From the Reagan to the Bush Administration." In *Environmental Policy in the 1990s*, edited by Norman Vig and Michael Kraft. Washington, DC: Congressional Quarterly Press, 1990.

Weaver, James, and Kevin O'Keefe. *The Evolution of Development Economics*. Washington, DC: American University Press, 1991.

World Bank. *Towards the Development of an Environmental Action Plan for Nigeria*. Washington, DC: World Bank, 1990.

World Bank. *Development and the Environment*. New York: Oxford University Press, 1992.

Zewdu, Medhin. "Government initiated Community Based Natural Resources Management." Paper Presented at a Workshop on Community Based Natural Resources Management, 2000.

Zewdu, Medhin. "Sustainable Development in Ethiopia." Addis Ababa, Ethiopia: Heinrich Boell Foundation and Institute of Biodiversity Conservation and Research, 2002.

Chapter 6

NGOs and Development in Botswana and Nigeria

Robert A. Dibie and Saliwe Kawewe

Many critical sustainable development issues in sub-Saharan Africa such as environment, economic development, human resource development, health care, and education transcend national and regional governments in the continent. These issues have become so diverse that they now require alternative resource mobilization approaches (Handelman 2006). In Botswana and Nigeria, one major response has been the intervention of non-governmental organizations (NGOs). Foreign and domestic NGOs are now serving an increasing important function in the sustainable development processes of these two nations. Among the many functions played by NGOs in Nigeria and Botswana are (1) provision of services in health, environment issues, education, welfare, and research; (2) addressing the dynamics of decentralization, redistribution of infrastructure and national planning; (3) providing the opportunity for the national governments of Botswana and Nigeria to serve its citizens better than ever in their respective history.

In this chapter NGOs refers to any international organization that is not established by intergovernmental agreement. Post independence NGOs in Botswana and Nigeria began as relief and welfare organizations and evolved into development agencies that are concerned with poverty alleviation, education, health, the environment, legal rights for women and human rights protection in general. In the past two decades NGOs have moved into the areas of fostering democracy in Africa. NGOs have also initiated direct and indirect interventions in the provision of technical assistance and funding to indigenous nonprofit organizations or NGOs (Dichter 2001; Handelman 2006).

The nature of public bureaucracies in Botswana and Nigeria is such that are understaffed. Poorly paid and operate with insufficient resources and outdated equipments. These two African states can no-longer keep up with the demands of the rapid growing cities for proper sanitation, policing, schools, transportation, electricity, health and water supplies. Most African nations including Botswana and Nigeria do less for their rural areas that provide it with food and revenue. Corruption and abuse of power are so widespread that citizens regard their nation's political leaders and bureaucracies with suspicion at best, hostility at worst (Smith 2001; Rapley 1996). In most African nations local and international NGOs have moved beyond the mere design of development policies to the strategy of involving grass-root organizations in elevating the life of and fighting inequality and poverty in the society. This grass-root approach, however, sometimes fall short in meeting the needs of women, the poor and general empowerment of the average citizens.

In Botswana and Nigeria citizens do their best to avoid public officials by not paying taxes, ignoring the law and smuggling. The World Bank (2000) contends that African states that are short of power, deprived of bureaucratic resources and distance from their citizens can do little to spread development. This situation has galvanized and attracted NGOs into Botswana and Nigeria. The aftermath, however, is that most NGOs agenda and interests sometimes run at crossroad to one another. In the past five decades NGOs have began to take on former public task, especially in the area of environmental control, education, health care provision and research.

Dynamics of NGOs and Development

There is a well established and growing literature on the new role of nonprofit organizations and NGOs in the economies of developed nations. In general, these studies have concluded that NGOs have been doing a lot in the development process. In the context of development in Africa, however, there are only very few literature on the role of NGOs in the development process (Ndegwa 1994; Ditchter 2001; Riddeli and Robinson 1995; Smith 2001).

Mark McPeak (1999) contends that NGOs can scale up their growth and operations by building their institutions, multiplying outreach by working with and through other organizations, diffusing their experience by influencing other actors, increasing their geographical reach, and mainstreaming their experience into the official policy framework. In the context of operations in Botswana and Nigeria, NGOs persistence presence depends on both domestic and international variables. On one hand, domestic variables range from government support to ethnic and social conflicts. On the other hand, international variables reflect continued support of foreign donor organizations.

The proliferation of domestic and internal NGOs in Africa is an indication of the internationalization of public welfare and the inability of African states to effectively handle the affairs of their economy. The internationalization of the NGOs is not a new phenomenon in Africa. Pre-independence and post-independence African nations have been linked to religious institutions such as the Catholic Church, Anglican Church, Methodist Church, Baptist Church, the Red Cross and Islamic organizations. Helmut Anheier and Kusuma Cunningham (1994) and Howard Handelman (2006) pointed out that these religious institutions have operating in different political, economic and cultural systems around the world. The period between 1970 and 2000 witnessed the growth of NGOs operations in education, health, human rights, development, environmental issues, food and democracy in the continent. The growth in the activities of NGOs in Botswana and Nigeria has been accompanied by a decline in the traditional activities of the national and regional governments in African states (Handelman 2006; World Bank 2000). The increasing dependency on food aid in Ethiopia, Democratic Republic of Congo and some East African states due to famine has also attracted foreign humanitarian NGOs to those regions of the continent. The humanitarian role of NGOs has been encouraged by the increasing willingness of the industrial nations' government to direct official aid away from African governments by using NGOs as alternative sources for the provision of aids to the poor people of the continent (Ditchter 2001; Jameson and Wilber 1996; Steven 2001).

One important feature of the NGOs in Africa is that, a number of them are originally established abroad and are organized or managed by expatriate in Botswana and Nigeria. These organizations have also increased their operations in the development and relief activities in the African continent. The series of structural adjustment policies implemented by successive African governments in the 1980s and 1990s had a destructive effect upon the middle and lower income groups as well as reduced the employment prospects of many secondary school and university graduates (Wallace 1999: Thomas 1992). Helmut Anheier and Kusuma Cunningham (1994) contend that developed nations interests in providing aid through NGOs to African nations can be largely because of the inability of several countries in the continent in bring about equitable and sustainable development. NGOs are therefore, seen as an alternative to state-led and national government controlled development processes. Despite the efforts put forward by the national governments of Botswana and Nigeria the World Bank continues to advocate the need for NGOs to help these African nations to promote local reforms and institution building (Ditchter 2001). Several developed nations have also joined the World Bank to commend NGOs as the only institution that could help African nations to build civil societies and strengthening their democratic values. Unfortunately, the few capital-intensive technology investment in Botswana and Nigeria has not "trickle down" development. Lack of skills has also prevented women from effectively participating in the development process. In the twenty-first century Botswana and Nigeria should attempt to focus more on using the basic need approach to pursue their sustainable development goals. Non-governmental organizations and national government institutions will have to focus more training women on basic self-reliant skills to enhance their ability to participate more in the sustainable development processes. NGOs have been highly commended to be very effective in initiating the basic human needs approach to sustainable development activities.

Research Methodology

The data on which this analysis was derived is from questionnaires that were administered by the authors in Botswana and Nigeria. The selection of these two nations is based on three important criteria: (1) the existence of a democratic government; (2) the existence of NGOs and functional national government; and (3) the ability to administer a questionnaire that has greater validity.

The first part of the project involved the analysis of NGOs documents available in the United States. This was following by in-depth interviews of citizens and public servants in both Botswana and Nigeria. The responses from the in-depth interview were be used to determine NGOs roles in the development process in both nations under study. This research involved the two African nations. In Botswana and Nigeria, the in-depth interview and data analysis were conducted in cities where NGOs had operations. Such cities include Gabarone, Lagos, and Abuja.

The second part of the research would involve administering questionnaires. Three hundred questionnaires were administered to citizens of each country. In Botswana 216 response was received. In the case of Nigeria 238 participants responded. The survey was conducted in the summer of 2004 and 2005. The data collected from the respondents were analyzed using the SSPS computer program. Combining the in-depth interviews and questionnaire data analysis of the role of NGOs in the development processes, enables us to systematically compare how two different African democratic political systems handle their sustainable development processes and service provisions in lieu of government and NGOs.

The objective of this research is to examine the perception of the citizens about the role NGO play in the development process of Botswana and Nigeria. The specific research questions addresses by this chapter are:

1. What the major role of NGOs in the development processes of Botswana and Nigeria?
2. What are the perceptions of the citizens of Botswana and Nigeria about the role of NGOs in their respective nation?
3. What is the appropriate framework for collaboration between the government, NGOs, the private sector and community based organizations towards sustainable development in Botswana and Nigeria.

Data Analysis and Discussion

Table 6.1 shows perception of the citizens of Botswana and Nigeria of the role of NGOs in their respective nation. Thirty five percent of the respondent in Botswana agreed and sixty-five disagree that foreign NGOs do not understand the nature of their development. In Nigeria ten percent agreed while ninety percent disagree that NGOs do not understand the nature of development trends and needs in the nation especially in the oil producing areas of the nation where foreign Multinational Corporation frequently pollute the rivers and agricultural lands.

In was very interesting to note a great irony in both nations. While forty-five percent of the respondent in Botswana stated that Foreign NGOs were part

Table 6.1
Perception of the Citizens of Botswana and Nigeria of the Role of NGOs

Statements about NGOs in Botswana and Nigeria	Botswana (216)		Nigeria (238)	
	Agree	Disagree	Agree	Disagree
Foreign NGOs do not Understand the real Nature of Africa's Development Problems.	35	65	10	90
Foreign NGOs are part of the underdevelopment Problems in Africa.	45	55	49	51
Foreign NGOs are very helpful to African nations.	62	48	50	50
International NGOs seem to impose foreign models of Solving domestic problems on indigenous people.	45	55	48	52
Foreign NGOs staff highly respect the culture and values of the African people.	55	45	60	40
The national government treats foreign NGOs staff better than local citizens.	67	33	81	19
Foreign NGOs are important instruments of Development in Africa.	62	48	59	41
Most foreign NGOs staffs are not 100% concerned about the African people they are supposed to be helping	48	52	49	51
Foreign NGOs have helped African nations in the area of Education.	70	30	85	15
Foreign NGOs have helped African nations in the area of Agriculture.	38	62	20	80
Foreign NGOs have helped African nations in the area of Technology Transfer.	15	85	21	79
Foreign NGOs have helped African nations in the area of Environment	56	44	12	88

Source: Derived from survey data 2004 and 2005

of the underdevelopment problem in the nation, forty-nine percent of the respondents from Nigeria felt the same way. The irony, however, is that most of the NGOs staff interview indicated that they were immensely help in the development process of both nations. Another interesting observation is that sixty-two percent respondents in Botswana indicated that foreign NGOs were very helpful to their nation in various ways for example health and education. In Nigeria, however, the positive response was fifty percent. It appears that Nigerians are not very happy with the role of NGOs. What seem apparent is that most respondents assumed that the multinational petroleum corporations operating in the nation were NGOs. Despite several attempts to correct this notion, most respondents did not change their perception.

While fifty-five percent of respondents agreed in Botswana that NGOs staff do not respect their culture and values only forty percent disagreed in Nigeria that NGOs staff undermine that traditional beliefs. Sixty percent of the respondents in Nigeria stated that some NGOs staff were very arrogant and often put down the Nigerian values. Sixty-seven percent of respondents in Botswana agreed that their national government highly respect foreign NGOs staff more than citizens working for the public sector. In figure in Nigeria was higher, eighty-one percent of the respondents felt that the national and regional governments seem to favor foreign NGOs staff than indigenous staff.

In the area of education and health care provision, there was a general consensus among the respondent Seventy percent in Botswana and eighty percent in Nigeria that NGOs have contributed tremendously to these sectors. The respondents in both nations, however, pointed that foreign NGOs have done very little in the areas of Agriculture and technology transfer to help their nation. Consequently, thirty-eight percent agree and sixty-two percent disagreed in Botswana on agricultural improvement, and fifteen agreed and eighty percent disagreed on technology transfer. In Nigeria 20 percent agree on agricultural support, while only eighty disagreed on technology transfer assistant by NGOs.

In both Nigeria and Botswana several of the respondents indicated that lack of strategic development plans have made foreign NGOs to impose international models of solving domestic problems in to their respective nations

They blame their national and regional governments for not giving NGOs any specification in the way they should handle or implement their projects in Botswana. They contend that in certain situation were NGOs have to monitor the operations of Multinational Corporation; they often do a poor job in conducting a clean investigation or holding such multinational corporation to high levels of accountability. This situation is often associated with the gold mines in Botswana and the oil industry in the Niger Delta areas of Nigeria. As a matter of fact several respondents indicated that NGOs seen to be involved in corrupt and unethical practices in these industrials areas.

Framework to Collaboration in Development

The process of sustainable development in Botswana and Nigeria should focus on collaboration between various stakeholders. The governments of both nations as well as NGOs that have stake in the two nations are often affected by global system of economics and production. As a result of this factor NGOs and most private sector organizations are committed to establishing sustainable excellence as their goal and culture. Thus by forming collaboration NGOs, government, the private sector would adapt the principles and practice of excellence and continuous improvement. This is very important for these stakeholders to meet the growing needs of the citizens of Botswana and Nigeria. As a result to collaboration, the government that is not use to practice excellence will be forced to move in the new direction of sustainable excellence. On the long run, when the public sector has been fully assimilated into the culture of NGOs, it would find it difficult to shy away from its new passion for sustainable excellence.

In the twenty-first century sustainable excellence must become the basic culture not only within NGOs, but among government institutions, community base organizations and civil society organizations (Handelman 2006). Although Botswana and Nigeria are developing nations, they must establish self-renewing organizations that could promote a market-friendly approach for the delivery of goods and services to its citizens. These ministries, public agencies and private sector institutions must simultaneously address management areas such as strategic planning, process improvement, change management, technology application and resource conservation.

Leaders of government ministries, agencies, NGOs and civil society organizations must find it very important to develop a culture and an environment supportive of change (Eade 2000). Unlike currently practiced in both nations public sector, leaders at all levels of the collaboration need all the help they can get to ensure that hard-won gains in productivity, effectiveness, mission readiness and accountability are sustained. Knowing where the government stands in its development plan and in relations to national and NGOs standards enables both nations to prepare plans and strategies to help it overcome its development impediments.

An appropriate approach for achieving sustainable development should begin by viewing the nations respectively as a positive force in the dynamic community of collaborators. With this approach the government should be able to evaluate and understand its strength and weaknesses, then prepare a plan to address these weaknesses and enhance the strength (Til and Salve 2001). The changing values of NGOs and government through globalization are also very important in the development process of Botswana and Nigeria. Globalization would help both nations to increase their competitive edge as well as put pressure on them to develop the potential demise of organization through the shrinking market (Kotter 1996; Steven 2001).

Further, it is also very necessary for the leaders of Botswana and Nigeria to introduce a leadership method called change leadership. This leadership style could be used to address the shifting needs of public organizations and the community. It would help the governments to manage their ministries and agencies as well as keep alert to the constant newness of the public task.

One of the impediments to development in Botswana and Nigeria is getting people to change. Corrupt public officials, individuals and communities get caught in their comfort zone. These two African nations need dedicated and transformational leaders who are steadfast with competent managers, who can keep alive the process of change. Such changes could be made possible through collaboration. Through collaboration stakeholder would share information, ensure that the necessary processes are available for community change, and making good decisions, the government agencies and NGOs advances the welfare of the citizens that they serve.

There different types of collaboration in order to achieve sustainable development in Botswana and Nigeria are described in Table 6. 2. Table 6. 2 show three important types of collaboration that might be useful in the development process of both nations. The table shows three types of collaboration which would be ideal for Botswana and Nigeria to implement in the process of seeking sustainable development. According Susanne Feeney (2001) collaboration is used to describe any kind of partnership, cooperation or coordination activity. What is crucial, however, is the adoption of any particular form of collaboration, the borne of contention is the ability of stakeholder to use of this forms of collaboration to reach a shared agreement, working condition and what the collaboration means to the members. Below is an explanation of the different forms of collaboration:

Table 6.2
Types of Collaborations

Board Activities	Coordination	Joint Venture	Collaboration
Executive–Board Intersect	Assessment and Planning	Review/approve contracts and determine control mechanism	Hand-in-hand Planning
Stakeholder Outreach	Little if any activity	Assess partner and stakeholder interests	Assess partners, information gathering communication with key stakeholders
Fiduciary & Financial	Assess risk potential and resources commitment	Assess risk and locus of control	Risk assessment resource commitments, governance issues
Policy Development and Monitoring	Program and mission alignment	Purpose and mission alignment	Mission congruence
Organization Health	Monitor staff and morale and program	Morale and service delivery	Monitor organizational impact/staff

Source: Susanne Feeney. "Governance Framework for Collaboration and Merger," in The Nonprofit Handbook: Management, ed. Tracy Daniel Connors. New York. John Wiley & Son, (2001) 119.

1. *Coordination:* This entails formal relationship between organizations or stakeholders. It involves planning and division of roles as well as the establishment of communication channels. Resources and staff should be made available to partners in the collaboration. Authority may rest with individual organizations, but must be willing to cooperate with other members of the consortium.
2. *Joint venture*: This means the collaboration of two or more organizations. It involves no consolidation of the organizations; however, it can change the character of control of the organizations involved. Organizations involved in joint ventures must share risks and reduce inter-agency competition.

3. *Collaboration*: This involves a mutually well defined relationship entered into by two or more organizations. The partnership involves a commitment to definition to mutual relationship, goals, a jointly developed structure and shared responsibility. Organizations in the collaboration also share mutual authority, resources, rewards and accountability for success (Feeney 2001).

If Botswana and Nigeria are committed to achieve sustainable development, three crucial questions need to be addressed. These questions are: how do public sector performance and development of actions by citizens affect accountability in the public sector? What is the relationship between performance and citizenship participation in the national and regional governments' development process? How can the nations' public servants better serve their communities? Some suggestion and possible answers to these questions is presented based on the analyses of my survey data.

Further, unless Botswana and the Nigerian governments improve pay of public servants, it will be impossible to attract, retain and assure the integrity of highly skilled public officials. Thus revitalizing public service in both nations will require transparent, merit-based recruitment procedures, promotion based on performance, sound management, in-service training and career development, and interlocking checks and balance to counter corruption.

According to Peter Haruna (2001) and Howard Handelman (2006) African nations governments need to introduce policies that are crafted on the assumption that the responsibility of the government is to promote citizenship and public discourse. Further, the public interest will require a democratic public administration that invites participation from and collaboration with citizens, the private sector and NGOs. Haruna (2001) contends that there is no doubt that dialogue among scholars, practitioners, and citizens will not only help to bridge the gap between theory and practice, but also to explore and test new possibilities for a better understanding of public administration and the management of non-profit organizations in Botswana and Nigeria.

Quality standards and performance indicators for all aspects of the public sector need to be defined and valid consumer satisfaction measures developed. Qualitative research methods have been proposed as solutions to these measurements concerns. Avis, Metcalfe and Richards (1990) used in depth interviews and qualitative analysis to determine the relationship between patient expectations and their satisfaction with the health care service. They concluded that those expectations alone were not an adequate model for understanding patient satisfaction. They observe that the way in which patients evaluate care changed with additional contact, and that ultimately satisfaction was based on how well the practitioner assisted them. They suggested that the qualitative approach to customer evaluation and the process of "surveying through customer's stories" provide invaluable information about the function of public service delivery.

As Botswana and Nigeria governments continue to experience widespread change, many administrators struggle with the problem of how to maintain or improve service quality. Developing appropriate quality indicators is a good place to start. For example, the change in the public electricity and water systems need a change in mission that will provide an opportunity for a comprehensive organization and re-engineering. These efforts would be well served by beginning with the understanding of consumer's perspective on service delivery.

Further, public institutional infrastructure in Botswana and Nigeria needs to cover a wide range of requirements, such as finance, training, development of quality standards, generation of necessary information, promotion of performance monitoring and development of applied research in appropriate fields for industrial development. (1) Government should take steps to prescribe stiff penalties for individual and corporate entities that conceal information or refuse to respond to data request from the respective national governments. (2) The national government's office of statistics needs to reorganize its data collecting and analysis methods in order to overcome the problem of substantial lags both in published data and time of their release. (3) Activities and programs of the various NGOs, statistical agencies and research institutions should be properly coordinated. This will minimize duplication of efforts, ensure optimal utilization of scarce statistical manpower and material resources, and evolve nationally accepted standards of data collection, analysis and presentation to facilitate meaningful aggregation of government statistics into a national data bank. (4) The government office of statistics and other data collection agencies in Botswana and Nigeria should be provided with adequate funding to conduct their essential field surveys and purchase facilities such as up-dated computers to process their data.

Public education and dissemination of information were found to be among the most significant functions of NGOs and civil society organizations. Continued state domination of the media also reduced the possibility of objective, nonpartisan reporting of political information. To change this practice at the national and regional governments in Botswana and Nigeria, there should be an expansion of independent radio and television services in order to increase public access to information. Although newspapers and magazines have become an important source of information in both nations, the difficulties in distribution couple with low literacy means that radio is still the primary way of reaching mass audience.

As for people's rights, the commitment of governments, NGOs, and development agencies to popular participation as a necessary ingredient of sustainable development and accountability. Accountability and transparency should be the heart of efforts to improve governance in Botswana and Nigeria. Anti-corruption strategies must be realistic, achievable, and consistently implemented. Both nations should make progress by reforming tax laws and investment codes, eliminate price control, reduce permits and licenses, and revise public procurement procedures. Constitutional and legal requirements for assets disclosure by political leaders and senior officials should be demanded by the citizens to increase accountability and transparency.

Finally, governance, as a term is different from government (Handelman 2006; McCarney et al. 1995). Given this definition, when applied to Botswana and Nigeria, it should include the private sector, civil society associations, NGOs, community organization and social movements. These are elements, which are often considered to be outside public policy process. Community based organizations and NGOs should be encouraged to participate in all public affairs. NGOs and community base organizations could provide the medium by which the people of these African nations could help themselves to keep their environment clean and to help extend infrastructure and services to their community. Collaboration of NGOs, public servants, private sector, citizens and residence could benefit these nations in various ways both in cash and in kind. By participating in community base organization's decision-making and by helping to implement specific projects and other planned activities. This will help to empower the communities to improve their standard of living in many respects. In this way, the communities and NGOs would have played a role in the management of their government and, hence, in the promotion or advancement of their respective sustainable development goals.

Conclusion

This chapter has examined the role of NGOs in the development process of Botswana and Nigeria. It argued that while the development problems facing Botswana and Nigeria's are tremendous, maintaining and nurturing an effective collaboration that requires all members of the consortium to be attuned to potential change, both within the partnership and in relation to its clients is very important for Botswana and Nigeria to achieve sustainable development. Joint venture between government, NGOs and civil society organizations as well as the private sector is also very crucial for both African nations to achieve sustainable development.

An attempt was made in this study to stress that the extent to which Botswana and Nigeria pursue change in organizations would intensifies if they find niche markets, tailor their purchase of services and goods in an increasingly selective and competitive manner. The idea that both governments must change their management approach just NGOs dose is center to the argument this chapter present. A changing approach that is more responsive to social and environmental goals must be determined by the resources available to the government of Botswana and Nigeria. It is paramount stress that managing public goods involve planning, budgeting, staffing, controlling and problem solving. While NGOs leaders are more involved in a set of processes that create organization and adapt them to significant changing circumstances, the public sector in both nations has been rather engulfed with people with the attitude that they might fail or left behind in the globalization and sustainable development process.

Modification of development policy and management practices that would reflect the dynamics of sustainable excellence is very crucial for Botswana and Nigeria to achieve development. Understanding why NGOs participation is so important in large-scale efforts to develop technology, health care, education, the environment, agriculture is the key to identifying the adjustments and changes necessary so that policy directions are accompanied by appropriate actions. Notwithstanding development predicaments that Botswana and Nigeria currently face it seems worthwhile for collaboration, coordination and joint venture to take place between the respective government agencies, foreign NGOs, grassroots support organization, membership support organization, local non-profit organizations and civil society organizations in an attempt to achieve sustainable economic development and effective goods and services delivery to the citizens.

References

Adamolekun, Oladipo, ed. *Public Administration in Africa: Main Issues and and Selected Countries Studies*. Boulder, CO: Westview, 1999.

Anheier, H., and Kusuma Cunningham. "Internationalization of the Nonprofit Sector." In *Jossey-Bass Handbook of Nonprofit Leadership and Management*, edited by R. D. Herman and Associates. San Francisco: Jossey-Bass, 1994.

Balogun, Jide, and Gelase Mutahaba. "Redynamising the African Civil Service for the Twenty-first Century: Prospect for a Non-Bureaucratic Structure." In *Bureaucracy and the Alternatives in World Perspective*, edited by Keith Henderson and P. Dwivedi. New York: St. Martin's Press, 1999.

Botswana National Conservative Strategy. *National Policy on Natural Resources Conservation and Development*, no. 1. Gaborone: Botswana, Government Printer, 1990.

Connors, T. D. *The Nonprofit Handbook*. 3rd ed. New York: John Wiley & Sons Inc, 2001.

Ditchter, T. "Globalization and Its Effects on NGOs." In *Understanding Nonprofit Organizations*, edited by Steven Ott. Boulder, CO: Westview Press, 2001.

Eade, Deborah, ed. *Development, NGOs and Civil Society*. Bloomfield, CT: Kumarian Press, 2005.

Eade, Deborah, ed. *Development, NGOs and Civil Society*. Bloomfield, CT: Kumarian Press, 2000.

Fisher, Julie. *NGOs and the Political Development of the Third World*. Bloomfield, CT: Kumarian Press, 1998.

Feeney, Susanne. "Governance Framework for Collaboration and Merger." In *The Nonprofit Handbook: Management*, edited by Tracy Daniel Connors. New York: John Wiley & Son, 2001, 119.

Handelman, Howard. *The Challenge of Third World Development*. Upper Saddle River, NJ: Prentice Hall, 2006.

Haruna, Peter. "Reflective Public Administration Reform: Building Relationships Bridging Gap in Ghana." *African Studies Review* 44, no.1 (2001): 37-57.

Kotter, J. P. *Leading Change*. Boston: Harvard Business School Press, 1996.

Jameson, K. P., and C. K. Wilber. *The Political Economy of Development and Underdevelopment*. New York: McGraw, 1996.

Leather, Allan, and Deborah Eade, ed. *Development NGOs and Trade Unions*. Bloomfield, CT: Kumarian Press, 2005.

McPeak, M. "How Should an International NGO Allocate Growth?" *Journal of Nonprofit Management and Leadership* 10, no. 2 (1999): 185-207.

Metcalfe, L., and S. Richards. *Improving Public Management*. London: Sage, 1990.

Ndegwa, Stephen. "Civil Society and Political Change in Africa: The Case of Non-Governmental Organizations in Kenya." *International Journal of Comparative Sociology* 35, no. 1-2 (2002): 19-40.

Olowu, Dele. "Public Service Delivery." In *Public Administration in Africa: Main Issues and Selected Countries Studies*, edited by Oladipo Adamolekun. Boulder, CO: Westview, 1999.

Onimode, Bade. *African Development and Governance Strategies in the 21st Century*. London: Palgrave Macmillan, 2004.

Republic of Botswana. "Botswana's National Report for the United Nations Conference on Environment and Development." Department of Town and Regional Planning, Ministry of Local Government and Lands. Gaborone, Botswana: Government Printer, 1992.

Republic of Botswana. "National Settlement Policy." Final Draft Report, Department of Towns and regional Planning, Ministry of Local Government, Lands, and Housing. Gaborone, Botswana: Government Printer, 1996.

Rapley, J. *Understanding Development.* Boulder, CO: Lynne Rienner, 1996.

Riddeli and M. Robinson. *Non-Governmental Organizations and Rural Poverty Alleviation.* London, England: Oxford University Press/Oversea Development Institute, 1995.

Smith, B. "Nonprofit Organizations in International Development." In *Understanding Nonprofit Organizations*, edited by Steven Ott. Boulder, CO: Westview Press, 2001.

Steven, O. *Understanding Nonprofit Organizations Governance, Leadership and Management.* Boulder, CO: Westview Press, 2001.

Thin, Neil. *Social Progress and Sustainable Development.* Bloomfield, CT: Kumarian Press, 2002.

Thin, Neil. *Social Progress and Sustainable Development.* Bloomfield, CT: Kumarian Press, 2002.

Thomas, A. "Non-Governmental Organizations and the Limits to Empowerment." In *Development Policy and Public Action*, edited by A. Thomas. London, England: Oxford University Press, 1992.

Til, Jon Van, and David P. Swalve. "Change Leadership or Change Management." In *The Nonprofit Handbook: Management*, edited by Tracy Daniel Connors. New York: John Wiley & Son, 2001, 65.

Wallace, D. "The Role of Multi-lateral Institutions in African Development." *Journal of Law and Policy in International Business* 30, no. 4 (1999): 697-715.

World Bank. *Can Africa Claim the 21st Century?* Washington, C: World Bank, 2000.

Chapter 7

Motivation and Volunteerism in NGOs in Ghana and Nigeria

Josephine Dibie and Robert A. Dibie

The desire for non-governmental organizations (NGOs) to provide health care, education, medical research, humanitarian aid, and international development in Ghana and Nigeria has been viewed as a critical element of motivating civil society (Hudson 2005). Motivation in NGOs is not only concerned with the set of processes that arouse, direct, and maintain behavior toward a goal, it is increasingly been recognized as a crucial variable to economic, community, social, and cultural development in Ghana and Nigeria. Motivation is not equivalent to job performance but is one of several determinants of job performance. Today's work ethic motivates people in NGOs to seek interesting and challenging jobs instead of just money.

In the past fifty years there has been a steady increase in the number of NGOs and civil society groups in Ghana and Nigeria. These NGOs can be divided into humanitarian, relief and private development assistance organizations, and interest associations. In recent times these NGOs have been referred to in both countries as NGOs. Majority of the NGOs in both countries are formed by religious institutions, monastic orders, missionary societies, hospitals and universities. These NGOs are also linked to different political, economic, and cultural systems of both nations as well as European and North American countries. One common fact about the NGOs in Ghana and Nigeria is that, they are mostly subsidiaries of international non-governmental organizations (INGOS) or global civil society groups. Although their activities are domestic in nature, their grant-making sources are located internationally. NGOs such as Africare, Technoserve, Catholic Relief Service, the Red Cross, Country Women's Association of Nigeria (COWAN), the Methodist Church, Save the Children Federation, Anglican Church, Aid Care Society, Bible Missionary Society, Association of Women in Agriculture, Afaataba Cooperative Society, and Ford Foundation's International Institute of Tropical

Agriculture (IITA) are prominent in the provision of humanitarian services to the people of Ghana and Nigeria.

The idea of volunteering for the benefit of others has long been a tradition in Ghana and Nigeria. In an attempt to revitalize their economies and societies Ghana and Nigeria has experienced decline in security, democratic governance and lack of improved human development. Their national civic service engagement programs have been mired with nepotism, corruption, mismanagement, and gender bias policies (Patel and Wilson 2004). The economic and political situation in both countries has been considerably weakened as government faced increasing pressure from citizens to meet their basic needs. Ghana and Nigeria are examples of nations faced with multiethnic societies and practice clientele politics and economies that continue to serve the needs of the urban areas at the expense of the rural population. Both nations also have weak institutions and increasing citizen's expectations that never met. This weakened political and economic situation often resulted in conflicts between ethnic and religious groups and those who have and who have been deprived. Sometimes the situation gets difficult that the rich cannot sleep because the poor are a wake (Dibie 2003). The major impediments for civil society groups in Ghana and Nigeria have been how to create an effective and complementary partnership with local, informal community-based organizations and how to be involved in civic engagement without compromising their social and economic development (Jaskyte 2004; Hudson 2005).

It has been estimated that the religious NGOs in Ghana have a network of over 1.5 million volunteers. On the other hand the volunteers in Nigeria are estimated to be over six million (Enemuo, 2001; Fowler 1998; Patel and Wilson 2004). Further, the administrative instrument for managing services of several volunteers working for NGOs in Ghana and Nigeria has been left in the hands of paid workers from diverse backgrounds. Some of these paid staff are foreign employees who sometimes serve as members of the board of directors are guided by the articles of incorporation or bylaws, civil rights laws, state and national tax laws of their respective institutions. Despite pragmatic domestic policies in Ghana and Nigeria, power elites have dominated their political and economic decision making process and institutions that protect human rights and advance human development have failed the majority of volunteers in both nations.

The nature of NGOs operations in both countries has made scholars to regard them as an alternative to state-led and state-dominated development institutions (Anheier and Cunningham 1994; Patel and Wilson 2004: Fisher 1998). Julie Fisher (1998) contend that the United States Agency for International Development (USAID) has been providing funds to NGOs in Africa to cover a wide range of projects such as agriculture, child services, education, human resources, socio-economic development, rural development, nutrition, health, disaster relief and technical assistance. The extent to which NGOs manage and motivate the personnel that work for them constitutes how successful their programs have been in Ghana and Nigeria.

NGOs in Ghana and Nigeria are often confronted with the problem of reconciling the demands of their regular employees, volunteers, clients, board members and donors. This complex task is sometimes very cumbersome and precarious when it has to do with the local culture and political environment. To some extent, NGOs have been successful in Ghana and Nigeria because they have been able to accommodate the problems associated with cultural diversity, geographical distance in operations, economic barriers and political fragmentation (Anang 1994; Ndegwa 1996). Despite this success story, Sandberg (1994) and (Anheier and Cunningham (1994) pointed out that NGOs in Africa still confront problems associated with insufficient institutional planning, poor human resource management, lack of motivation of volunteers, lack of project evaluation, bad information management, weak fundraising, inefficiency in project implementation and lack of data processing. The human resources problem, which is the main focus of this study, involves a whole range of issues, such as recruitment, training and motivation of volunteers (Patel and Wilson 2004). Although NGOs have been able to recruit well-trained and educated staff in Ghana and Nigeria, their regular staff are also learning to build on indigenous volunteers in addressing the problems in the civil society. Most of the human resources problems would be resolved if an important and socially justifiable mission is established. An ideal motivation policy will also serve as a source of inspiration to key stakeholders, particularly regular employees and volunteers. The search for new and more effective ways of service delivery is also paramount to the success of NGOs operations in both nations (Jaskyte 2004). Failure to establish such motivation policy in NGOs operating in Ghana and Nigeria has often resulted in a non-conducive working environment and reduced motivation and participation of employees.

This chapter examines some of the human resources problems that NGOs confront in Ghana and Nigeria. It explores what motivates the behavior of volunteers in several nonprofit organizations in both nations. It argues that the existence of a psychological contract combined with well-known difficulties in mandating volunteer behavior might cause volunteers to perceive a breach of such contract seriously. Consequently, such perceived breach would affect the level of participation and withdrawal from the activities of the organization. This study attempts to find out the extent to which volunteers enter their working relationship with specific expectations and to what extent nonprofit organizations in Ghana and Nigeria fulfill these expectations. It assumes that a personal motivating factor is the stimulating value that fosters his or her continuity in voluntary work. The major questions addressed in the study are: In what ways can the psychological contract and extrinsic and intrinsic motivational factors be used to understand the behavior and performance of volunteers working for NGOs in Ghana and Nigeria? What motivates volunteers and what does it mean to them. Further, what role does personal, societal and organizational factors play in motivating a volunteer? The last section of the paper considers the application of the findings to both Ghana and Nigeria. It attempts to provide an insight to members of the board of directors and chief executives of NGOs that they ought to pay more attention to ways in which volunteer contracts are largely being fulfilled. It also strongly suggests that administrators of non-governmental organizations should make changes that would help to motivate and retain volunteers and dedicated employees.

Contract and Expectations of Employees

Research has shown that NGOs staff will improve their performance when specific, acceptably difficult goals are set and feedback about task performance is provided (Greenbarg and Baron 2003) Thus, performance to outcome expectancy is the belief that effort will lead to performance. In other words volunteers in NGOs will be motivated to work towards a goal if they want it and think that they have a chance of achieving such goal. The task of selecting goals that are acceptable to employees is facilitated by allowing employees to participate in the goal-setting process. According to Gregory Moorhead and Ricky Griffin (2004) motivation theories proposes that people have only three basic needs: existence, relatedness, and growth. Following from these theories, NGOs are encouraged to do several things to motivate their employees. Notably, NGOs should promote a healthy workforce, provide financial security, provide opportunities to socialize, and recognize employees' accomplishments.

Contract as used in this chapter refers to an agreement between two or more people enforceable by law. Psychological contract as used in this chapter is a contract, which exits between a person and another party. The contractual agreement might be between an employee and an employer. What is important about the psychological agreement is that there is a reciprocal exchange of agreement between the employee and employer. Each party is required to fulfill his or her obligation. Farmer and Fedor (1999) contend that both parties believe an agreement exists and that some sort of promise has been made. The fact that a promise has been established makes both contract holders to be bound to a set of reciprocal obligations. So many NGOs have failed in Ghana and Nigeria because they ignore, or tried to circumvent, or even tried to contradict the contractual agreement between management and employees (including volunteers).

Steers and Porter (1998) and Nylunds (2001) contend that altruism, personal interests, emotional needs and social contact are some of the factors that motivate volunteers to participate in NGOs. What is important about these studies is that the multiple goals of an individual usually stimulate their desire to engage in volunteerism. Anne Yeung (2004) and Omoto and Snyder (1993) provided more insight in this discourse by arguing that personal motivation should sometimes be viewed as an inner factor, and it is a phenomenon that should include an individuals reflection of his or her environment. In this respect motivation can be perceived as interconnecting both motives and the individual commitment to work as a volunteer. Their findings provide an important insight to this study.

Rousseau (1990), and Farmer and Fedor (1999) pointed out that on the one hand, the important element of the psychological contract to an employee is that the contract might include loyalty, extra-role behaviors, overtime, minimum stay, willingness to accept transfers and so on. On the other hand, the contract might mandate the employer to provide extrinsic and intrinsic motivational variables such as high pay, training, job security, advancement and career development.

Shore and Tetrick (1994) and Nylund (2001) exert that although psychological contract is based on trust, it develops from the interaction of volunteers and the environment of the NGOs. Each member of the contract has some expectations of one another. Rousseau (1989) rightfully argued that if the expectations of both parties are violated, trust and faith in the relationship will be considered undermined. Therefore, if for example, the NGO violates the contract, that could result in lower volunteer contribution and investment. The aftermath might be lower performance, high turnover, irregular attendance, low retention, and precarious citizenship behavior. Omoto and Snyder (1993 and 1995) contend that this is true because people volunteer to fulfill a number of needs. These needs include value expression, social adjustment, ego defense and gaining knowledge. Omoto and Snyder's argument suggests that volunteers enter into a work related contract with an NGO with specific expectations.

Waldschmidt et al. (1994) pointed out that an NGO, who has a contract obligation with an employee but fails to pay such staff regularly, will not expect such an unpaid employee to perform exactly like a well-paid worker. They argued that volunteers have different reasons for joining an NGO and because of these reasons they could show different patterns of behavior in their involvement. The bone of contention is that volunteers should not be subject to the same performance standards to which paid employees in the NGO are held.

Psychological contract is used in this study to highlight how volunteers working in an NGO could hold the organizations accountable to its contract in Ghana and Nigeria. This study attempts to show that the level of volunteer participation in or withdrawal from NGOs operations in Ghana and Nigeria is dependent on how the NGOs fulfill their contract with their regular staff and volunteers.

Motivation has at least two connotations in the field of organizational behavior in NGOs. It is viewed as a management strategy to induce paid workers and volunteers to act in ways that would produce the desired result anticipated by the NGO. Properly motivated employees, who feel that their expectations are being met by the NGO, will perform efficiently and effectively. When contractual obligation and expectations are not met, employees will find reasons to stay away from work and perform poorly when at work. Abraham Maslow (1954) pointed out that if people grow up in an environment where their needs are not met, they will be unlikely to function as healthy, well- adjusted individuals. Therefore, unless volunteers get their needs met by NGOs they will not function as effectively as possible.

Individual differences, job characteristics, and organizational practices are three of many factors that influence motivation. In order to develop an effective motivation program, managers must consider how the interaction among these factors affects employee performance on the job (Pearce 1993; Ban and Ruccucci 2002).

According to Greenberg and Baron (2003) and Moorhead and Griffin (2004), individual expectations such as personal needs, values, attitudes and interests will determine what kind of behavior they will bring to their jobs.

Because these characteristics vary from person to person, so will what motivates people. One employee may be motivated by money and hold out for a job paying a high salary. Another may be motivated by security and accept a lower paying job that involves few risks of unemployment. Thus, volunteers working in NGOs will be motivated to do so if they think that they have a good chance of achieving their goal.

Greenberg and Baron (2003) stated that Frederick Hertzberg's two factor motivation theory stipulated that motivators and hygiene factors operate independently of each other. The absence of dissatisfiers will not motivate workers; motivation arises only in the presence of satisfiers. According to this formulation, NGOs would need to reduce dissatisfiers and increase satisfiers in order to produce a motivated work force. Frederick Hertzberg was among the first behavioral scientists to look at employee motivation from a different angle (Dresang 2002; Moorhead and Griffin 2004).

Hertzberg's results led him to conclude that two separate and distinct kinds of experiences produce job satisfaction and job dissatisfaction. Thus, the model based on his research has been called the "two-factor model." The factors associated with positive feelings about the job, Hertzberg labeled motivator factors (Greenberg and Baron 2003). The factors associated with feelings of dissatisfaction were labeled hygiene factors. Motivating factors are those that are intrinsic (internal) to the job, including the challenge of the work itself, responsibility, recognition, achievement, advancement and growth, while hygiene factors are those that are extrinsic (external) to the job including working conditions, company policies, supervision, co-workers and salary, status, and job security (Greenberg and Baron 2003).

Managers of NGOs who recognize that subordinates are striving to satisfy their expectation needs should act in supportive ways. They might encourage regular staff to cooperate with volunteers more closely as well as foster more participation in the NGOs social activities such as picnics and end-of-year parties. According to Farmer and Fedor (1999), the special nature of the volunteer and NGO psychological contract is likely to be reflected in ways such as: (1) how violations are perceived and responded to; (2) expectations that volunteers hold; and (3) the nature of the contract.

Research Method

This study analyzed what motivates NGO staff and volunteers' behavior, notably the level of commitment and efficiency in service delivery to citizens in the communities in Ghana and Nigeria. It also identifies the specific motivational activities adopted by various NGOs in both nations. It attempts to examine the extent to which these motivational activities correspond to the ones expected or favored by the employees.

The field research was conducted in Ghana and Nigeria. A series of semi-structured interviews were conducted with regular NGO staff and volunteers in Ghana and Nigeria. The data for this study was collected through both semi-structured interviews and a survey administered personally by the authors in cooperation with NGO staff who provided valuable feedback concerning what drives their behavior at work and the meaningfulness and readability of those issues created for the study. Combining interview and data analysis techniques offered significant advantages to those other research methods that do not. It allows the authors to collect more accurate data than other methods.

The study was conducted in Ghana and Nigeria in the summer of 2005. The research project relied on two sets of information sources in Ghana and Nigeria: (1) A structured personal interview with over four hundred foundations and NGOs managers, volunteers and regular (paid staff) in both nations; (2) administration of five hundred questionnaires. The total number of employees of these forty NGOs in both nations is estimated to be about 900 volunteers and 210 paid staff.

Five hundred questionnaires were administered to regular NGO staff and volunteers. Two hundred (250 or 50 percent) of the questionnaires were administered in Ghana, while another 250 were administered to NGO employees in Nigeria. Two hundred and five NGO employees responded to the questionnaire in Ghana, while 227 employees responded in Nigeria. A total of 432 responses where received out of the 500 questionnaires administered to employees of forty active NGOs randomly selected from a list of NGOs in Ghana and Nigeria. The data collected from the 432 respondents were analyzed using the SPSS computer program. Table 7.1 shows the names of the NGOs in Ghana and Nigeria who participated in the survey. The following specific research questions provided the basis of this study:

1. In what ways have NGOs' violation of your employment contract affected your contribution, performance, attendance, retention, and citizenship behavior on the job?
2. What are the most important distinctions between NGOs regular staff expectations and those of volunteers in the organizations?
3. Can the employees' perception of NGOs support of their volunteer staff lead to heightened attendance, performance, and innovation?

A detailed search of the motivation literature was conducted to identify all the major motivational activities. The following list of motivational variables and techniques was then obtained. The first ten variables are *extrinsic* motivation factors: (1) Gifts and material benefits outside regular salary; (2) Status; (3) Salary; (4) Good supervision; (5) Good working environment; (6) Lunch subsidy; (7) Privileges; (8) Good rules and regulations; (9) Free medical care; and (10) Affectionate relationship at workplace between managers and workers (Dresang 2002; Greenberg and Baron 2003).

The next ten variables are *intrinsic* motivation factors as used in the survey are: (11) Provision of job security; (12) Respect; (13) Promotion; (14) Challenging work; (15) Independent decision-making; (16) Job rotation; (17) Job enlargement; (18) Recognized remarkable achievement; (19) Competition; and (20) Praise (Dresang 2002; Greenberg and Baron 2003).

On the questionnaire, respondents were asked to rank the motivational activities in their order of importance or preference. The activity they thought to be most important would be ranked one, while the activity that are lest important would be ranked ten.

The questionnaires given to the volunteers and regular staff were collected from them before the personal interviews were conducted. During the interview sessions, NGOs employees were asked to rank the same motivational activities again. The purpose of this was to find out what motivates employees and the extent to which volunteers enter their working relationship with specific expectations. We attempt to find out the extent to which nonprofit organizations fulfill these expectations. At the end of the interview it was found that there was no significant difference between the rankings of the regular and volunteer employees. Effort was made to ensure that the workers fully understood the meaning of the motivational activities before ranking them.

Using the interview method in research allows the authors to study a complex situation in great depth, providing the opportunity to gain insights that may not be possible if other methods were used.

Table 7.1
Names of NGOs that Participated in the Study

NGOs in Ghana	NGOs in Nigeria
Actionaid, Accra	Africare, Lagos
Afaataba, Bolgatanga	Technoserve, Abuja
Amanside Tree Planting and Rural Development Association, Bekwa-Ashanti	Catholic Relief Services, Lagos
Aid Care Soceity, Accra	The Red Cross Society of Nigeria, Lagos
Anti-Aids Volunteers	Methodist Hospital, Eku
Beware of Aids, Offinso-Ashanti	Anglican Church of Nigeria, Ibadan
Bible Society of Ghana, Accra	Jesus Women, Benin City
Bible Missionary Society, Accra	Save the Children Federation, Lagos
Assemblies of God Development and Relief Services, Accra	Bible Missionary Society of Nigeria, Lagos
Association of Women in Agriculture, Brong Ahafo.	Ford Foundation's International Institute of Tropical Agriculture, Ibadan
Nandom Agriculture Project, Wa	Country Women's Association of Nigeria (COWAN), Lagos
Nandom Food Farmers Women, Nandom	Cocoa Farmers Association, Ibadan

Data Analysis and Discussion

In analyzing the data for this study, the ranks given to each activity by all the respondents were added and the mean calculated to give the average rank. The average ranks were, in turn, ranked from 1 to 10, 1 being the activity with the lowest average rank (signifying the most favored motivational activity) and 10 (the least favored activity) being the activity with the highest average rank.

Table 7.2 shows the profile of the respondents to this survey. The total number of respondents was 432. Two hundred and five respondents were from Ghana (100 from regular NGOs staff and 105 from NGOs volunteers). There were 227 respondents from Nigeria (100 from regular NGOs staff and 127 from

Ghana (100 from regular NGOs staff and 105 from NGOs volunteers). There were 227 respondents from Nigeria (100 from regular NGOs staff and 127 from NGOs volunteers). Table 7.3A and 7.3B provides a detailed analysis of motivational factors and the expectations of both regular and volunteers NGOs staff who responded to the survey. Table 7.3A and 7.3B also summarizes the most important differences between regular staff and volunteers of several NGOs in Ghana and Nigeria. The differences can be divided into reason for affiliation, extrinsic and intrinsic factors, and structural and employee role expectations. Further, the table shows the level of expectations of motivational factors between regular NGOs staff and volunteers in Ghana and Nigeria. While 96-98 percent of volunteers stated that they sought employment in NGOs because of their religious faith, only 20-31 percent of regular staff indicated that their religious belief was a major factor why they sought employment with the NGOs in both nations. Although most of the regular NGOs staff had fairly good educational qualifications, an average of twenty five percent of the respondents in both nations indicated that they joined the NGOs because of their religious belief. Similarly, an average of ninety-seven percent of the volunteers in Ghana and Nigeria indicated that they joined the NGOs because of their religious belief.

Table 7.2
Profile of NGO Staff and Volunteers that Responded

Position /Title in GO	**Nations**			**Total**
	Ghana	**Nigeria**	Missing Variables	
Regular Staff				
Directors	10	05	0	015
Priest	07	10	0	017
Asst. Director	08	10	0	018
Manager	10	09	0	019
Asst. Manager	08	08	0	016
Field Staff	57	58	0	115
Sub-Total	100	100	0	**200**
Volunteers				
Supervisor	22	25	0	047
Field Staff	83	102	0	185
Sub-Total	105	127	0	232
Total	**205**	**227**	**0**	**432**

Source: Computed from Survey Data 2005.

The survey result reveals that an average of fifty percent of both regular NGOs staff and volunteers in Ghana and Nigeria indicated that their job satisfaction was moderate. They also indicated that they would continue to work for their respective nonprofit organizations. This finding helps provide an understanding of why the performance of most NGOs regular staff and volunteers at work is based on the limited motivation factors that are available to them. The findings in this study also revealed that variables such as the reasons for affiliation, intrinsic and extrinsic motivational activities are factors that influence the performance of

NGOs workers in Ghana and Nigeria.

Findings and Discussion

Table 7. 3A
Motivational Factors and Expectations of NGO Staff and Volunteers

Variable	Ghana NGO Staff (100 = 100%)	Volunteers In Ghana (105 = 100%)		Nigeria's NGO Staff (100 = 100%)	Volunteers In Nigeria (127 = 100%)		Differences in Expectations
Reasons for Affiliation							
Religious Belief	20	96	(76)	31	98	(67)	High
Job Satisfaction	47	60	(27)	55	70	(15)	Moder-ate
Affective involvement	50	48	(2)	65	51	(14)	Moder-ate
Extrinsic Factors							
Gifts Outside Regular Salary	40	42	(2)	51	56	(5)	Low
Good Supervision	60	55	(15)	70	67	(17)	Moderate
Good Working Environment	90	88	(18)	76	80	(16)	Moder-ate
Performance and standards	30	39	(9)	33	36	(3)	Low
Good Rules and regulations	88	55	(33)	70	27	(43)	High
Affectionate Relationship at workplace	90	87	(17)	92	80	(12)	Moder-ate
Intrinsic Factors							
Job Security	87	30	(57)	90	45	(45)	High
Challenging work	85	88	(3)	81	75	(6)	Low
Respect	50	30	(20)	60	45	(15)	Moder-ate
Job Enlargement	0	0	(0)	0	0	(0)	None
Recognized Achievement	0	0	(0)	0	0	(0)	None
Competition	25	36	(11)	30	33	3)	Low
Praise	28	31	(3)	40	37	(3)	Low

Table 7.3B
Motivational Factors and Expectations of NGO Staff and Volunteers

Structural and Employee Role Expectations							
Role Uncertainty	33	37	(4)	27	31	(4)	Low
Power to Enforce Role Expectations	80	57	(23)	89	56	(33)	High
In-Role Behavior	50	49	(1)	55	51	(4)	Low
Extra-Role Behavior	10	90	(80)	31	88	(57)	High
Division of Labor in Task Allocation	75	35	(40)	80	31	(49)	High
Status Distinctions	70	15	(55)	80	21	(51)	High
Primary Basis of Control and Compliance	72	89	(17)	90	81	(11)	Moderate
Informal Social Influence	45	50	(15)	32	44	(12)	Low
Organizational Controlled Social Influence	73	67	(8)	82	77	(5)	Low
Level of face-to-face Contact	84	76	(8)	98	81	(17)	Moderate
Status as a Member of the Organization	83	65	(18)	80	68	(14)	Moderate

Source: Computed from Survey Data 2005:
Key (12) – Percentage of Differences

Although these findings are closely related with Frederick Herberg's two factor motivational theory, the reason for affiliation is also a major factor that motivates volunteers in these NGOs. The result of the findings in this study is summarized below.

There are major differences (High expectations 67-76%) between the perception of regular staff and volunteers about their reason for affiliation in the operations of NGOs in Ghana and Nigeria. There are low differences (2-5%) between the perceptions of regular staff and volunteers about extrinsic variables such as free medical care, gift outside regular salary and performance standard. There are moderate difference of (15-18%) between the perception of regular staff and volunteers about extrinsic motivational activities such as good supervision and good working environment. There is major difference (45-60%) between the perceptions of regular staff and volunteers about intrinsic motivational activities such as job security and promotion. There are minor differences of (3-11%) between the perceptions of regular staff and volunteers about intrinsic motivational activities such as praise, competition and challenging work. There is moderate difference of (8-18%) between the perceptions of regular staff and volunteers about structural and employee role variables such as primary basis of control and compliance, level of face to face contact, and status as a member of the organization. There are also minor differences of (23-25%) between the perception of regular staff and volunteers about variables such as power to enforce role, division of labor in task allocation and status distinction in their non-governmental organizations. There are major difference of (57-80%) between the perception of regular staff and volunteers about variables such as "extra-role behavior."

Table 7.4
Levels of NGO Employees Expectations and Attitudes

Behavior	Strongly Agree	Agree	Not Sure	Disagree	Strongly Disagree	Total
NGOS meeting the Expectations of Volunteers	120	50	30	100	132	432
Participation in Organization's Activities	204	106	22	75	25	432
Turn over if there is an Alternative Job	275	50	25	50	32	432
Perceived NGOs Support of Volunteers	232	75	25	60	40	432

Source: Computed from Survey Data 2005.

The volunteers that were interviewed stated that almost all volunteer functions were extra-role since the regular staff of the NGOs rarely mandated their rather than perceived organizational support. Majority of the volunteers in Nigeria expressed that it was very important to their religious orientation that their efforts improve the quality of life of clients. Their expectations and rewards extended beyond personal and organizational support, they include strong religious beliefs.

This analysis of various expectations of NGOs employees in Ghana and Nigeria shows how psychological contract can affect regular staff and volunteers in their NGOs. Figure 7. 1 indicates, that volunteers will participate more and be willing to spend a longer duration in an NGO if the organization creates conducive environment as well as motivates its employees. The interview result indicates very strongly that there is a two-way relationship between the regular staff, volunteers and their non-governmental organizations.

This study provides an insight to members of the board of directors and chief executives of NGOs that they ought to pay more attention to ways in which volunteer contracts are largely being fulfilled. It also strongly suggests that administrators of non-governmental organizations should make changes that would help to motivate and retain volunteers and dedicated employees (Balogun and Mutahaba 1999).

Figure 7.1
Relationship between Met Expectations and Perceived Organizational Support

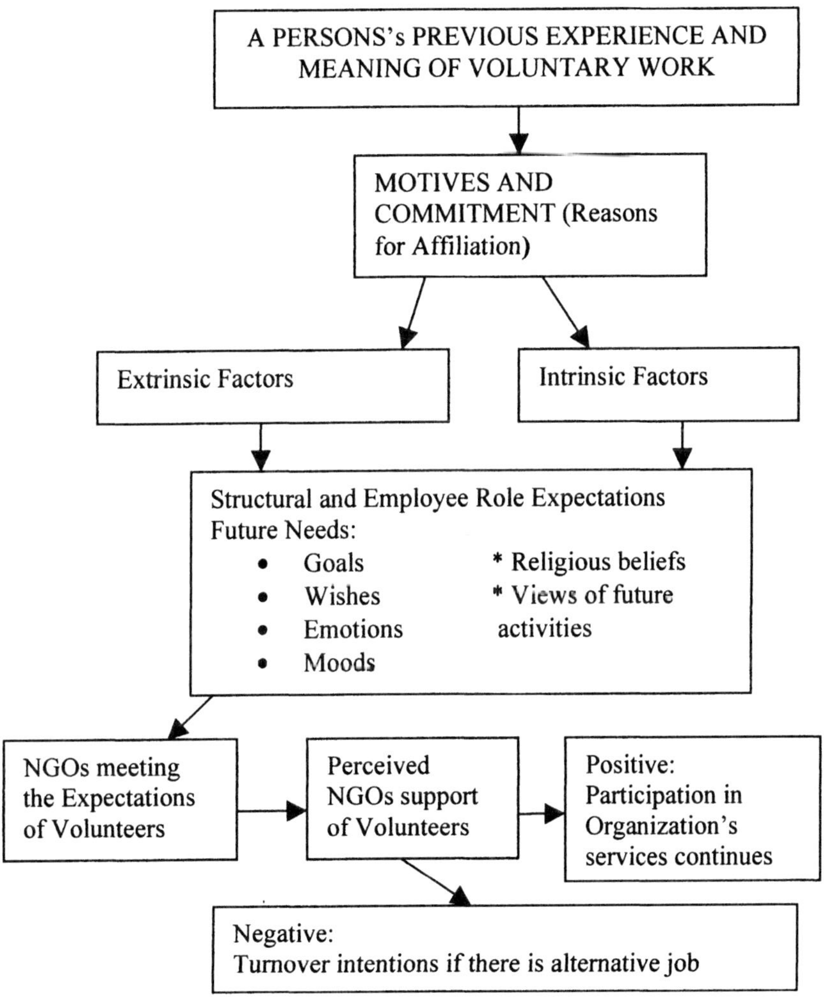

The study also reveals that a number of variables or situations are likely to affect motivation and productivity. Among these features, the nature of the job is paramount (Bonjean et. al 1994; Hudson 2005). Also important, is the social group in which the task is performed, the positive and negative experiences and the role the volunteers and regular staff play in performing the task. Volunteers in NGOs are not just products of the past; they are also creatures of the present productivity (Snyder and Ridges 1992; Hyden 1995). The chief executives of NGOs in Ghana and Nigeria should search for a balance between the goals of their organization and the expectations and aspirations of their volunteers by attending to individual expectations, preferences, valuing relationships and feelings (Ban and Riccucci, 2002). This framework would help to encourage open communication, team building and collaboration in the organization. It will also foster the personal growth and career development of volunteers.

The study strongly reveals and recommends that both extrinsic and intrinsic motivational factors would account for improved performance of volunteers and regular staff in NGOs in Ghana and Nigeria. Based on these findings, NGOs in Ghana and Nigeria should not limit themselves to cash compensation such as salary/wages. They should also reward employees financially through retirement plans, health and life insurance schemes, and other fringe benefits. These financial rewards are intended to encourage employees and promote positive performance-related behaviors as well as make employees feel they are being supported by their organizations. Further, the study reveals that volunteers' initiatives are crucial and appropriate in addressing the risks to human security in Ghana and Nigeria (Hudson 2005; Kiggundu 1989; Willard and Johnson 1990). In light of this finding it is recommended that future research on volunteerism should explore the important role they play in the ongoing sustainable development processes in both nations. There are inevitable strong correlation between motivation and performance. Although regular staff management controls are necessary in NGOs, the direction of change should favor reforms that relax the application of motivational factors and provide greater opportunity for the exercise of volunteers and staff initiatives. The implementation of tasks away from rigid procedures is one such method. Encouraging initiatives and experiences of regular staff and volunteers, orienting performance to results rather than conformity with rules and procedures are other factors that NGOs in Ghana and Nigeria should consider. Finally, it is paramount that NGOs facilitate communication and coordination across their organizations and operations because interpersonal relations will help their staff to cope with tasks that are characterized by considerable uncertainty. Any motivational factor that is implemented must be compatible with the maintenance of essential managerial accountability and control not only results that NGOs staff must achieve.

Conclusions

This chapter examines what motivates volunteers and regular NGOs staff in Ghana and Nigeria. It contends that volunteers' performance might lead to a variety of intrinsic and extrinsic rewards and if employees perceived these rewards an equitable they could lead to satisfaction. It explores how psychological contracts and motivational activities could affect volunteers and regular NGOs staff behavior. The chapter argues that volunteers participation and withdrawal in NGOs activities or operations is contingent on their perception or perceived expectation of organizational support. It further contend

Thus, of volunteers' expectation are closely tied to performance outcome. Organizational support could take different forms, such as extrinsic and intrinsic motivational activities.

The general thrust of the theories on motivation and performance discussed in this study focuses on causes of employee behavior at the work place. Each theory uses different psychological concepts to explain behavior and the need for greater flexibility in leadership styles and organizational support of employees. There is substantial evidence that supports a link between fulfilling volunteers' expectations and their level of participation in NGOs operations in Ghana and Nigeria.

The findings of this study show that significant differences existed between the choice of extrinsic and intrinsic motivational activities by volunteers and regular staff of non-governmental organizations in Ghana and Nigeria. What seems to be needed then is administrative style that will help chief executives of NGOs to determine and nurture a truly supportive relationship between the organization, its volunteers and regular employees. Such mutual or two-way relationship will help the organizations in achieving their missions.

Finally, development in Ghana and Nigeria involves social transformation that promotes political, social, and cultural as well as economic. NGOs and their staff should be part of the transformation mechanism in both nations. However, while development also implies modernization, in respect of secularization, industrialization, and urbanization it is not necessary to be westernization has most foreign NGOs seem to be promoting in Ghana and Nigeria. The effective implementation of a social development approach in Ghana and Nigeria would incrementally address the predicaments facing volunteers because they can make a significant contribution to social development in both nations if their expectations are met and an integrated strategy is adopted to promote civic engagement. In addition, volunteers also are concerned about the fairness of the manner in which NGOs treat them in Ghana and Nigeria. This is sometimes referred as organizational justice or distributive justice. These concepts suggest that NGOs should avoid intentionally underpaying or overpaying employees, that managers should follow fair procedures (e.g., ones that are consistent and correctible), and that managers should explain the basis for outcomes in a thorough and socially sensitive manner.

References

Anang, Federick. "Evaluating the Role and Impact of Foreign NGOs in Ghana." In *The Changing Politics of Non-Governmental Organizations and African States*, edited by Eve Sandbarg. Westport, CT: Praeger, 1994.

Anheier, Helmut, and Kusuma Cunningham. "Internationalization of the Nonprofit Sector." In *The Jossey-Bass Handbook of Nonprofit Leadership and Management*, edited by Robert D. Herman and Associates. San Francisco: Jossey-Bass Publishers, 1994.

Anheier, Helmut. "Non-Governmental Organizations and Institutional Development in Africa." In *The Changing Politics of Non-Governmental Organizations and African States*, edited by Eve Sandbarg. Westport, CT: Praeger, 1994.

Balogun, Jide, and Gelase Mutahaba. "Redynamizing the African Civil Service for the

Africa." In *The Changing Politics of Non-Governmental Organizations and African States*, edited by Eve Sandbarg. Westport, CT: Praeger, 1994.

Balogun, Jide, and Gelase Mutahaba. "Redynamizing the African Civil Service for the Twenty-first Century: Prospects for a Non-bureaucratic Structure." In *Bureaucracy and the Alternatives in World Perspective*, edited by Keith Henderson and P. Dwivedi. New Pork: St. Martins, 1999.

Ban, Carolyn, and Norma Riccucci. *Public Personnel Management: Current Concerns, Future Challenges*. New York: Longman, 2002.

Bonjean, C. M., W. T. Markham, and P. O. Macken. "Measuring Self Expression in Voluntary Organizations: A Theory-Based Questionnaire." *Journal of Applied Behavioral Science* 30 (1994): 487-515.

Clary, E. G., M. Snyder, and R. Ridge. "Volunteers' Motivations: A Functional Strategy for the Recruitment, Placement, and Retention of Volunteers." *Nonprofit Management and Leadership* 2, no. 4 (1992): 333-350.

Dibie, Robert. *Public Management and Sustainable Development in Nigeria*. Aldershot, England: Ashgate, 2003.

Dresang, Dennis. *Public Personnel Management and Public Policy*. New York: Longman, 2002.

Enemuo, F. C. "Youth Mobilization for Nation-Building: The Case of the National Youth Service Corps Scheme in Nigeria." Paper Presented at the Ford Foundation's Workshop on Youth Involvement as a Strategy for Social, Economic and Democratic Development, Costa Rica, January 2001.

Farmer, Steven, and Donald Fedor. "Volunteer Participation and Withdrawal: A Psychological Contract Perspective on the Role of Expectation and Organizational Support." *Nonprofit Management & Leadership* 9, no. 4 (1999): 249-367.

Fisher, Julie. *Non-Governments and the Political Development of the Third World*. West Hartford, CT: Kumarian Press, 1998.

Fowler, A. "Non-Governmental Organizations in Africa: Achieving Comparative Advantage in Relief and Macro-Development." Institute of Development Studies Discussion Paper, United Kingdom, 1998.

Greenbarg, Jerald, and Robert Baron. *Behavior in Organizations*. 7th ed. Upper Saddle River, NJ: Prentice Hall, 2003.

Hudson, Mike. *Managing at the Leading Edge: New Challenges in Managing Nonprofit Organizations*. San Francisco: Jossey-Bass, 2005.

Hyden, G. "Bringing Volunteerism Back In." In *Service Provision under Stress in East Africa*, edited by Semboja and Therkildsen. Nairobi: Center for Udviklingsforskning, 1995, 35-49.

Jaskyte, Kristina. "Transformational Leadership, Organizational Culture, and Innovativeness in Nonprofit Organizations." *Nonprofit Management & Leadership* 15, no. 2 (2004): 38-63.

Johnson, Willard R., and Vivian Johnson. *West African Governments and Volunteer Development Organizations*. Lanham, MD: University Press of America, 1990.

Kiggundu, Moses. *Managing Organization in Developing Countries: An Operational and Strategic Approach*. West Hartford, CT: Kumarian Press, 1989.

Maslow, Abraham. *Motivation and Personality*. New York: Harper and Row, 1954.

Moorhead, Gregory, and Ricky Griffin. *Organizational Behavior: Managing People and Organizations*. Boston: Hougton Mifflin Press, 2004, 144-146.

Ndegwa, Stephen. *The Two faces of Civil Society: NGOs and Politics in Africa*. West Hartford, CT: Kumarian Press, 1996.

Nylund, M. "Mixed Motives of Young Nordic Volunteers." In *Youth, Citizenship and Empowerment*, edited by Helve and C. Wallace., Aldershot, England: Ashgate, 2001, 91-109.

Omoto, A. M., and M. Snyder. "Basic Research in Action: Voluntarism and Society's Response to AIDS." *Personality and Social Psychology Bulletin* 16, no. 2 (1990): 152-165.

Omoto, A. M., and M. Snyder. "AIDs Volunteers and their Motivations." *Nonprofit Management and Leadership* 4 (1993): 157-176.

Omoto, A. M., and M. Snyder. "Sustained Helping without Obligation: Motivation, Longevity of Service, and Perceived Attitude Change among AIDS Volunteers." *Journal of Personality and Social Psychology* 68, no. 4 (1995): 671-691.

Patel, Leila, and Theresa Wilson. "Civic Service in Sub-Saharan Africa." *Nonprofit and Voluntary Sector Quarterly* 33, no.4 (2004): 22-38.

Pearce, J. L. *Volunteers: The Organizational Behavior of Unpaid Workers*. London: Routledge Press, 1993.

Rousseau, D. M. "Psychological and Implied Contracts in Organizations." *Employee Responsibilities and Rights Journal* 2, no. 2 (1989): 121-139.

Rousseau, D. M. "New Hire Perceptions of Their Own and Their Employers Obligations: A Study of Psychological Contracts." *Journal of Organizational Behavior* 11, no. 5 (1990): 389-400.

Rousseau, D. M., and J. M. Parks. "The Contracts of Individuals and Organizations." In *Research in Organizational Behavior*, edited by L. L. Cummings and B. M. Staw. Greenwich, CT: JAI Press, 1993.

Sandbarg, Eve, ed. "The Changing Politics of Non-Governmental Organizations and the African State." In *The Changing Politics of Non-Governmental Organizations and African States*, edited by Eve Sandbarg. Westport, CT: Praeger, 1994.

Shore, L. M., and L. E. Tetrick. "The Psychological Contract as an Explanatory Framework in the Employment Relationship." *Trends in Organizational Behavior* 1 (1994): 91-109.

Steers, R. M., and L. W. Porter. *Motivation and Work Behavior*. 4th ed. New York: McGraw-Hill, 1998.

Waldschmidt, D. M., D. R. Ilgen, A. Katke, C. C. Sagi, S. L. and Tellez. "Volunteers in the Workforce: Some Motivational Implications." Paper Presented at the Annual Meeting of the Academy of Management, Dallas, August 1994.

Yeung, Anne Brirgitta. "The Octagon Model of Volunteer Motivation: Results of a Phenomenological Analysis." *Voluntas: International Journal of Voluntary and Nonprofit Organizations* 15, no. 1 (2004): 21- 46.

Chapter 8

NGOs and Development in Cameroon

Wilfred Gabsa

Civil society is no doubt an issue that the regime in Cameroon is still grappling with. Within this ambit is a new phenomenon that the government is obliged to deal with at virtually all levels of societal organization? This phenomenon has become so strong and intrusive that it has left no sphere of societal organization untouched. With the advent of democracy in the early 1990s in Cameroon and most parts of the World, nongovernmental organizations (NGOs), the subject of this research have gained more salience in the day-to-day running of the affairs of the country. The phenomenon that emerged sometime in the early 90s has become a corner stone of the civil society organizations in the nation. This judgment is also espoused by analysts (Edwards and Hulme 1992) who claim, "if the 1980s can be described as the decade of NGOs. It is interesting to speculate how the 1990s will be defined" because in reality it is the current decade that truly deserves this label.

That aside, one thing is certain with NGOs are that they have become useful instruments of development. Notwithstanding the role NGOs apparently play in their respective societies (Tabetsing 2003) they still do not have the status they deserve and are not well known in the domain in which they exist and operate. Besides they have so many problems that thwart their effectiveness.

One may be tempted to think that the proliferation of NGOs in the early 1990s is because the nongovernmental arena had not been discovered yet. This of course is not true. In making this analogy, it is vital to give a thought to the democratization process and how this may relate to the advent of NGOs.

As far as the political system is concerned there is no disputing of the fact that the people in their majority no longer trust the government of Cameroon, to the extent that they would cling to anything that has no connection with the government or its institutions for survival. The level of trust in the regime is so low (Tabetsing 2003) that the aphorism "I believe in the devil I know than the saint I don't know" does not seem to have a place in the country anymore (Mbita 1998). People are ready to surrender their rights and resources to any individual and/or institution outside of the government that gives them any form of assurance of a better and healthier life, whether this is backed by concrete actions or not. Consequently people in Cameroon rely more in the organizations that exist outside of the government and its affiliated institutions than on the government and the institutions it represent. It is perhaps for this reason that there is an over proliferation of these organizations in the country. Even though if asked, Cameroonians would surely have a different rationale to explain this rise in NGOs, the involvement of the international community in some of these societies accounts for why they are more Cameroon and for the poor performance of the government as well.

Furthermore NGOs are more flexible than the government or its institutions. As a result of the ties these groups have with the local communities (in which they are based and from where their activities are coordinated), they tend to know the people better and are better able to adjust to their needs and aspirations (Livernash 1992) than any government will do. In a similar perspective, their size and the number of people they employ and work with makes it easier for them to adapt to new situations, particularly those that relate to overhead costs, financial obligations and the list continues.

In addition, the sources of their revenue are much wider than that of governments, to the extent that it is hard for NGOs that are well establish to run out of resources, and shut down altogether. Some of them get money from international organizations, States other than the host State, and still some get it from donor organizations other than international organizations. In the similar perspective, these organizations are better placed to help the poor in many more ways than the government can ever do. In fact they are well placed to create personal relationships with the poor and interact with them in more ways than they can with the government or its institutions.

Given the several reasons just outlined about the comparative advantages of NGOs over the government and its institutions, the question that accrues there from is whether it is possible for these organizations to replace the government? The answer is of course no, it is not possible for this to happen because after everything these institutions need protection from the political system, and the people that these structures are created to serve need a lot more protection as well. In fact, the government can provide the kind of protection they deserve because it exists to serve the interest of the whole society. Whichever way one looks at it, the services that NGOs provide are bound to be supplementary to that of the government (The Herald 2004).

This chapter contends that the proliferation of NGOs is just one of those ripple effects of the wind of democracy. It addresses the question: can NGOs replace the government in the management of the affairs in Cameroon? What responsibilities do they have and how are these responsibilities separated from those of the State? How do NGOs compare to institutions of the government? Is it possible for these organizations to play the role of the government? Do they stand a better chance of serving the people better than the government does? These are some the questions that will be answered as this analysis progress.

The Rise of NGOs

There is no doubt that the rise of NGOs in Cameroon like elsewhere had long been exponential over the past thirty years. Although these organizations have today flooded the society in an alarming manner, their existence creates more problems apparently than provide solutions to the problems they are apparently created to take care of. Whereas this is an issue we would be addressing in a later part of this work, it is important to delve into some of the reasons why NGOs or what the text governing them in Cameroon calls Common Initiative Groups Laws of 1992 and 1999 came into being and why they exist in such great numbers today in the country.

To begin with, the political history and evolution of the country is a fundamental factor in the renaissance of NGOs in Cameroon. This should not be confused with the colonial history of Cameroon, although they are closely connected. What I am referring to is the political evolution of Cameroon since independence in 1960 with the reunification of Eastern and Southern Cameroons. After independence, there was a massive proliferation of NGOs, unfortunately very few of them were in the area of economic development. In most cases they were attached to specific individuals, the majority of whom went on self-exile. The organizations that kicked off with the independence of the country were created by the French to ensure the economic status quo while at the same time making sure that they enjoyed all the economic advantages that accrued from colonialism (Ngoh 1996). *The* French company for the development of textiles, the association of chemical and road network in Cameroon, and the list continues were some of the first NGOs in the nation. There are all structures that are economically oriented but that were formed not only to foster the economic well-being of the French in Cameroon but were created to forcefully tie the colonial economy to its overseas counterpart in France.

In Southern Cameroon, the Youth League, and the Cameroon Welfare Union, are some NGOs in the early colonial days that finally decided to go political by merging to form the National Council of Cameroon and Nigeria (NCNC) (Koge 1985). When Ahidjo finally came to power in 1960 and succeeded subsequently to bring both Cameroon's together as one country, he prohibited the existence of all forms of civil society organizations, claiming that they are anti-patriotic groups of Cameroonians whose interest "is to take Cameroon back its pre-independence days" (Ahidjo 1976). This pattern continued until the early days of the democratization process, a process that opened up the public space for the formation of NGOs. Basically, the massive creation of NGOs in Cameroon came with the democratization process that went into full gear in the 1990s. Like N'Diaye this study argues to the effect that "le boom des ONG au Cameroon date des annees 90" (1990 is the year of the spread of NGOs in Cameroon) (N'Diaye 2005). The extension of freedoms in Cameroon made this possible, but whether this has helped the society at all in its development efforts is what is still to be determined.

Additionally the economic crisis is responsible for the proliferation of NGOs in Cameroon. The Structural Adjustment Program (SAP) with its accompanying measures worsened the economic crisis in Cameroon. It worsened the situation because of the unintended effects of the application of the program on peoples who were not at the origin of the program and who had no alternative but to be subjected to the dictates of financial institutions (great beneficiaries of the program too) whose economic prowess sometimes surpass that of some developing states. Whereas analysts in African political economy see the program as the only outlet for the continent to get itself out of poverty the fact remains that it has done more harm to the continent than the good it was intended to bring (Kempe 1997). Even though most of the problems that the continent faces today can be traced back to the post-independence period, the SAP did by every indication aggravate the economic situation in Cameroon. Among other things, "poverty and socioeconomic inequalities increased, the external debt burden became heavier, capital flight deepened, balance of payment weakened, unemployment and crime escalated, famine and malnutrition increased, budget deficits soared, agricultural productivity declined, political and civil strife worsened, and environmental degradation expanded (Kempe 1997). Some of these factors were aggravated by the demand by the international community obliging recipient countries to open their political institutions up for democracy that they were still not ready for. Whereas good governance and democracy is a fundamental requirement for economic recovery (Meier 1995), and development (albeit debatable), it goes without saying that good governance and democracy has to be introduced sequentially, that is in respect of principles that are particular to the society concerned, what was not the case in most of the Third World in general and Cameroon in particular. The deepening economic crises in Cameroon provided the imperative for policy reform. Among the many reforms that the government undertook are changes in government policy, institutional structure, or administrative procedures (Perkins and Roemer 1991) and of course textual reforms. One of the immediate consequences was the opening up of the civil society, whose spill over effect turned out to be the proliferation of nongovernmental organizations. Besides the fact that government provided the space needed for the proliferation of civil society, the support (both financial and moral) that these organizations received from international organizations is not to be discounted in this process.

These reasons aside, social deprivation, poverty, clienteles networks are also factors that have driven the proliferation of NGOs in Cameroon. As we shall discover, it is evident that the practices of the government and its cronies in the early and later part of the democratization process did push for the establishment of NGOs. The people came to realize that once the political environment was liberalized, one good way of constraining the government or making the government cautious in its way of doing things is via competition that is by creating institutions and structures that can cater for some of the responsibilities of the government. As already indicated to compete with the government these organizations relied significantly on the support (mostly financial and some times capital support) of the international society on which the bulk of them depend (some exclusively) for survival and continuity.

A multitude of factors are responsible for the creation and proliferation of NGOs in Cameroon. These factors range from the economic crisis to the process of political liberalization, to the way governmental runs its affairs, to the Structural Adjustment Program, and the list continues. Whereas these may not be an exhaustive list of the factors responsible for the proliferation of NGOs in Cameroon, they nonetheless give a broad apercu (an indication) of the situation as it is in the country today. With that we beg to switch gear to the dynamics of NGOs in Cameroon.

The Dynamics of NGOs in the Nation

The meager economic status of a country like Cameroon may make some analysts of NGOs to conclude that the nation might not have enough NGOs. This would be a big mistake; in fact it will be grossly incorrect. Cameroon has lots of NGOs, actually it should be said that it has a lot more NGOs than expected given the history of their existence. If one takes for instance into consideration the fact that their existence dates back in the early 1990s and that the country right now is unable to keep tract of its NGOs. This is proof that a lot still has to be done to for the existence of a healthy environment for NGOs in the country. The dynamics of nongovernmental organizations in Cameroon is two fold: these organizations have different appellations that mean one and the same thing, and the fact that their domain of activity is diversified.

There is actually a lot of confusion with regard to the existence of NGOs in Cameroon. The society (perhaps with outside inspiration) has generated several appellations (Fisher 1994) of NGOs in Cameroon today to the extent that one gets lost in the semantics of nongovernmental organizations. Whereas it is common to hear names like grassroots organizations (GRO), nongovernmental organizations (NGO), grassroots support organizations (GRSO), and common initiative groups (CIG) within the NGO phraseology. The Law on the organization and functioning of these organizations in its Article 1 makes explicit allusion only to NGOs that are "created and exercise their activities within the framework of the law" (Law of 1999) on the liberty of association. Even though the President of Cameroon signed the 1999 Law, there exists another piece of legislation signed by the Prime Minister that relates to another kind of organization known as the Common Initiative Group. Although the text of the President is hierarchically superior to that of the Prime Minister, government authorities as well as citizens and managers of NGOs use any of the appellations mentioned above to designate a NGOs. It is our hope that a text would be drafted in the near future to settle this issue.

Diversity is another phenomenon that characterizes NGOs in Cameroon. These organizations operate in virtually all works of life ranging from agriculture, to forestry or in short the environment, food service, human rights and the list continues. In the terms of the Law on nongovernmental organizations, Article 3, states, "the mission of public interest that is assigned to these organizations is determined by the State in the judicial domain, the economic, social, cultural, sanitation, sports, educational, humanitarian, and environmental domains or the domain of the protection of human rights" (Law of 1999). Basically NGOs exist in all of these domains today in Cameroon. In terms of the missions of NGOs therefore, it can be alleged that their domain of activity is very diverse, lets take a look at how this diversity is reflected in the role these organizations play in the development of the society.

NGOs and Economic Development

The economic development of Cameroon is of major concern to the government. The standard of living of the people, their lifestyles and the possibility of every one to fulfill his or her aspiration in life are of concern to the government. Economic development, Meier (1995) says "involves something more than economic growth plus change: there are essential qualitative dimensions in the development process that extend beyond the growth or expansion of an economy through a simple widening process."

Based on this contention, economic development does not only feature in the development of institutions and change in attitudes and values, it can also be "interpreted as a rise in productivity, social and economic equalization, modern knowledge, improved institutions and attitudes, and a rationally coordinated system of policy measures that can remove the host of undesirable conditions in the social system that have perpetuated a state of underdevelopment" (Crush 1995). Given these definitions of economic development, what is the impact of NGOs in the economic development of the country? Their impact in the economic development of Cameroon can be analyzed from various standpoints: their impact in the field of participation, education, change in the life style of Cameroonians, and the list continues.

Before getting into the role that NGOs play in the economic development of the country, it is important to give an indication of some of the NGOs that are directly involved with activities that relate to economic development. The multiplicity of groups in Cameroon directly involved in the development process of the country lends credence to the fact that the State alone cannot be the sole custodian of development (Onana 1994). Although this translates the idea that these groups are working in different parts of the economy, one wonders though where some of them get their resources or financial support. This should be a major concern for those groups that have as objective the provision of aid to local citizens. How they conducted fund raising is a question no one in the country is willing to deal with. Some of these organizations are involved in poverty reduction initiatives that are vital for the people to get themselves out of poverty.

A look at the poverty index of the country over years or rather since the existence of these organizations is confusing with regard to the effect that NGOs are having on the economy of the country and life of the people. The positive tendency we notice with the Human Poverty Index of 50 percent between 1987 –1997, to 31.99 percent in 1999, and then to 30 percent in 2000 (Boston

University 2005) make a criticism of the role of these organizations in economic development difficult if not impossible.

Table 8. 1
NGOs in the Domain of Economic Development

Name of NGO	Domain of Competence
ONG Afrique Agricole	For agricultural production
Amazones de Development Rural	For rural development
Association for Social Aid	For multiple help to the needy
Youth Development Association	For the development of the young in need
Manyu Palm Kernel Industry	For the production of Palm Kernel
Humanitarian Rehabilitation Organization	For the poor and needy
Aide et Developpement du Bassin Forestiere du Sud	For development Aid

Although this study does not control for the effect of other variables, it is still possible to assume that the work of NGOs must have been instrumental to the good performance of Cameroon with regards to the Human Development Index. Furthermore, the fact that the GDP per capita moves from negative 0.6 between 19975-1999 to positive number (UNDP 2005) is proof that things are not the same in Cameroon and that everyone is working hard to change the standard of living, and improve upon the well being of the people. NGOs are having significant economic development impact in Cameroon.

NGOs and Popular Participation

The proliferation of NGOs in the country has increased the participation of Cameroonians to the development process, although this is not as visible as one would expect. These organizations have made the people to realize that they are and should be the agents of their own development (Roff 2004; Kohl 2003). They have moved from parochial philosophies of life to a participatory lifestyle in which they are made to understand that their pleasures; their well-being and that of their neighbors depend on them and not on the government as the belief has always been. It is common in Cameroon to see women, youths, and the elderly performing major decision-making roles in various NGOs and helping the society in various ways via these mechanisms to achieve their best. If one thing is certain, it is the fact that they can be no change without concrete action (Mama 2000) and general participation. In situations where team work is required with governmental institutions, the people are now working together with the government rather than fighting against it. This is what most African governments would love to see take place. For one thing Cameroonians are more than ever before concerned about what takes place around them, and they are ready more than they have ever been to take part in activities that can bring some improvements in the life they live. National human rights groups, national rural participatory groups, and national environmental groups are some of those associations that are out to encourage the average Cameroonian to engage in efforts that that can bring about the change they expect for themselves. The usefulness of being involved is that it creates room for individuals and some of these nongovernmental organizations to be accountable to the people, a thing most them are not comfortable with.

NGOs and Education

For development to be actually considered as freedom as the noble prizewinner in economics holds, people have to be well educated to cater for themselves, their interests and those of the community in which they thrive. Education is the bedrock on which society grows and reproduces itself. Sen (1999) in the same fashion claims, "the expansion of education and literacy in a region can facilitate social change (even the reduction of fertility and mortality) and also help to enhance economic progress from which others too benefit."

Table 8.2
An Indication of Feminist Associations

Description/Name	Educational Objective
Federation of Rural Women	Promotion of rural activities for women
Federation of Poor Women....	Taking poor women out of poverty
Environment sans frontiere	Healthy environmental practices
Group Bamenda Aghem Women	Economic empowerment for women
Health Women's Association	AIDS, and other health issues
Women Human Rights Group	Take the woman out of slavery
Association for the fight against violence on women	Protecting the woman
Reseau des femmes activates Pour le developpement du Nyong et Soo	Feminist activities geared toward development of the Woman
Torch Bearers in Bamenda	Women's rights defense group
Nbengwi Social Women's Group	For the societal integration of the woman

There are lots of NGOs in Cameroon that have helped the society in becoming more economically oriented in their way of living and thinking. As an example, the National Association of Female Jurists has been so instrumental in the life of the woman in Cameron to the extent that women are now beginning to own and manage landed property what was formerly not the case in Cameroon in the 1980s.

Among the NGOs that have been active in the education of women in Cameroon the following can be distinguished. Although just the tip of the iceberg, these are a sample of feminist associations that exist to cater for the needs of the woman in Cameroon. Actually, there exist more that one hundred of such associations in Cameroon today. How to operate without duplicating each other is the topic of another paper. So far in the country, women are becoming more and more active in the social, economic and political life of the society what was not the case earlier in the late 1970s and early 1980s (Awasum 2002). HIV/AIDS organizations are other organizations that are created to educate the people on the dangers of the HIV/AIDS virus, how it is transmitted, how we can avoid it and how to interact and live with infected persons without hurting their feelings. The later is a vital part of HIV/AIDS education and it is only through the work of NGOs working in this domain that we can get to know the behavior pattern to adopt vis-à-vis victims of this terminal virus. Table 8.2 presents a clear picture of what we are talking about.

NGOs and Economic Development Activities

It is difficult to establish a correlation between the number of NGOs that exist in the country today and economic development. However the assessment that we make of the impact these organizations have on the economic development of the society relates to the issues already discussed above. To give an indication of the effect they have on the development of the society, we resolved to use some numbers that is time series data on Cameroon from various international sources. These are useful in that through them we can attribute the changes over time to the effect of the proliferation of NGOs. The areas that are examined are those in which we were able to verify that NGOs are more active, that is involved in. These include such sensitive areas like AIDS and devastating effect it is having on the Cameroonian society, education, poverty, the population, and the economic growth rate of the country given that these are all interconnected. Needless to say that this analysis of the relationship between NGOs and economic development is done in respect of the definition we gave of economic growth. The constitutive elements of economic growth were very useful in making this decision.

HIV/AIDS is one of those domains in the world that has become the number one killer disease. Health the saying goes is the primary duty of life. A healthy society is a prosperous society. In fact, the health of the society is fundamental in the determination of the level of development of that society. HIV/AIDS related death toll in Cameroon is very extensive to the extent that one wonders if NGOs are having any effect at all. A joint project on HIV/AIDS (UNAIDS, UNICEF, and WHO 2004) gives a good perspective on this phenomenon. The data indicates that "HIV prevalence among workers tested in the Nations capital Yaoundé increased from 5.6 percent in 1990 to 45.3 percent in 1993, and declined to 34 percent in 1997/1998" (UNAIDS, UNICEF and WHO 2004). Although the decline is not enormous, it clearly divulges a mark reduction compared to the situation as it was in 1990 when NGOs were just being created. There is every reason for one to assume and correctly too that the educative and supportive role of NGOs contributed to this decline. Assuming that this is a true reflection of the situation as it was in the country and assuming that the trend continues in the same direction, it is possible that the rate will reduce to a less alarming level hopefully. However it becomes frightful when the same data asserts that in 2000, in spite of the mammoth work of AIDS NGOs, women were more likely than men to be infected with HIV. This fear becomes even more apparent when one takes into consideration the registered infected cases from 1990 through 1998.

Table 8.3
The Evolution of AIDS Infection from 1990-1998

Year	1990	1991	1992	1993	1994	1995	1996	1997	1998
Infected Cases	183	604	1308	1385	1761	2766	1485	3950	5410

Source: UNAID UNICEF and WHO 2004.

Table 8.3 definitely does not speak well of HIV/AIDS NGOs in Cameroon. The 2004 data is even more frightening. It purports that HIV/AIDS cases have globally reduced in African countries with the exception of Cameroon and The Ivory Coast (Africa Focus 2004). This data notwithstanding, HIVAIDS NGOs should be given a pat in the back because it is probable that things might have been much worse were it not of the activities of these organizations.

Another element that has a big role to play in the development of the country is the population. The population growth of the country serves a useful tool in determining the level of development of the society. There has been a discernible change in population growth as international data presents it. According to an estimate by a United Nations Development Program (HDR 2005) data, the population growth rate that stood at 2.4 million between 1975 and 2002 is expected to decrease to 1.8 million for the years 2002 to 2015 (HDR 2005). The meaning one reads from this is that NGOs have been instrumental in educating the people to understand and see the merits of family planning and small size families-an issue that is anti African as the history books tell us. The problem with this assessment though is that there are other contributory factors like AIDS, poverty and the list continue that we did not control for. Overall NGOs are very active in the domain of the population in Cameroon, especially as some of them think that the Cameroonian woman has been subjected to childbearing against their wish for too long (Andrew Sopi, 2002).

In spite of the feminization of poverty that characterizes most of the Third World, poverty is one of those areas that have registered some improvement over the years, but whether this can be attributed to the impact of NGOs is a question that is open to debate. Whether defined in relative or absolute terms, the notion of poverty includes the situation of the household, average income per person usually one half of two thirds of GDP person, food intake for survival, (International Fund for Agricultural Development 2001) the number of people living below poverty and the provision of basic human necessities. Even though research has it that the rate of poverty in the continent continues to grow, what I find difficult to believe, is why poverty is on the increase in spite of the positive economic indicators that Cameroon continues to register over the years.

Whereas International Fund for Agricultural Development (IFAD) has it that research shows that Africa has improved if analyzed as a continent, but that the situation is different if looked at on a case-by-case basis (International Fund for Agricultural Development 2001). Whereas this may be a true assessment of the situation as it is, the fact is that a look at the life Cameroonians live today and the way they do things compared to what has always been there is every reason to believe that the rural population and the backward uneducated few have evolved a great deal (Africa Focus Bulletin 2004). NGOs have to some degree to be praised for the positive GDP growth rate that stood at 4.3 percent for 2003 and 4.6 percent for 2004 (Africa Focus Bulletin 2004). If the growth rate of the country is higher than its population growth rate then there reason to believe that some of these organizations are having a positive effect on family planning. Even though this cannot be attributed totally to the work of nongovernmental organizations, it is likely that they did make their presence felt to a degree that research is still unable to demonstrate. The life the rural population of the forest zone is living today bears testimony to this assessment. In the Eastern part of the country for instance, the people are now able via environmental organizations to live without too much dependence on wood, wildlife, and plant species as the situation was earlier on before the proliferation (Africa Focus Bulletin 2004) of these organizations. The same argument can be made of other parts of the country.

NGOs have also been very active in the domain of political development through the influence they bring to bear on public policy in Cameroon. By political development we mean the decision making influence. The policy advice they give to the government on issues pertaining to the education, lifestyles, and the habit of the people both in urban and rural areas is significant to this effect. Whereas NGOs are useful in the mobilization of the civil society (Ma 2002) they are also useful in making the government take the best decisions for its citizens or in the interest of the nation as a whole. Some of these NGOs have been very useful in promoting performance in the public sector (Fisher 1993) through the various training sessions some of them do have with government employees. This is especially the case with HIV/AIDS organizations, election monitoring or politically oriented organizations and those that work with the environment as well. The role they play in the decision making process is important because these organizations are not created for the sake of it, but to make sure things in their domain of existence are different from what they were before they came into existence. Talking on the occasion of a forum known as "Programme Initiative de Renforcement du Secteur des ONG du Cameroon" (IRSOC), organized by pro development NGOs in Cameroon, Tsala Messi, Secretary of State of Public Investment and Territorial Organization intimated (N' Diaye 2005) "les ONG sont des partenaires a part entiere qu'il faut associer a la formulation des politiques de developpement" (NGOs are major partners that should be associated to the formulation of the politics of development).

From this analysis it is evident that there are several loose ends that will only be taken care of with time. However it is useful to indicate that some of the conclusions we make here are debatable considering that the study was not able to control for the effect of other variables. Although most of the problems inherent in this work have already been raised, it is useful to indicate however that just as it is difficult to establish causality in a clear manner between these organizations and NGOs, the impact of these structures on the development process can be inferred given especially that these organizations have become a major economic partner of the State in Cameroon. Furthermore, whereas it is impossible for us to control the effects of other variables whose effect in this process is indisputable. Like the contribution of the International Community through its organizations and members, the impact of the new governance initiatives, the role of the democratic process, and many others, the fact remains that these organizations have been active enough in the life and development of the people. It would therefore, be wrong by not giving them some credit for the improvements that Cameroon has experienced in its economic indicators over the years, especially the years following the mass creation of NGOs. On another count, in spite of these limitations, this analysis although a case study of NGOs in Cameroon, applies in many ways to other countries of the continent. The impact and challenges of these organizations on the developmental efforts of Cameroon is one of those items that can travel across African boundaries.

Challenges of NGOs

An analysis of the role of NGOs in the development of Cameroon is a very crucial one, especially at this time when it has been proven beyond reasonable doubt that the State no more has the capacity to carry out its traditional responsibilities such as the provision of social amenities to its citizens and provide employment to everyone as it did before. The people are today obliged to turn elsewhere for support and assistance and NGOs come in handy in this regard. Whereas NGOs have without doubt been very instrumental in promoting and patronizing local development initiatives, their contribution nevertheless has not been all roses. In spite of the significance of these organizations in the Cameroonian society, there is no denying that the role they play in the development process in Cameroon is fraught with daunting challenges. Some of these challenges are created by the NGOs themselves while others are challenges proper to the environment within they operate. For a better grasp of these challenges they would be viewed under two main titles: endogenous, that is challenges that are proper to NGOs as well as exogenous challenges.

Challenges proper to NGOs in Cameroon suggests that there exist a paradox with regard to the contribution of NGOs in the development of Cameroon. The paradox is that just as NGOs are apparently the answer to the development of Cameroon, they are at the same time responsible for the crisis of development.

The operation of any human organization depends a great deal on the structure of is personnel. By every measure this is the primordial factor on which the effectiveness of an institution (Mercer 1999) can and should be measured. The situation in Cameroon just as it is in other parts of the World, particularly in the developing world, is characterized by a colossal lack of manpower to help these organizations in fulfilling the duties for which they are created. This is a problem that confronts virtually all-nongovernmental organizations in Cameroon. From environmental, health, poverty related, education proper and other domains of activities, the plight is the same. The problem does not end at the level of manpower alone, those that are available to help the organizations carry on with the role they are created to play but are not well trained. How can one help people solve problems associated with the way the live in the forest zone if he or she does not know or cannot tell precisely how their life styles impact the environment? In the same fashion, how can one teach people how to run elections if he or she has not been taught the dynamics of the electoral process?

Similarly how feasible is it for an individual to teach people how to protect themselves against the HIV/AIDS virus and how to deal with infected victims if that person has not been trained specifically for that purpose? Let us for instance consider the case of the National Student Union for the Control of Aids (NASUCA). Although created in the early 1990s with the duty of educating the student population on the dynamics of the HIV/AIDS virus, it was only able to have its members, founding fathers trained for the mission for which it was created four years into its existence. The lack of "organizational skills" (Binns and Motteux 2001) is a fundamental challenge that the majority of these organizations have to deal with. The lack of trained human resources (Fayemi, Jaye and Yeebo 2003) makes it difficult for these organizations to do the job for which they are created. The connection between this handicap and the overall effectiveness of these organizations is strong. If a judicial system does not have well trained personnel it is impossible for one to expect any good decisions to come from the system they represent. Simple economics teaches us that the factors of production: land, labor, capital and entrepreneurship together determine the success of any enterprise, the absence of one of these factors makes production ineffective or accounts for low productivity, and loss of profit among others.

Human resource challenges are just one amongst the many challenges that these organizations are faced with. The scarcity of financial resources (Trivedy 1999) makes the work of these organizations extremely hard. One thing that stands out clear with the creation of most of these NGOs in Cameroon is the fact that they emerge from the post-Structural Adjustment Program, a period during which the government and its citizens realized although grudgingly that the government alone could no longer serve the country as the sole employer. The effect this has in this process is that most Cameroonians see the opportunity to create NGOs as a way of gainfully creating employment for them. In making this decision they hardly gave thought to how they were to raise money to manage them and make their organization useful in its area of activity. It is not until after most of them got on their feet that they suddenly realized they needed financial assistance to realize the objectives for which they exists. On the whole, the dearth of financial resources is one of the biggest handicaps that NGOs currently face in Cameroon (Eloundou and Parfait, 2002).

Other challenges that these organizations face in their daily operations range from the absence of effective accountability (Ebrahim 2003) to the distortion of NGO objectives that is reduced to that of personal aggrandizement. Also clienteles practices that plaque the political system spills over into NGOs. If one were to take a close and critical look at the way most of these structures are managed and how their members are recruited, the clientele's tradition they operate under becomes all the more visible. An example of what I am referring to (although not documented) is a situation where the government gets into a lucrative NGO and replace the leaders with hand picked government employees, with the sole aim of having free access to the financial resources of the organization.

Exogenous Challenges to NGOs

The absence of financial autonomy brings to light the serious problem that these organizations face in Cameroon and in most of the continent that of dependence on foreign institutions that *dependencitas* claim is responsible for underdevelopment (Chilcote 1994). The dependence of these organizations on foreign assistance, both in monetary terms as well as in capital make their existence and effective operation contingent on them. Usually, some of these organizations "are so dependent on foreign aid that we hardly have a mind and policy option of our own" (Member of FEDORAC talking in Yaoundé) (*The Herald* 1998).

Furthermore, the neo-liberal economic tradition that most International Organizations and Western countries espoused with enthusiasm in the 70s and 80s only worsened the situation, as multinational institutions are more prepared to solicit NGO inputs in their programs and policies than those of the governments (Collins, 1995). It created a paradox that unfortunately produced a boomerang effect. This theory encouraged the minimalist State theory that meant the transfer of State responsibility to organizations other than public institutions. Against this backdrop, State capacity was reduced to the extent that it has become incapable of performing its duties (Clough 1999). It would not be an exaggeration to suppose that the State's incapacity to create an effective functional environment for NGOs in Cameroon is because of its limited powers. Besides the policies of the State are themselves not adequately transparent.

Also, government practices and the relationship they entertain with these organizations have to be specified and well defined. Instead of what one observes in the country is public officials particularly the ruling elites have become so blinded by the ethnic concept that they want to reserve the best and very lucrative NGOs for members of the ruling ethnic group only. NGOs that work in the domain of HIV/AIDS and poverty, and the environment are typical examples of NGOs that have suffered fundamentally from biased decision-making on the part of government authorities. Another sector that has suffered a great deal in this regard is research. The situation is so rampant in the country that when individuals get together to form an NGO they have to make sure they stay away from the regime as much as possible. Although this practice is not documented, it is nonetheless tearing down the noble objectives and good ambitions of NGOs in Cameroon. Mediocrity, lack of interest, mismanagement, and the list continue are result of these practices. The regimes' responsibility should be nothing short of creating or rather providing an appropriate arena within which NGOs operate.

Corruption is another cankerworm that has eaten into the political and economic life of the Cameroonian society. Whereas corruption is not something that is peculiar to the Cameroonian society, or to countries of the African continent, it is an issue that has tremendously tarnished the image of certain countries; Cameroon for instance is a case in point. The problem in the developing world is that of degree, its nucleus is so extensive that some observers have been tempted to assert that it is a behavioral pattern that has become part of the decision making process. As some analysts of the situation posit "corruption has become like an un-written law which nevertheless exerts power over the people who submit to it, knowing nothing can be done to improve the situation. This is a serious situation" (*Effort Cameroonians* 1997). Although a real problem in the country, it is prudent to indicate that this is an inflated assessment of the status of corruption in Cameroon. This notwithstanding, corruption is a problem that handicaps the work of nongovernmental organizations in the country as its pervasiveness spills over into the management of organizations some of which are not familiar with simple principles of accountability. The fact that the institutions of the Republic are not able to make these organizations accountable is itself problematic. In the long run they exist and operate more like private businesses that seek foreign aid for purposes of personal enrichment. This certainly is the reason why most of these organizations die immediately after their first foreign assistance (Sipa 2004). When this organizations canvass for resources, they should be able to account for how these resources are used, they should be able to demonstrate to the government that their activities do not duplicate each other. It is only in this way that the regime can generate the confidence that can be put to the service of its NGOs.

Conclusion

This chapter has examined the role of NGOs in Cameroon's development processes. It argues that NGOs are without doubt making a plausible contribution to the development process in Cameroon. The boom that the society experienced in this domain in the 1990s although causing problems of competence might eventually be a good thing for the economy. The positive impact could lead to specialization that is an invaluable stage in economic growth (Rostow 1971). One advise that these NGOs must heed to in Cameroon is that because they are apparently poised at improving the lot of humankind, they are obliged to support all movements that challenge the political system that benefits only a few and impoverish the many. To do this successfully, they must endeavor to internationalize those philanthropic tendencies that such human related activities require. Respect, selflessness, humility, openness, and transparency are some of these philanthropic related tendencies. As they do this, they have to realize though that they cannot replace the State. NGOs, therefore, need an orderly environment where competition is allowed and where they are allowed to operate to the fullness of their abilities.

Given the scramble to form NGOs in Cameroon today, and the difficulty these organizations have in raising the revenue needed to carry on with their activities (Charlton 1995). The government might have to form partnership with NGOs, the private sector and community based organizations in dealing with the challenges that they face in their day-to-day operation; the question then becomes whether NGOs are institutionally and politically sustainable in the long run? From the analysis provided in this chapter we can conclude that NGOs have been able to make a positive contribution to the Cameroonian crisis of poverty, crisis of the environment, human rights, and the crisis of population growth. Acting together the answer to this question could be resounding yes. Until this happens, the best option is just to wait and see.

References

Africa Focus Bulletin, Dec. 3, 2004, 5.

Ahidjo, A. *Fondements et Perspectives du Cameroon Nouveau.* Paris: Saint Lambert 1976, 97.

Andrew, Sopi. *Cameroon Post,* no. 278 (20 June 2002), 2.

Anonymous. "Economic Growth in Cameroon at Risk." www.afrol.com/artilces/15085 (December 2004).

Charlton, Roger. "Sustaining an Impact? Development NGOs in the 1990s." *Third World Quarterly* 16, no. 3 (September 1995).

Chilcote, R. *Theories of Comparative Politics: The Search for a Paradigm Reconsidered.* Boulder, CO: Westview Press, 1994.

Chretien, Tabetsing. "Une Guerre Civile est Possible au Cameroon" [A Civil War is Possible in Cameroon]. In *Le Messager*, no.1572 (October 10, 2003).

Crush, J., ed. *The Power of Development.* London: Routledge, 1995.

Collins, C. "NGOs: They Are Everywhere, but What Are They?" *National Catholic Reporter* 31, no. 29 (1995): 3-5.

Clough, M. "Reflections on Civil Society." *Nation* 266, no. 7 (1999): 7.

Ebrahim, Alnoor. "Accountability in Practice: Mechanisms for NGOs." *World Development* 31, no. 5 (May 2003): 78-94.

Edwards, M., and D. Hulme, eds. *Making a Difference: NGOs and Development in a Changing World.* London: Earthscan Publications Ltd, 1992, 25.

Effort Camerounaise, no. 106 (October 13-19, 1997): 23-27.

Eloundou, E., and M. Parfiat. "Will Economic Crisis in Africa Weaken Rural-Urban Ties? Insights from Child Fosterage Trends in Cameroon." *Rural Sociology* 67, no. 2 (June 2002): 3.

Fayemi, J. K., T.Jaye, and Z. Yeebo. "Democracy, Security & Poverty in Ghana: A Midterm Review of the Kufour Administration." *Journal of West African Affairs* 3, no. 2 (2003): 39-57.

Fisher, Julie. *The Road from Rio: Sustainable Development and the Nongovernmental Movement in the Third World.* Westport, CT, and London: Praeger, 1993.

Fisher, Julie. "Third World NGOs." In *Environment* 36, no. 7 (Sept. 1994).

Human Development Reports. /hdr.undp.org/statistics/data/indic/indic (February 14, 2006).

International Fund for Agricultural Development (IFAD). *Assessing Rural Poverty: Western and Central Africa.* Rome: IFAD, 2001, 13.
Kempe Sr., Hope R. *African Political Economy: Contemporary Issues in Development.* London: M. E. Sharpe, 1997, 3-14 and 128-130.
Koge, E. *Change in Cameroon.* Alexandria, VA: ARC publications, 1985, 89.
Kohl, Ben. "Nongovernmental Organizations an Intermediaries for Decentralization in Bolivia." *Government & Policy* 21, no. 3 (June, 2003).
Law No. 92/005/006, Prime Ministerial Degree No. 92/455/P, November 23, 1992.
Law No. 99/014 Regulating Nongovernmental Organizations in Cameroon, December 22, 1999.
Livernash, R. "The Growing Influence of NGOs in the Developing World." *Environment* (June 1992).
Mama, A. "Strengthening Civil Society: Participatory Action Research in a Militarized State." *Development in Practice* 10, no. 1 (February 2000): 2
Manji, Firoze, and Carl O'Coill. "The Missionary Position: NGOs and Development in Africa." *International Affairs* 78, no. 3 (2002): 567-83.
Mbita, M. L. "Cameroon: Number One in World Wide Corruption." *Peace Link*, no. 357. Http://ospiti.peacelink.it/anb-bia/nr357/e02.html (1998).
Meier, Gerald M. *Leading Issues in Economic Development.* 6th ed. New York: Oxford University Press, 1995, 45
Mercer, C. "Reconceptualizing State-Society Relations in Tanzania: Are NGOs 'Making a Difference'?" *Area* 31, no. 3 (1999): 247-58.
N'Diaye, B. "ONG et. Pauvrete au Cameroon: Des Strategies Communes." In http://www.wagne.net/ecovox/eco17/actual2.html (accessed February 14, 2006)
Nel, E., T. Binns, and N. Motteux. "Community-Based Development, Non-Governmental Organizations and Social Capital in Post-Apartheid South Africa." *Geogr. Ann.* 83B, no. 1 (2001).
Ngoh, Victor. *History of Cameroon since 1800.* Limbe-Cameroon: Presbook, 1996.
Onana, Hughes. *Les Transitions Democratiques en Afrique: le Cas du Cameroun.* Yaoundé: SOPECAM, 1994.
Perkins, D., and M. Roemer, eds. *Reforming Economic Systems in Developing Countries.* Cambridge, MA: Harvard Institute for International Development, 1991.
Qiusha, Ma. "The Governance of NGOs in China since 1978: How Much Autonomy?" *Nonprofit & Voluntary Sector Quarterly* 31, no. 3 (September 2002).
Reports and Letters of the Cameroon Ozone Club (CAMOC). www.eeiu.org/chapters/cameroon/reports.html (accessed January 4, 2006).
Roff, Shem. "Nongovernmental Organizations." *International Social Work* 47, no. 2, (April 2004).
Rostow, W. Whitman. *The Stages of Economic Growth; a non-Communist Manifesto.* 2nd ed. Cambridge: Cambridge University Press, 1971.
Sen, Amartya. *Development as Freedom.* New York: Anchor Books, 1999.
Sipa Joshua. Phone interview by Wilfred Gabsa on the "Life and management of NGOs in Cameroon," January 9, 2004.
Trivedy, R. "NGOs in a Global Future." *Development in Practice* 9, no. 5 (2004). *The Herald*, Reporting from Kumba-Cameroon, (November 14, 2004).
UNAIDS, UNICEF, and WHO. "Epidemiological Fact Sheets on HIV/AIDS and Sexually Transmitted Infections 2004 Update." http://www.who.int/hiv or http://www.unaids.org (14 February 2006).
www.undp.org/hdr.2001/indicator (February 12, 2006).
www.finfacts.com (February 14, 2006).

Chapter 9

NGOs and Religion in Zimbabwean Uncertain Times

Johnston Akuma-Kalu Njoku

The affirmation of human rights on a comprehensive scale in Zimbabwe has been the cornerstone of several non-governmental organizations (NGOs) in the nation. Before and after its independence from Great Britain in 1980, the government of Zimbabwe has not been able to effectively provide social welfare programs for its citizens. The national government has also been unable to provide adequate resources for the provision and maintenance of rural and urban infrastructure and services. The effectiveness of any regime depends on a number of variables especially the manner that urban and rural cities are organized, administered, and managed. In these respects, the urban and rural sectors of Zimbabwe has been found wanting. The national and regional governments in Zimbabwe have not been able to make any significant impact on the provision of welfare services, infrastructure and in the performance of the basic municipal functions. This dismal performance of the national and regional governments has also spilt over to poor economic, political, and social development of the nation. Political instability and crisis of legitimacy has immensely made it difficult for the national government to manage its resources equitably to the satisfaction of all interest groups. In the past two decades Zimbabwe national government has been cracking down on NGOs who support opposition party leaders. Despite the fact that NGOs have served and positively influenced the citizens' experience of Zimbabwe the national government continues to curtail their operations in the nation.

Zimbabwe was plagued with drought in the late 1980s and 1990s. This environmental disaster worsened the farming situation and caused the unemployment rate in the nation to increase tremendously. The consequences of the environmental problems range from poverty to illness, from hunger to epidemics, from the inability of women to own land to the defense of children, and from banning the hunting of special animals to saving the ecology. Other related problems range from agricultural productivity decline to famine and malnutrition increase. Several religious NGOs have been very instrumental in helping the national government in the provision and delivery of social goods and services to the disadvantage and poor citizens of Zimbabwe. Despite the hostile policies of the government toward NGOs in the past two decades the Catholic Church—based groups have played very important role to mobilize various communities, women groups, ethnic groups and various community-based organizations to have their voices heard as well as assert their identities in the nation.

Even though, as Roberts (1979) has pointed out, the mandate of the Catholic Church was to evangelize and convert the indigenous peoples of Zimbabwe on Western terms "The Catholic Church in Zimbabwe can proudly claim to have done as much as anyone to fulfill the Pope's injunction to become African in Africa. Johnston Njoku (1992) confirmed that the Church has continued to be native in Zimbabwe where the indigenous peoples use term such as "Roma" to describe the Catholic Church with delight. In other words, the use of the term Roma makes the Catholic native. The term Roma is indeed an integral part of Zimbabwean life. As such, the Church has always been there during all the major struggles and moments of prosperity in the nation. Right from its beginning, the Catholic Church has always helped to enhance the quality of life in Zimbabwe by spreading Christian ideals and by establishing and carrying out training, skill development projects, and provision of essential opportunities to citizens. Over many decades many mission stations were established as Zimbabweans accepted the Word. Along with their spread of the Christian message the Church translated its Catholic doctrines into citizens' lives through health care, academic and vocational training for Zimbabweans from different regions and various linguistic groups.

During the war of independence the Catholic Church and other religion-based NGOs provided charity, hospitality, and incentives to rural populations in Zimbabwe. With financial resources from international funding agencies and Church bodies both local and international NGOs have continued to provided much needed assistance in the social, economic and political development processes in Zimbabwe. After the war, in the 1980s, the religious NGOs combined its Christian force into drought relief and care of displaced people. In fact, during the apartheid regime in South Africa, the Catholic Church, along with other religious NGOs both local and international took on a wider regional responsibility as thousands of refugees from South Africa flooded Zimbabwe. To meet the demands of the extended responsibility, the Zimbabwean Roma and other NGOs in Zimbabwe made a combined use of their resources to provide charity, hospitality, and public incentives. The Church became outspoken on justice and the right of the oppressed, help political prisoners and their families. During the 1990s, the Zimbabwe's National Association of Non-Governmental Organizations (NANGO) continued to coordinate the collaborative activities of the NGOs in the nation, including the Catholic Development Commission (CADEC) and the Poverty Reduction to enhance human development knowledge.

In the past decade, the Roma continued to play positive roles in national development programs working with laity and grassroots organizations under the coordination of the Bishop Conference, which legislate the laws of the whole Catholic Church in Zimbabwe. The mandate of the parishes and local churches is not only to preach the word of Christ, but also to take care of the people, look after the sick, the displaced, the homeless, and the uneducated. In 1996, the efforts of Roman Catholic Bishops of Africa began publicly to denounce debt payments made at the expense of providing basic healthcare, education, and other social services to the poor in several countries in the continent. According to Mark Engler (2005) this action of African Catholic Bishop instigated Bishops from Latin America as well as the late Pope John Paul II to make similar statement to fight against poverty in Africa.

This chapter examines the role of religious NGOs in Zimbabwe. It argues that the autonomy of its citizen depends on the strength of its public and civil society consciousness. Further it identifies the types and nature of civil societies in Zimbabwe and the linkages they have with their communities. It describes the contemporary problems facing NGOs in Zimbabwe. The concluding section discusses the sustainability of religious NGOs activities in the development process of the nation and makes some recommendation.

The Legacy of Religion, Civil Society, and Development

One of the outcomes of the Berlin conference of between 1884 and 1885 is the scramble and partition of the African continent into the present day fifty-four nations. This partition of the African continent also led to a plethora of problems. The characteristics of the problems range from nationalism movement to ethnic conflicts, from irredentism to boundary conflicts, from sustainable development dilemma to regional cooperation dialogue and from Islam dominance to Christian paradigm. The history of the African people reveals that there are variable evidence of strong nationalism and patriotism that was rekindles later by both the pan-Africanism movement, Organization of African Unity (OAU) and the present day African Community.

The legacy of the continent also comprise nations and communities, the existence and acknowledgement of common traditions of origins, traditional cultures and values, ensured social cohesion, patriotism, and nationalism. Despite the lack of unity among African nations during the pre-colonial period, there were active trading activities among the various regions. Robert Dibie (2001) pointed out that Christianity and education mechanism was part of the colonial legacy in Africa. After colonial administration was established in Zimbabwe, the missionaries and colonial authorities forged a very close working relationship. European religion instilled submissiveness by stressing that life on earth was temporary and to be used only as exercise for external life. The European missionaries thought African in their schools that in order for one to qualify for external life they have to practice the Christian virtue of forgiveness, submissiveness and patience. In the process of spreading the distorted European values several international NGOs established projects in Zimbabwe and several other African nations. Khapoya (1994) and Ali Mazrui (1986) contend that we could tie the relationship between the church missions and colonial regimes as a conspiracy to promote under develop in the continent. Frank Gunder (1969) exerts that the deindustrialization and the disruption of the African continent with slave trade and subsequently colonialism are examples of how Europeans manifested the under development of several African nations including Zimbabwe. Post independence operations of international NGOs and religious organizations might be argued to be another hiding agenda of the developed world to either correct the aftermath of exploitation of the continent or the promotion of the new global civil society.

In pre and post independence Zimbabwe civil societies have played very crucial roles in the governance, economic and social sphere of the nation. Civil society activities in the nation have taken three dimensions. First are the grassroots organizations. This type of civil society activities has included community groups, labor union and interest groups. These groups have defended the local and ethnic interests of specific values beyond the formal political processes of Zimbabwe. These groups have also assisted in shifting its members from the political system to informal political and formal associations of interests and values as a source of collective action to weaken the national policies. The second kind of civil societies in Zimbabwe are international NGOs. According to Manuel Castells (2005) these kinds of NGOs could be call the global civil society. He contends that global civil society is made up of NGOs and other forms of aggregation of interests. According to him, global civil society organizes popular expression and representation of the citizens. Such civil societies are also connected to the government as advocates of democratic projects and demand the public institutional system to effectively implement such policies. The third type of civil societies that are prominent in Zimbabwe is what John Clark (2003) and Mary Kaldor (2003) describe as social movements that are aimed at controlling the process of globalization. This type of civil society builds networks of action and organization to mobilize people to demand justice. Thus this type of civil society is characterized by the expression of the crisis of political legitimacy. They have also transformed into oppositional and religious movement against the government in Zimbabwe. For example the catholic religious group in Zimbabwe has been a social movement preaching against the economic, social and cultural effects of the Robert Mugabe's administration policies in the past two decades.

The problem of legitimacy is also one of the major problems facing the administration of Robert Mugabe. Legitimacy is a major requirement to political development, institutionalization, order, and stability. Popular participation in the political process encourages democracy to rein in any nation. The problem in Zimbabwe is be less if the people of the nation believe that they own their country and that will have a greater emotional attachment to it and a greater responsibility to support its sustainable development process. The process of getting the people of Zimbabwe to become emotionally connected to the nation's administration invariably entails transparency and accountability of the ruling party and national government. Since Zimbabwe attained its independence in 1980, the nation democratic test has failed. In this regard, the people, especially those in the rural areas seem to be unresponsive to the government's mobilization endeavors of any sort. This unresponsiveness is particularly noticed in the land reform dilemma that faces the nation at present.

Political legitimacy brings us to one the crucial problems in Zimbabwe. This problem has also spillover to the inefficiency in governance. An effect of this major problem is the inability of the current administration to maintain order and simultaneously solve the development problems that confronts it without the necessity of corruption, ethnic conflict and uneven distribution of resources, and excessive use of state powers. One major question to address at this point is: can government of the government Zimbabwe effective gain legitimacy as well as enter the international and global civil society movement without suffering the agonies of slave trade, colonialism, exploitation and the humiliation of European controls of their land and natural resources? One possible answer to this question could be drawn from Japan's history. Japan is now a major power in the world political system without having to undergo the agonies of European colonization and imperialism. Japan was able to acquire European and North American tools and education without succumbing to subjugation. The is one the reasons why Andre Frank (1969) pointed out that development of the underdeveloped nations will be greatly stimulated by the indiscriminate transfer of capital institutions and values from developed North American and European countries to African nations especially Zimbabwe that has been extensively exploited during its pre and post independence history.

The crucial role of NGOs in development in African countries is increasing due to the shift in their focus from the traditional approach of spreading the Word to economic growth and human development. Deliberate attempt by international agencies such as the United Nations, World Bank, International Monetary Fund and others makes it inevitable that more attention should be paid to the activities of NGOs around the world as the resources to promote development are being channeled through them. Further, the process of reducing the roles of national and regional government have created a serious poverty gap that cannot be filled by other types of organization and this have enhanced the recognition of NGOs in the development processes of several African nations.

There are several other NGOs that have emerged recently in both the rural and urban areas. Most of them are not registered as required by the national government of Zimbabwe. The majority of them have been formed in order to confront the problems of environmental management, particularly, sanitation and waste management in their neighborhoods. This is because environmental, sanitation services, infrastructural services like roads, drainage, electricity, water and community services like schools, market, health facilities are in short supply in the old as well as new communities. Other NGOs such as the Roma religious groups have been very effective in helping the poor to survive during the uncertain times. Community based organizations like resident association have become so important in meeting these needs. In order for Zimbabwe to achieve sustainable development it might the wise for the national government to collaborate with the religious NGOs, the private sector and community based organization in its development process.

Contemporary Problems Facing NGOs in Zimbabwe

Today, the very government that NGOs had made determined efforts to support in the past is seriously curtailing their ability to effectively function in the nation. Local and international NGOs face constant threats in Zimbabwe where the absence of justice is constant. Consequently, political instability and corruption in the nation has made developments in the areas of economic, education, health, and food production to decline.

Due to corruption, those in decision making level have misallocated large sums of money meant for the general public. Funds often earmarked for new schools, hospitals and other institutions to serve the needy are often channeled into projects of negligible social value by public officials receiving kickbacks from commercial contractors. According to the Human Development Index Report (HDIR) (2003) corruption in Zimbabwe has reaching unprecedented levels that it is robbing the general population of their human rights, democracy and development. Zimbabwe has almost 80 percent of its population living in rural areas; of this number about 61 percent live under the Poverty Datum Line (HDIR 2003). Corruption impacts on public administration in ways, which debilitates its capacity to provide service to the public. It distorts decision making and choices, where contracts go to those who offer illicit gains rather than the best products and price. Corruption is therefore among the greatest challenges of current times in Zimbabwe.

The critical issues confronting the everyday life of the people, national government of Zimbabwe as well as NGOs are the crisis of efficiency, legitimacy, ethnic identity and the crisis of equity. Due to the fact that the national government of Zimbabwe has not been able to effectively address these crisis NGOs have become the voice and the movements that defend the needs, interest and values of the citizens of Zimbabwe. The weak role of the government has made the citizens to undermine the policies of the national public institutions.

A western human rights group has released a damning report accusing the Zimbabwean government of withholding food aid from Zimbabweans who voted for the opposition party in the controversial March 2002 elections. Furthermore, the report warns Donors to "be aware of the possibility that their donations could be used by the government of Zimbabwe to repress its political opponents and reward its supporters. Careful monitoring must take place down to the most local level," in Matabeleland South, where NGOs responsible for food aid delivery in Zimbabwe corroborated the findings in the report. The report of the Training and Research Support Centre, which was last updated July 30, 2004, makes a similar accusation of the Zimbabwean government to the effect that government supporters use food aid as political instrument of intimidation of people queuing for food aid. No matter what form of intimidation that takes place in Zimbabwe, the success of the government is measured by its ability to promote economic development. The major goal of economic development is to increase the number and variety of jobs opportunities available to its citizens. In refusing to perform these activities, the present government of Zimbabwe has failed its people because of excessive corruption, ethnic conflict and lack of transparency and accountability.

In essence, the national government lacks the ability to mobilize community participation and use the resources of existing community-based institutions to promote economic potentials. On the other hand NGOs have been able to assess the potentials and marshal the necessary resources to design and develop the local or rural economy and human rights of the citizens. At the same time national and regional governments and civil societies are beginning to realize that most of the initiatives for human development in the nation are been promoted by international NGOs. The foreign NGOs have had tremendous impact upon all public and private decision. In an attempt to aggressively correct this crisis the government of President Robert Mugabe introduced policies to vindicate NGOs in the nation. The national government accused NGOs for supporting political opponents. The government also stated that such foreign NGOs activities constituted a breach of national security. As a result of strict government policies, NGOs have now restricted their activities to the traditional housekeeping services. This new dimension of NGOs operation has affected the economic development in several communities.

Many NGOs have probably acted unwittingly to restrict employment opportunities without understanding or assessing the economic consequences of their action. Similarly, neighborhoods level community based organizations in Zimbabwe have had dramatic impact on private investment. Further, neighborhoods with active churches and civil society organizations that work toward the constructive development of their community have continued to reluctantly act as beacons to developers and investors.

As at the present time the number of NGOs in Zimbabwe has doubled compared to early 1980s. Prominent among them are Green-peace, Amnesty International, CARE, World Wildlife Federation, Save the Children, International Committee of Red Cross, and the International Famine Center. These NGOs staff composed of both foreign and indigenous citizens. Their operations or projects are related to human rights, environmental, poverty alleviation, peace and women liberation.

The borne of contention, however, is the inability of the government of Zimbabwe to solve its citizens social and economic problems. This shows that the over centralized government of President Robert Mugabe is no the most effective way to address the nation's problem. Many citizens of Zimbabwe that I interviewed indicated that the government is simply to far remove from local communities to understand nature of a particular problem and to offer pragmatic solutions. While advocates of civil society are encouraged by the dramatic increase of NGOs in Zimbabwe, opponents of the government believe that local community based organizations efforts alone cannot solve the nation's problem.

The process of achieving sustainable development in Zimbabwe has been frustrated by the lack of pragmatic constitutional checks and balances system in the country. Since the 1980s, the government of Robert Mugabe has constantly use state powers to prevent opposition parties from effectively contributing to the democratic development of Zimbabwe. Mugabe's administration focus has been that of establishing a one party state. When this idea of one-party state was partially abandoned in the 1990s for a multiparty system the ruling party has been very reluctant in responding to the call for a constitutional reform by civil society organizations and NGOs in the nation. This attitude of the leaders of Zimbabwe has undermined the notion of globalization and the new dimension of democracy that has been taking place around the world. Democracy cannot takes place in Zimbabwe if there are no popular trust and support for constitutional order.

Since the 1990s, and after the drought that plague the nation, the economy of Zimbabwe has been deteriorating in such a way that it has affected the popularity of the ruling party. Although the 1995, 1999, 2002, 2005 elections results have not shown this lack of popularity of the ruling party, NGOs and several civil societies have continued to provide channels for criticism (Laakso 2002). NGOs and civil society organizations in Zimbabwe have been accusing the ruling party headed by Robert Mugabe for elections irregularities, such as vote-buying and rampant rigging. Prominent of these NGOs are the Catholic Commission for Justice and peace (CCJP), various private sector and business interest groups, and the Zimbabwe Congress of Trade Union (ZCTU) (Laakso 2004). Every election in Zimbabwe has been followed by disillusion and apathy. It was not until the elections of 2000 and 2002 that the Movement for Democratic Change (MDC) emerged as an active opposition party in Zimbabwe. According to Liisa Laakso (2004) and Susan Booysen (2004) the emergence of MDC was stemmed from the twenty years experience of NGOs, community based civil groups and labor union members who were not happy about the way the ruling party has been silencing its critics. In 1993, for example, the government of Zimbabwe used the compulsory purchase powers under the new Land Acquisition Act to seize Mr. Sithole's (an opposition leader) farm near Harare and four thousand families were brutally evicted. In 1995 Mr. Sithole was arrested by the government and accused of an assignation plot against Mugabe. The presidential elections of 1996 were an embarrassment for the government because the official turnout in the whole country was below 32 percent (Sithole 1997). The government also used the same tactics to antagonize Mr. Tsvangirai (another opposition party leader and president of MDC) since the formation of MDC in 1999 (Tsvangirai, 2002). The extensive use of state powers by Mugabe administration against the wish of NGOs, civil society groups and trade unions led to a tense period in Zimbabwe. The aftermath of the tense period were workers demonstration, strike and property damaged or looted by rioters. The period also witnesses the first farmers strike in the nation.

Liisa Laakso (2004) pointed out that the pressure to check the powers of Robert Mugabe culminated in the formation of the National Constitutional Assembly (NCA). The call to check the use of state powers by the ruling party headed by Mugabe was led by NGOs such as the Zimbabwe Council of Churches, the Catholic Commission for Justice and Peace (CCJP), the Legal

Resources Foundation, Zim-Rights and the ZCTU. Despite the opposition of these NGOs to excessive use of state powers the elections of 2002 and 2005 would mark real battle over government power.

Zimbabwe citizens continue to experience government harassment, intimidation and excessive use of police force against opposition parties. While participation in elections is stronger in the urban cities, in the rural areas intimidation has often discouraged participation. During the 2005 elections, several citizens were disenfranchised by the reduction of polling stations in many cities, yet the ruling party celebrated the wining of the rigged elections. The urban protest and the rural reluctance to support Robert Mugabe's administration in 2002 and 2005 elections reflect an era when NGOs and community based organizations wanted to promote good governance, human rights and democracy in Zimbabwe. In the twenty-first century, it is the popular participation, rule of law and support for constitutional order that can make democracy work in Zimbabwe. The discontent with poor economic performance and Robert Mugabe are only some of the problems. In order for Zimbabwe to strive for the achievement of sustainable development, the government must look beyond electoral competition between political parties. There is the urgent need for the nation to create a peaceful environment where the citizen's rights are respected and the rule of law is equitably enforced without respect of persons or party or political positions.

According to Joshua Goldstein (2003) the most prominent approach to understanding why international non-governmental organizations INGOs establish operations in African or around the world is the desire to create international cooperation. Goldstein (2003) use the functionalist theory to explain the notion that growth in nonpolitical issues for example, human rights, human development, technology, trade, cultural exchange, education and so on, will create pressures for states like Zimbabwe to cooperate in international organizations. Functionalist contends that nations begin cooperation in technical and relatively non-controversial areas because these are often low political issues. Cooperation in these limited areas might spillover to more controversial political issues in the long-run. The notion of economic development in Zimbabwe and the question of integration among African nations, explains the extent to which such cooperation could contribute to development and the promotion of accountability and transparency. Since it is assumed that cooperation among African nations might lead to regional economic development, will such integration also promote efficiency in the public sector? Although the functionalist theory is compelling, it fails to effectively address the role of NGOs in the development process of several nations. On this basis, integration among nations should therefore, be seen as only a supplement to the development of Zimbabwe. Partnership among the national government, NGOs, community base organizations and civil society organizations in addition to integration of nations might be a better panacea capable of solving all the problems facing the government and people of Zimbabwe.

Future collaboration among NGOs, the private sector and community based organizations would foster good community schools that are both public and private. Private decisions and public economic activity are intimately related and affect employment opportunities for all rural and urban residents. This concept should lead the government, NGOs and community based organizations to take a new and different perspective toward planned coordinated development initiatives. The national government of Zimbabwe need to understand that no matter how depressed or arrogant they are, the public sector, NGOs, community institutions and civil societies are essential partners in the sustainable development process of any nation.

Counting on Roma in Uncertain Times

While it is true that kids are being turned away from food queues in some parts of Zimbabwe, Christian Aid program officers attest to the fact that they have been fortunate that their feeding programs in schools has continued without such incidents. This clearly suggests that the Church still has some kind of influence or legitimacy in carrying out its NGO activities in Zimbabwe, without much difficulty (FOSENET Report). The Catholic Church of Zimbabwe has the tract record of being neutral and can, therefore, be counted on to monitor essential NGO projects.

Since independence, especially when I was working in Zimbabwe in the late 1980 and early 1990s, the Catholic Church has continued to become more and more native—Roma. Zimbabweans Catholics are more like a family of converted people of God—"sons and daughters of God, and brothers and sisters of Jesus Christ the Son of Mary and thus truly catholic. Through baptism Zimbabweans become the children of God, which automatically implies the acceptance of Mary as the mother of Jesus to whom they turn in difficult times. What this means to the member of Roma is that over and above the traditional heads of their families is a new leader who is Christ. Every male ordained minister of Christ becomes a new Father and everybody including the president of the country (himself a Roma) calls him *baba*—the Shona word for father. The Bishop becomes *sekuru*, which stands for grandfather. Above all is the Mwari—the Father in heaven who remains the supreme filial deity—God. The Zimbabwea Catholic Bishop's Conference (ZCBC) is the legislative body for the entire country. The Archbishop of Harare is the Papal representative in Zimbabwe. "In fact, the Holy See and the Republic of Zimbabwe established diplomatic relations on June 26, 1980 at the level of Apolitic Nunciature on the part of the Holy See, and of Embassy on the part of the Republic of Zimbabwe" (Catholic Directory 1990).

Under the ZCBC are six Dioceses of Bulawayo, Chinoyi, Gweru, Hwange, Mutare, and the Archdiocese of Harare. Each Diocese or Archdiocese is made up of many deaneries, districts, parishes, and churches with a hierarchy of religious and lay personnel. One of the strengths and selling point of the Catholic Church is that it is always catholic—does not discriminate in carrying out its mission among the people. As one commentator in a video documentary puts it:

> The Church did not discriminate in providing its services because Christ asked it to serve all people regardless of their religious affiliations. The Church concentrates on the disadvantaged. . . . The Church was also responsible for the setting up of the Justice and Peace Commission, a body that defended the right of people and dignity of man. The Catholic Commission on Justice and Peace continues to play the role it played in pre-independent Zimbabwe. The role includes monitoring Human Rights in the country.

The benefit of Catholic Comprehensive Education includes:

- Establishment of pre-schools, primary, secondary, vocational schools and seminaries
- Equipping Zimbabweans with essential experiences and practical employment skills especially in the rural areas
- Providing education for living
- Coordinating volunteers both local and international that spend up to two or more years providing services and imparting special skills to young Zimbabweans to achieve meaningful adult employments.

The division of Zimbabwe into dioceses of Harare, Gweru, Chinhoyi, Hwange, and Bulawayo as administrative headquarters illustrates how change can be seen as the realignment of ethnic or linguistic groups into one catholic identity. The elaborate organization and practice of involving every class of the indigenous people from the Archbishop to the lay grassroots has turned the Roman Catholic Church in Zimbabwe into Roma. As Roma the Church is involved at every level of rural development. Roma has managed to incorporate into its evangelizing agenda the roles of education, healthcare, social work, and skill development. People in the rural areas (both catholic and non-catholic, everywhere I visited during my fieldwork, receive equal attention in Catholic schools, health clinics, and other social services provided by the Roma. In some locations, for example Chishawasa, members were formed into communities and encouraged to engage in self-help farm projects. The same was true of Doyden, Muzururu, Fainham, Stapefor, and Gokemore. In addition to acting as a teacher training institution, Gokemore provided education from elementary to secondary levels.

The CACEC working with Caritas International is concerned with the wellbeing of the human beings throughout the world and has been in Zimbabwe. Through its well established educational institutions and mission-based poverty reduction schemes it has provided services to all Zimbabweans regardless of their regional, political, and religious affiliation. Therefore, it stands a good chance of providing the safest way to ensure that there is no discrimination in discharging essential duties in this trying moments in Zimbabwean history.

Based upon the basic condition created by Roma and drawing from track record of CADEC, I recommend the following approaches in the present uncertain times in Zimbabwe:

- The Roma's CADEC and Lutheran World Federation, working with lay volunteers should continue the business of visiting dioceses and parishes and mission stations to help people in Zimbabweans in very practical ways. Together, they can help with the spiritual and physical needs of Zimbabweans.
- Encourage self-help schemes with the young, the old, and the destitute in Zimbabweans who are being denied the chance to survive by the government that suppress NGO activities. Evidence shows that this important approach helped CADEC to deal with acute poverty situations, where they work side by side with other Church-based NGOs to provide need-based welfare projects including supplementary feeding programs—gardening, poultry, and bakery. Encouraging people to fend themselves through self-help projects will not be difficult to do in Zimbabweans because such a communal method is traditional to the people of the nation.
- The Roma and other Churches in Zimbabwe at the instance of CADEC should combine their resources to teach the poor, hungry Zimbabweans how to get out of poverty and get rid of dependency.
- CADEC should be the coordinating agency of all the local, regional, and national relief efforts in Zimbabwe in this uncertain time.
- While all this is going on, the Church in Zimbabwe should not shy away from the role of advocacy. The CADEC should coordinate ecumenical efforts to petition the various government agencies on behalf of the people in the rural areas of Zimbabwe.

Several religious NGOs in Zimbabwe must be seen as partners in the development process of the nation. As a result national and regional governments in the nation must forge closer links with them in order to encourage these religious groups in their support efforts to work side-by-side with the government in the provision of humanitarian services to the citizens of Zimbabwe. Regional governments need to build bridges by which it can effectively and efficiently collaborate with community based organizations in order to provide the necessary support for many services they perform in the rural and urban governance of the nation. The national government need to decentralize more in order to show some seriousness in its approach to reaching out to the rural population of Zimbabwe.

In the twenty-first century, the effectiveness and the long-term viability of community based organizations will depend on the level of commitment of their members, leaders and the communities they serve. The national government must endeavor to promote the principles of shared governance and encourage the popular participation of citizens and all stakeholders in its sustainable development process. Such principles would help to mobilize financial and other forms of obligations to the needed project or infrastructure.

There is also the need for transparency and accountability of all leaders in the political and development processes. This would definitely help to ensure the sustained efforts of stakeholders in serving their respective constituencies or communities. Already the Roma is performing that role, however, the pattern have to be equitably spread around the nation. In the communities where there are no viable NGOs or CBOs the national and regional governments must step in to address the citizens' social, humanitarian and economic needs. These communities should not be the only focus of the government, it is mandatory for the national government to reach out to all constituencies in the nation.

There is the urgent need for the government of Zimbabwe to collaborate with the private sector, NGOs, community based organizations and other civil societies in the nation in its development processes. It is only by this that they can come to grip with the solutions to the problems of development in Zimbabwe. While networking among these public, private, religious and international sectors is good in itself, NGOs and other associations will need to foster close cooperation with local government and the rural areas in other to spread development evenly. Grant and Keohane (2005) and Chaskin and Garg (1997) contends that the government, NGOs and civil society groups must give meaning to local or rural participation in decision-making, formulation of development projects and their implementation. It is only by encouraging popular participation from these rural sectors that development can become real indigenous and the citizens would be proud to be agents of change in the twenty-first century.

Conclusion

This chapter has examined the role of religious NGOs in Zimbabwe. It argued that the various political and environmental predicaments facing citizens of the nation has somewhat attracted NGOs activities. Over the past three decades religious NGOs especially the Roma have changed aspects of their activities purely in line with the felt needs of the communities they serve. Most NGOs have tried to collaborate with the indigenous community based organizations but the linkages have been weak and little benefits have been derived from them. Therefore the government of Zimbabwe would have to put in a lot of efforts to encourage more interaction between all stakeholders.

The civil society in Zimbabwe is described as a bridge between community-based organizations and the central government. This channel if well established could enables Zimbabwe to transform to a representative democracy where citizens can actively transcends their political interests into that of national growth. It is very important that the national government stop denying the citizens their constitutional rights or use public institutions to intimidate members of civil societies and community based organizations.

The government and its institutions of governance in Zimbabwe are either insufficient or plague with corruption. These problems are further engulfed in the crisis of governance that is related to political legitimacy. The consequences of the crisis of legitimacy in Zimbabwe have been an increasing distance between citizens and their representative. Due to the distance between citizens and their representatives, social movement and the Roma as well as a variety of international and indigenous NGOs are trying to fill the current void representation and legitimate policy making process in Zimbabwe. Therefore before the end of the twenty-first century a global civil society network would be established in the nation. Thus, for an effective governance system that would help Zimbabwe to achieve sustainable development to take place, the nation must find ways other than the its current centralized approach to encourage collaboration among NGOs, the private sector, community base organizations and other civil societies in the Zimbabwe.

References

Beach, D. N. "Chimurenga: The Shona Rising of 1896-1897." *Journal of African History* 20, no. 3 (1997): 395-420.

Berliner, P. F. "Political Sentiments in Shona Songs and Oral Tradition." *Essays in Arts and Sciences* 6, no. 1 (1977): 1-29.

Booysen, Susan. "The Dualities of Contemporary Zimbabwean Politics: Constitutionalism versus The Law of Power and the land 1999-2002." *African Studies Quarterly* 7, no. 2 and 3 (2004): 9-21.

Brand, C. M. "African Nationalists and the Missionaries in Rhodesia." In *Christianity South of the Zambezi, II*, edited by Anthony J. Dachs. London: E. C. Bourdillon Press 1977, 69-85.

Carroll, Thomas. *Intermediary NGOs: The Supporting Links to Grassroots Development.* West Hartford, CT: Kumarian Press, 1992.

Castells, Manuel. "Global Governance and Global Politics." *Political Science and Politics* 38, no. 1 (2005): 9-16.

Catholic Directory of Zimbabwe. Harare, Zimbabwe: Catholic Press, 1989 and 1990, 1-3.

Chaskin, R. J., and S. Garg. "The Issue of Governance in Neighborhood Based Initiatives." *Urban Affairs Review* 32, no. 5 (1997): 632-661.

Clark, John. *Civil Society and the Battle for Ethical Globalization.* West Hartford, CT: Kumarian Press, 2003.

Dibie, Robert. *Politics and Policies in Sub-Saharan Africa.* New York: University Press of America, 2001.

Engler, Mark. "Debt Cancellation: Historic Victories, New Challenges." May 17, 2005.

FOSENET. *National NGO Food Security Network.* August 2, 2004.

Frank, Gunder. *Latin America: Underdevelopment or Revolution*? New York: Monthly Review Press, 1969.

Fry, Peter. *Soirits of Protest, Spirits-mediums and the Articulation of Consensus among the Zezuru of Southern Rhodesia, (now Zimbabwe*). Cambridge: Cambridge University Press, 1976.

Goldstein, Joshua. *International Relations*. Harper Collins College Publishers, 2003.

Grant, Ruth, and Robert Keohane. "Accountability and Abuses of Power in World Politics." *American Political Science Review* 99, no. 1: 29-43.

Kaldor, Mary. *The Global Civil Society*. London: Routledge, 2003.

Khapoya, Vincent. *The African Experience: An Introduction.* Upper Saddle River, NJ: Prentice Hall, 1994.

Laakso, Liisa. "Opposition Politics in Independent Zimbabwe." *African Studies Quarterly* 7, no. 2 and 3 (2004): 21-37.

Laakso, Liisa. "The Politics of International Election Observation: The case of Zimbabwe in 2000." *Journal of Modern African Studies* 40, no. 3 (2002): 437-464.

Mazrui, Ali. *The African: A Triple Heritage.* London: BBC Publication, 1986.

Njoku, J. Akuma-Kalu. "Nature and Organizing Principles of African Music and the Emergence of Shona Catholic Mass Music in Zimbabwe." Ph.D. diss. Indiana University, 1992, 167-192.

Pongweni, A. J. C. *Songs that Won the Liberation War*. Harare: The College Press, 1982.
Report of the Training and Research Support Centre. *The Catholic Church and Zimbabwe*. July 30, 2004.
Roberts, R. S. "The Catholic Church." In *The Catholic Church and Zimbabwe*, edited by A. J. Dachs, and Rea W. F. Gweru: Mambo Press, 1979.
Sithole, Masipula. "Zimbabwe's Eroding Authoritarianism." *Journal of Democracy*, 8 no. 1 (1997): 127-141.
Snarr, Michael, and Neil Snarr, eds. *Introducing Global Issues*. Boulder, CO: Lynne Rienner, 1998.
Tsvangirai, Mogan. "President Morgan Tavangirai Addresses MDC Parliamentarians." December 18, 2002.
World Bank. *Human Development Index Report*. Washington, DC: World Bank, 2003.

Chapter 10

NGOs and Development in the Democratic Republic of Congo

Francois N. Muyumba

A comprehensive study of the nongovernmental organizations (NGOs) in Democratic Republic of Congo (DRC) requires a re-examination and understanding of the Congolese community in general and more specifically its socio-ethnic divisions and their competing political and economic interests. The existence of such a varied ethnic communities constitute a very critical and complex configuration in the study and understanding of the obstacles that will need to be overcome on the road toward the development of national consciousness and the building of a cohesive national culture, and especially with regards to the integration of all ethnic groups within a nation which is eighty – times larger than Belgium and thirty time larger than France. Accordingly, as a vast country with immense economic resources, the DRC has been at the centre of what could be termed African world war.

The five-year conflict pitted government forces, supported by Angola, Namibia and Zimbabwe, against rebels backed by Uganda and Rwanda. But despite a peace deal and the formation of a transitional government in 2003, the threat of civil war remains. An overview of the history of the war reveals clearly that they war has claimed an estimated three million lives, either as a direct result of fighting or because of disease and malnutrition. It remains difficult to determine the real direct causes, but the war situation always bring with it additional causes that cannot be ignored nor avoided, unless some peaceful resolutions of the conflict are quickly implemented. It is usually possible to argue that the war creates conditions that are not usual, and thereby compels anyone to look into the war as a source of both particular economic and political problems. The war in the Democratic Republic of Congo, like in much African country for example, Sierra Leone, Liberia etc was primarily fuelled by the country's vast mineral wealth, with all sides taking advantage of the anarchy to plunder its natural resources.

For this study, it is possible to briefly establish that the history of DR Congo has been one of civil war and corruption. After independence in 1960, the country immediately faced an army mutiny and an attempt at secession by its mineral-rich province of Katanga. A year later, its prime minister, Patrice Lumumba, was seized and killed by troops loyal to army chief of staff Joseph Mobutu, who was indeed sponsored and supported by Western powers.

In 1965, Joseph Mobutu seized power, and in 1973 changed the name of the country from Democratic Republic of Congo to Republic of Zaire, and established a policy of authentic identity under which he changed his own names from Joseph to Mobutu Sese Seko. Under the instigation of CIA and other Western Secret services, Mobutu turned Zaire into a springboard for operations against Soviet-backed Angola and thereby ensured US backing. But he also made Zaire synonymous with One Party system, corruption, dictatorship, and autocracy.

After the Cold War, both Zaire and Mobutu ceased to be of interest to the US. Therefore, in 1996, when neighboring Rwanda invaded it to flush out extremist Hutu militias, it gave a boost to the anti-Mobutu rebels, who quickly captured the capital, Kinshasa, installed Laurent Kabila as president and renamed the country back to DR Congo.

Nonetheless, DR Congo's troubles have continued. American government and other Western powers did not get along with Laurent Desire Kabila, and they orchestrated a rift between him and his former allies sparking a new rebellion, backed by Rwanda and Uganda. Angola, Namibia and Zimbabwe took Kabila's side, turning the country into a vast battleground. Kabila a Congolese nationalist, who was inclined to follow some of Patrice Emery Lumumba's orientations, was killed in January 2001 and was quickly replaced by his thirty-year-old son, Joseph Kabila as the President. Despite coup attempts and sporadic violence a fragile peace has held since the formal end of the war in 2003. As at the time of writing in 2006, the national government with headquarters in Kinshasa has no control over large parts of the country and tension remains high in the east and south.

Moreover, the socio-economic and political fabrics of the state is devastated and has left the Congolese citizens is a much worse condition. The Crisis Group, a Brussels-based think-tank, said in 2005 that 1,000 people were dying every day from war-related causes, including disease, hunger and all sorts of abuses and violence.

What is more astonishing to the observes is the tenacity of the Congolese mass which tries by all mean to stay united despite the efforts by external forces and western powers to use all the terrorist tactic to find a way to divide them and waken their resolve to maintain a healthy, dynamic state. DRC today has a population of some 56 to 65 million people, and it occupied an area of 2.34 million square km, or (90, 5354 sq miles). The Congolese speak many languages and their official ones include French, Lingala, Kiwahili, Kikongo, and Tshiluba. Congolese are religiously traditionalist with a growing population of Christian and Islamic communities. Their economic is still strong relying itself upon the export of Diamonds, copper, cobalt, coffee calton, timbers and crude oil. The World Bank (2005) estimated that the Congolese GNP per capita is $120.00.

The history of DRC reflects both the resilience of the people to exist as an independent nation, and the efforts by alien forces, especially Westerners with their Congolese allies who are dissatisfied and seek to overthrow the existing regime, or those who want to create confusion and take advantage of the situation in order to gain access to the rare minerals they need. The fact is that the march of history cannot realistically be stopped. Today DRC has both state controlled and private television stations throughout the country including Radio Television Nationale Congolaise (RTNC), state controlled terrestrial and Satellite TV, Television Congolese, government commercial station run by RTNC, Antenne A, private, commercial; Canal Z, commercial, Canal Kin-Private, Raga TV-private and Radio-television Kin Malebo (RTKM), private. These media are also supported a set of radio programming including "La Voix du Congo, a state controlled and operated by RTNC, broadcasting in French, Swahili, Lingala, Tshiluba and Kikongo. Radio Okapi United Nation backed politically independent network, on FM and shortwave has also been used to promote peace and integration of people from different ethnic and civil society groups. Raga FM-private network has also been operating just like Radio Okapi. There are also print media including, Le Potential, La reference plus a daily, L'Avenir, le Soft, le Palmares, L'Observateur, Boyoma daily, Elima evening daily, and Mjumbe daily. In addition to these there are BBC and Radio France International broadcast, which listeners can capture in Kinshasa and in other cities. These diversified communication resources constitute a significantly powerful source of new ideas, and aspirations as it liberate the people from depending on the state controlled agencies, they are able to get information from other place. It is this liberalization that I project as the factor in the development and promotion of the Congolese NGOs (Martin 2002).

This discussion must consider the status and operations of NGOs in the Democratic Republic of Congo as a new phenomenon. Contrary to Alexis de Toqueville's experience in America, the DRCongo, like many African nations, emerged from colonial domination without well-defined private organizations similar to the current NGOs. The colonial administrations across the world limited all venues of free expression including the number of "political associations" as Alexis De Tocqueville called them in 1831 in America. In the Belgian Congo, the political colonial situation was worse as we know it, especially with regard to King Leopold's design of the so-called Civilization Mission. Since its independence, and most recently, the Congolese charitable and community organizations, as separate from the state owned enterprises and socio-political associations have increased in number and as in many other countries, the NGOs constitute primarily a modern and contemporary development.

This new development is phenomenal because with the downing of democratization movement after the fall of Berlin Wall, DRC as well as other countries such as Cameroon saw a slower and gradual extension of citizenship rights from 1980s to the 1990s. Even former President for life, Joseph Mobutu

Sese Seko, who had remained in power for thirty years until 1996, experienced political pressure to disengage from the "One Party State" to multiparty State, opening as such a possibility of allowing Congolese to fully participate in their own enhancement, protection and defense of their fundamental liberties. Since then, individual peoples, institutions, and labor organizations, and religious confederations took the opportunity to not only establish private organizations as instruments and mechanisms through which they could meet community needs, defend and promote new relevant and effective policies, but also to express themselves freely with regard to their governance. According to James A Paul (2000), Alexis De Tocqueville, believed that "the importance of the "political associations" lies in their being regarded as institutions of democracy, uniquely numerous and influential in the United States at the time of his famous visit in 1831 (Hochschild 1998).

It is fundamentally critical to establish once and for all that the structural organization of the Congolese population is gradually being reflected by the quality and quantity of Congolese NGOs as they struggle to represent the society's many faces and many aspirations. It is theoretically possible to argue that the examination of the rise and development of Congolese NGOs will result in our understanding of socio-economic and political imperatives that will lead further to the appreciation of the principled ideals that underlie the rise of NGOs in DRC. Such investigation of the consequential outcome of this development may also make an allowance for understanding the causal factors of the socio-economic and political imperatives that are shaping the Congolese community and from which the destiny of the state itself can surely be predicted.

Presently, the overwhelming international presence under the UN Peace Keeping forces known as MONUC represents a clear socio-political and economic pressure that has compelled the Congolese authorities, government and people to be sensitive to their own future. Though such international presence of UN forces is to bring peace and to encourage Congolese political elites to become more interested in peaceful resolution of conflicts, it has at the same time pushed the Congolese to realize that they are indeed facing a dangerous national crisis that might certainly disfigure DRC's national image. The Congolese national crisis as some believe, originated in what has come to be known as African World War I. The war is so called because at the time it started in 1998, it brought together several African nations to support the belligerent factions that opposed then the Lawrence Kabila's regime. For this author, the political crisis in DRC is not new nor did it begin with Kabila's regime. It should be important to establish for our discussion that the DRC has been embattled for many decades by external elements that sought to either weaken its resolve to remain united, or to establish policies that favored its independence and self-reliance, rather than the policies that continued its colonial status and economic structures as a county of children needing white fathers and mothers as was abundantly reflected by the Belgian paternalistic colonial policy. Even Mobutu, as the darling of the Western powers during the Cold war, struggled to remove the blanket of paternalism, as he issued his famous 1973 Zairianization appeal. Mobutu labeled the Belgian "BANOKO" or

"White uncles" who forever desired to remain in charge of Congolese Affairs from business enterprises, social institutions, government, and country clubs.

The 1998's war was a product of a growing envy of the neighboring African states that have functioned as channels by alien European powers to have access to the Congolese rich soil with all its natural beauties and bounties, its forests, gold mines, diamond, copper and Coltan or Columbite-tantalite, a metallic ore that, once refined, is heat resistant and stores an electrical charge (Foster 2005). It has been shown that Coltan is a key ingredient in circuit boards that operate cell phones and laptops. Ironically, one kilo of Columbite-tantalite can be bought for $15.00 from the Congolese diggers, while the same can be sold in the global world market at $600.00. The war by any name possible (tribal war, belligerent war, or rebellion war or civil war) cannot be understood in all its propensities by focusing only on its 1998s' origins.

It is therefore possible to argue that this discussion is an attempt to identify and delineate the socio-economic and political imperatives that have spurred the Congolese NGOs. It is also possible to hypothesize that under the conditions that threatened the civil liberties fought for by such prominent figures as, Etienne Tshisekedi and his "Union Pour la Democratie et le Progrès Sociales (UDPS) in the 1980s, Congolese people sought to increase and diversify not only their abilities to play a decisive role in the search for peace and harmony for their nation, but also to rise to the challenge of defending, correcting, and voicing their positions, stands, and reactions to the particular form of government that exists within their country. Accordingly, it is entirely possible that the Congolese NGOs today address every conceivable issue and operate in every part of the nation. Such a large proliferation of these organizations suggests two major socio-economic and political evolutions. First, that the Congolese government in recent days, is moving toward a gradual liberalization and transformation of the way in which it relates to its governed mass and is finding it necessary to assist such mass to be organized in order to operate efficiently. Modern governments in world tend to privatize by creating competitive tendering and giving agencies freedom to ménage reforms (Osborne and Gaebler 1992). Secondly, the well-organized people are regarded as actively seeking to have voice in all affairs of their nation, and to develop and acquire powers that allow them to be active participants in the management, control and production of their societies. As is well known, the historical development of these organizations elsewhere in the world was influenced first of all by the connections and international relations that individuals and institutions in one country established with other individuals, institutions and organizations in other nations. Thus most NGOs are found operating in one locality, country, or region of the nation, or are really international entities. There is also a great deal of coalition of efforts among NGOs.

Meanwhile, international NGOs have their own agenda and a growing influence in other places. Much such organization can easily pass as if they were transnational agencies. This is perhaps very well illustrated by the growth and expansion of the International Red Cross, the World Alliance of YMCA, the London–based Amnesty International with networks in over ninety countries and territories. According to James A. Paul 2000, Amnesty International Secretariat in London has about three hundred staff and specialists. It should be observed that there is a great need for us to make certain that the new spurge of Congolese NGOs is following the theoretical and ideological orientations which have guided NGOs elsewhere.

As the discourse about democracy and accountability continues, it becomes increasingly necessary that NGOs role be frequently assessed to determine their effectiveness in what they claim to do and especially in the areas of peaceful resolution of the conflicts and or the crises that confront in the modern Congolese society. Congolese problems today can not be regarded as simply tribal or national, they are indeed the product of Globalization process that has created cross-border communities of interest that only NGOs can address effectively. It is apparent that national governments have been shown to be unable to represent or to address the interest of particular communities. The NGOs will thus have role and functions they cannot relinquish.

Conceptual Framework

Four variables provide a framework for conceptualizing how the Democratic Republic of Congo can attain sustainable development in the future. These variables include the provision of basic needs, social reforms, development of human capital and economic reforms. Can the government alone provide these needs? As the situation is right now in the nation the answer is no. Who then can provide these needs for the citizens of the Democratic Republic of Congo? Figure 10.1 illustrate the critical need for the government of the Democratic Republic of Congo to form partnership with NGOs, the private sector, community-based organizations in the process of providing these needs to the people of the nation.

Further, individuals would have to learn how to depend less on government and establish community-based organizations to help provide their basic needs. The broad-based partnership advocated between the governments, the private sector and NGOs will provide a wider scope of public activities that would mobilize citizens into frequent contact with various competing institutions. This partnership will in turn foster and increase socialization among citizens, promote political participation, education, good health, change in citizens' attitude, increase economic growth, and reduce income as well as inequality gap in the nation. Figure 10.1 also shows a viable part to democracy, transparency and accountability via the interaction of government, NGOs, the private sector and civil society groups. The structural persistence phase of the partnership will help to engage actors in developing and consolidating democratic principles that are currently missing in the nation.

The appearance of international non-governmental organizations (INGOs) activities in the nation can also foster a significant role in developing a democratic mind set among the citizens of the Democratic Republic of Congo. Participatory citizenry begins with the understanding that democratic progressions will only be realized by opening up the political process regardless of citizens' ethnicity, clan, kinship and religion (Bradley 2005). Just as the government alone cannot propel the nation to achieving sustainable development, NGOs will not be able to do so alone either, both parties will have to work with the private sector and various civil society groups and community based organizations. Thus, the people of the Democratic Republic of Congo can be mobilized to engage in social actions to oppose militia groups that flourish as a result of poverty and hunger of the masses. Genuine education can advance egalitarian, sustainable agriculture geared towards local consumption needs. This partnership will reinforce the empowerment of the masses in the Democratic Republic of Congo. Figure 10.1 is predicated on the assumption that rational choice is part of sociological explanation of human actions. Politicians for example, act only because they believe they have a good reason or motivation underlying such action. Quite often such choice is influenced by the expectation of a society.

In the other hand, neo-institutional economic approach suggested by Williamson (1989), Pratt and Deckhouse, (1991) recognizes the pressure emanating from the public choice. Mweller (1989 and 1997) claims that all theories underlying NGOs development are based on the presence of a rational actor model of man. To ascertain the rise, development and rapid spread of Congolese NGOs, it is necessary to determine under which conditions these semi-private, semi-public associations have expanded. Sandra Van Thiel (2004: 180) suggests that politicians and political situations may influence the establishment of NGOs as they are expected to become executive agents of certain state tasks as opposed to the government bureaucracy. In other words, the behavior of individuals is often time rational in that it attempts to achieve well-established goals. That is, the NGOs arc created to meet certain important goals. And in achieving these goals, actors can maximize their expected utility.

Based on social production function approach, dating back to Adam Smith, two universal goals pursued by all individual actors can be fiamed to be (a) a search for a rational way to achieve one's physical well being and (b) a way to achieve social approval as suggested by Lindenberg and Frey (1993). More revealing is the fact that these universal goals are not achieved until one has developed intermediary or instrumental goals. The achievement of goals is often constrained or controlled by the quantity and quality of resources an actor has at his disposal and the constraints he faces. It fallows that this analysis relies heavily on the developed society model where there are an abundance of financial resources. It does not fail however to capture what now exists in the developing African societies. The resources are not necessary financial they may be non-financial. It is thus possible to hypothesize that a constrain-driven approach can offer a simplified way of modeling individual behavior.

It is apparent that NGOs do not develop easily in society where dictatorship exists. Nevertheless, it has been found that other aspects of NGOs or umbrella organizations of the states can be established to extend the arms of the state for example a politician, legislator, or Presidents may want to create intermediary executive agencies and place his preferred friends or relative to run them. For example in a legislative context, a good legislator is one who is re-elected several times and has been able to achieve a satisfactory level of physical well-being goals as well as his social approval goals. He must have the ability to maximize that he has been able not only to live well, but also to accomplish things or tasks that his constituency value and appreciate.

Figure 10.1
Partnership Model

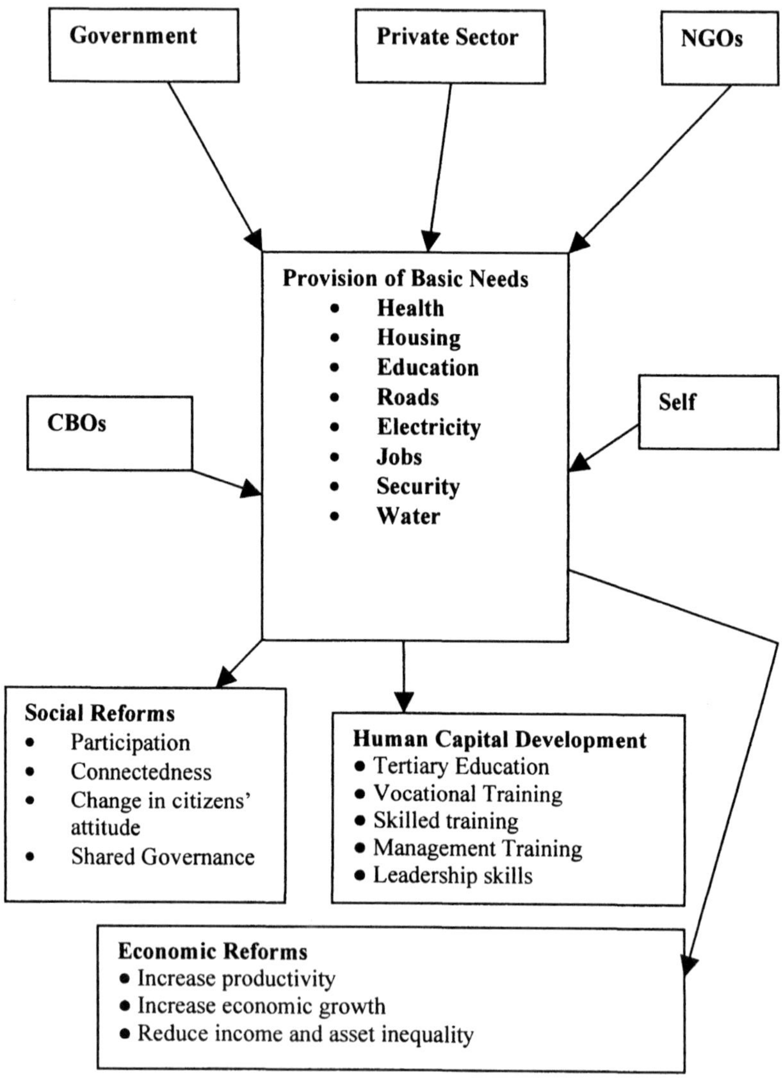

One can thus theorize that NGOs are engendered by the pressure that emerges from differences in political aspirations and the actors desire to have developed a rapport with the public through social approval. Such ideal constraining factors include challenging pressures and urgencies reflecting the demands and obligations engendered by the actor's response to political ideology, economic conditions, electoral challenges, corporatism, collective goods, specific investments, imitation of peers, and desire to monitoring the implementation of the output of his legislative initiatives, laws, programs, and policies. It is my assumption that NGOs or agencies like them, are not all private or public, some are indeed functioning in both sectors, and can, as I have stated earlier become the extension of the arm of the state.

Theoretically, NGOs do not all fit within one definition. They must however meet certain acceptable standards, and respond to certain criteria, which distinguish them from any other organization. Such rules or techniques constitute a body of regulations. Such ideas, principles, and approaches must apply to their overall mission, objective and purpose, especially as they are considered to be different from the actual practices. Theory in this instance is the hypothetical conceptualization of circumstantial principles that are not practical at all. For example what conditions are necessary for NGOs to exist in a society? One is compelled to hypothesize a society that is tolerant to civil disobedience and in which dictatorship is not possible. Is this possible or practical? Who can survive in such autocracy and create NGO that does not create conflicting situation?

So, in theory, there is agreement that NGOs must meet some fundamental criteria. They must for example be independent from direct control of any government. Furthermore, they must have three other generally accepted characteristics that exclude particular types of bodies from consideration. "An NGO will not be constituted as a political party; it will be non-profit-making organization, and it will not be a criminal group, in particular it will be non-violent (Lindenberg and Frey 1993). While the United Nations recognizes that the defining boundaries of these organizations can sometimes be blurred: some NGOs being in practice closely identified with political party; many NGOs generating some income from commercial activities, notably consultancy contracts or sales of publications; and a small percentage of NGOs becoming associated with violent political protests, it remains true that an NGO is never constituted as a government bureaucracy, a party, a company, a criminal organization or guerrilla group (Lindenberg and Frey 1993; Muyumba 2001). For our purpose here anyhow, an NGO should theoretically be readily recognized as an independent voluntary association of people acting together on a continuous basis for some common purpose, other than achieving government office, making money or illegal activities. This basic definition should probably guide us better to delineate the controversial and ambiguous features of Congolese NGOs.

It is possible furthermore to hypothesize that Congolese government is moving toward liberalization of its polity, especially as the number of private

NGOs is growing, and each is seeking governmental recognition of its status as non profit organization, and yet with sufficient liberties and determination to become much more involved in the social, economic, cultural and political debate. In order to be much more effective, the theory encourages specialization. In this perspective, each NGO must have an area or domain of specialization and concentration of its actions as to be a very efficient and effective executor of its agenda. As civil organizations, NGOs practice civil disobedience especially when the civil liberties of their compatriots' members are violated or about to be violated. They may work on defense of civil rights, civil servant and civil service and are prone to promote labor organizations that strive to enforce civil law and protection of workers. They are indeed civil libertarians as they seek to provide higher level of freedom in all aspects of their nation's life. Such NGOs also could be temporary or ad hoc in nature, other is really permanent agencies and institutions of a society and they function according to acceptable international standards or institutional rules that have been formally set up. Consider the foundations that are established with an endowment fund, for example a school, research establishment or charitable trust or hospital. Theoretically, such organizations are guided by theorems, and or provable logical propositions that can be tested by a set of axiomatic assumptions.

It is therefore possible to speculate that the nature of assumptions adopted by any particular NGO must reflect its underlying theoretical frame of reference. And this is the defining principle that distinguishes one NGO from the other because of the constraints and limits that such NGO pursues. One can also theorize that in country as the DRC, Nigeria, Egypt and or South Africa with large population, NGOs will tend to reflect regional, state or provincial, and or national interests. It is thus important to examine the nature of the DRC society.

Socio-Ethnic and Geopolitical Settings

Briefly, the DR C is situated in the middle of Africa, and extends itself almost equally on both sides the equator and is completely located within Torrid Zone. It is fair to say that the Democratic Republic of Congo's cultural topography is by a variety of ethnic groupings, and that members of these ethnic groups are no longer located in specific geopolitical area, given the fact that population from these ethnic groups are now found in its eleven provinces where they did not originate. This is due to the growth and development of new and large urban communities represented by the largest cities: Kinshasa, Mbuji-Mayi, Lubumbashi, Kananga, Matadi, Kamina, Kolwezi, Bukavu, Goma, MBandaka Kisangani, Kindu, Bukavu, Goma, and Banded, etc. The exact population and the number of ethnic groups in the Democratic Republic of Congo have never been scientifically established. The difficulty does not come from the census or from the intricacy to count them arithmetically, rather than from theoretical order where, the definition of "ethnic group" has not found a total agreement among the linguists, anthropologists and political scientists. Nevertheless the tacit and implicit consensus is pushing the Congolese scientists to present the following ethnic groups as major characteristics of the population of the

Democratic Republic of Congo. We have adopted these divisions from the work of the Institut Géographique du Congo published in the *Cahier Economic et Sociaux, vol. 23, no. 1-4, août, 1989.* The country's population has been divided by eleven provinces and appears as this:

1. Kinshasa Province has a surface of 9,965 square kilometers with a population estimated conservatively to be 5.5 million people with a large percentage of people belonging to the ethnic group of Humbu and Teke. Kinshasa administrative headquarters are found in the city of Kinshasa itself.

2. Bas Congo Province administrative capitol is Matadi. Bas -Congo has a population of 3.5 million people and its major ethnic groups include Kongo (Ntandu, Ndibu, Mbata, Yombe, Besingombe, Manteke, Mnianga, Woyo and Bamboma).

3. Bandundu Province has a capitol city known as Bandundu (former city of Kikwit). Bandundu occupies an area space of 259,658 square kilometers with a population of 5.5 million people. This population is subdivided into the following ethnic groups: Pende, Yaka, Yansi, Mbala, Sakata, Mboma, and Tshokwe.

4. Occidental Kasai Province has its administrative in the city of Kananga. It occupies an area space of 154,741 square kilometers with a population of 3.5 million people. The major ethnic goups found in Occidental Kasai include: Lulua, Kuba, Tshokwe, Tshilele and Lunda.

5. Oriental Kasai Province has its capitol at Mbuji-Mayi. It occupies an area of 170.302 square kilometers with a population of 1.5 million people. The major ethnic groups found in Oriental Kasai Province include: Luba, Songhye, Kanyok, Kanintshina, and Tetela.

6. Katanga Province capitol is located in the city of Lubumbashi. The province of Katanga occupies an area space of 496.877 kilometers with a population of 4.5 million people. Its major ethnic groups include: Baluba, Ruwud, Bemba, Hemba, Sanga, Tshokwe, and Tabwa..

7. Maniema Province has its capital at Kindu, and occupies areas of 132.250 square kilometers with a population of 1.5 million people. Its major ethnic groups include Tetela, Kusu, Bangubangu, Kumu, Zimba and Lega.

8. South Kivu Province capitol is Bukavu. The province occupies an area of 65.070 square kilometers with a population of 3 million people. Its major ethnic groups include: Shi, Lega, and Fulero.

9. North Kivu Province capital is Goma. The province occupies an area of 59.583 square kilometers with a population of 3.5 million people. Its major ethnic groups include: Nande, Nyanga, Hunde, Banyarwanda, and Kumu.

10. Oriental Province capitol is Kisangani. It occupies an area of 503.239 square kilometers with a population of 6 million people. Its major ethnic groups include: Lokele, Topoke, Mbole, Boa, Ngbetu, Alur, Logo, Lugwara, Hema, Lenda, Wagenia, and Twa.

11. Equatorial Province capitol is Mbandaka. It occupies an area of 403.292 square kilometers with a population of 5 million people. Its major ethnic group includes: Mongo, Budja, Ngombe, Ekonda, Libinza, Ngbandi, Ngbaka, and Batshwa (Muyumba 2001; Lindenberg and Frey 1993).

It is possible to argue that the search for peaceful resolution of conflicts, peace building and reconstruction of the Congo cannot be left in the hands of the belligerent factions alone including the present government of DRC for that matter. There appears to be a real opportunity to mobilize ordinary citizens to develop the capacity and propensity to become advocates for peaceful resolution of conflicts. To that extent, there is a grand chance for the Transition government led by President Joseph Kabila to share the stage with Congolese NGOs and domestic civil society groups. There is a growing awareness that the central authorities and the civil society groups must involve themselves into the resolute educational programs aimed at the development of positive aptitudes toward peaceful resolution of conflicts. Karl Marx advanced the notion that conflicts of interests were in essence the motor behind any significant social change. DRC has experienced political problems since day one of its independence, and it seems just logical that it should move toward the acquisition of advocacy skills, strategies, and approaches that might promote peaceful resolutions of conflicts and wars. This perspective suggests that DRC cannot divert from involving itself into the creation and establishment of capable NGOs and local civil society groups that would develop expertise in the field of peaceful conflict resolution, including NGOs, Interest groups, pressure groups, lobbies and private voluntary organizations Such endeavor entails the institution of periodic training of personnel and specialists in the areas of critical investigative research, methodologies, and strategies for analysis of information, and transparent ways to report the results and ensuring equitable distribution of goods and services derived from such investigation throughout the nation.

In this perspective, the foreseeable challenge is to transform peoples fear into courage, to ensure that every citizen of the Democratic Republic of Congo will no longer equate sustainable development process with ethnocentrism, but to participate fully towards the creation, promotion and development of peaceful political and social environment in the nation. The sheer numbers of ethnic groups in DRC has been regarded as the main source of all socio-political, cultural economic and civil conflicts. Yet, so far anyhow, Congolese political crises since 1960s have not been ethnic in nature. It is very possible that the country has not had a strong private sector that would have been capable to counterbalance the behavior and actions of the governing authorities. Hence the emergence of domestic NGOs that are managed by Congolese citizens and their allies can certainly be regarded as salvation and a mechanism for checking the excessive powers of the government. It establishes a good beginning of a political discourse that will be expected to be at times mutually supportive and at other times oppositional to the monopoly of power without consent of the governed. These NGOs will both extend and augment the power of the Congolese people, especially in configuring and reconfiguring of its democratic institutions, processes and balancing acts.

Advocacy for Human Rights in DRC

Perhaps, in order to make a dent within the study of what is developing now within Africa in general, and more particularly in the DRC, it might be wise to begin by a brief historical discussion of the origins and status of the NGOs in the DRC. Interests in the democratization process and democracy require the development and adoptation of a new way to pursue peace through negotiation. Such negotiations cannot be successful without ideological and methodological strategies of peaceful resolution of conflicts. It must be said that in order to be truly successful, any approach to peaceful negotiation may inspire the cultivation, promotion, and institution of a way of life and not just an impromptus response to historical events. For a people that have lived under the tough colonial structure, and under successive autocratic regimes (Mobutu/Kabila-Kalbila), resorting to peaceful resolution, negotiated settlement, and bargaining seem to suggest themselves as credible ingredients that one might want to espouse. Historically, as early as 1937 during the Belgian Congo's colonial experience, both the Christian Protestant Council and the Catholic Church started to carry the laden flag of defenders and protectors of the indigenous rights. This avocation in advocacy was actually disputed between the Christian Churches and the Colonial government that regarded the foreign Missionaries societies as interfering within the colonial governmental domain. It was assumed then that the responsibility of the Colonial government and governing authorities included the obligation to provide a Colonial Charter that would establish a code of conduct that protected the rights and privileges of all colonial subjects. One needs to remember that the Christian enterprises looked at their theology as teaching the code of Christian ethics and behaviors that all Christians should follow and they should treat one another with respect and love. African traditional beliefs suggest that one's neighbors are indeed one's brother and /or sister.

In fact, the Church of Christ in the Congo started out as the Congo Protestant Council of Church, a representative body of all Protestant Denominations of Churches in the Congo. Today in the DRC, the Catholic and Protestant Church Communities are well established, and they claim close to forty million members. They started to confront the Colonial authorities on the basis of its greedy contradictions aimed at confusing the world community about the real interests of King Leopold in the Congo. Leopold II's mission statement emphasized the civilization of the Congolese, yet his real interests laid on his commercial and business enterprises. Instead of civilization, the missionaries found out that the king was engaged in forced labor including all tactics and strategies to kidnap and abuse women whose sons and husbands did not obey the dicta to collect and bring a large quantity of wild rubber. Congoleses human and civic rights became the concern of such prominent pioneer missionaries as William Sheppard, William Morrison, and E.V. Sjöblom, and others who discovered that the Leopold II's agents had ordered Congolese soldiers and other chiefs at their service to show how severe they were toward Congolese who refused to bring their quota of rubber. Congolese lost parts of their body as evidence that they were punished.

The rise of the Protestant NGOs can thus be found within the overall protest movement against Leopold II's rule of terror. The Presbyterian Mission archives retain primacy in recorded writings of William Sheppard, the first to have his views of despicable behaviors of King Leopold II in the Congo. Both William Phipps (2002) and Adam Hoschschikld (1999) point out that Dr. William Sheppard, an African-American Presbyterian Missionary to the Congo, from early 1890s to late 1930s, was the first recognized religious leader to take upon him the burden to stand up for the rights of the Congolese people. He literally wrote an article in which he exposed his discovery of eighty-one human hands severed from Congolese men who had refused to bring in the required quota of rubber. Another Baptist Missionary from Sweden, Sjöblom, published in Swedish press, detailed description of the comportment of Leopold agents in the Congo. "He told how the African Public Force soldiers (under Leopold Congo Free State) were rewarded for the number of hands they collected" (Lindenberg and Frey, 1993). They further pointed out that [one] agent told him that he had himself seen a State Officer at one of the outposts pay a certain number of brass roads (local currency) to soldiers for a number of hands they had brought (Lindenberg and Frey 1993).

As a child, growing up in Belgian Congo in the late 1950s one could not avoid following the positioning by the State as well as by the Churches about their role within the future of the Belgian Congo. Of course, the search for more freedom under the colonial rule was both a preoccupation of the Protestant church as it was far more resisted by the colonial authorities, and yet, the rising Congolese middle class demanded such protection. Generally, the process was painfully restricted and controlled. Nevertheless, there is an understanding that the Churches would demand more freedoms than it will be possible to get, and the state would only grant those rights that did not work against its best interests. As the Newspaper, *The Potential*, of June 20, 2005 reports:

> "The Roman Catholic Church of DRC has just brought, once again, its contribution to the relaxation of the worrisome situation of the moment. By the voice of its president, Mgr. Laurent Monsengwo Pasinya, the national Episcopalian Conference of Congo [(CENCO)] has, during a press conference likened on Friday the interfaith Centre of Kinshasa, invited the political actors' government and those that are except institutions for the reassurance and for the

dialogue. A realistic and responsible message from the Catholic Church was based on peace and unity in the Democratic Republic of Congo" (*The Potential*, of June 20, 2005).

The power of religious NGOs is reflected by their broadening voice. Once the National Episcopal Conference has spoken, the prelates or Mgrs in different provinces and localities carry the same message through their direct contacts with Church congregations in particular places. Hence one can note that Mgr. Cibangu Cishiku, Archbishop of Mbuji-Mayi, repeated the same message as Mgr. Mosengwo. The concern over the rising tides of popular, more or less lively reactions sometimes expressed with violence was registered in the DRC capitol city and in the provincial sits of government, forced the Catholic prelates to react by issuing their own recommendations and directives. Reactions which, it is advisable to examine and to estimate seriously and in depth, notably in what they seem widely pressed on base of frustrations, exasperations because of the generally deteriorating socio-political conditions of life, and the growing impatience over the promised happier future which always seems delayed before becoming a reality (Lindenberg and Frey 1993).

According to the diagnosis of the national Episcopal Conference of Congo (CENCO), DRC has been facing the excitement that focuses on the approaching date of June 30, 2005. For example, Mgr. Laurent Monsengwo Pasinya, chairman of CENCO, likened the DRC to the interdiocesan Centre of Kinshasa. It is this appreciation of the ministers of the universal Church, which justified the elaboration and implementation of their appeal in the reassurance, launched several weeks before June 30, 2005.

Perhaps it is best to chronicle just how to the date of June 30, 1960 acquired great significance and importance within the context of Congolese nationalism and cultural history. June 30, 1960, was indeed the Independence Day. It was the King Baudouin of Belgium who was to declare in a major speech before Belgian colonialists, the Congolese, and the entire world community the historical end and cessation of formal Belgian colonization in Congo. It was also the day Joseph Kasavubu made his mild speech accepting the challenge of Independence. But for most radical Congolese, it is the day the flamboyant Premier Minister of Congo, Mr. Patrice Emery Lumumba upstaged both the King of Belgium and the President Joseph Kasavubu in an impromptus and memorable independence speech on the meaning of independence? Every June 30 since then, the entire nation celebrates by participating in public festivities organized by the state as well by individuals. However, June 30, 2005, became infamous because it was projected as a special day the Congolese mass would forcibly end the period of transition. The political opposition, namely the Union for Democracy and Social Progress Party, and affiliated organizations proclaimed it to constitute the legal end of the Transition Government. This stand by the Opposition parties created a new type of conflict and challenged the Transition Government.

It is possible to visualize how the prelates' appeal could remind the Congolese to remember the previous statement made by the permanent

Committee, entitled, *Congo Belongs to us*. This was published on February 5, 2005, and its underlying quest was to establish a real leitmotiv of measures intended to bring a happy outcome of the transition government by the preliminary organization of free and democratic elections. At first glance, the Roman Catholic Church of DRC appeared to exhort the political parties, government and people to return to the dialogue to defuse the crisis that was clocking on the horizon. Better than the politicians, the Church wanted to make it plain that it was not any longer a question of continuing to take the Congolese people in hostage, rather than to move forward and never move back, as well as it had recommended this to the South African President, Thabo Mbeki visit to DRC in summer 2004.

In fact, the Newspaper, *Potential* reports that, as the most important ONG, the Catholic Church's actions are critical challenges to the decision-makers and to the other political actors. They incite people and their political leaders to calm the storm and to privilege dialogue. It is absolutely necessary to reassure spirits, the prelate said. This dialogue is authoritarian at the level of structures, leaders of the State, and the international Community, at the level of the political parties and social organizations, it is necessary to make everything possible to guarantee that, by the date of June 30, 2005, and beyond, the conditions of a positive dialogue, a peace will prevail as a psychological reassurance to all.

Furthermore, the Catholic Conference stands free of the political parties such as UDPS (Union for Democracy and Social Progress), PPRD (People's Party for Revolution and Democracy) and MLC (Movement de Liberation Congolais) and the transition Government to take seriously the occasion presented by the symbolic date of June 30, to invest themselves into the process of national dialogue and reconciliation to promote peace and development. Otherwise, the Catholic NGOs ask all and all to refrain from any violent crimes whether or not it is coming from the polices and or from the civil population: slaughters, thefts, burglaries and armed raids, confrontations and armed conflicts, destructions of the properties and individual possessions and physical abuses are all negative forces and contrary to the spirit of national dialogue. As Mgr. Mosengwo observed, ' to be engaged in such acts of violence would be equivalent to dishonor the memory of the million men and women of our country fallen and pointlessly sacrificed (Martin 2002; Lindenberg and Frey 1993).

It seems that by this appeal in the reassurance, the Roman Catholic Church of DRC, reminds everybody that it is easy to want to have the blood on hands of the sacred character of the human life and that the wishes of the Church were that in conjunction with the date of June 30, 2005, there be no acts of violence or vandalism. A state established and governed by law excludes anarchy and disorder; it imposes the respect for the law, which every citizen must follow in order to shape ones life and act soundly. The Congolese Catholic Church promotes thus the notion that if a people have plausible reasons to express its opinion, it should do it legally, without breakage or plunder, because there is nothing more beautiful than a peaceful demonstration (Muyumba 2001; Lindenberg and Frey 1993).

On basis of this historical background, it is possible to estimate that the greatest number of Congolese NGOs has originated from, and or are derived, from the confessional organizations. All the Catholic, Protestant and Islamic organizations place a heavy emphasis on private business ownership, and have traditionally encouraged the development of private enterprises, private venues for free expressions such as free press, and media which are not dominated by the Government, but which may work in frank cooperation, and collaboration with the state. It should not be surprising that even in the annals of the United Nations of 1998, evidence abounds that one of the leading humanitarian NGOs, advocated early recognition of the Rwandan genocide and swift and resolute action to stop it (Muyumba 2001). Hence for the greatest majority of the Congolese NGOs, are confronted with the dilemma of establishing their essential orientation, and their importance and necessity as representatives of the civil society or a religious community.

The scholars and activists have thus an obligation to determine how effective they are able to counterbalance not only the power of the state, but also the growing influence of discourse of politico-economic, religious, and socio-pathological globalization which people across the world readily admit openly, is capable of corrupting them. Muyumba (2001) contends that though such globalization allows scholars to frame their arguments for or against trans-nationalization as a way of thinking about movement that by nature, extends our vision of reality beyond the borders of a nation- state, it is apparent that NGOs have the obligation to remain vigilant in the defense of their people's highest interests, even though, sometimes, their visions may become localized and particular. The lesson from the past decades however, is that such leaders as Mobutu and his authoritarian regimes used the people's silence as a symbol of unity and tolerance to their archaic political butchery. Suffice it to conclude hence that the Congolese NGOs view intents of the Transition government of DRC today, in all matters, as suspect. Currently the, Congolese NGOs comprise of:

1. *NGOs* that are non-government Organizations that developed uniquely to work with a civil society group or groups of people outside of the government, and without government involvement.

2. *Local Self-Help NGOs* are those NGOs that are developed within a state to implement projects that are usually financed through their own organizations or from local and (sometimes) international sources. These can certainly include lay religious groups.

3. *Church Organizations as NGO*: These refers to non-government organizations usually developed by a nation state or an international Church denomination or religious sect, to provide free services for its members or for the people using donated resources and/ or collected

special offerings within the church community. (Sometimes this includes access to ecumenical resources from the World council of church or other missionary organizations).

4. *Multinational NGOs* are usually those NGOs that are financed and supported by several nations or multinational corporations.

5. *International NGOs* are those that help several countries in the international community. They may function in some parts of the world depending on their interests (International Red Cross).

6. *Transnational NGOs* are those that are supported by several nations to help a multitude of countries. The international business community also many times backs these. The major concept is to hide the identity of the nations from which the NGOs are derived.

7. *Indigenous NGOs*. Those are non-government organizations that are created with little organization and resources but can have a powerful voice if connected to other NGOs. Local issues and concerns are very unique and particular, although they may have parallels elsewhere.

8. *Donors.* This may be a corporation, a company, an individual, or a government agency that provides grants, scholarships, legal aid, and resources for self-development of people to qualified NGOs.

Generally, the roles of the Congolese NGOs have often time shifted and altered depending on the political climate and economic conditions that affect DRC and define the state of its well being and that of its people. Since most African NGOs are complex organizations, it is plausible to posit that Congolese NGOs face tremendous challenges, because they usually have limited resources and therefore may be incapable of achieving some of their bona fide objectives. Majority of these NGOs are however learning quickly to stay aloof and not make their ideological precepts more rigidly unyielding and overly transparent so as to allow them to protect themselves by managing safely their relationships with the international organizations, state governments, and other influential powers that may intend to manipulate them, and or deter them from their most significant objectives and goals. That is, the international organizations, or donors do not act in vacuum; they do not give without expecting something in return even an influential hand from the recipient. As one of my student once observed I am distressed to discover that Africa in general and DRC in particular, struggles at the same time to keep control of its state affairs, as well as to find reliable partners in development (Muyumba 2001).

The complex nature of NGOs has been very well defined by their goals. They are needed as counterbalancing organizations within a society, especially in those societies struggling to provide their people with diversified and self-determining voices, as independent socio-political and economic actors, as well as builders of their nation, its governing institutions, its infrastructures and its rule of the law. The NGOs represent the second level of power in a society, but without which the primary responsibility of citizens to organize in defense and protection of their sovereign and human rights cannot be guaranteed. It is from these conflicting interests between the perceived power of the state and its corruptive capacity that the defense and protection of human and civic rights of the sovereign people that the NGOs derive their mission and power to speak on behalf of many who are voiceless.

Political Parties as NGOs

As early as 1960s, Congolese saw political parties as reliable organizations that could voice their desires and aspirations. Such Parties as the Association of Bakongo (ABAKO), the Movement National Congolais (Lumumba's Party) and the other organizations were created to present a panorama of voices in defense of Congolese rights. But Political parties become vilified by the Mobutu regime as early as 1961, moving away from political debate and encouraging militarization of politics and autocratic regimentation. From the 1980s to 1990s however, under the autocratic regime of Mobutu, the Congolese people were definitely struggling to have voice. Aspiring politicians and lay leaders of the community went to prison and to their death. But the essential of their struggle, was to create and establish political structures that promoted democracy, and they did that by secretly creating and establishing free political parties. Mobutu as a despot faced a growing dissidence from the opposition politicians who were willing to sacrifice themselves to re-establish the multiparty system. Political opposition was silenced, many, including Etienne Tshisekedi, the National President of UDPS, carry on their body the painful symbols of torture inflicted upon them by Mobutu cronies. Such things as branding of MPR symbols on their backs, stomachs or chests were done. In 1996, Mobutu fail from power under the double pressure of his failing health and powerful threat of physical elimination by the invading liberation armed forces under Kabila.

Communication, Press, and Media as NGOs

One area of development, which demonstrates the best of the fruits of that early societal re-organization, is the communication media. According to Stephan Hobe (1998),

> At the threshold of the twenty-first century, the concept of the state is subject to profound challenges. Among Western European States, one can watch in owe the gradual transfer of tasks from the public to the private sector, such as the well-known example of the privatization of state owned businesses (Hobe 1998).

Congolese have developed a network of mass media which include Government sponsored TV, and magazines, newspapers, etc, and privately owned radio and television broadcasting systems. All of which clearly reflect the earning of the Congolese people to remain free, and to provide once again free channels of news and their interpretation, which will be free of state's interference. This implies that the Congolese NGOs like their counterparts elsewhere claim to be transparent organizations, and sometimes one may find one individual belonging to more than one NGO. This is very important because in many cases NGOs have tendency to work in coalition with other NGOs in order to have the greatest impact. As Hobe (1998) demonstrate, "the growing importance and legal recognition of the activities of NGOs are indicative of a changing paradigm [in national as well as] international systems and in international law. Within the international system, the state is losing its formerly dominant position. Other organizations representing community interests are becoming increasingly important."

Elsewhere, international governmental organizations serve to help states fulfill all those tasks they cannot readily handle easily, and thus they solve those problems whose scope transcends the states capacity. According to Hobe (1998), this evolution has accurately been characterized as "internationalization," while in reality it contributes toward our understanding of denationalization.

The trend described above reflects a new definition of the future tasks of at least some national as well as international NGOs. They stand as entities that are needed to represent global interests, e.g. if they are really international in nature, or local or national interests if they are indeed local or national in character. In this regard, depending on the assumed roles and mission of NGOs such as representation of public interests, whether international or local, are spelled out in some details within the norms of international law, and recognized by the united nations as players or agents of the public interest. Hobe (1998) concludes with Jost Delbrück (1993) that the importance of NGOs can only grow in the future. In such a case, one must recognize at least partially, the characteristic quality of international NGOs. Such recognition demonstrates even more clearly the important challenge to statehood posed by the proliferation of NGOs in the world. This accounts for the fear and concerns of unstable governments where NGOs are just about to become competitors to the state not only in factual but also in legal terms.

In my most recent visit to DRC, in July 2004, it was possible to note the existence of many types of non-governmental organizations. Almost in every city, commune district and towns, being either organized or organizing their interest groups. These groups are distinguished by their bylaws or statues, and have unique civic personality or identity where as they stand up as collective NGOs that not only function independently, but also compete for resources that are available through the church, the United Nation agencies dealing with issues of Children and Youth, or educational issues through, Unesco, and labor related through the International Labor Organization, or from international organizations such as the International Red Cross. Hence, the country is experiencing an uplifting in terms of multiplicity of voices that speak to people's aspirations, needs for education, reliable employment, religious freedom, free press, advocacy for the rights of Journalists to write and express their opinions and or advocacy for freedom of expression including religious, political, social and economic discourse. This is an important dimension of the shifting of the role of representation of the people. The Congolese state in no longer the only one recognized representative of its citizens; citizen organizations are also now becoming able to speak on behalf of their people.

Based on this interpretation, the Roman Catholic Church of DRC can be regarded as capable of reaching out and informing an elaborate segment of the Congolese community. Its positions or stands are clear and informative to every sector of the society. For example in addressing itself to the Independent Electoral Commission (IEC), the Conference of Bishops recommended that IEC establishes a clear calendar defining and determining prerequisites as well as dates foreseen for terms referendum and electoral: identification and recruitment of the voters, date of the referendum and the elections. This calendar should be accompanied by realistic commitments, based on viable feasibility studies, not to owe, once again, to put back elections and to prolong pointlessly transition. IEC owes, besides, a break with the deficit of communication, which leaves independent civil societies groups and political parties with doubt and confusion.

One further example of Catholic NGOs recommendation is that the dates of various ballots to come presidential elections, legislative and municipal should be generally considered and communicated earlier enough to inform the public, and prepare the participants. In other words, the Roman Catholic Church invites IEC to proceed with preparation for general elections without waiting for the decision of continuation of the transition emanating from the Parliament. The churches fear is that waiting without a plan could make it possible for IEC to be accused of duplicity to the people and complicity with the representatives of the institutions of the transition. This is a powerful voice not only because it is coming from the Congolese Catholic Church, but because these church communities are among the most sophisticated, well educated and very experienced religious leaders who have a great deal of contacts throughout the world.

On other aspect of the Freedom of expression within the Episcopal National Conference is reflected by the dissenting opinion expressed by Mgr. Tshibangu Tshishiku, the vice President of the Episcopal Conference of Congolese Bishops who argued that he does not see why one should hesitate to proclaim from now on, with the advent of the Third Republic, the "federal" character of the republic-while greeting the proposition of the Project of constitution creating the Council of economic, socio and political institutions at both the provincial and national levels. He argues that:

- The citizens of the DRC must be enlightened well, before they can pronounce themselves, notably on constitutional Referendum.

- The moment came definitely today to cross the threshold of liberty and face the catalyst challenge for the future, that is to take decisive step for a greatly decentralized federal or of federal type structure; Conceived well and adequately formulated, this structure far from leading to drift and conflicts and dissensions, can only contribute on the contrary to the actual national development of the base and in the blooming of each of the provinces or big regions of Congo (Bamporiki, 2005).

The former Rector of the University and Archbishop of Mbuji-Mayi endorsed the proposed draft of the constitution and advised the authorities to work toward the reduction of the number of political parties by clear demarcations indicating whether or not a party is a regional, provincial, or national organization. He welcomed the proposition to create fourteen new provinces besides the eleven existing presently as a way of creating opportunity to empower the citizens of these provinces. The Catholic NGOs as represented by these two archbishops exhorted the Church to remain vigilantly committed in spite of, and more the current worrisome circumstances, to focus with confidence and a great hope towards the close and distant future of our country (Bamporiki 2005).

The above section reflects clearly the role of Catholic NGOs and place both religiously or politically and socially. They are the integral part and parcel of the people. Another characteristic of the Congolese NGOs is that they are predominantly urban organizations, which claim to be private, and yet they seem to have some well-established connections to some governmental department and agencies. Some NGOs have national character that they are represented in all the provinces, regions, or local or rural territories and or small towns.

In the area of mass media and Communication, the Congolese NGOS are the largest organizations and they stand as the veteran organizations that have had his test of time. They are the most experienced groups because they were involved in the Struggle for independence, and some became the voice of the emerging Congolese Petits bourgoiesies or *la class moyenne*. These NGOs are grouped under an umbrella organization known as ACP-Agene Congolaise de Presse or the Congolese Press Agency.

This agency has almost five hundred journalists working for its varied specialized services. Fifty of these are all located in Kinshasa where they graduated from IFASIC. In the provincial capital offices the number of journalist's alternates between five and ten units among which one finds a Provincial director, a Permanent Secretary for Redaction, and the reporters. Almost eighty other (fifty in Kinshasa and thirty in provinces) have already benefited from in-service training Seminars organized by IFASIC and its partners, such as the Friedrich Naumann Fondation. Fifty other journalists of ACP found in Kinshasa and the thirty working at provincial level have also benefited from in training seminars organized by IFASIC and the Friederich Naumann Foundation or by other partners. Given these training, the overage level of training of the Congolese journalists is equivalent to six years of Secondary Education, in the provinces, and of three years of College and University Studies in Kinshasa. In their globalization pursuit, the ACP produces and distributes newspapers, their publications are critically important to the government which from time to time, relies on ACP to get its message to the public despite the availability of the state national radio and television broadcasting systems, and a multiplicity of departmental publications. ACP provides strong leadership in defense of the freedom of press, and thus is respected among all Congolese NGOs because of its experience and rich background. Often ACP works cooperatively with state but most of time they oppose one another.

For the DRC, the private newspapers constitute a dynamic group of private enterprises to which the public enterprises return also to pass their messages. One thing shared by all privately owned enterprises are that they do not have a large diffusion of information, and thus, their budgets do not support regular production and dissemination of news and newspapers. Thus a dependency of sort exists where the private enterprises are found publishing for government agencies. The conflict of interest is not really factual here since the state in this fashion becomes simply a client. It is estimated that depending on its budget, each NGO in this category can produce, and disseminate information according to its budget. For example while the National Corporation dealing with post office and telecommunication is usually able to produce only five hundred copies of its journal, the other national giant company, MIBA can produce about six thousand copies of its journal, *Mbongo or Diamonds.*

The other category of NGOs includes church related civilian organizations that focus on many interesting areas of Congolese life. Among the few collected data received recently, is a list of 121 NGOs located within Katanga provinces, which are difficulty to categorize. Only their ideological leaning, specialized focus and concentration, makes it difficult to limit assistance, given the fact that some are clearly involved in more than one activity. For the moment however, I intend to discuss their stated involvement in the sectors that interest them the most.

Using their number as a significant indicator of their concern, I will now outline and categorize them as follow:

1. *Focus on Agricultural Activities:* In this category, 89 NGOs out of a total of 121 NGOs or 68 percent indicate that they are involved in *Agricultural development projects*, and that they consider agri-businesses, and agriculture to constitute an area of great concern, especially if the people must develop alternative to develop their region, and respond to peoples needs. It is easy to see this as a matter of conscience that Africans of the twenty-first century are now attempting to return to the land to raise their own food, and to do so with the understanding that African development may depend heavily on the outcome of their new technology and methodology of food production, dissemination, and sale.

2. *Focus on Educational activities:* In this category 47 NGOS out of a total of 121 NGOs or 26 percent are dedicated to promoting educational enterprises at localities found in the Katanga Province. These non-governmental organizations are involved in scholastic education and its place in the transformation of a society. Education for them appeals to both young and adult people. Those who have knowledge to organize

and manage schools succeed to contribute to the emancipation and development of their people. Education requires freedom of thoughts, expression, and literacy. And these NGOs will go out of their ways to facilitate the creation and establishment of privately educational enterprises, or they will work almost as syndicate (labor Unions) to protect the rights of teachers.

3. *Focus on Animal husbandry or Breeding:* In this category 35 NGOs out of a total of 121 NGOs, or 14 percent indicate that they are more concerned with *animal breeding or husbandry.* This is directly related to Agriculture, which encompasses animal husbandry and breeding. Both of which are related processes to increase the production and the protection and dissemination of consumable protein.

4. *Focus on Health Issues and Rights:* In this category 30 NGOs or 9 percent indicate that they are attempting to deal or resolve the issue related to Congolese people health problems and treatments. They would probably work the rights of the retirees to receive coverage of their health expenses and to make certain that the implying companies, government, and national health insurances are able to meet their obligations to the workers, and that public health institutions (hospitals, clinics and dispensaries), as well as private enterprises are able to respond timely to the needs of the Congolese people.

5. *Protection of Women, Children and other:* This category includes organizations established to focus on the protection of women, children, and other vulnerable persons who have not had voice in the past. This category or less than 1 percent of the organization appears to be one of the lesser groups, and yet in reality is a significant mile stone in the ways to the defense and protection of the most susceptible among us.

6. *Focus on Water and Sanitation*: This category focuses on people's right to have clean water on regular basis and to maintain certain acceptable standards for sanitations both in rural and urban settings. Many African Nations have and continue to face challenge to produce, maintain, and equally distribute clean water, and at the same time hold acceptable standards of sanitation. Many diseases and epidemics are derived by bad hygienic habits and lack of clean drinking water. It is possible to conceive the availability of clean water to be a human right issue.

7. *Focus on Community Development:* This category focuses primarily on issues related to community Development. They seek assistance from International agencies such as USAID, PNUD, and other continental organizations that deal with development issues and or that can land a

hand with financing, to accomplish minimal outputs of development, self-development, and community based projects that are not personal, but involve a participation of entire community, or a segment of it. The most popular so far are small projects such as community health care, dispensary, or birthing room. Some agency has founded the establishment of new secondary school or clinics. Rural as well some quarters or districts in the expanding urban community may need a nearby clinic or dispensary.

8. *Focus on civic education and literacy*: This category or closer to 0.9 percent of all NGOs places heavy emphasis on civic and literacy education. They feel strongly that the people citizen needs to know their government, their rights and their obligation to voice their opinions in all matters regarding their governance. One cannot be able to do so without acquiring some level of literacy that equip them to read, understand and comprehend what is at stake in their community or nation. This is where the majority of high school drops outs, the women and men who need to learn to read and write go. Sometimes this is given freely; sometimes they may charge some fees, as it is necessary to provide qualified teachers and assistants.

9. *Other Collectives Focuses*: This category include all other small organizations but focusing in such areas as food and nutrition, gender and women' issues, environmental problems, crafts, information technology, Humanitarian assistance, Transportation, Food security, agro-business, commerce and micro-finance, vocational technical training, moral consciousness, culture and arts-teachers rights, youth works, and leadership training and sports. These small focuses are as important in what they do as any other organizations. It seems to me that many of these small ones are still in a very early stage of their development.

Two other well respected nongovernmental organizations are the syndicates: The Federation of Teachers and the Federation of Civil Servants in DRC have recently teamed together to bargain for better salaries and benefits from their public employer, the Transition Government. Since both teachers and civil servants are workers and functionaries of State, they have been recognized as federations representing the laborers. Recently however, they have decided to break away from their silent trust of the authorities, and have begun to defend and protect their fundamental rights as laborers, especially in light of revelations that the administrators from executive presidential space down to the lowly assistant to the Ministers are being rewarded timely and abundantly than poor civil servants and teachers. Many in these ranks have been working for many years without regular salaries and benefits being paid. These two organizations are now expanding their appeal to include major enterprises such as Federation of Minors at MIBA in Mbuji-Mayi, Tshikapa, and Kilo-

Moto, as well as the forest developers of Equator, Bandundu and Bas Congo provinces. According to the sale leaflet developed by the agents and civil servants of the State, any production or accumulations of the wealth, which take advantage only in a handle of the citizens of a country, are unbreakable.

According to the federations of teachers and civil servants, wealth produced or accumulated in these conditions in DRC should be stopped because they damage the nation in the same ways as the persons to whom they are provided or to those who take advantage of them (Muyumba 2001). Furthermore, the syndicates of teachers and Agents and Civil Servants seems to become even more radical by their bold effort to have the government recognize that they are citizens, and would not want their rights and privileges trampled. They are now aiming at the belly of the beast, the sources of state powers that is they want to mobilize workers as to refuse to facilitate even the services at the ministries for which they often provided and maintained minimal governmental activities without the due rewards.

Irritated by governmental inflexibility, and failure to respect contracts it has signed, they federations have opted to strike and to mobilize other workers to block all internal sources of revenues by which the leaders in powers raise money to deceive the people whom they are nevertheless supposed to serve and not harm. Clearly, in the traditions of Congolese labor organizations that had worked so hard to harness good incomes for workers in the last decade of colonization, today, the Federations of Agents and Civil Servants is applying the same principles and programs to mobilize and gain (win) the agents and the executives of the financial state control over the State at the cause of the people which condemns them for their indirect support for the animals of prey of economics by agreeing to bail out the boxes which are transformed finally into Danaïdes's barrels to the detriment of the national community (Muyumba 2001).

Overall, it can be established once and for all, that the more the NGOs in major cities become functional, the more they will influence development in provincial capitols, rural towns, and large village communities and districts. Presently, the expansion of wireless communication technology in the country is allowing for the first time, the availability of and access to information that were traditionally rare. The most important role of the Congolese NGOs appears to be involved in the education of their members. The millions of their country folks need such education and training. There is a higher expectation that once educated, these millions will be able to voice both their displeasure and pleasures in unison, or in particular so as to promote a clear and appreciable level of rededication of individuals and collective groups and civic organization to the defense of their human rights. Though many NGOs are still in infancy state, many other emergent organizations including the confessional organizations, labor Unions, and syndicate as well as federations of teachers health NGOs, etc., are turning into more experienced and savvy organizations that they are especially able to leave and return to the country for the purpose of further training, workshop, conferences, and seminars that prepare them to be even more organized and more efficiently effective.

In summary, the Congolese NGOs are gradually developing every year, and are determined to face courageously and boldly the multitudes of challenges. They will not however return to the 1970s era where Mobutu dominated and controlled everything. Most of decisions made about whether or not to get involved with certain countries, depend on the political stability and the level of democratization of the state.

Presently, the Transitional government is confronting its own political pressure from the NGOs as well as from the political parties and the people to move rapidly toward the organization and the implementation of transparent, and democratic elections at all levels so as to empower the people to participate in the decision-making process and identify and elect their governing authorities, the constitution, the type of state and government, and the political divisions of country (provinces or federated states) which would bring power back to them. While Western donors are still needed to assist in the development of NGOs, their influence and impact must be measured so that it does not overwhelming reach the level where the Congolese themselves might loose interests, or their unique capabilities to defend their own highest rights. Given that many African nations are squeezed by the decreasing number of donors willing to provide sufficient amount of dollars, and some are in return cutting off their commitment to provide resources for certain important services to the citizens, it is important that Western donors be encouraged to work cooperatively with local NGOs or to enable them to establish their own organizations to funds their preferred projects and render the private sectors more actives then before. Such use of local talent and skill, which uses the allocated funds, has a great performance track. It includes local people in projects to promote democracy, rather then granting such funds to the state directly. This resort to the grassroots organizations will require continuous training and assessment to determine just how effective the movement toward democracy is accomplishing its tasks.

Clearly, the role of democracy in transition in African nations is a significant milestone in road toward the final victorious day. Congolese NGOs are sensing it, and are forever involved into the development of a future, which will not see the people left out of their nation rendezvous with glorious destiny. Local NGOs such as Churches, Law Offices, have risen to oppose authoritarian rule in many places, countries and societies in hopes to achieve both physical well-beings for their people and social approval. That is in essence the real outcome of a successful democratization process.

In recent days, the Union for Democracy and Social Progress (UDPS) has under the leadership of Etienne Tshisekedi has accepted to participate in the planned general elections and presidential elections scheduled for March and April 2006. It is challenging the transition government, the people, the armed forces etc to line up and work toward democratization of the society. The UDPS itself had become the exemplary actor, by democratizing its own agencies and ways of electing officers, and institutionalizing its organs. It is carefully listening to the critical mass, to the critics of its actions, and it enjoys a large following between both the Catholic and Protestant Christians, just as solidarity was in Poland some years back.

The presence of the Protestant leaders within the governmental institutions such as House of Representative and Senate raises serious questions concerning Religious NGOs, but such presence could also be a balancing act. There is however a concern that NGOs general plans must not remain fixed at being contestants and defenders of human rights but that they must strive to become the consummate enforcers of human and civil rights. It is not possible to conclude this discussion without reiterating the fact that the Congolese society in indeed in transition from Mobutu's day of autocracy to a more democratic situation where the NGOs themselves exemplify the road toward shared governance between the state and the people. Depending upon the location of the analyst, the situation is not evenly distributed as the towns, cities and provinces located far away from the capital city Kinshasa may still reflect their marginalization and their peripheral existence. Nevertheless, a shift is observable, the state is having a very difficult time holding to its traditional roles as the sole voice, and it is gradually being provided with opportunity to extend its arms and share some of its traditional tasks with emergent organizations such a NGOs. It is important to recognize here the impact of UN Peace keeping forces, and especially the preponderant role of UN administrative system, which is recognized as part of the accompanying authority within this period of the transitional government in DRC has encouraged he proliferation of the NGOs, but, they are indeed changing the fabric of the nation.

There is a brief refrain of a new song in DRC about Africa, and it is sung by youthful choirs and congregations and it says repeatedly: Et l' Afrique sera sauvée, (bis) or And Africa will be saved. Perhaps the salvation of DRC and the Great Lakes region lies in its future or within its uncorrupted youthful NGOs.

References

Bamporiki, Chaira. "Black November Projected by the Congolese Labor Organization." *The Potential Newspaper*. Kinshasha: Laja bulela-unsubscribe@yahoo.com, November 2, 2005.

Dibie, Robert. *The Politics and Policies of Sub-Saharan Africa.* Lanham, MD: University Press of America, 2001.

Economic Report on Africa: Accelerating the Pace of Development. Ethiopia, Economic Commission For Africa, 2003.

Fanon, Frantz. *The Wretched of the Earth.* New York: Grover Press, 1993.

Foster J. Todd. "Out of Africa and Into History Books For Waynesboro's Sheppard." *The News Virginia*. Waynesboro, VA, July 24, 2005, A7.

Griffith, Phoebe. *Removing the Shackles: Strategies to Tackle Globalization*. London, International Communications, 2003.

Hobe, Stephan. *Global Challenges to Statehood: The Increasingly Important Role of Nongovernmental Organizations.* New York: Global Policy Forum, 1998. Globalpolicy @Globalpoly.org.

Hochschild, Adam. *King Leopold's Ghost: A Study of Greed, Terror and Heroism in Colonial Africa*. Boston: First Marine Book/Houghton Mifflin, 1999.

Institut Facultaire des Sciences de l'Information et de la Communication (IFASIC). La *Situation de l'Information et de la Communication en Republique Democratique du Congo.* Ministère de l'Education Nationale et Fonds des Nations Uninies pour l'Enfant. Kinshasa: UNICEF, 1999.

Lindenberg, S. M. "The New Political Economy: Its Potential and Limitations for the Social Sciences in *General and for Sociology in Particular.*" *Okonomische Erkldrung sozialen Verhaltens,* edited by W. Sodeur. Duisburg: Verlag dersozialwisschaftlichen Kooperative, 1983, 1-68.

Lindenberg, S. M., and B. Frey. "Alternatives, Frames and Relative Prices." *Acta Sociologica* 36 (1993): 191-205.

Martin, Guy. "Reading of Rwandan Genocide." *African Studies Review* 45, no. 3 (December 2002): 17-29.

Mueller, D. C. *Public Choice II.* Cambridge: Cambridge University Press, 1989.

Mueller, D. C., ed. *Perspective on Public Choice: A Handbook.* Cambridge: Cambridge University Press, 1997.

Muyumba, Francois N. "Environmental Policy in the Democratic Republic of Congo." *The Journal of African Policy Studies* 7 no. 2 and 3 (2001): 61-87.

Muyumba, Francois. "Politics in the Democratic Republic of Congo." In *The Politics and Policies of Sub-Saharan Africa,* edited by Robert Dibie. New York: University Press of America, 2001, 259-306.

Ndegwa, Stephen N. *The Two Faces of Civil Society: NGOs and Politics in Africa.* West Hartford, CT: Kumarian Press, 1996.

Nzongola-Ntalaja, Georges. *Class Struggle and National Liberation in Africa: Essays on Political Economy of Neo-Colonialism.* Roxbury, MA: Omenana, 1982.

Nzongola-Ntalaja, Georges. *The Congo From Leopold to Kabila: A People History.* London: Zed Books, 2002.

Nzongola-Ntalaja, Georges, and Margaret C. Lee, eds. *The State and Democracy in Africa.* Trenton, NJ: Africa World Press, Inc., 1997.

Osborne, P., and T. Gaebler. Reinventing *Government: How the entrepreneurial Spirit is Transforming the Public Sector.* Reading, MA: Addison Wesley, 1992.

Paul, James A. *NGOs and Global Policy-Making.* Global Policy Forum, New York. *Globalpolicy@globalpolicy.org* (January 6, 2006).

Phipps, William E. *William Sheppard: Congo's African-American Livingstone.* Louisville, KY: Geneva Press, 2002.

Sanberg, Eve. *The Changing Politics of Non-government Organization and African States.* New York: Praeger, 1994.

Welch, Claude. *Protecting Human Rights in Africa: The Roles and Strategies of NGOs. Ethiopia.* Lanham, MD: University of America Press, 2000.

Wilson, Richard A. *The Politics of Truth and Reconciliation in South Africa: Legitimizing the Post-Apartheid State.* Cambridge: Cambridge University Press, 2001.

World Bank Organization. www.worldbank.org (January 7, 2006).

Chapter 11

Strategic Repositioning of NGOs for Sustainable Development in Africa

Felix Moses Edoho

In African countries, there is estrangement between the governments and the governed (Hyden, 1983; Bratton, 1994). The masses lack access to public goods. Governments are often impervious to the plights of the citizens and unresponsive to their needs. Consequently, "a phalanx of . . . (NGOs) arise to fill the gaps left by governments" (Bratton, 1990:888). Unresponsiveness to local needs often heightens if the governments are unelected and accountability nonexistent. This has been the case during much of the post-independence era that military regimes have seized the political center stage and dotted Africa's landscape. In such instance, a genre of NGOs called "gap fillers" (Dicklitch, 1998) often steps in to provide essential services which, in many cases, have made the difference between life and death. The third sector designation also connotes the notion that NGOs represent one of the three vectors of the society, enjoying coequality and at par with the public and private sectors.

Growing interest in NGOs reflects their increasing importance and popularity as an empirical phenomenon (Mercer, 2002). Such interest also reflects the normative belief that NGOs are potentially institutional mechanisms of development alternatives (Drabek, 1987; Tandon, 2001). NGOs can function better where "market failure" and "state failure" have occurred (Hulme, 1994:253). Liberals celebrate NGOs as mechanisms for remedying the institutional weaknesses of the state and private sector and promoting socioeconomic development (Korten, 1990; Hulme, 1994). However, neo-liberals claim that NGOs are part of the private sector, noting their socioeconomic significance in delivering services to the poor cheaply, equitably, and efficiently (Hyden, 1983; Uphoff, 1993). "If there were to be a single statement which symbolized the fundamental message of neo-liberalism," Colclough (1991:7) averred, "it would be this . . . imperfect markets are better than imperfect states."

In Africa, there is a built-in disconnect between the government and the governed. Hyden (1983:19) remarked that postcolonial African states appear to be "suspended balloon-like in mid-air." Debilitating crisis ravaging sub-Saharan African countries has been attributed to the "deep estrangement between state and society" (Bratton, 1996:231, 1994:255; Hyden, 1983). Estrangement means unresponsiveness of state to demands for basic social welfare. Therefore, NGOs help to fill the institutional vacuum caused by unresponsive political system (Dicklitch, 1998). Bratton (1989:573) contrasts the ideological orientations of government vis-à-vis NGOs. "Whereas the state is driven by the organizational imperatives of administrative command and control, NGOs generally seek to inculcate autonomous and participatory action." The accessibility of NGOs' services to the masses earns them trust and legitimacy more than governments (Williams, 2003; Kaldor, 2003). Marie-Claude Smout observed that international NGOs derive "their legitimacy from their ability to make demands in terms of collective needs . . . [and] from their innovative capacity to suggest ways to meet those needs" (Mundy and Murphy, 2001:91).

Exacerbating the debilitating economic crisis have been natural disasters: droughts, poor harvest, and resultant famine and food crisis. This puts Africa in a position of perennially needing food aid. Statistics alone do not actually capture the scale of human suffering in the region. However, television frequently brings to limelight the vivid dimension of the human catastrophes in Africa. Pictures of dehydrated, malnourished, dying, and dead children are not happy sights. As I am writing, Niger is facing these dilemmas. This situation stirs the conscience of both the governments and NGOs in industrialized countries. While governments commonly provide aid through official channels, NGOs have been in the fields providing humanitarian relief: food, clothing, drugs, etc. In addition to directly providing assistance, international NGOs help nationals in various African countries to establish their local counterparts through which they channel relief materials and financial assistance (INTRAC 2004).

The world has recorded an upsurge of NGOs, but the trend has been particularly remarkable in Africa, Asia, and Latin America (Clarke, 1998). Growth of NGOs in Africa has been described as "explosive" (Williams, 2003). The worldwide phenomenal growth of NGOs and scale of their operations led Salamon (1994:109) to assert that "we are in the midst of global 'associational revolution' that may prove to be as significant to the latter twentieth century as the rise of the nation-state was to the later nineteenth century." A burgeoning literature captures the exponential growth of NGOs and pervasiveness of their operations in Africa (e.g., Bratton, 1989, 1990; 1996; Bornstein, 2002; Chazan, 1994; Dorman, 2003; Fowler, 1991; Hearn, 2002; INTRAC, 2004; Kaplan., 1994; Manji and O'Coill, 2004; Reuben, 2002; Salih, 2002; Waiguchu, 1999; Welch, 2003; Weiss, 2002).

This chapter proposes a strategic management paradigm for African non-governmental organizations (NGOs). This focus is grounded in the premise that for African NGOs to contribute to sustainable development, they must redefine themselves by adopting strategic vision and refocusing their energies. Kaplan

(1994:1) posits "the lack of adequate strategy to give effect to organizational vision" as one of the major factors militating against the effectiveness of NGOs in South Africa. Many NGOs in industrialized countries embrace private sector management techniques and systems to improve their operations (Oster, 1995:3). Embracing strategic management ideas will help African NGOs to prioritize their activities, realign their resources, and improve performance. Repositioning African NGOs for the challenges of sustainable development in the twenty-first century is a strategic imperative.

Elaboration of the central thesis in this chapter is organized into seven sections. Following this introductory segment is conceptual framework and theoretical assessment of NGOs. It provides both a frame of reference for understanding the phenomenon of NGOs and theoretical review of literature on the field. In section three, various reasons are adduced for the phenomenal growth of NGOs in Africa. Section four lays out a strategic management model that would be beneficial to African NGOs. Section five articulates the benefits of strategic management, while section six makes a case for building supportive capacity to facilitate the institutionalization strategic management in African NGOs. The last section provides a concluding summary for the paper.

Framework and Theoretical Assessment

NGO is an amorphous construct that subsumes a universe of multifaceted organizations of different origins and sizes undertaking diversified interventionist activities with varying levels of resources. NGOs are private, nonprofit entities endowed with distinct legal attributes, and they are concerned with public goods (Clarke, 1998). They cover a whole gamut of human engagements—arts, economic, educational, cultural, political, and social. Literature is inundated by various nomenclatures of what these organizations are and what they do. In this chapter, we will use NGOs to subsume all entities that fit the description on Table 11.1. NGOs range from private voluntary organizations, philanthropic foundations, to those entities committed to human rights, civil liberty, environmental issues, economic development, and humanitarian relief.

Charitable NGOs provide relief to refugees or endeavor to meet the needs of the poor, by distributing food, clothing, and medicine (e.g., International Red Cross, Doctors without Borders, American Refugee Committee). They also provide housing and schooling (e.g., Habitat for Humanity International, Save the Children). NGOs with policy analysis and community development focus serve to strengthen and enhance the capacity of local organizations and communities by collaborating with and empowering or helping them to initiate social and economic development activities. Environmental NGOs work to create, and sensitize communities to, sustainable social and economic development by using sound environment practices and policies. Services-oriented NGOs provide educational, family planning, and health programs for the needy. Human rights and civil liberty NGOs seek to open up the political space for mass participation.

Even within given specie of NGOs, there are sub-species. Within the human rights genre, for instance, Welch (1995) distinguished six different types of NGOs in terms of their strategies: education, empowerment, enforcement, documentation, democratization, and development. Our focus is decidedly limited to those NGOs that are constituted for the specific purpose of promoting community economic development. Activities of such NGOs are geared toward building the African communities as the foundation for sustainable development. Such NGOs, as Bratton (1989:569) noted, "promise to strengthen . . . people's abilities to improve their own lives."

Table 11.1
Descriptive Understanding of NGOs

Acronym	Description
BONGO	Business Organized Non-Governmental Organization
FONGO	Funder Organized Non-Governmental Organization
NFP	Not For Profit
NPO	Nonprofit Organization
NGDO	Non-Governmental Development Organization
NFGO	Not for Gain Organization
NGO	Non-Governmental Organization
PONGO	Political Non-Governmental Organization
PVO	Private Voluntary Organization
GONGO	Government Organized Non-Governmental Organization
QUANGO	Quasi Autonomous Non-Governmental Organization

These NGOs not only mobilize and harness local resources, but also leverage international resources and work toward changing the existential realities in African communities. NGOs in this group seek to enact change by working to improve the social and economic conditions of the populace—be they in terms of helping people to develop skills set for productive employment; training farmers to adopt modern farming techniques and providing technical assistance, mobilizing communities to pave access roads; or sinking boreholes to provide portable drinking water for communities. Evidence shows that such NGOs have been quite successful in improving access to water, sanitation facilities, and primary health services in Africa (Bratton, 1989:572).

Another operational differentiation of NGOs in Africa is their origins and locus of control—the determinant of power and location of decision-making authority. Research found that although NGOs from North America and European countries (Northern NGOs) may depend on partnership with African NGOs to obtain funding from their donors, "the power in the relationship remains outside Africa" (INTRAC, 2004:8). Hulme (1994:258) offers a typological delineation of NGOs based on their geographic origins: northern NGOs (NNGOs) based in donor countries and almost always directed by northerners; intermediate southern NGOs (SNGOs) that operate at the national level or across several regions within a developing country; and membership organizations (MO) comprising members from a localized area and managed by the membership.

It is imperative to note that foreign NGOs in Africa have external locus of control even when they are managed by nationals of African countries. Thus, we focus on SNGOs (Hulme, 1994), or what are actually national NGOs (Bratton, 1990:106). These NGOs are established and managed by nationals of African countries. These nationals have full power and decision making authority. National NGOs have internal locus of control. Contextually, our proposal of strategic management is targeted at the national NGOs. Building the strategic management capacities of these NGOs is the key to actualizing sustainable development in Africa.

Conceptual Framework

NGOs have been broadly conceptualized as "the mediating structures" (Berger and Neuhaus, 1990) and as constituting the "third sector" (Hulme, 1994; Van Rooy, 2001; Werther and Berman, 2001) of society. Figure 11.1 captures these twin notions of NGOs. The mediating structure conceptualization suggests a void in the society that neither the public nor private sector fills, or can fill. Thus, NGOs emerge as the third sector, essentially straddling both sectors, carrying out activities left undone or done inefficiently and ineffectively, by the public and public sectors. The inherent inability of the private and public sectors to meet societal needs lies at the heart of state and market failures (Hulme, 1994). The public, private, and third sectors all derive impetus and legitimacy from the society. However, the degree of freedom that NGOs enjoy at a given time in any society depends on the nature of government in power. Bratton (1989:572) noted that "the amount of space allowed to NGOs in any given country is determined first and foremost by political consideration, rather than by any calculation of the contributions of NGOs to economic and social development." The vicissitudes of NGOs in Kenya (Copestake, 1993) and Zimbabwe (Dorman, 2003) amply illustrate the point.

Nonetheless, literature considers NGOs more as a vital component of the civil society (Hearn, 2002; Kaldor, 2003; Kaplan, 1994; Van Rooy, 2001). As a construct itself, civil society appears to encompass all residual organizations that, by virtue of their activities, cannot be easily classified as either belonging purely in the public or private sector. As Dwayne Wood observed, civil society is "becoming an all-encompassing term to refer to social phenomenon putatively beyond formal state structures, but not necessarily free of all contact with the state" (quoted in Chazan, 1994:255). Civil society covers all "organizations and institutions that stand outside of state structure" (Kaplan, 1994:2). These organizations occupy the "middle ground between communal groups and state structure" (Chazan, 1994:255). NGOs are a mechanism that "mediate[s] between State and market excesses" (Van Rooy, 2001:27).

Theoretical Assessment:

There is ample theorizing on the logic and phenomenon of NGOs—why they persist and even thrive (e.g., Ben-Ner, 1986). Hansmann (1987) identified four theories advanced to explain the presence of NGOs in the market economy: public goods, contract failure, government subsidies, and consumer control. First is that NGOs produce public goods beyond those produced by governments (Weisbrod, 1974)? Second is contract failure. As articulated by Hansmann (1987), "nonprofits of all types typically arise in situations in which, owing either to the circumstances under which a service is purchased or consumed or to the nature of the service itself, consumers feel unable to evaluate accurately the quantity or the quality of the service a firm produces for them" (p. 29). Third are government subsidies. Fama and Jensen (1983), among others, argued that various government subsidies, such as tax exemption, reduced postal rates, and other favorable regulatory treatments, contributed to the presence and growth of NGOs. Fourth is consumer control. Hansmann (1980) and others argued that for mutual-benefit entities that provide services solely to their members, the desire for control by members explains the choice of nonprofit as organizational form.

In the context of the New Policy Agenda (Commins, 1997; Hulme and Edwards, 1997), organized around the twin pillars of neo-liberal economics and liberal democratic theory, NGOs are preferred channels for service provision in deliberate substitution for the state (Edwards and Hulme, 1995:4). Rooted in this framework, Colclough (1991) contended that governments should not be directly involved in providing social services; their role should be limited to providing and maintaining an "enabling environment." Korten (1990) distinguished among three generations of NGOs: the first is committed to relief and welfare activities; the second to small-scale, local development projects; and the third to community organization, mobilization, and coalition-building. This typology highlights the central ideological propensity of contemporary NGOs and draws attention to second and third generation NGOs the fastest growing category. Relief and welfare NGOs, the largest group in the developing countries, are engaged in charitable activities and are apolitical.

Development NGOs seek to weaken and overcome the dependency of their "first generation" counterparts. They use activities such as primary health care programs and agricultural cooperatives to organize and mobilize peasants, helping them to challenge the local elite. These NGOs are politically engaged. Lastly, the "third generation" NGOs are those that focus on conscientization and mobilization leading to direct intervention in political conflicts (Clarke, 1990). In her critical study of Uganda, Dicklitch (1998) identified three major varieties of NGOs based on their relations with government. First, "gap fillers" operate in the absence or weakness of government institutions. Second, "people's organizations" are often opposed to particular regimes, mobilizing popular support as a means. Finally, "voluntary organizations" seek to act as intermediaries between the state and affected individuals and/or grassroots NGOs that represent them.

Figure 11.1
The Structural Role of NGOs in Society

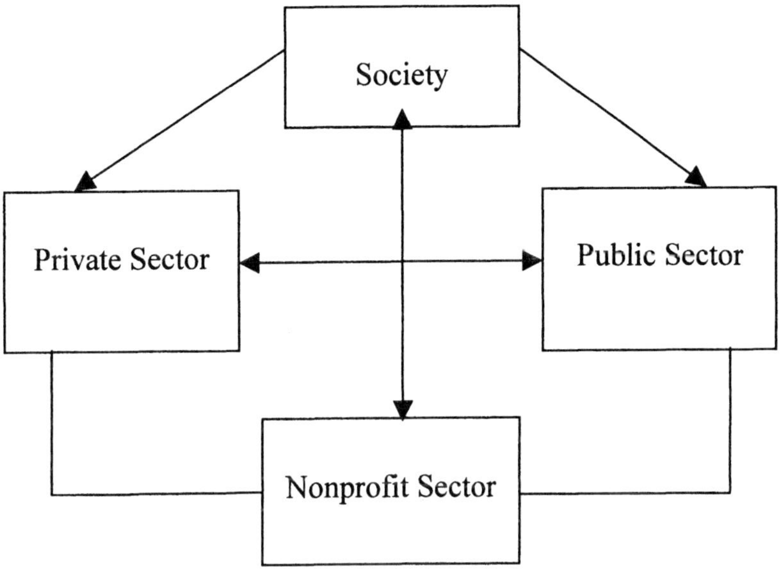

There are conflicting findings relative to the intriguing question of whether or not the proliferation of NGOs has resulted in political change and economic development in the developing countries. Hirschman (1987:98) contends that it is impossible to prove a relationship between the withering of the authoritarian state in Latin America and the rise of NGOs and grassroots social movements. Sanyal (1994:40) argues that "the political impact of bottom-up [NGO] projects has been . . . less striking than their economic impact." If NGOs do not contribute to political change, the reason is not far-fetched. NGOs may have voice, but not vote (Williams, 2003).

A study by Alan Fowler concluded that Kenya's NGO community is unable to hasten fundamental political change, because of its fragmentation, competitiveness, and unrepresentative structure. Thus, NGOs are more likely to maintain status quo than change the political landscape (Clarke, 1998). Welch (2003:325) found that: "African human rights NGOs ameliorate rather than transform situations. They monitor and analyze, rather than achieve rapid, blanket changes. They take gradual steps rather than massive leaps." However, NGOs are believed to have played a "vital role in [the] process" of political change (Chazan, 1994:276) in Africa, where they have also been instrumental in pluralizing the institutional environment by encouraging political participation (Bratton, 1989). Edwards and Hulme (1995:20) contend that dependence on official funding "emasculate[s] NGO attempts to serve as catalysts for the poor."

Yet, successes of NGOs in securing policy reforms are widely acknowledged. Clark (1991), Edwards (1993), UNDP (1993), and Storey (2001) all noted that working in concert, Northern and Southern NGOs have contributed to influencing policy changes by their governments as well as multilateral agencies like the World Bank and IMF. Clark (1991:150) documents NGOs' involvement and successes in influencing various policy changes: the baby-milk marketing code, the drafting of an international essential drugs list, trade liberalization for clothing manufactured in the South, an EU emergency food reserve for the provision of famine relief, action on global warming and rainforest destruction, debt relief to African countries, and the imposition of sanction to combat apartheid in South Africa.

Edwards (1993:116) enumerated the influence of NGOs on World Bank policies relative to gender, participation, poverty, and the environment; cancellation of, or modification to, World Bank projects; movement away from vertical interventions in health-sector investment; improvement in food regimes for refugees and displaced people; modification of IMF-imposed structural adjustment programs to take greater account of their social ramifications. Storey (2001) argues that "Adjustment has generated a great deal lobbying and campaigning effort on the part of NGOs around the world, aiming to highlight the claimed misconceptions, shortcomings, and failures of structural adjustment."

Despite their humanitarian credentials, however, African intellectuals increasingly view foreign NGOs with skepticism and suspicion. They see foreign NGOs' operations in Africa through the prism of their colonial antecedents (e.g., Waiguchu, 1999; Manji and O'Coill, 2002; Welch, 2003). They assert that the role of foreign NGOs in African development represents a continuity of the work of their precursors, the missionaries and voluntary organizations that cooperated in Europe's colonization and control of Africa" (Manji and O'Coill, 2004:2). With particular reference to missionaries, Welch (2003:317) states that many Africans like to summarize their colonial experience into two sentences: "First they had the Bible and we had the land. Then we had the Bible and they had the land."

African Environment and Proliferation of NGOs

A plethora of literature examines the phenomenon of NGOs, their activities, and their exponential growth in Africa (e.g., Bratton, 1989, 1990; Bornstein, 2002; Fowler, 1991; Hearn, 2002; Manji and O'Coill, 2002; Salih, 2003; Waiguchu, 1999; Welch, 2003). Africa is widely acclaimed for a strong tradition of charity, community self-help, and welfare institutions. This partly accounts for unqualified receptivity of African countries to NGOs. Bratton (1989:571) traced the origins of the contemporary NGOs in Africa to the period of emergent nationalism. During this period, NGOs sprang up "in the forms of ethnic welfare groups, professional associations and separatist churches which articulated the demands of newly modernized Africans."

The global image of Africa is that of poor leadership, mismanagement, and official corruption. As a result, Africa has become synonymous with poverty, political instability, social unrest, and genocidal civil wars. Thus, to think of

Africa is to think of poverty (O'Connor, 1991:1). Proliferation of NGOs in Africa needs to be understood in this context. As interventionist agencies, NGOs are perceived as efficacious institutional mechanisms to help change this Afro-pessimistic environment. This partly explains why Africa is region where "the best and the worst examples of NGOs can be found" (World Resources Institute, 2003). This has fueled a concern about the emerging trend toward "NGO-isation" (Hearn, 2002:35) of African society. Our primary focus in this segment is to discuss the magnitude of NGOs in Africa and to identify the factors that have contributed to their proliferation and blossoming in the region.

Magnitude of NGOs in Africa:

It is difficult to determine the actual number of NGOs in Africa. Part of the difficulty lies in the classificatory schemes that may either include or exclude certain organizations. Overall, determination of the actual population of NGOs in Africa would require census in individual countries. Absent this approach, whatever figure is used would be only an estimate at best and should be used with caution. Waiguchu (1999:374) estimated 600,000-800,000 NGOs in Africa. This figure encompasses all organizations that exhibit characteristics of nonprofit or voluntary organizations. Over one-half of the figures are religious-based, while the rest represent nonsectarian nonprofit variety (Waiguchu, 1999:374).

Most of the NGOs in Africa are concentrated in a few countries. Nigeria, Kenya, Egypt, South Africa, Ethiopia, Ghana, Cote d'Ivoire, Zimbabwe, Uganda, Tanzania, Zambia, and Senegal are axis of heavy concentration of NGOs in Africa (World Resources Institute, 2003; Waiguchu, 1999). However, it is estimated that Nigeria and Kenya are homes to larger numbers of NGOs in Africa (Waiguchu, 1999:374). Data show that between 1980 and 2000, NGOs in 17 African countries increased from 1,854 to 5,896. In Nigeria, they increased from 1,350 to 4,028. During the period, Islamic NGOs also increased from 138 to 891 (Salih, 2002: Table 1).

During 1980-1988, grassroots self-help organizations in Kenya surged from less than 5,000 to 26,000 (Fowler, 1991). The number of foreign NGOs in Kenya almost tripled to 134 from 1978 to 1988 (Fowler, 1991; Williams, 2003). About 40 percent of development NGOs in Kenya is foreign, representing 204 out of 511 NGOs. The Friedrich Ebert Stiflung Foundation data shows that between 1961 and 1980, there were only 25 registered NGOs in Tanzania. By 1990, the number increased to 41. Between 1990 and 1993, the number surged to 224, and since 1996 over 6,000 NGOs have been registered. According to the Registrar of Societies, Tanzania had 8,499 NGOs as of September 1998. By December 2000, there were over 10,000 registered NGOs. In Uganda, there are over 1,000 NGOs (in Reuben, 2002). Data cited by Van Rooy (2003:33) indicates that there were 800 registered NGOs in Ghana in 1998.

Church and Growth of NGOs:

Clarke (1998) observed that Catholic Church has been a major force behind the proliferation of NGOs in Latin America, the Philippines, and Africa. A recent study by Hearn (2002) indicates significant growth of evangelical NGOs in Kenya. Salih (2002) also indicates growth of Islamic NGOs in Africa. Missionaries came to Africa *pari passu* with colonial incursion, conquest, subjugation, and occupation of the continent. While colonial regimes were busy establishing infrastructure of the political economy for surplus extraction and appropriation, the missionaries were engaged in evangelizing and proselytizing the natives. The role of churches in Africa reflected the normative theme of the civilizing mission or *mission civilisatrice* (Welch, 2003:317) that was used to justify colonial intervention in Africa.

Missionaries built churches for the new converts; schools to teach and inculcate in students the basic Christian religious ethos, beliefs, and values; and community health centers to attend to the physically sick (Bornstein, 2002; Waiguchu, 1999; Welch, 2003). For religious NGOs, realms of the material and spiritual are joined, and economic development and salvation are coterminous. The welfare propensity of religious NGOs is rooted in the theology of holism. Thus, "holistic development is the preferred solution to any problem: do not just take care of people's material needs, feed them spiritually as well" (Bornstein, 2002:10). This orientation, coupled with the need to expand faith-based activities, contributed to the growth of NGOs in Africa. Religious-based NGOs, local welfare and self-help institutions, and ethnic associations were the dominant expressions of NGOs in Africa in the 1960s.

Table 11.2 shows the statistics cited by the World Resources Institute (2003) tend to capture the magnitude of NGOs and their activities in Kenya:

Table 11.2
NGOs Activities in Kenya

NGOs Activities in Kenya	Statistics
Number of voluntary nonprofit organizations (including informal Organizations), 2002	150,000
Number of government-registered NGOs, 2003	2,511
Percentage of hospitals run by NGOs, 1999	50.2%
Percentage of health clinics/medical centers run by NGOs, 1999	87.1%
Percentage of nursing/maternity homes run by NGOs, 1999	100%

Military Regimes and Political Alienation:

For Africa, the 1960s were a watershed and an extraordinary decade because it ushered in decolonization tidal waves that reverberated throughout the region. Concomitant political independence of many African countries that were hitherto colonial territories evoked widespread rhetorical optimism. However, the euphoria was premature as military personnel seized the control of political authority. Ever since then, the legitimacy of military rule had been seriously contested (Joseph, 1996:193). Military regimes are antithetical to democratic culture of competitive politics and democratic participation. They proscribed political parties, banned political activities, restricted civil liberty, limited freedom of expression, and infringed on human rights of the citizens. NGOs have emerged to press military regimes to open up political space; respect the basic human rights of their citizens; and to grant them civil liberty.

This had been the case in Nigeria during the 1980s. The proliferation of human rights and civil liberty NGOs in Nigeria climaxed with the annulment of presidential election in the early 1990s. In many instances, and against all odds, these NGOs held mass rallies to protest military brutality. Given the history of prolonged military interventions in African politics, coupled with the decay of political parties and institutions, NGOs have helped to "pluralize the institutional environment and . . . encourage participation in decision making [and] promote democratic culture" (Bratton, 1989:570); they have also helped to strengthen civil society by contributing to differentiation of structures and expansion in political participation (Clarke, 1998). Since the military left the political scene, in what has been termed the "wave of the second independence" in the 1990s (Welch, 2003:318), these NGOs have become accountability watchdogs for civil liberty and human rights.

Depressing Economic Environment:

The 1970s were touted as a decade of economic nationalism. Yet, Africa was worse off to the extent that the 1970s were declared the "lost decade." Even the World Bank that had been overly optimistic about the prospects of economic growth in Africa had to admit that on the average, African people were "as badly off at the end of the decade as they were at the beginning" and the region had "the most disturbing outlook" compared to other regions (World Bank, 1980). This grim economic scenario was exacerbated by recurrent droughts and civil wars in Angola, Chad, Ethiopia, Mozambique, Sudan, Somalia, and Uganda (Salih, 2002). Foreign humanitarian NGOs responded to the resultant refugee crisis and human tragedies by providing relief and working through local NGOs (INTRAC, 2004).

The 1980s were a decade of widespread disillusionment and unrelieved Afro-pessimism. Whatever was left in Africa as a vestige of "hope for development had turned into prospect of decay (Glickman, 1988: 9). This environment led to a marked mushrooming of both local and foreign NGOs during the 1980s. Dubbed the "decade of NGOs" (Bratton, 1989:569; Nelson and Wright, 1995:181) and "NGO revolution" (Hearn, 2002:44), the 1980s witnessed exponential "increase in foreign NGO activities, particularly in relief and rehabilitation in war-torn countries" (Salih, 2002). National economies in African countries during the 1980s witnessed increasing disparity between the few that benefited from the neo-liberal economic restructuring and the masses for whom structural adjustment policy meant economic hardship (Bond, 1998). The World Bank (1986:9) observed that: "For the first time since World War II a whole region has suffered retrogression over a generation." This explains why NGOs proliferated and their humanitarian activities gained prominence in Africa.

Every decade has witnessed deteriorating economic conditions in Africa. By 1990, most African countries were on the brink of collapse. In 1985, 45.6 percent of the population in the region lived below poverty line; by 1990, that increased to 47.8 percent; and 49.7 was projected for 2000. Of the thirty-three countries the World Bank classified as low-income economies in 1992, twenty were African countries. In 1992, there were forty-three low-income economies of which twenty-eight were in Africa. Data also indicated that Africa also contained eight of the twelve poorest countries in the world, and eleven of the twelve countries with the lowest average life expectancy (World Bank, 1992).

A United Nations Development Program (UNDP, 2003:38-41) report indicated that, in the 1990s, children under five were nineteen times more likely to die in Africa than in industrialized countries; but in 2003, they were twenty-six times more likely. During 1990-1999, the percentage of people living on US$1 a day in Africa increased from 47.4 to 49 percent. Three out of four countries that experienced a drop in their human development index (HDI) during 1980-1990 were in Africa, while thirteen out of the twenty-one countries that saw a sharp drop in their HDI during 1990-2000 were also in the region. The same report concluded that although the number of poor people increased in all developing regions, it was staggering in Africa "where an additional 74 million people, the population of the Philippines, ended the decade in extreme poverty" (p. 41).

Environmental Crisis:

African countries have mono-product and extractive economies. As such, they are dependent heavily on one product for their foreign exchange, and in many cases the product is mineral. For example, Nigeria obtains over 80 percent of its foreign exchange income from export of crude oil; Sierra Leone depends on export of diamond for over 60 percent of its foreign exchange; while copper provides Zambia with 85 percent of foreign exchange earnings. Extractive industries are capital-intensive, and they are dominated by transnational corporations. These corporations do not exercise due diligence and do not practice corporate social responsibility.

Extractive industries are major sources of environmental degradation, particularly groundwater contamination and air pollution. These issues have galvanized communities into action. Various environmental NGOs have emerged around the issue of environmental protection. In the Niger Delta region of Nigeria, numerous NGOs have been established to tackle oil companies and to put the Nigerian government to task on environmental protection. In this region, oil firms have rendered farmland wasteland; local communities have declared war against oil firms as a result of prolonged gas flaring, frequent oil spills; blowouts; oil pipeline explosions; and fire outbreaks. Working in alliance with their international counterparts, environmental NGOs have exposed the recklessness of oil firms in the Niger Delta region, drawing attention of the global community to the environmental disasters and human rights abuses (Wright, 2002).

Foreign Aid:

Proliferation of NGOs in Africa has been attributed to the international aid regime (INTRAC, 2004). A good number of development NGOs in Africa have been established by funds supplied through foreign aid. Governments of the industrialized countries have become disenchanted with corrupt African governments who have mismanaged and, in most cases, embezzled foreign aid. Consequently, they see NGOs increasingly as viable institutional alternative (Drabek, 1987; Tandon, 1997) that could help to register positive impact of foreign aid. NGOs today is a prominent part of the "international aid regime" (INTRAC, 2004:6) or "development machine" a vast institutional and disciplinary nexus of official agencies, practitioners, consultants, scholars, and other miscellaneous experts producing and consuming knowledge about development world (Manji and O'Coill, 2002; Williams, 2003).

This development machine is propelled by the New Policy Agenda (Edwards and Hulme, 1997; Macdonald, 1997), sometimes called "Washington Consensus" (Joseph, 201:149). The Director of Policy and Planning at the World Vision, largest evangelical NGO, posits that:

> NGOs . . . are faced with the emergence of the New Policy Agenda (NPA) . . . The donor-driven NPA emphasizes the central importance of free markets, efficient use of limited government resources, a reduced role for the state and the need for good governance in the low income countries . . . As NGOs consider the impact of global trends and their linkages with the New Policy Agenda, a serious complication is the growing incorporation of NGOs into the policy agendas of donor agencies . . . The New Policy appears to call NGOs to . . . serve as implementers of public sector donor priorities (Commins, 1997:141).

Donor-driven and grounded in neo-liberal democratic ideology and market theology, the new agenda canvasses rolling back the state and increasing role for non-state entities, such as NGOs. The symbiotic relationships between the governments of industrialized countries and NGOs from their home countries are defined by the new policy framework. In addition to individual governments, the European Union and multilateral institutions, such as the United Nations, the World Bank, and the International Monetary Fund (IMF) strongly promote

NGOs as development alternative in developing countries (Clarke, 1998; Hearn, 2002; Werther and Berman, 2001). They "not only promote the idea of NGOs as legitimate institutions in policy design and implementation but also fund them" (Hearn, 2002:34).

NGOs form part of the "aid chain networks linked to international aid and cooperation, and channeling funds and other resources and other resources for the purpose of fostering social change" (Bebbington, 2004:727; INTRAC, 2004). In the early 1970s, less than two percent of NGO income came from official sources; but by mid-1990s, that surged to 30 percent (Williams, 2003). It is estimated that during 1980-1993, the total spending by NGOs in the OECD countries surged from US$2.8 billion to US$5.7 billion in current prices (Edwards and Hulme, 1995). In 1994, CARE, the largest NGO in the world had a budget of US$400 million, Catholic Relief Services, US$300 million, and World Vision, US$300 million (InterAction, cited in Hearn, 2002:44).

Leading other Western countries is the U.S. government that disburses some 40 percent of its global development assistance via NGOs; 90 percent of the U.S. aid program, administered by the USAID in Kenya, is channeled through NGOs and private sector organizations, such as evangelical churches (Hearn, 2002). The British Overseas Development Institute reported that, in 1992, NGOs distributed between 10 percent and 15 percent of all aid transfers to developing countries (Williams, 2003). The British Department for International Development allocates about eight percent of its aid budget to NGOs. During 1984-1994, the British Government increased its funding to NGOs by 400 percent (Fowler, 1991; Williams, 2003). Reports of the World Bank indicate that 12 percent of the foreign aid to developing countries was channeled through NGOs in 1994. In 1996, the total amount involved was US$7 billion worldwide. Today, NGOs in Africa manages about US$3.5 billion in foreign aid. In 2002, NGOs were involved in 70 percent of the World Bank projects, compared to 50 percent in the previous years (*New York Times*, March 22, 2002). The magnitude of foreign aid channeled to non-state actors has fueled the phenomenal growth of NGOs worldwide.

A Strategic Management Model for African NGOs

Strategic management embodies executive decisions and actions that inform the long-term performance of an organization (Wheelen and Hunger, 2004:2). The process of strategic management can be conceptualized as comprising four interrelated stages: articulation of vision and mission statements, strategy formulation, strategy implementation, and strategy evaluation and control. Figure 11.2 provides a simplified strategic management model for African NGOs. The model contains the major components that give strategic management its distinctive identity.

Vision and mission: An organization's vision statement captures the ostensible aspirations of its leadership and provides a panoramic view of where the organization is heading (Thompson and Strickland, 2003; Pearce and Robinson, 2005:37). It expresses the organization's strategic intent. It is ennobling statement of what NGOs are and what they are striving to become. It provides a glimpse into what the NGOs' world would look like if they achieve their mission. Organizations commonly realign their energies and resources with their strategic intent. Vision should create a shared meaning and purpose. It should inspire and spur people to action, and it should be empowering. There is a view that developing a vision statement is the first step in strategic planning, even preceding mission statement (David, 2005:9).

Whereas vision statement is more futuristic and embodies NGOs' aspirations, mission statement provides an existential rationale for the NGOs. It expresses the reason that organization exists and the products or services it provides to the society. The mission of most NGOs typically to fill an observed need in some defined community in altruistic manner.

Figure 11.2
Strategic Management Model

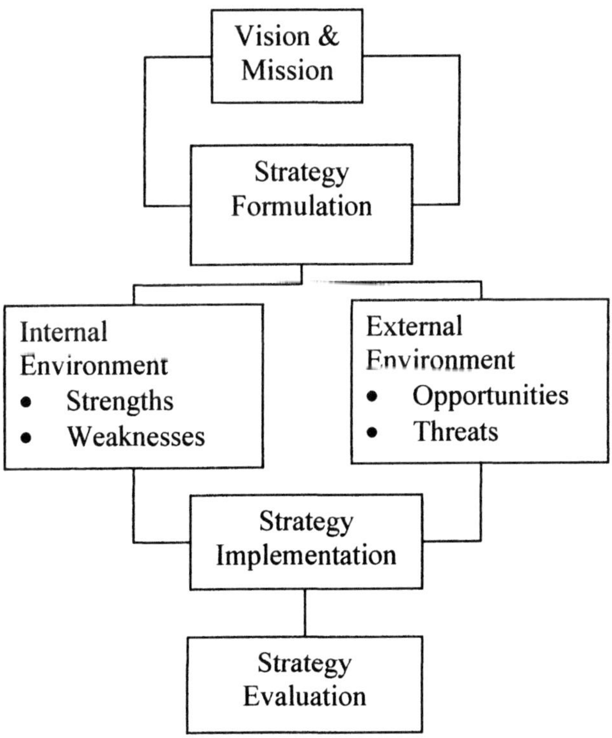

As NGOs mature, their mission may need reevaluation and modification. In fact the success of maturing NGOs is bound to affect, and almost always change, the needs and expectations of beneficiaries (Drucker, 1989). Generally, mission differentiates one organization from the others (Wheelen and Hunger, 2004:10-11).

African NGOs needs to articulate and elaborate on both their vision and mission, which should embody their strategic aspirations, uniqueness, distinctiveness, and corporate identity. Today, African NGOs are falling over themselves in an effort to be relevant; they try to be all things to all communities. Most of them hardly know why they exist and where they are heading. In an attempt to be everything at all times, without actually defining their visions and developing the strategies to actualize them, they tend to overextend themselves by becoming embroiled in issues that are either mundane or beyond their capacity and limited resources.

Strategy formulation: This stage of the strategic management process entails determining strategic objectives for the purpose of crafting strategies for the entire organization. A typical hierarchy of objectives for African NGOs would be: corporate objectives, which articulate organization's overall direction and attitude toward growth and management of various units; business objectives, which establish what individual units should strive to achieve; and functional objectives, which define the level of support to be provided for the NGOs to achieve strategic objectives. Strategies are crafted at three corresponding levels: corporate-level strategies deal with what the NGOs intends to do to achieve their corporate objectives; business-level strategies focus on. How they intend to compete; while functional-level strategies involve actions taken by the functional units to support corporate- and business-level strategies to achieve objectives. Associated with this is determination of policies.

To actually formulate effective strategies, however, NGOs must conduct in-depth study of their internal and external environments. A popular framework for undertaking such a study is SWOT (S = strengths; W – weaknesses; O = opportunities; T = threats) analysis. Within the internal environment, NGOs must identify their strengths and weaknesses. Strengths would enable NGOs to take advantage of the opportunities and respond to threats in the external environment. Strengths involve internal capabilities are abilities that become the tools or building blocks of strategy (Prahadad and Hamel, 1990).

NGOs internal capabilities are competencies that can easily be imitated by competitors. However, core competencies are capabilities that are unique to individual organizations and cannot be easily duplicated, and are central to the mission attainment (Prahadad and Hamel, 1990; Wheelen and Hunger, 2004). By contrast, weaknesses expose NGOs to external environmental threats and impede their ability to achieve their strategic goals.

External environmental analysis enables NGOs to assemble information and data that would enable them to identify both actual and potential opportunities and threats. NGOs exist in a larger general operating environment, encompassing cultural, sociological legal, technological, governmental/political, and regulatory dimensions. Changes in any of these dimensions can impact the vision, mission, and strategies of NGOs. For example, changes in the regulatory dimension may affect fundraising. The logic of environmental analysis is to match NGOs' internal strengths with external opportunities, and to minimize internal weaknesses relative to external threats.

Until NGOs understand the nature of external threats facing them and the opportunities they could exploit, on the one hand, and the internal capabilities and resource base they have, on the other, it would be extremely difficult if not impossible for them to formulate appropriate strategies. While the vision defines what the NGOs strive toward and the mission defines what it will do to get there, strategies address how NGOs will go about achieving their mission (McLaughlin, 1999). Strategy formulation enables NGOs to generate information that would help them make strategic choices and decisions, and to translate them into strategic plans. Strategic plan is the blueprint that embodies NGOs' strategic goals as well as game plans specifying how the goals would be achieved.

Strategy implementation: This is the process of putting into action the strategies and policies that NGOs formulated. It involves developing programs, budgets, and procedures to be followed by all employees at all levels. To ensure successful implementation of strategies, it might be necessary to change or modify the NGOs' leadership, culture, and structure. Strategy implementation may warrant a reappraisal of the entire management system to determine a "fit" along several dimension: between the strategic vision/direction and key personnel (how do they fit in); between strategies and culture (are the strategies compatible with the traditional ways of how things are done); and between strategy and structure (is the existing structural configuration adequate/suitable for present strategies). The result of these inquiries might require significant realignment of resources to achieve strategic goals.

Strategy evaluation: This stage of the strategic management process involves monitoring activities, generating feedbacks, and assessing the results of corporate operations, performance, and productivity. NGOs must measure the results of their performance against established strategic goals and objectives. Productivity must be measured against standards. Performance is the end results obtained from a given activity. Strategy evaluation system enables NGOs to determine whether or not they have achieved their goals; whether or not their strategies work; and whether or not they need to fine-tune their management systems given the feedbacks.

Benefits of Strategic Perspective for African NGOs

Certain benefits will accrue to African NGOs by institutionalizing strategic management paradigm. Such benefits stem from the fact that NGOs that begin with clear and simple objectives are most likely to be effective at achieving their goals.

Pragmatism: Strategic management is an exercise in pragmatism. Adopting the paradigm will enable African NGOs to be more pragmatic and proactive, rather than passive and reactive in defining and shaping their own future. From a historical standpoint, the major benefit that accrues to organizations that adopt a strategic management framework has been to help such organizations to formulate better strategies by using logical and rational approach to making critical choices (David, 2005). Strategic perspective is empowering in the fundamental sense that it equips organizations to initiate and influence, rather than passively respond to, changes in the external environment. In this regard, African NGOs will be better positioned to anticipate and influence environmental changes as well as exert control over their own destiny.

Culture: Embracing strategic management view will enable African NGOs to put in place a culture that will inform corporate behavior. Consequently, the executives will commit themselves to systematic, periodic, and critical management review and audit of their operational performance on a continuing basis. Strategic management creates a functional culture that is empowering. When people are empowered, they are more likely to take initiatives; they will also poise to be creative and innovative. Institutionalizing the strategic management culture in African NGOs will concomitantly condition their mindsets relative to acceptable behavior and level of performance. Research indicates that the process, rather than the decision or blueprint *per se*, is the more important contribution of strategic management perspective to organizations (Langley, 1988).

Competition: African NGOs operate in a competitive global environment. They compete in the global network for financial assistance and information sharing to support their operations in an age that the traditional funding sources are dwindling. Within this global network are NGOs from other developing regions (for example, Latin America, South America, and Asia). African NGOs also compete with the private sector for recruitment and hiring of qualified personnel. On both cases, the intensity of competition, even among African NGOs themselves, is escalating. The implication is that NGOs that demonstrate strategic orientation and posturing are more likely to earn credibility to attract external financial support. Those NGOs will readily utilize their strategic management blueprints as a marketing tool. They will have competitive advantage over those without it.

Efficiency: Strategic management will encourage operational efficiency of African NGOs. It will help them to optimize the allocation of their limited resources. Evidence in the private sector indicates conclusively that organizations that use strategic management approach are more profitable and successful than their counterparts that do not (Schwenk and Schrader, 1993; Miller and Cardinal, 1994; Peel and Bridge, 1998; Smith, 1998). Although such findings apply to research in the profit-making entities, the essential principle is that internal operational efficiency is a contributory factor to high performance and success. Having in place policies and procedures that employees understand and follow tend to enhance efficiency by lowering costs.

Non-financials: Greenley (1986) had provided a robust list of the non-financial benefits of strategic management to organizations. These include: identification, prioritization, and exploitation of opportunities; allocation of time and resources to identified opportunities; providing a framework for improved coordination and control of activities; encouragement of forward thinking; constituting a basis for clarifying individual responsibilities; and offering a cooperative, integrated, and enthusiastic approach to tackling problems and opportunities. These non-financial benefits will also accrue to African NGOs if they embrace the strategic management.

Building Supportive Capacity for Strategic Management

For African NGOs to contribute to sustainable development, they need to build and enhance their capacities in order to institutionalize strategic management process. African countries lack capacity (see Edoho, 1998). In Kenya, Bratton (1990) found that performance of local and national NGOs is impeded by "a common set of management problems such as, vague goals, a lack of skills for project preparation and unreliable system of financial control." To evolve guidelines that will help African NGOs to adopt strategic management perspective, however, we draw on Glickman and Servon's (1999, 2003) definition and measurement of capacity of nonprofit organizations based on a typology of five components: resource management, organizational, programmatic, networking, and political.

Resource management capacity: To achieve their strategic objectives, African NGOs must develop the capacity to generate revenues through grants, contracts, loans, services, and so forth. Akin to this is the capacity to attract, hire, retain, and develop human resources to implement their strategies. They need to enhance their human capacity to attract, acquire, and maintain funding to achieve their objectives. African NGOs need the capacity to manage and leverage their limited resources to achieve their strategic goals.

Organizational capacity: African NGOs need effective management frameworks to implement their strategies in order to realize their visions; they need to design responsive organizational systems; develop policies and procedures; apply modern management techniques and technology; and invest in human capital development (technical training and management development).

Programmatic capacity: African NGOs must develop capacity to conceptualize, initiate, design, and implement their programs. In conjunction with this, they need to ensure the coherency of their programs. In other word, each project their initiate ought to either complement or elaborate on the existing programs. Resource availability should determine the scale of their programs. Overall, their programs should be informed by their corporate vision and mission statements.

Networking capacity: In order to access resources necessary to carry out their strategic objectives and goals, African NGOs must develop a networking capacity. They need to relate to and establish relationships with a host of constituencies, both inside and outside their geographic locale. They need build bridges and collaborative relationships across all divides: governmental agencies, private sector firms, foundations, other NGOs, and international organizations and agencies. Such networking relationships will help African NGOs to diversify their sources of financial assistance, rather than depend heavily on a few sources.

Political capacity: African NGOs need to develop political capacity. They should develop the ability to work with government. Bratton (1990:111) posits that the extent to which national NGOs are able to influence policy is dependent upon "the nature of their relations with government."

Certain African NGOs see every efforts emanating from the governments through the prism of confrontational politics. Political capacity also means that African NGOs should be constructive in criticizing wrong-headed policies of the governments. They also need to develop access to elected officials and facilitate relationships with the corporate executives.

Strategic Leadership and Management of African NGOs

Articulating of vision and mission of NGOs; formulating and implementing strategies; and evaluating performance all require effective management and leadership. Thus, the success of African NGOs would be ultimately dependent upon managerial talents and leadership acumen. Some writers differentiate between "management" and "leadership" (Bass, 1990; Blunt and Jones, 1992; Kotler, 1990; Quinn, 2000; Tichy, 2002). Blunt and Jones (1992) note that an individual articulates a vision of what the organization should be. Such an individual "communicates this vision and creates organizational conditions conducive to entrepreneurial performance. This is leadership." It is believed that management is concerned with maintaining the status quo, while leadership is concerned with change. As expressed by Kotler (1990:104), management "is about coping with complexity," whereas leadership "is about coping with change."

Emerging view is that although the distinction between management and leadership may have been appropriate in the previous decade, it is no longer applicable useful in contemporary environment (Quinn, 2000; Tichy, 1999). Quinn (2000) identified what he called eight "seeds" of effective management and leadership, which executives of African NGOs should consider: envision the health productive community; first look within; embrace hypocritical self; transcend fear; embody the vision of the common good; disturb the system; surrender to the emergent process; and entice through moral power. Managers cannot be successful without being good leaders and vice versa. An executive needs good managerial and leadership skills to succeed.

A leader of African NGOs must play multiple roles. The individual must provide ennobling and empowering vision that is, a vision that is widely shared among members and spearhead the institutionalization of strategic management process. The person must understand the complexity of the global environment and be able to provide strategic guidance and direction to the organization. Leaders of African NGOs must have the ability to empower subordinates. Formulation and implementation of strategic plan require discipline. This is a function of the organizational culture. The NGOs' leadership must establish a culture that promotes disciplined behavior to ensure compliance with policies, procedures, and rules. Such a culture would elicit commitment to compliance from members of the organization.

Conclusion

The phenomenal growth of NGOs in Africa can no longer be ignored. African NGOs should no longer be treated pejoratively as belonging in the fringe, and therefore marginalized in the quest for sustainable development scheme. African NGOs need to be mainstreamed in the national development process. However, for African NGOs to earn respectability of the policy makers, they need to demonstrate that they can contribute toward sustainable national development. This chapter has argued that African NGOs can do so by adopting the framework of strategic management. This framework will enable them to improve efficiency and performance.

It is imperative to state that strategic management is not a panacea for all problems confronting contemporary organizations or African NGOs for that matter. The uniqueness of strategic management is inherent in the fact it will prepare NGOs for eventualities because it provides a framework for anticipating and dealing with such eventualities. However, African NGOs may be reluctant to contemplate, not even mentioning actually adopting, strategic management perspective. Yet, such reluctance in the African context is quite understandable, but nonetheless inexcusable.

Some of the obvious reasons that African NGOs may hesitate and not easily embrace strategic management are that the concept itself is intimidating. Some organizations consider strategic management as encompassing esoteric knowledge that is not readily accessible to ordinary mortals. Not too long ago, this view of strategic management gained prominence among small business entrepreneurs in the United States. This mode of thinking contributed to the bogus belief that strategic management was the unique province of major corporations (Edoho, 1996).

Reinforcing this mindset is the fact that African NGOs are organizations in a hurry. First, most of them are hurriedly established to confront the burning issues of the moment. Consequently, they are deeply embroiled in crisis management and firefighting that does not allow them time for planning. Second, thinking about and envisioning the future and formulating coherent strategies require time, efforts, expertise, and above all dedication. These call for commitment of resources—a luxury that most African NGOs cannot afford.

As in legal services, African NGOs can find professionals who can assist them to crystallize visions and provide technical assistance for them to develop strategic plans, either for minimum costs or *pro bono*. For African NGOs, strategic management is the key to the future.

References

Bass, B. *Handbook of Leadership: Theory, Research, and Managerial Application.* 3rd ed. New York: Macmillan, 1990.

Bebbington, Anthony. "NGOs and Uneven Development: Geographies of Development Intervention." *Progress in Human Geography* 28, no. 6 (2004): 725-745.
Ben-Ner, A. "Nonprofit Organizations: Why do they Exist in Market Economy." In *The Economics of Nonprofit Institutions: Studies in Structure and Policy*, edited by S. Rose-Ackerman. New York: Oxford University Press, 1986.
Berger, Peter, and Richard J. Neuhaus. "To Empower People: The Role of Mediating Structures in Public Policy." In *The Nonprofit Organizations*, edited by David Gies, et al. Pacific Grove, CA: Brooks/Cole Publishing, 1990.
Bornstein, Erica. "Developing Faith: Theologies of Economic Development in Zimbabwe." *Journal of Religion in Africa* 32, no. 1 (2002): 4-31.
Bratton, Michael. "The Politics of Government-NGO Relations in Africa." *World Development* 17, no. 4 (1989): 569-587.
Bratton, Michael. "Non-Governmental Organizations in Africa: Can they Influence Public Policy?" *Development and Change* 21 (1990): 87-118.
Bratton, Michael. "Peasant-State Relations in Postcolonial Africa: Patterns of Engagement and Disengagement." In *State Power and Social Forces: Domination and Transformation in the Third World*, edited by J. Migdal, A. Kohl, and V. Shue. Cambridge: Cambridge University Press, 1994, 231-254.
Blunt, P., and M. Jones. *Managing Organizations in Africa*. New York: Walter de Gruyter, 1992.
Bond, Patrick. *Uneven Zimbabwe: A Study of Finance, Development, and Underdevelopment*. Trenton, NJ: Africa World Press, 1998.
Chazan, Naomi. "Engaging the State: Associational Life in Sub-Saharan Africa." In *State Power and Social Forces: Domination and Transformation in the Third World*, edited by J. Migdal, A. Kohl, and V. Shue. Cambridge: Cambridge University Press, 1994, 255-289.
Clark, J. *Democratizing Development: The Role of Voluntary Organizations*. London: Earthscan, 1991.
Clarke, Gerard. "Non-Government Organizations (NGOs) and Politics in the Developing World." *Political Studies* 17 (1998): 36-52.
Colclough, C. "Structuralism vs. Neo-liberalism: An Introduction." In *State or Market? Neo-liberalim and the Development Policy Debate*, edited by C. Colclough and J. Manor. Oxford: Oxford University Press, 1991.
Commins, S. "World Vision International and Donors: Too Close for Comfort." In *NGOs, State and Donors*, edited by D. Hulme and M. Edwards. Basingstoke: Macmillan Press, 1997.
Copestake, James G. "Kenya: Country Overview." In *Non-Governmental Organizations and the State in Africa*, edited by Kate Wellard and James G. Copestake. New York: Routledge, 1993, 87-99.
David, Fred R. *Strategic Management: Concepts and Cases*. 9th ed. Upper Saddle River, NJ: Prentice Hall, 2004.
Dicklitch, S. *The Elusive Promise of NGOs in Africa: Lessons from Uganda*. New York: St. Martins Press, 1998.
Dorman, Sara Rich. "NGOs and Constitutional Debate in Zimbabwe: From Inclusion to Exclusion." *Journal of Southern African Studies* 29, no. 4 (2003): 845-863.
Drabek. A. G. "Development Alternatives: The Challenge of NGOs." Supplement. *World Development* 15 (1987): 9-15.
Drucker, P. "What Business Can Learn from Nonprofits." *Harvard Business Review* (July-August, 1998): 89-93.
Edoho, Felix M. "Management Capacity Building: A Strategic Imperative for African Development in the Twenty-First Century." In *Capacity Building in Developing*

Countries: Human and Environmental Dimensions, edited by Valentine U. James. Westport, CT: Praeger, 1988. 228-251.

Edwards, Michael, and David Hulme, eds. *Non-Governmental Organizations: Performance and Accountability, Beyond the Magic Bullet*. London: Earthscan, 1995.

Fama, E., and M. Jensen. "Agency Problems and Residual Claims." *Journal of Law and Economics* 26 (1983): 327-350.

Glickman, H., ed. *The Crisis and Challenge of African Development*. New York: Greenwood Press, 1988.

Glickman, Norman J., and Lisa J. Servon. "By the Numbers: Measuring Community Development Corporations' Capacity." *Journal of Planning Education and Research* 22, no. 3 (2003): 240-256.

Fowler, A. "The Role of NGOs in Changing State-Society Relations: Perspectives from Eastern and Southern Africa." *Development Policy Review* 9 (1991): 53-84.

Greenley, G. "Does Strategic Planning Improve Company Performance?" *Long Range Planning* 19, no. 2 (1986): 106

Hansmann, H. "The Role of Nonprofit Enterprise." *Yale Law Journal* 89 (1980): 835-901.

Hansmann, H. "Economic Theories of Nonprofit Organizations." In *The Nonprofit Sector: A Research Handbook* edited by W. W. Powell. New Haven, CT: Yale University Press, 1987.

Hearn, Julia. "The NGO of Kenyan Society: USAID and the Restructuring of Health Care." *Review of African Political Economy* 75 (1998): 89-100.

Hearn, Julia. "The 'Invisible' NGOs: US Evangelical Missions in Kenya." *Journal of Religion in Africa* 32, no. 1 (2002): 32-60.

Hirschman, A. O. *Getting Ahead Collectively: Grassroots Experience in Latin America*. New York: Pergamon, 1987.

Hulme, David. "Social Development Research and the Third Sector: NGOs as Users and Subjects of Social Inquiry." In *Rethinking Social Development: Theory, Research and Practice*, edited by David Booth. London: Longman, 1994.

Hulme, David, and Michael Edwards, eds. *NGOs, State and Donors: Too Close for Comfort?* Basingstoke. Macmillan Press, 1997.

Hyden, Goran. *No Shortcut to Progress*. London: Heinemann, 1983.

INTRAC. "Institutional Co-operation between African NGOs and External Partners: Current Constraints and Ways Ahead." Background Paper for the International Symposium on Building the Capacity and Resources of African NGOs. African Union Conference Centre, Addis Ababa, Ethiopia, December 5-7, 2004.

Joseph, Jaime. "NGOs: Fragmented Dreams." In *Debating Development: NGOS and the Future*, edited by Deborah Eade and Ernest Ligteringen. Oxford: Oxfam, 2001.

Kaldor, Mary. "Civil Society and Accountability." *Journal of Human Development* 4, no. 1 (2003)

Kaplan, Allan. "NGOs, Civil Society and Capacity-Building: Towards the Development of Strategy." 2004, 1-17. http://www.cdra.org.za/articles/NGOs (accessed May 3, 2005).

Korten, D. C. *Getting to the 21st Century: Voluntary Action and Global Agenda*. West Hartford, CT: Kumarian Press, 1990.

Kotler, John P. "What Leaders Really Do." *Harvard Business Review* (May-June, 1990): 104.

Langley, Ann. "The Role of Formal Strategic Planning." *Long Range Planning* 21, no. 3 (June, 1988).

Macdonald, L. *Supporting Civil Society: The Political Role of Non-Governmental Organizations in Central America*. Basingstoke: Macmillan, 1997.

Manji, Firoze, and Carl O'Coill. "The Missionary Position: NGOs and Development in Africa." *International Affairs* 78, no. 3 (2002): 567-583.
McLaughlin, T. A. "Elements of Strategy." *The Nonprofit Times* (April, 1999): 20-22.
Mercer, C. "NGOs, Civil Society and Democratization: A Critical Review of the Literature." *Progress in Developmental Studies* 2 (2002): 5-22.
Miller, C. C., and L. B. Cardinal. "Strategic Planning and Firm Performance: A Synthesis of Two Decades of Research." *Academy of Management Research* 6, no. 27 (1994): 1649-1665.
Mundy, Karen, and Lynn Murphy. "Transnational Advocacy: Global Civil Society? Emerging Evidence from the Field of Education." *Comparative Education Review* 45, no. 1 (2001): 85-126.
Nelson, N., and S. Wright, eds. *Power and Participatory Development: Theory and Practice*. London: Intermediate Technology Publications, 1995.
New York Times. "NGOs Show their Growing Power," March 22, 2002. http://www.globalpolicy.org/ngos/role/globdem/credib/2002/0322/power.htm (accessed May 3, 2005).
O'Connor, A. *Poverty in Africa: A Geographical Approach*. London: Belhaven Press, 1991.
Oster, Sharon M. *Strategic Management for Nonprofit Organizations: Theory and Cases*. New York: Oxford University Press, 1995.
Pearce, John A., and Richard B. Robinson. *Strategic Management: Formulation, Implementation, and Control*. 9th ed. Boston: McGraw-Hill/Irwin, 2005.
Peel, M., and J. Bridge. "How Planning and Capital Budgeting Improve SME Performance." *Long Range Planning* 31, no. 6 (1998): 848-856.
Prahadad, C. K., and G. Hamel. "The Core Competence of the Corporation." *Harvard Business Review* (May-June, 1990): 80-81.
Quinn, R. E. *Change the World*. San Francisco: Jossey-Bass, 2000.
Reporter "Transforming Government-NGOs Collaboration and Complementarily in Ethiopia," May 28, 2003.
Reuben, Janet. "NGOs and Africa in the New Millennium: Lessons from Tanzania." Presentation at the Panel on Re-thinking African Development. CODESRIA General Assembly, 2002.
Salamon, L. M. "The Rise of the Nonprofit Sector." *Foreign Affairs* 73, no. 4 (1994): 109-122.
Salih, M. A. Mohammed. "Islamic NGOs in Africa: The Promise and Peril of Islamic Voluntarism." Occasional Paper, Center of African Studies, University of Copenhagen, 2002.
Sanyal, B. "Cooperative Autonomy: The Dialectic of State-NGOs Relationship in Developing Countries." *Research Series 100*. Geneva: ILO, 1994.
Sergeant, Adrian. *Marketing Management for Nonprofit Organizations*. New York: Oxford University Press, 1999.
Schwenk, G. L., and K. Schrader. "Effect of Formal Strategic Planning in Financial Performance in Small Firms: A Meta-Analysis." *Entrepreneurship and Practice* 3, no. 17 (1993): 53-64.
Smith, Julia. "Strategies for Start-Ups." *Long Range Planning* 31, no. 6 (1998): 857-872.
Storey, Andy. "The World Bank, Neo-liberalism, and Power: Discourse Analysis and Implications for Campaigners." In *Debating Development: NGOs and the Future*, edited by Deborah Eade and Ernst Ligteringen. Oxford: Oxfam, 2001, 104-128.
Tandon, Rajesh. "Riding High or Nosediving: Development NGOs in the New Millennium." In *Debating Development: NGOs and the Future*, edited by Deborah Eade and Ernst Ligteringen. Oxford: Oxfam, 2001, 44-59.

Thompson, Arthur A., and A. J. Strickland. *Strategic Management: Concepts and Cases.* 13th ed. Boston: McGraw-Hill/Irwin, 2003.

Tichy, N. M. *The Leadership Engine.* New York: Harper Business, 2002.

United Nations Development Program [UNDP]. *Human Development Report.* New York: Oxford University Press, 1993.

United Nations Development Program. *Human Development Report.* New York: Oxford University Press, 2003.

Uphoff, N. "Grassroots Organizations and NGOs in Rural Development: Opportunities with Diminishing State and Expanding Markets." *World Development* 21 (1993): 607-622.

Van Rooy, Alison. "Good News! You may be Out of a Job: Reflections on the Past and Future 50 Years of Northern NGOs." In *Debating Development: NGOs and the Future*, edited by Deborah Eade and Ernst Ligteringen. Oxford: Oxfam, 2001, 19-43.

Waiguchu, J. Muruku. "Rethinking and Managing Nonprofit Organizations in Africa." In *Management of Organizations in Africa: A Handbook and Reference*, edited by J. M. Waiguchu, Edward Tiagha, and M. Mwaura. Westport, CT: Quorum Books, 1999.

Weisbrod, Burton. "Toward a Theory of the Voluntary Nonprofit Sector in a Three-Sector Economy." In *Altruism, Morality and Economic Theory*, edited by Edmund Phelps. New York: Russell Sage, 1974.

Weiss, Holger. "Reorganizing Social Welfare among Muslims: Islamic Voluntarism and Other Forms Communal Support in Northern Ghana." *Journal of Religion in Africa* 32, no. 1 (2002): 83-109.

Welch, C. *Practicing Human Rights in Africa: Rules and Strategies of Non-Governmental Organizations.* Philadelphia: University of Pennsylvania, 1995.

Welch, C. "Human Rights NGOs and the Rule of Law in Africa." *Journal of Human Rights* 2, no. 3 (2003): 315-327. http://www.tandf.co.uk/journal (accessed February 22 2006).

Wheelen, Thomas L., and J. David Hunger. *Strategic Management and Policy.* 9th ed. Upper Saddle River, NJ: Pearson/Prentice Hall, 2004.

Williams, Michael. "Global Civil Society: Expectations, Capacities and the Accountability of International NGOs. 21st Century Trust." 2003. http://www.21stcenturytrust.org/williams2.html (accessed May 3, 2005).

World Bank. *World Development Report.* Washington, DC: World Bank, 1980.

World Bank. *World Development Report.* Washington, DC: World Bank, 1986.

World Bank. *Governance and Development.* Washington, DC: World Bank, 1992.

World Resources Institute. *World Resources 2002-2004: Decisions for the Earth: Balance, Voice, and Power.*UNDP/UNEP/World Bank/IMF, 2003.

Wright, Brian. "Non-Governmental Organizations and Indifference as a Human Rights Issue: The Case of Nigerian Oil Embargo." *Journal of Human Rights* 1, no. 2 (2002): 231-245.

Chapter 12

Current and Future Roles of NGOs in the Empowerment of Women in Africa

Josephine Dibie and Robert A. Dibie

Since the beginning of the twenty-first century African women have been struggling to achieve equity with men in leadership and decision-making. The drafting of the communiqué for the Eradication of all Discrimination Against Women (CEDAW) in 1979 by the United Nations, has also galvanize gender NGOs in several nations in sub-Saharan Africa. Although the Fourth World Conference on Women (FWCW, Beijing 1995) had help to mobilize women all over the world, several nations in Africa has been very slow in introducing policies that would help to eradicate all forms of gender related discrimination and abuse. Just after ten years of the Discrimination Against Women declaration, African nations that were part of the 189 countries who indicated that there no ambivalent contradiction in the pledge to promote the equity of women in decision-making and in strengthening the national machineries for enabling women as co-equal in governance with men have now taken steps back due to the emergence of a more difficult political and challenging economic environment (Kuye 2003; Vargas 2000; Antrobus 2004).

Despite the fact the most African governments have come to accept that women's rights are human rights, the national and regional leaders have lacked the will to put in place structures and policies that could strengthen and protect the rights of women in both the public service and the private sectors. Poverty reduction policies of most African nations no-longer talk of women but stress human capital development, right-sizing, devolution, privatization of public corporation and out-sourcing. The most troubling aftermath across the African continent includes disturbing indications on the overall status of women. The spread of poverty from Sudan to the Democratic Republic of Congo, Rwanda, Ethiopia, Chad, Niger and several other African nations have also increased the practice of women trafficking, the high incidence of material morality and women illiteracy (World Bank Report 2005; Meekers and Richter 2005). Women's poverty has also led to children malnutrition in several African nations. In most African countries women and their children have become losers in the production industry that are affected by trade liberalization policies. As a result of lay off of their husbands as well as withdrawal of social support by the government, women's domestic and economic responsibilities have increased. In the democratic Republic of Congo and several other African countries women, for example, have suffered from rape in communal conflicts. In general women have become the victims of society while men play the role of political control and major decision makers of the state and family.

The history of women in the African continent presents an account of tremendous diversity in the roles women play in the social and economic development of each nation. Historically, religion and cultural patterns of educational development in the sub region have also helped to shape the present representation of talented women in senior management positions in the public and private sectors. In some African nations where constitutional amendments and new electoral laws on gender quotas have been enacted there has been little evidence of compliance. On one hand, most electoral gender quotas have turned out to be purely symbolic due to religious and cultural factors. On the other hand, quotas have become more symbolic if NGOs and gender capacity building organizations are not organized by women's movement. Lack of sanctions for non compliance and effective rules about ranks order of candidates has also made the few elected women to be powerless (Dahlerup 2005).

HIV/AIDS continue to be one the greatest challenges to sexual and reproductive health and rights among women in most parts of the African continent. The most vulnerable to the deadly disease are younger girls, poor people, and married women. According to the International Family Planning Perspective (2002) young women are up to seven times more likely than men to contract HIV in east Africa (2-3). Further, lack of economic opportunities for women has caused a rise in often unprotected, transactional sex. Life expectancy across the African continent is decreasing at an alarming rate as HIV/AIDS continue to wipe out more than one million people every year as well as the present and future human capital of several nations. Sexual violence to women, unwanted pregnancies and lack of access to medical services and information are also predicaments that women in rural Africa face. In some east African countries, conflict situation and wars often lead to population displacement of women and children (Meekers and Richter 2005). This displacement disproportionately affects women and their children and further compounds the problem of poverty.

While women constitute about 60 percent of the African population, there are till a disproportionately low number of them in senior leadership positions in both the public and private sectors. It is therefore clear that women are less present in sizable numbers in education, business and industry, and government, however, despite their larger population in the continent. Today, female senior public administrators are relatively rare. Recent studies show that only 2 percent of senior public administrators are women in the civil service of most African nations (Kuye 2003). While it appears that there are more women than men in the national, state and regional governments in sub-Saharan African nations, there are more men in the apex of leadership.

Priscilla Kuye (2003) contends that prejudice continues to exist, as does the glass ceiling that limits women from enjoying truly equal opportunities in several African governments public service. Although sufficient time may not have passed to allow more women to work their way into the senior positions in the African public service, there appear to be more formidable barriers. Most notably are the gender stereotypes that postulate inaccurate and myopic beliefs about the kinds of tasks for which women are most appropriately suited. These beliefs originated from some religious and in some cases parochial cultural practices.

The few studies that mentioned gender helplessness in sub-Saharan African countries argued that gender does shape the opportunities and constraints women and men face in securing positions in government (Thomas-Sayter and Rocheleau 1995; Adepoju 1994; Kalu 1993). Moreover, as Adepuju (1994) and Hyden (2006) pointed out, the systematically inferior position of women inside and outside the public service and household in the continent points to the necessity of treating gender as a force of its own in sustainable development issues in Africa. Although the relative deprivation of women when compared with men varies around the fifty African nations, it is very important to note that giving qualified women more senior public management positions in government organizations will galvanize the continent's bit for sustainable development. If economic, health and social developments are expected to reach men and women equitably across the African continent, government and NGOs will have to engage as well as restructure their interest to address women issues. The government, private sector and NGOs will have development new mechanism to redistribute public resources to the urban and rural communities equitably with effective prescriptions and action for sustainable management to men, women and children.

This chapter examines the predicament of prejudice that women face in countries in sub-Saharan Africa. It explores the factors that militate against the integration of women into senior administrative and political leadership positions in the continent. It contends that if women are under represented in Africa because of open or indirect mechanism of exclusion and discrimination, then educating women and girls is not enough, and may even result in little change if the public and private sectors institutions are not changed simultaneously. Further it stressed that the public, private sectors and NGOs in Africa need to introduce diversity management programs as a policy at the national and regional governments in order to engage talented women in its process of seeking sustainable development. The chapter also argues that in offering women the opportunity to access economic resources as well as to disentangle their identities from those of their families they will contribute immensely in the sustainable development process of Africa. If the problem is not women's lack of resources, but lack of acknowledgement of those resources and experiences that women actually bring with them into the public and private sectors, then there is no need to wait for women to be more educated or experienced. It contends that no development process will be totally beneficial to a nation if it does not involve women.

This chapter also presents some theoretical perspectives of the role of women in the development process of a nation. It develops theoretical and practical understandings of gender issues and its important process of social transformation in Africa. Given a labor force and culture with male dominance, is the present use of women in the African society the best possible one for the continent? The concluding section calls for an equal opportunity and sexual harassment policies that would effectively reduce discrimination against women in the public service as well as stimulate and integrate talented women interests in the social, economic, leadership, and political development of Africa. National governments, the private sector and NGOs would have to do more in the twenty-first century to promote women's right and equity for all citizens in the continent.

Citizenship, Women, and Equal Opportunity

The study of feminism and equal opportunity in Africa is still in its infancy. Citizenship of a nation is crucial in the relationship between an individual and the nation state where they reside. All over the world man and women have been incorporated into citizenship of different nations. Gender inequalities are therefore buried within the state. According to Georgina Waylen (1996) through the state dynamic process gender relations are partly constituted by public policy, culture or religion. Therefore a nation's practices construct and legitimate gender divisions and identities that are in part constructed by the law and public discuss which emanates from its government. Consequently while some African governments have for the most part acted to reinforce women subordination, the space can exist within the public sector to act to change gender relations (Alvarez 1989). Recently, attention to the impact of gender and ethnicity on public institutions has focused largely on the perceptions of discrimination. The notion of representative democracy, equal opportunities and sexual harassment are still very new concept in several African nations.

The Secretary General of the United Nation Kofi Annan recently postulated that discrimination or violence against women is perhaps the most shameful human rights violation and it is perhaps the most pervasive. He contends that discrimination and human rights violation against women knows no boundaries of geography culture or wealth. As long as it continues, human beings cannot claim to be making real progress toward equality in development and peace (Aderibigbe 2004). In sub-Saharan Africa, discrimination and human rights violation against women take the form of blatant refusal to hire women in certain positions, gender based violence that results in physical, sexual or psychological harm or suffering to women. This also includes threats to women and girls, sexual harassment, and arbitrary deprivation of liberty in both their private and public life. Physical violence of women in Africa also involves all forms of physical abuse such as punching, kicking, shoving, or other assaults that involves knives, acid bath or other harmful objects. On the one hand sexual violence in several African nations is associated with rape, indecent assault, and incest. On the other hand, psychological violence involves verbal attacks, threats of violence from men, humiliation, harassment and deprivation of access to employment, economic and career development. Therefore, the extension of the remit of African governments into the realm of the private has the effect of politicizing women issues, for example through matters such as abortion, rape and domestic violence. This politicization would then help to mobilize NGOs and women movements to handle popular campaign around the continent in order to influence the political agenda and public policy (Waylen 1996).

There is a widespread acceptance of the critical role played by women and public institutions in the development process (Abdullah, 1995; Bank, 1994; Dennis 1987; Konjo 1976 and 1991; Ofei-Aboagye 1994; Wallace, 1999; Turner and Hulme 1997; World Bank 1997). Women act as major actors in the transformation process, whether in terms of their direct involvement in the economy or their more tempered role as catalyst, facilitator and regulator of economic activity (World Bank 2005). At the same time, there has been a growing concern with the representation of women and the management of diversity within the Africa's public sector (Adepuju 1994; Kuye 2003). The concern of unequal representation of women in the public sector has affected reform efforts that stresses human resources management issues such as capacity-building, participatory management styles, cross gender mentor-protégé relationship, constant innovation, entrepreneurial initiative, teamwork, strategic thinking and planning as crucial.

World Bank (1997 and 2005) report pointed out that when women are not offered equal opportunity in the public sector there is the danger that some skills and talents in a nation could be wasted. The idea that recruitment and promotion are based on gender rather than merit can contribute significantly to a decrease of morale and performance among talented and innovative women.

As Dahlerup (2005) and Esman (1997) have pointed out, that ethnic politics largely ignores public administration or socioeconomic development, in much the same way that the literature on economic development overlooks ethnic cleavages. Yet in many societies across the African continent, ethnicity and gender stereotype plays such a pervasive role in the development process. This is why Adepoju (1994) and Matland (2006) describe gender and ethnic politics as "an important dimension in public affairs, pervading the environment in which public administration functions in sub-Saharan Africa."

The report of the civil service reforms in several African nations addressed the issue of quota system and perceptions of discrimination against women in the public sector. Some African scholars have also strived for what is known as a representative bureaucracy in several sub-Saharan African nations (Green 1999; Kalu 1993). The notion of quotas and discriminatory attitudes and practices as well as unequal power relations that led to women's under representation in political decision-making was also addressed by the Beijing declaration. The concept of a representative bureaucracy is attributed to Kingsley (1944), Krislov (1974) and Meier (1993), among others. Kingsley's argued that, for an administrative system to respond to changes in the political climate of a nation, it had to represent children, young adults, women and men equally. It should be noted that Kingsley was referring specifically to the homogeneous British society where social classes exist in the Marxian sense, rather than ethnic groups, were it is used as the units of analysis.

Carol Harvey and June Allard (2002) describe diversity in the workplace as the racial, ethnic, and gender differences in an organization. The concept of diversity in the public service of most African nations mean that the public bureaucracy should broadly reflects the gender, religious, social, economic, cultural and development interests of the respective nations. In this regard, all the religious, social class and gender members of the nation should be well represented (Gentile 1996). In this respect, top management should comprise talented men, women and young adults in the country. These groups should share a common national interests and values with the political leaders of the country (Isekhure 1998). This idea is closely related to the current discourses on public sector reform, that the bureaucracy must be more responsive to the policy direction of the government of the day instead of being purely neutral and impartial.

Lijphart (1977) describes the passive and active representation approaches in a society. According to him the passive approach presents a more or less sociological/demographic argument. It suggests that the bureaucracy should mirror society as a whole. This approach according to Lijphart is known as proportionality. It means that all groups in a society should be represented in decision-making organs and institutions. All groups in the society should be represented proportionally. Appointments to the bureaucracy should therefore be allocated among men, women and the other different segments of the population in direct proportion to their numbers. In this way, the administrative apparatus of several African nations will become a microcosm of the wider society.

This approach is clearly impractical in several African nations for three main reasons. In the first place, it fails to recognize that social groups may not be equally predisposed to seeking careers in the public service. To the extent that this is true, the public service of several African nations will never be fully representative on the basis of proportionality. This had always been the main explanation offered to describe the absence of talented women in senior management positions in the public service. It was argued that most women in the rural areas do rarely applies for positions in the public services because they prefer to seek employment in agricultural or commerce sectors (Kalu,1993). Second, not all groups (especially women) are qualified to seek employment in the public sector due to either quotas or on merit. As Otobo (1999) and Oluwo (1999) pointed out representative bureaucracy in most African nations depend on an even distribution of formal education. That is, women in most African society may be underrepresented in the public sector due to historical, religious and cultural patterns of educational development.

The level at which the bureaucracy ought to be representative is a third problem. Modupe Kolawole (1998) argued that socialization experiences among women within the public service tend to diminish the influence of pre-employment experiences, and that upwardly mobile public servants are likely to hold different values and opinions from others with the same social origins. Jerald Greenberg (2003) contend that when one think of a mentor, the image that comes to mind is an older male senior executive helping a younger male junior executive work his way up the public service ladder by introducing him to the "old boy network." By definition, any old boy network is sexist. Indeed, women in most African nations' public sector often seem to have less access to suitable mentor than do men because there are few or no women in senior management positions that could serve as mentors.

Jerald Greenberg (2007) and Modupe Kolawole (1998) presented three reasons why men have more access to mentor than women. First, there are simply fewer female executives available to serve as mentor for young female employees. Second, women are less willing to enter into mentoring relationships because they anticipate greater risk than men in doing so. Recent survey in some African nations found that women expressed more concern than men did about the potential for negative exposure that might come from the increased visibility they assume because of their protégé status. This is specifically very important because most African nations do not have sexual harassment laws. Third, barriers to mentoring exist not only between men and women, but also between members of different religious and ethnic groups. Insofar as mentor and protégé often get together because they have similar backgrounds and share similar attitudes, it is not surprising to find that people from different ethnic and religious groups face difficulties in their mentor-protégé relationships if they form one at all.

Adamolekun (1999) and Kim Reimann (2006) pointed out the current wave of public sector reform efforts that tacitly approves of an expanded role for technocratic advisors from outside the public sector to improve the situation. The reform policies certainly reduced the role of senior public servants as the sole source of policy advices and almost banishing them to implementation and administration issues. This role also makes it difficult for them to introduce programs that would eliminate discrimination against women. Far from being loyal to their nation, these senior public administrators are more likely to be loyal to their ethnic group and the political hand that feeds them. Thus, prejudice against women continues to exist in the public and private sectors of most African nations, as does the glass ceiling that limits all women from enjoying true equal opportunities and a working environment free from sexual harassment in the nation. Thus, gender balance will not come about by itself except government and NGOs take some crucial actions (Dahlerup 2005). Therefore, the responsibility for dealing with the under representation of women rests with the government, the private sector and NGOs. It is therefore paramount that the understanding of women's under representation should be addressed by public policy such as electoral gender quotas for the recruitment and election of female candidates. It will be optimistic to predict that progress for women will come in the twenty-first century inevitably in several African nations with the intervention of foreign NGOs and reform in public policy.

Women at the Workplace and their Family

The obvious question however is, why aren't there more women in positions of power and leadership in most African nations? What explanations satisfy the debate about who is qualified to lead in African nations? In most African nations the hiring of men into senior management positions can be described as an instrument of controls over female employees (Aderibegbe 2004). Although this may not be treated by a society as legitimate, the practice still continues. In some ethnic groups where these practices are deemed legitimate their treatment as forms of gender abuse has stirred a huge debate. Often this debate boils down to arguments for cultural relativism versus universal human rights (Beneria 2003; Dahlerup 2005; Ibe 1994). In most African families a husband uses this same idea as a reason to physically abuse or discipline his wife. This practice is an acceptable behavior among several African ethnic and religious groups.

As stated above several African nations have a strong patriarchal structure that maintained the sexual division of labor in the household and families. This same structure directly restricts women's availability for wage work and indirectly affects the terms of employment for those women who enter the public and private sectors. As discussed earlier, there is a clear gender differentiation, in terms of occupational status and work condition in several African nations. Specifically, women in the public service and private sector are characterized by limited and insecure employment opportunities and marked substandard wages, poor work conditions, unstable hours and disadvantageous employment contracts (Ifedi 1994; Karanja 1987; Mba 1982). Women are predominantly employed in low wage jobs or extremely small-scale venture, which shunt them into segregated occupation and repetitious manual production.

Despite the fact that majority of the women who work in the public service and private sector in several African nations occupy junior positions, there are few women who hold position of power in the government. In the private sector, there are also a hand full of women who are entrepreneurs and directors. There are, however, few women who are handicapped with the lack of affordable childcare, escalating rate of spousal abandonment, an increasingly high cost of living and gender stereotyping. These conditions deny women in the public and private sectors the requisite skills, training, and capital to secure more lucrative and secured employment (Nweke 1985; Ifedi 1994; Obadina 1985). Moreover, because most African women tend to be concentrated in transitory, low-paid, and low status jobs they typically replicate their household tasks, proper place as well as of their activities as survival victims.

In most African public and private sectors, the marginalization of women in the continent has two contrasting gender ideologies, which ironically produce the same outcome. The first is related to the aforementioned state- promoted gender identity. The state rhetoric and action imply that women in most African nations do not need to engage in income-generating activities and that those who do engage in such activities do so for reasons other than economic necessity. The second gender ideology under girding the marginalization of women micro-entrepreneurs is related to gender bias embedded in development practice that perceive women as vulnerable and isolated groups and their activities as a collection of inconsequential endeavors (Aderibege 2004; Waylen 1996; Dahlerup 2005; Reimann 2006). Gender specific ideologies; such as these, which underpin the marginalization of women within the public and private sectors in African, are often nuance by cultural, ethnic and religious undertone.

In several African nations, the rigid and hegemonic nature of prevailing notions of work not only denigrates the work of women but dis-empowers women producers themselves. Interview conducted in several African nations in the summer of 2006 reveals that, although women consider themselves to be producers of goods and providers of services for a large segment of the society, like the society women have a low estimate of the value of their own labor. Hence, it would seem that the particular constructions of gender to which some African working women are subject and which inform their notions of self not only deny them the value of their daily activities but also undermine the potential of their private sector or public agencies as well as discourage them from developing enabling the concept of self worth.

The exclusion of women from senior public management and political position at the national and regional government levels as well as private sectors reinforce the argument that women do not have economic and political power in several African nations. After almost six decades of independence how can women in most African nations be empowered to participate in economic, social and political aspect of their society and nation? The implementation of appropriate strategies to enhance women empowerment in Africa is one of the major steps for the continent to achieve sustainable development.

Policies toward Women's Empowerment

No doubt women are the pillars of the African family. Generally men acknowledge that the physical, psychological health and mental health of each member of their family depends on the woman in the family. This assumption leads us to argue that the promotion of a woman's well-being is the solution to the ills of society in the African continent. Thus, empowerment of women in the continent with education, technical skills, enhanced self-worth and economic independence will lead toward equality and full participation life. Training in personal and family hygiene, knowledge about safe food preparation and inclusion of vitamins and micro-nutrients in food, freedom from harmful activities including smoking and drug use and sexual and reproductive choice, including the right to have safe sex will help to empower women in the African continent to be the primary care giver and health providers for their family.

While the passive approach emphasizes the sociological or demographic representatives of women in the public and private sectors of Africa, the active approach places the accent on the cultural, religious and political determination of discrimination against women (Waylen 1996; Dahlerup 2005; Reiman 2006)

Table 12.1
Policies for Women's Empowerment

Policy Variable	Description
Equal Employment Opportunities	Equal opportunity and other ethnic-conscious instruments designed to benefit the marginalized girls and middle age women.
Gender Discrimination	Take action to stop gender discrimination in the hiring and promotion process.
Child Day Care Assistance	Public and private institutions should be encouraged to provide child day care facilities around their location.
Women Participation in Politics	Create an environment that will encourage women to participate in politics and occupy key positions in political parties.
Diversity in Women Education	(a) Girls and middle age women should be encouraged to complete at least high school diploma. (b) Women should be encouraged to be Scientists, Engineers, Pilots, Computer Experts and Doctors.
Law Against Women Abuse	Take action to prosecute men who abuse their wives.
National Sexual Harassment Policy in the workplace	Prosecute men especially senior administrators who use their position to intimidate junior female employees or demand sex as a condition for continuous employment or promotion.
Women Co-operative Societies and NGOs	Encourage the consolidation of women economic power through co-operative societies and NGOs around the nation.
Public Education Campaign to change traditional, social, cultural, and religions stereotype on women.	Introduce civil society campaign to educate both rural and urban communities that the time is right for the nation to change some of its outdated values about girls and women.

From this perspective arise policies such as equal opportunity and other ethnic-conscious instruments designed to benefit the marginalized groups. Equality of opportunity is predicated on the idea of fair competition on the basis of merit, and the role of public policy is to ensure that all qualified individuals (men and women) may enter the competition and be judged according to the same criteria. Thus the state must act to (1) ensure that the competition is equal, and (2) equalize starting points where necessary (Lovenduski 1989: 8; Steinman 1991; Weisner 1997). Table 12.1 shows a framework of how women empowerment can be achieved in Africa.

Political leadership:

There is the need for all African governments and NGOs regardless of culture, religion, political system, history and custom, to protect the universally recognized human rights all nations have agreed to as well as the Beijing declaration to protect women's right. African governments need to prosecute those who violate the human rights laws. African governments must enforce laws that has to do with rape, gender based violence, murder and torture. No African nation should condone discrimination against women or any form of sexual abuse.

It is also important that the government, the private sector and NGOs operating in the African continent elevate the priority for women in development. In the twenty-first century development should not only focus on power plants, good roads, health care, technology, dams, and defense, rather governments need to put people and families first. They can do this by investing in women, young girls, welfare and education, women's needs, in women's opportunities, and in women's rights. It is therefore paramount for NGOs, the public and private sectors to ensure that women are their number one priority in achieving sustainable development in Africa.

Protection of Women from Disease:

The problem of the spread of HIV/AIDS in Africa is alarming. It is therefore essential that governments, NGOs and the private sector unite to form a sexual and reproductive health movement in seeking solutions to address the HIV/AIDS disease in the continent. NGOs should collaborate with local health departments and family planning agencies and clinics on the front lines in preventing the spread of sexually transmitted infections. It is not enough to condemn illiterate African women who are affected because of indifference to science and by failure to provide tools for their own protection. Doing so will insinuate blaming the victim and denotes crime against humanity and thus negligence towards humanity. African governments and NGOs must collaborate to fight back and mobilize a comprehensive prevention program that experts estimate could prevent the HIV/AIDS epidemic from further spreading in the African continent. There is also the need for the manufacturing of female condoms. These condoms should be made more affordable and acceptable. Through this technique condom might simultaneously prevent unwanted pregnancy, sexually transmitted infections and AIDS virus itself. It is crucial that NGOs, CBOs, the private sector, all relevant stakeholders collaborate in the design and implementation of health sector reform alongside the government. Access of health services to vulnerable groups especially women in the rural areas must be ensured.

Culture, Tradition and Religion:

There are over one thousand ethnic groups and languages in Africa. Nigeria for example, has nearly 250 different languages and ethnic groups, while Tanzania has more than 100. Kenya alone has more than forty ethnic groups and languages (Khapoya 1998). The interesting thing about the different ethnic groups is that they all have distinct or specific cultures and traditions. In several parts of Africa the values of culture and tradition are both dynamic and affected by changing legal, economic and political forces (Akinboye 2004; Khapoya 1998). In some cases these African cultures could serve as impediments to human rights and development in the context of the twenty-first century. Therefore it is paramount for African governments and NGOs to walk together in the elimination of those culture and religious values that infringe upon women's rights. They should also strengthen the exiting positive cultural values that promote gender equality and human dignity. The strengthening of positive cultural practices could be done through reinforcement of human rights education and law reform. Traditional methods of dealing with sexual and life-skills education need to be reevaluated. There is also the need for partnership or collaboration with religious, customary laws and traditional stakeholders to realize the rights of vulnerable groups especially women and young girls that are affected by parochial traditional practices such as female mutilation, child marriages and obnoxious initiation and widowhood rites. National governments should introduce reforms in customary laws, constitutional and judicial laws pertaining to marriage, land inheritance rights and family life.

Equity and Women's Citizenship:

In any nation men and women contribute to the development process. Like in most western industrial countries, African nations must recognize that equity, equality and women empowerment as the necessary pre-requisites for women's ability to enjoy the right to the highest attainable standard of sexual and reproductive health. In most western industrialized countries women are encouraged to be equal partners to men. This practice should be encourage in Africa, in order to transformed gender relations and achieve sustained equity and social justice. Therefore African nations should introduce groundbreaking public policy that would encourage progressive measures that will ensure the fulfillment of women's rights. NGOs and government institutions should promote popular education campaign on gender rights, gender-sensitive issues and the socialization of children. In addition, African governments and NGOs should promote women's sexual rights, including their rights to bodily integrity, their freedom to determine their sexual lives and their freedom from sexual violence, coercion, discrimination and ostracism. The current practice of entrenched structural gendered inequities and inequalities manifest in economic powerlessness, and in inadequate law protection from violations such as gender based violence. These current practices in several African nations have resulted in women and girls not being accorded their equal rights and citizenship. Passing public policy that allocates seats for women called quotas, and engaging in electoral politics are the leading models for reaching the goals of achieving women's citizenship across the African continent.

Diversity and Equal Opportunity:

There has been much debate and political controversy surrounding equal opportunity policies and quota system in several African nations. At the heart of the debate is the question of whether preferential treatment is justified and, if so, on what grounds. While accepting that there may be reason to challenge the arbitrary criteria on which preferences are to be allocated, there is no alternative but to support Edwards' (1995) position that, in principle at least, they (i.e. preferences to one or other group) are acceptable once they are designed to remove inequality and do not create greater injustices than those they seek to overcome.

Diversity ought to be an end in itself and not a means to achieving some less noble, politically motivated objective (Harvey and Allard 2002). Second, if equal opportunity is intended to serve as compensation for past injustices, then it is flawed as a form of redress since there is seldom anything that links past victims and present beneficiaries. What it does, in effect, is to seriously devalue (or certainly undervalue) the qualifications of those whose forebears stand accused of discriminating against previous generations of the new "in-group." This is surely tantamount to replacing one system of injustice with another.

African nations government and NGOs not only must understand the dynamics of family abuse, but also be prepared to offer support and guidance to victims as they move through the difficult period in their life. Repairing the body and spirit is only half the battle; society must be able to make the victims of family abuse completely whole. This has to include financial reimbursement from the offender. The people of Africa are beginning to accept the fact that victims of crimes in general and victims of family abuse in particular, have rights and need to be active participants in the criminal justice system. This includes giving their input during sentencing of offenders. The use of victim impact statements is a giant step forward for victims of family violence.

The various policy instruments for ensuring women development are not exclusive to the government's official policies. Legal aid and legal literacy are the most popular components of government's effort to reduce family abuse. To rectify this situation in several African nations, the Family Law Center is a legal services advisory center offering free legal advice on all family legal problems to low income people. The center's founders were careful not to restrict its services to women because of fears that it would be stigmatized as another "women's liberation project." Such a label might have jeopardized the center's existence for a number of reasons. To be more inclusive the center publishes booklets in four of the main languages in some African nations. These publications are free and target school-age children in the hope that they will read it to their mothers while also learning on their own (Akande and Kuye 1986; Kuye 2003).

In recent years, some NGOs have become increasing proactive in their attempt to eliminate prejudice. Their approach is not just to hire a broader group of people than usual, but to create an atmosphere in which diverse groups can flourish. The NGOs above are not merely trying to obey the law or attempting to be socially responsible, but they recognize that diversity is a public issue that needs to be addressed. The government should therefore make sure that all its agencies introduce appropriate diversity management programs that will give women access to senior management positions. As Otobo (1999) pointed out, the success of the government is increasing been determined by its managers' ability to naturally tap the full potentials of a diverse workforce that comprise of women, men, young adults and so on.

The introduction of diversity management program in African nations' public service would constitute an effort to celebrate diversity by creasing supportive work environments for women and minority ethnic groups in the continent. The national and regional governments should adopt the underlying philosophy of diversity management programs so that they may crack the glass ceiling preventing women and minorities groups in the continent from excelling and contributing effectively to the nation's sustainable development process.

There are some non-official women organizations or associations that are committed to women development. These NGOs include; Association of Working House Wives, Association of Media Women, Army Officers Wives Association, and National Council of Women Society of Nigeria and so on. The interests of these groups are basically confined to the welfare of their members. In the future the government should encourage women groups to consolidate their economic powers by establishing co-operative societies that will enhance their quest for liberation. The current activities of the National Council of Women for example, include the operation of child welfare services scheme, and market nurseries to cater for the children of market traders. The council runs adult education programs aimed at increasing political awareness and participation of women in development with particular references to women franchise the right to vote and be voted for. It also runs a number of hostel accommodations for women in various towns and cities in Africa in order to alleviate accommodation problems for women in urban centers. These activities are not enough. New women co-operative societies should be formed around the African continent to further promote these causes.

Community Home Economics Program:

The formal instrument for women development in several African nations is the Ministry or Department of Social Development, Youth and Sports and the Ministry of Women Affairs. Broad policies and guidelines on women development emanate from these ministries. Prominent among such development programs is the Community Home Economics that include day care center management. This is designed to enlighten women in rural areas on modern methods of home keeping and childcare. Another women development program is the Community

Development Training Center. The center undertakes the training of rural women, teachers, and front line women leaders to enable them to motivate the citizens towards undertaking self help projects and to handle the various Day Care Centers (Buchanan 1993; Kuye 2003). Although women dominated the teaching and nursing professions in several African nations, the Ministry of Women's Affairs should do a better job in communicating their roles in the women empowerment process to both women and men.

Adult Education Program:

The Adult Education program of the Ministry or Department of Education though not an exclusive women policy affair has also presented policy instrument for enhancing women development. Women are largely illiterates in comparison with their male folks and would therefore benefit more from adult education programs of the national and various regional governments. It is pertinent to note that most African nations have set up a National Education Agency and, subsequently several regional governments have been directed to set aside some of their capital budget on education for the agency (Ibe 1994).

Some African nations government has started operating a scholarship scheme for interested female candidates that do exceptionally well in science; technology, mathematics and other sciences related subjects. Some technical colleges have been devoted to the enhancement of women development in a number of African countries (Buchanan 1993). Also indicative of government policy, is the use of mass media to propagate women education. In this vein, both the national education ministry and state governments seek to encourage parents to send their female children to school. In most rural regions, the official position is to prosecute parents who either withdraw their daughters from school for marriage, encourage their daughters to trade on the streets or farm. Several African nations' government has also established the Commission for Women's Affairs to enhance the status of women socially and economically. In addition, NGOs and several African nations' government has issued decrees abolishing abuses against women, improving their health status discouraging such practices as early marriage and female circumcision. The President of Nigeria, Olusegun Obasanjo announced the establishment of a new Ministry for Women Affairs in his 2000 budget speech. This is a continuation of General Sani Abacha's legacy of 1995. The rationale for the establishment of a women's ministry is that it will encourage women to enter the labor force and supply a wide range of talents and services that is required for the sustainable development of Nigeria. This in turn will improve productivity and economic growth of the continent. In the management of businesses and industries, however, women are conspicuously absent. The government and NGOs in Africa should establish an atmosphere where women will be seen as transformational managers and innovative entrepreneurs. It is not the technical, but the sociological aspects of industrial and business management that militates against success for women in the professional occupations.

Pressure from Civil Society Groups:

Further political pressure from NGOs, multinational corporations, civil society groups, governments, lenders and international donors by men and women dedicated to sexual equality will be vital to ensure that women's interests are not neglected. These groups range from rural co-operatives societies to professional occupational associations, to urban business enterprises, to social welfare, church, and entertainment groups. Although they may not have originated as such, many of these groups have developed an expressly political focus. Through the use of these NGOs or civil society groups, women's protest has assumed widely divergent forms. Some civil society organizations are seeking to politicize the private domain in certain contexts. Nonsexist education and training for women and men as well as equal access to jobs, property, and leadership positions must be provided. African nations will not achieve their development goals if women's full humanity and citizenship is not acknowledge and vigorously protected.

Even if legal reforms make the economic situation of wives more secured, African men must be educated on other ways to boost their ego, redirect their anger and curb their chauvinism. Beating ones' wife is surely not an option. The media should be used to educate the people of Africa, that cultural values that encourage family abuse are no longer valid in the twenty-first century.

African women should realize that the degree of success that they will experience in curtailing any opposition from men and in averting gender stereotype in their nation is dependent on their ability to enlist men as allies. The extent to which this would be possible in Africa hinges on women's ability to convince men that their new social space and new gender identities are non-threatening, mutually benefiting, and greater than a zero-sum game. In the twenty-first century African nations should change the notion of women as specialized homemakers and men as providers. Double waged families should be seen as a means to retain economic stability and a better way to weather the storms of family emergencies. There should be a mutual understanding that both women and men have the obligation to participate in the labor market regardless of gender and domestic responsibilities.

Gender Factor in Development:

African nations' government and NGOs that seek to defend the status quo have sometimes caused anxiety to their national development process. The ability of women to mobilize to the right shows that they could be involved in activities that would in turn empower them to be more active in the development process of their nation and in the public sphere. Doing things in the name of motherhood and womanhood is another way of promoting confident in their willingness to support men as partners in the development process. Most foreign NGOs in Africa have been using the concept of identity politics to promise women of different classes' security and meaning as well as offering stability in part through clearly defined sex roles, family life and religious orientations. In several African nations, the nature of the relationship between NGOs that support women's empowerment and the national government is another key area for investigation in the future. Such study will enable a better understanding of the strategies which can be employed to promote a nation's development agenda and the opportunities that might exist for women in the country.

In the twenty-first century, African nations need to promote women as agents of development. The concept of women as agent of development is a historical fact and it is a disservice for any country (including African nations) to ignore its women population in its development efforts. Therefore, the need for effective participation of women in development should be compelling. Equal opportunities should be provided to them and their male counterparts, both of whom should be seen as partners in, progress (Ebosele 1993; Adepoju 1994). This partnership role of women in development is, however, slowly being accepted in several African nations.

In several African nations feminism obscures the essential struggle and lumps together into interests that might even be practically opposed. The various professional bodies of women and those that are members of all the political parties should operate to further consolidate a system which opposes the interests of workers and peasants (men and women) alike. They should also work principally to advance their own corporate interests and not that of women in general and in abstraction. The "glass ceiling" and the "glass wall" are phrases that were coined to illustrate the obstacles that hinder upward mobility or lateral movement of women in the work place. Many articles offer explanations for the disproportionately low number of women in leadership positions, all of which focus on barriers that keep women from rising in corporations (Greenberg 2007; Beneria 2003; Dahlerup and Josefa 2005).

It is only when women are freed from the current property relations that they could be regarded as fully liberated. For other injustice which are largely psychological and social, such a humiliation, over-lordship, family abuse, etc., are formed on this basis. The World Bank (2005) summarizes well the economic plight of women: "Modernization has shifted the balance of advantage against women. The legal framework and the modern social sector and producer services developed by the independent African nation (and also most externally sponsored development project) have not serviced women well. Legal systems have discriminated in land titling . . . It is often more difficult for women to gain access to information and technology, resources, and credit. Agricultural extension and formal financial institutions are biased towards a male clientele . . . There is a wider gender gap in education. As a result, women are less equipped than men to take advantage of the better earning opportunities" (World Bank 1989: 86-87).

The process of development and urbanization has fortunately liberated a small minority of educated African women. Many of these professional women play prominent roles in international forums for equal rights, status redress and the emancipation of African women. At the African Conference on Women in Kenya, June 23-25, 2004, NGOs, Community-based organizations (CBOs), youth organization, policy makers, researchers, parliamentarians and donor from thirty

African countries noted that . . . "There are compelling reasons why African women must be integrated in the development process. First is their numerical strength . . . They are industrious and enterprising . . . They are good managers . . . No national development program will be meaningful and thorough if women are not fully involved" (Meekers and Richter 2005). African women want to be integrated on an equal footing in the ongoing development process for greater efficiency.

The constraining factors in the advancement of women to the same status as men in Nigeria are daunting in many respects. Therefore in eliciting women participation in development, their inhibiting factors need to be identified and removed in order to equalize access to opportunities.

In the past, women's role in several African nations was confined solely to the kitchen, trade and other domestic activities. This view of women's role is still largely held in most African countries. Women in Africa are consciously, deliberately and perpetually considered as subordinate to their male counterparts as a matter of tradition and culture that must be unchangeable. In this vein, the relationship between women and men in several African nations is that of unequal partners.

Some African nations have patriarchal culture. This means men usually exert maximum influence over decisions affecting income, family land, property and children. The economic empowerment of women in Africa means that they have to be given equal right and access to employment. The active participation of married women in the labor market of the Africa continent will contribute positively to the development of their nations respectively (Kuye 2003). One advantage derived from couples having professional careers is the improvement of the living standard of their family. In most cases men (husbands) in single-wage families often engage themselves in their job in a manner that might be detrimental to their family life.

Economic stability is very essential to family security. A nation will be considered to be developed when every family has the source to adequately support itself in terms of food, clothing, health, shelter and means of educating their children. Many families around the world as well as in several African nations own their family stability to the pivotal roles played by the woman (mother) in proving for the family. The importance of this assertion becomes clear when we take a historical excursion into the world's past and current women leaders.

Instances of women leadership roles are not peculiar to Africa. They could be found also in other parts of the world. Women have featured in the monarchical life of Britain and Netherlands of which Queens Elizabeth I and II, and Beatrice of the Netherlands respectively are examples. Contemporarily, the former Prime Minister of Britain (Margaret Thatcher) is a woman. Indira Ghandi was, until her assassination in 1984, the powerful Prime Minister of India, a country of over 800 million people (Mohanty et al. 1991). Golda Meir was also the Prime Minister of Israel for several years. Curazin Aquino and Benazir Bhutto were elected Prime Minister of the Philippines and Pakistan respectively. By her second election to office Benazir Bhutto has become the first female Prime Minister of an Islamic state in the world, a fact that was hither deemed as anathema by Muslim fundamentalist of Zia ul Haqs Pakistan (Egonmwan 1991). In the United States women leaders such Drs Albright and Dr. Condoleser Rice (an African-American) has been very effect as Secretary of State (U.S. Foreign Minister). Despite these achievements by women, gender typing of career and leadership in the fields traditionally occupied by males has yet to disappear in Nigeria.

The lack of cooperation between various government services such as police, courts, social welfare, and health only exacerbates women's problems. Abused women need many services that cannot be provided by only one agency. The lack of collaboration between agencies results in increased inaccessibility. Although some groups are working to rectify this situation by bringing together NGOs and governmental departments, government services for abuse women are virtually not enough in most African nations.

Finally, African nations would be able to strive towards achieving sustainable development if they could anchor the effective mobilization of women in politics and governance. The fact of the matter is that placing women in political position and leadership in governance constitutes but a piece of what is representative democracy. Politics and governance are not just about governments, states and elections. Politics encompass the broader questions of voices, identities, parity, justice and social change that women can benefit from across Africa.

Conclusion

This chapter has examined the current and future roles of NGOs in the empowerment of women in Africa. It argues that gender balance will not come about by itself, therefore the government, the private sector and NGOs has the responsibility for dealing with the under representation of women in the African continent. It calls for African governments to introduce diversity management programs. These policies should be adopted by the national and regional governments as a means for empowering women in economic, social and political aspects of life.

Women in the African continent can no longer wait fifty years to achieve equity and equal rights as men in contributing to the processes of sustainable development in the continent? If the problem of under represented is not women's lack of resources, but lack of knowledge of these resources and experiences that women actually bring with them into the political life and sustainable development processes, then there is no need to wait for women to be more educated or experience. There is therefore the need to government and NGOs in Africa to promote an effective popular education on gender and rights as well as gender-sensitive socialization of children programs. Because both men and women can contribute to Africa's development, governments, NGOs and other stakeholders should encourage initiatives with men as partners to transform gender relations and achieve gender equity and social justice.

The chapter also argued that in offering women the opportunity to access economic resources as well as to disentangle their identities from those of their families, diversity management programs will provide the space for women in

Africa to clearly define their role as equal partners in the sustainable development process of the continent. The chapter suggested ways in which subjective perceptions of discrimination can be minimized in Africa. Transparency in the affairs of treating women as equal members of the African society is critical. Public disclosure of entrance requirements and examination results, and even of the rationale for confidentiality where this is felt unavoidable, can ensure that injustice and unfairness are met with public censure. The composition of interview panels must be sensitive to issues of ethnicity as well as gender.

In the twenty-first century, African nations' government public service and private sector needs a new paradigm in the work place that links ability with skill, rather than ability with gender. The precise nature of the jobs assigned to men and women is not important in itself. What is important is that jobs should be given to the people with the right qualifications or skills. Gender typing will not help the African continent to attain its industrialization goals. Given Africa's critical economic and political problems, it appears increasingly obvious that suppressing the talents and skills of women in order to protect men's privileges is an enormous waste of human resources that the country can no longer afford. The present situation does not meet the criterion of "the best person for the job." It therefore implies a kind of prodigality that those concerned with public interest can hardly be viewed with equanimity.

A pragmatic gain toward gender equality suggests a reality at odds with seemingly fairer policy formulation. Although some bureaucratic structures are in place to provide for equal wages and equality of opportunity, women's economic position relative to men's have eroded. Enforcement of these myopic policies on gender equality clearly becomes problematic when left to men in top management positions. Culturally and religiously (in case of Muslim) prescribed role for women prevent them from asserting themselves as much as they are capable. It also prevents men from allowing women to function as equal partners. Gender balanced policies and women in senior policy making positions should serve as a model for changing cultural stereotypes. If women's program units are allowed to control significant resources, build useful alliance, and create appropriate incentives, other parts of the public and private sectors would be more likely to respond to policy mandates on gender equality. A look at the past shows clearly that positive strides will not be made without sustained and conscientious efforts by the government.

The various governments, NGOs, private sectors and other civil society groups in Africa must ensure that women are given equal opportunity to contribute in the national development process. With such concrete resolution of the constraints militating against women's participation in development, the African continent will move faster in its industrialization process.

References

Abdullah, Hussaina. "Wifeism and Activism: The Nigerian Women's Movement." In *The Challenge of Local Feminisms: Women's Movements in Global Perspective*, edited by

Amerita Basu. Boulder, CO: Westview, 1995.

Adamolekun, Oladipo, ed. *Public Administration in Africa.* Boulder, CO: Westview, 1999.

Adepuju, Aderanti. "The Demographic Profile: Sustained High Morality and Fertility and Migration for Employment." In *Gender, Work and Population in Sub-Saharan Africa,* edited by Aderanti Adepoju and Christine Oppong. London: J. Currey, 1994.

Aderibegbe, Yinka. "Women and the War Against Gender Violence." *The Guardian Newspaper,* Lagos, Nigeria: 21, October 2004, (15).

Akande, Jade O., and Priscilla O. Kuye. 1986. "Nigeria: Family Law Project." In *Empowerment and the Law: Strategies of Third World Women,* edited by Margaret Schuler. Washington, DC: OEF International, 1986, 335-345.

Akinboye, Solomon O. "Introduction: Paxadox of Gender Equality in Nigerian Politics." In *Paxadox of Gender Equality in Nigerian Politics,* edited by Akinboye Solomon. Lagos, Nigeria: Concept Publications Limited, 1-13.

Alvarez, S. "Contradictions of a Women's Space in a male Dominated State: The Political Role of the Commissions on the Status of Women in Post Authoritarian Brazil." In *Women, International Development and Politics,* edited by K. Staudt, Philadelphia: Temple University Press, 1989, 129.

Antrobus, P. *The Global Women's Movements: Origins, Issues and Strategies.* London: Zeb Books, 2004.

Badejo, D. L. *Women in Nigeria Today.* London: Zed Books Limited, 1985.

Bank, Leslie. "Angry Men and Working Women: Gender, Violence and Economic Change in Qwaqwq in the 1980s." *African Studies* 53, no. 1 (1994): 89–114.

Beneria, L. *Gender, Development, and Globalization Economics As If All People Matter.* London: Routledge, 2003.

Buchanan, Enid. "Women: Struggle for Change." *West Africa* (November 1-7, 1993): 21-23.

Callaway, Barbara, and Lucy Creevey. "Women and the State in Islamic West Africa." In *Women, the State and Development,* edited by Sue Ellen M. Charton, Jana Everett, and Kathleen Staudt. Albany: SUNY Press, 1989, 86-113.

Callaway, Barbara, J. *Muslim Hausa Women in Nigeria: Tradition and Change.* New York: Syracuse University Press, 1987.

Dahlerup, Drude. *Women, Quoatas and Politics.* London: Routledge, 2005.

Dahlerup, Drude, and Josefa Gigi Francisco. "Gender, Governance and Democracy." *Isis Monograph Series* 1, no. 1 (2005): 12-19.

Dennis, Carolyne. "Women and the State in Nigeria: The case of the Federal Military Government." In *Women, State and Ideology: Studies from Africa and Asia,* edited by Haleh Afshar. Albany: SUNY Press, 1987, 13-27.

Dolphyne, Florence Abena. *The Emancipation of Women: An African Perspective.* Accra: Ghana University Press, 1991.

Ebosele, Moses. "Political Emancipation of Women." *The Nigerian Observer.* Benin City, Nigeria: October 1993, 5.

Edwards, J. *When Race Counts The Morality of Racial Preference in Britain and America.* London: Routledge, 1995.

Egonmwan, Johnson. *Public Policy Analysis: Concepts and Applications.* Benin City, Nigeria: Aka and Brothers Press, 1991.

Esman, Milton. "Public Administration, Ethnic Conflict, and Economic Development." *Public Administration* Review 57, no. 6 (1997): 527-33.

Green, December. *Gender Violence in Africa.* New York: St. Martin's Press, 1999.

Greenberg, J. *Managing Organizational Behavior.* Upper Saddle River, NJ: Prentice Hall, 2007.

Gentile, Mary. *Managerial Excellence through Diversity*. Prospect Heights, Ill.: Waveland Press, 1996.

Harvey, C., and June Allard. *Understanding and Managing Diversity*. Upper Saddle River, NJ: Prentice Hall, 2002.

Hyden, Goran. *African Politics in Comparative Perspective*. New York: Cambridge University Press, 2006.

Ibe, Iro. "A Look at the Gender Conflict in Africa." *The Punch Newspaper*. Lagos, Nigeria: March 1994, 7.

Isekhure, N. *201 Solutions to Vision 2010*. Benin City, Nigeria: Oduna Communications, 1998.

Ifedi, Chuma. "Women Workers in Multinational Enterprises in Developing Countries." *Business Concord Magazine* 29, no. 2 (June 1994): 7.

International Family Planning Perspective (IFPP). "In Zimbabwe, Sexual Relationships with Older Men Put Young Women at high Risk of HIV Infection." *IIFPP* 28, no. 4 (December, 2002).

Kalu, W. J. "Battered Spouse As a Social Concern in Work with Families in Two Semi-Rural Communities of Nigeria." *Journal of Family Violence* 8, no. 4 (1993): 361-373.

Karanja, Wambuiwa. "Outside Wives and Inside Wives in Nigeria: A Study of Changing Perceptions in Marriage." In *Transformations of African Marriage*, edited by David Parkin and David Nyamwaya. Manchester: Manchester University Press, 1987.

Khapoya, Vincent. *The African Experience*. Upper Saddle, NJ: Prenctice Hall Press, 1998.

Kingsley, Donald. *Representative Bureaucracy*. Yellow Springs, OH: Antioch Press, 1944.

Kolawole, Modupe, ed. *Gender Perceptions and Development in Africa*. Lagos, Nigeria: Arrabon Academic Publisher, 1998.

Konjo, Kwame. "The Dual-Sex Political System in Operation: Igbo Women and Community Politics in Midwestern Nigeria." In *Women in Africa*, edited by Nancy Hafkin and Edna Bay. Stanford, CA: Stanford University Press, 1976, 45-58.

Konjo Kwame. "Nigerian Women's Participation in National Politics: Legitimacy and Stability in an Era of Transition." Michigan State University Working Paper. July 1991, 221.

Krislov, Samuel. *Representative Bureaucracy*. Englewood Cliff, NJ: Prentice Hall, 1997.

Kuye, Priscilla. "Economic and Political Empowerment of Women." *Nigeria Vanguard Newspaper*, 6 January, 2003, 2-3.

Ljjphart, Arend. *Democracy in Plural Societies*. New Haven, CT: Yale University Press, 1977.

Lovenduski, Joni. "Implementing Equal Opportunities in the 1980s: An Overview." *Public Administration* 67 (1989): 7-18.

Mba, Nina Emma. *Nigerian Woman Mobilized: Women's Political Activity in Southern Nigeria 1900-1965*. Berkeley: University of California, 1982.

Meekers, D., and Kerry Richter. "Factors Associated with use of the Female Condom in Zimbabwe." *International Family Planning Perspective (IFPP)* 31, no. 1 (March, 2005): 1-5.

Meier, Kenneth J. "Representative Bureaucracy: A Theoretical and Empirical Exposition." In *Research in Public Administration*, edited by James Perry, Greenwich, CT: JAI Press, 1993.

Mohanty, Chandra T., A. Russo, and L. Torres. *Third World Women and the Politics of Feminism*. Bloomington: Indiana University Press, 1991.

Nweke, Therese. "The Role of Women in Nigerian Society: The Media." In *Women in Nigeria Today*, edited by Elizabeth Obadina. London: Zed Books, 1985, 201-207.

Obadina, Elizabeth. "How Relevant Is the Western Women's Liberation Movement for Nigeria?" In *Women in Nigeria Today*, edited by Elizabeth Obadina. London: Zed Books, 1985, 138-142.

Ofei-Aoagye, Rosemary Ofeibea. "Altering the Strands of the Fabric: A Preliminary Look at Domestic Violence in Ghana." *Signs* 19, no. 4 (1994): 924 –940.

Olowu, D. "Accountability and Transparency." In *Public Administration in Africa*, edited by Oladipo Adamolekun. Boulder, CO: Westview, 1999.

Otobo, E. "Nigeria." In *Public Administration in Africa*, edited by Oladipo Adamolekun. Boulder, CO: Westview, 1999.

Matland, R. "Electoral Quotas: Frequency and Effectiveness." In *Women, Quotas and Politics*, edited by D. Dahlerup. London: Routledge, 2006, 275-292.

Reiman, Kim. "A View from the Top: International Politics, Norms and the Worldwide Growth of NGOs." *International Studies Quarter* 50 (2006): 45-67.

Robertson, Claire, and Iris Berger. *Women and Class in Africa.* New York: Africana Publishing Company, 1986.

Steinman Michael. *Women Battering: Policy Responses*. Highland Heights, KY: Academy of Criminal Justice, 1991.

Thomas-Sayter, B., and Dianne Rocheleau. *Gender, Environment and Development.* Boulder, CO: Lynne Rienner Press, 1995.

Turner, Mark, and David Hulme. *Governance, Administration and Development: Making the State Work.* London: Macmillan Press, 1997.

Vargas, V. "Democratic Institutionality and Feminist Strategies During the Nineties." In *About Women's Powers and Vision*, edited by V. Vargas. Montevideo: Dawn and Repem, 2000.

Wallace, Harvey. *Family Violence: Legal, Medical, and Social Perspectives*. Boston: Allyn and Bacon, 1999.

Waylen, Georgina. *Gender in Third World Politic.* Boulder, CO: Lynne Rienner Press, 1996.

Weisner Thomas, Candice Bradley, and Philip Kilbride. *African Families and the Crisis of Social Change*. Westport, CT: Bergin and Garvey, 1997.

World Bank. *Sub-Sahara Africa: From Crisis to Sustainable Growth: A Long Term Perspective Study*. Washington, DC: World Bank, 1989.

World Bank. *World Development Report.* New York: Oxford University Press, 1997.

World Bank. *World Development Report*. New York: Oxford University Press, 1998-1999.

World Bank. *World Development Report*. New York: Oxford University Press, 2005.

Chapter 13

Public Administration and Sustainability in Africa

Robert A. Dibie and Ogwo Jombo Umeh

The conduct of civil servants in several African nations constitutes the greatest impediment to the attainment of sustainable development in the continent. Ethics have totally disappeared from the public administration system of most African countries. The pervasive ambience of present day public administration and the African society could be described as one of corruption, malpractices, dishonesty, lack of integrity, absence of moral values and ethical conduct. The differences in values, beliefs, religion and culture have led to different forms of administrative and accountability styles. The collapsing state of the public sector in most African nations is due largely to leaders who are not committed to the development of their societies and who lack honesty and commitment to shared governance. While the government of a nation is expected to render social stability, regulate the market, make laws, determine the tax structure, create infrastructure, dominate key industrial sectors and deliver goods and services to its citizens, the situation is, however, not so in many African nations.

It has become very difficult for the government of several African nations to depend on their public administration and agencies to achieve development goals. Balogun et al. (1999), Adamolekun (1999) and Olowu and Sako (2003) contend that public administration in many Africa countries is confronted with problems such as (1) irregular payment of civil servants, (2) lack of office supply and equipment to effectively function, (3) rapid turnover of governments and political systems, (4) incompatible socio-cultural practices, (5) volatile economic performance, (6) too rapid change in the nature, size and complexity of task, (7) high rates of population growth and rapid urbanization, (8) government functions are often dispersed among an excessive number of ministries, authorities and agencies, and this result in inadequate leadership within the government for policy formulation, planning, and implementation, and (9) various public administrators and agencies do not have the sufficient competence to develop solid plans and projects for the citizens. Given the preponderance of the liberal democratic model inherited from past colonial regimes political reforms and relationship between politicians and civil servants has been allowed to degenerate in several African nations.

Kiggundu (1989) and Olowu and Sako (2003) argues that African countries lack organizations in the true sense of it. Their organizations, he suggests, are pre-scientific, and as such are not capable of bringing about development. While government and its public administration institutions directly and indirectly affects the life of every citizens, civil society organizations have not been given the opportunity to fully participate in the governance and development processes of their respective nations. Civil society as used in this chapter refers to all institutions that are not identified with the government. These range from NGOs such as chambers of commerce to voluntary organizations, community based organizations and religions groups.

With the introduction of Structural adjustment programs to several African nations in the past three decades by the World Bank and International Monetary Fund (IMF), newer collaborations are being formed between NGOs and African governments. The debt crisis that several African nations face has also made them to realize the tremendous potentials of NGOs as alternative instrument for providing social services to citizens. NGOs in African have been recognized for mediating clientele and donor needs in a way that accommodate the interests of poor African citizens and the donor organizations. For over eighty years NGOs have built long term capacity as service providers to communities in the rural areas of Africa. They have often built close relationships with those who use their services. Unlike the current system of public administration in several African nations, NGOs' process of bureaucratization has not interfered with the donors' goals of assistance in the distribution of resources to the disenfranchised in rural communities. In the midst of government institutions in Africa, NGOs have frequently been credited with providing resources and services that transform the daily lives of poor rural communities (Eade 2000; Thin 2002). In several African nations, NGOs are noted for fostering dynamic forms of economic dependence as well as ignoring the structural inequality of the marketplace. NGOs have also promoted new forms of gender equality and more pragmatic forms of women liberation than those associated with government policies of most nations in the continent.

The African economy, multiple perspectives on aid dependence and the role of NGOs as an alternative for economic change and social justice in the continent has insinuated the need for development administration in Africa. Post independence African states inherited a public administration system that constituted a mismatch between the civil service and what its society required. As a result, public administration system across the African continent has almost collapsed or has become ineffective. The small numbers of African nations that have survived some transformation have remained relatively insulated from the development process, elitist in orientation, and have continued to operate to satisfy the needs of very few members of their society. According to Adamolekum (1999) and Collins (2000) such public administration systems have failed to serve the needs of a rapidly changing society in the twenty-first century and to effectively discharge the traditional functions of government in a developing nation. The distinction between current public administration practices and development administration is mainly in the notion of inclusiveness of NGOs, market-regulated, privately controlled and voluntarily organized civil society organizations in the development process of the African continent (Leather and Eade 2005; Olowu and Sako 2003). Thus, African nations need development administration systems that would promote collaboration between government and civil society, as well as encourage shared governance and accountability. Development administration would foster and represent the varied interests of their constituents and encourage efforts to mobilize for political change.

This chapter examines why post independence public administration in Africa have not helped transform the continent into broad-based sustainable development and user friendly institutions. It argues that the failure of African governments to adopt development administration after independence has detracted from the ability of the continent to achieve sustainable development. It also discussed how NGOs have adequately transform themselves for tasks and performance in the post-independence period against the backdrop of political, social, and cultural conflicts, environmental impediments and debt crisis in the African continent. Then the chapter further argues that the mismatch between current public administration practice and the needs of the civil society has impaired the capacity of several national governments in Africa to function effectively. In closing, the chapter provides some suggestions on the need to establish broad-based sustainable development and development administration mechanisms that would promote collaboration among the government, NGOs, multinational corporations, the private sector and community based organizations in the sustainable development process of the African continent.

Framework for Sustainability

The concept of sustainable development was introduced by the World Commission on Environment and Development in 1987. This institution is also known as the Brundtland Commission Report of 1987 (WCED 1987). Pearce, Markandya and Barbier (1989) contend that the major premise of the sustainable development concept calls for citizens of the world to leave to the next generation a stock of quality of life assets no less than those that they have inherited.

The future of African countries would be greatly affected by the choice African elites make today as they attempt to cope with current crisis. To move Africa urban and rural dwellers out of poverty will require diversification, modernization, and expansion of urban and rural economies. It is indisputable that all African states have implemented processes of change, some incremental in nature and others radical. Since African nations have a shortage of domestic capitalists, the state must play a critical role in economic investment. Therefore, development in Africa could be argued to be sustainable only when it can meet the needs of its people without prejudice to those of future generation (Holmberg, Bass, and Timberlake 1991).

Sustainable development is used in this chapter in terms of current development processes that meet the needs of the present citizens of African's states without compromising the ability of future generation to meet their own needs (Dibie 2004). The sustainable development concept postulates that development could only take place when the per capita utility or well being of the African people has increased over time with free exchange or substitution between natural and man made capital. This could be measured only when the well being of the African people increase over time without declining the natural wealth of the continent. In the African context, sustainable development is the principle that will guide the various governments, NGOs, public officials, private sector and people of the continent as they proceed toward development.

Weaver, Rock and Kusterer (1997) used the term broad-based sustainable development to capture the process of equitable, participatory and environmental development. They contend that broad-based sustainable development should replace the narrow goal of economic growth that has been pursued for several years by rich and poor countries around the world.

The characteristics of economic growth are often tied with efficiency of the market. Market economy is a generating growth mechanism that leaves many people out and thus ignores them. This warrants African nations' governments to introduce policies to change market economy. The practice in most African nations is that governments often pursue economic policies that benefit only those in the public sector at the expense of the people. In several African nations, such practices have not only concentrated wealth in a few hands but have actually retarded the overall economic development of those nations.

According to Weaver, Rock and Kusterer (1997) broad-based sustainable development must involve four important factors: (1) it should be a healthy growing economy that constantly transforms itself to maintain and enhance the standard of living; (2) the benefits of economic growth are equitably shared; women, minorities, immigrants, the poor, and the handicapped get a fair deal from economic growth. (3) Respect for human rights, good governance, a healthy civil society of NGOs, and an increasingly democratic society. (4) A process of economic growth that do not destroy the environment for example, pollute the air and soil, poison the water, destroy forest and other places of natural beauty (van Klinken 2003; Weaver, Rock, and Kusterer 1997: 2). These factors are necessary to enable the future generation of the African continent to enjoy the same or a higher standard of living and civilization.

Collier Ruth and David Collier (1991) contend that the nature of path-dependent development might affect the political and social change of a nation. They pointed out that decision taken today will limit the choice of elites facing significant challenges in the future. That is, past reconfigurations of social-political structures constrain the possible path political transition may take in the future (Collins 2000; Olowu and Sako 2003; Huxtable 1998).

In order for African nations to be sustainable, national governments of various countries in the continent would have to introduce policies that are necessary to protect satisfaction of basic human needs and inalienable rights of their people. African governments need policies that would promote good governance and democracy. They also need to provide opportunities for all of their people to participate in political decision making process as well as the achievement of equity and social justice. African governments need to promote an environment for shared governance and the provision of self-determination and cultural diversity. While doing the above, they should also protect their environment for the future generation.

Making Development Sustainable in Africa

A number of theories and common themes have emerged at the critical interface between concepts and development action. While these themes fall short of consensus, they nevertheless represent common ground, which unites the interests of scholars and practitioners, and provide the basis for informed dialogue and mutual criticism and learning. Development as an instrument to influence the future has certain implications. First, it means paying attention to capacity. That is, to what needs to expand the ability and energy to make change. Second, it involves equity considerations, the fair distribution of benefits and opportunities among prospective clients. Third, it means participation (or empowerment); in the sense that only if people have some power will they receive the benefits of development. Fourth, it means taking seriously the interdependence in the world and the need to ensure that the future is sustainable (van Klinken 2003; Bryant and White 1982: 15). Fifth, it involves effectiveness considerations the degree to which public services actually reach clients and achieve their intended objectives. Sixth, it involves efficiency considerations the most favorable ratio of costs to outputs in the range of choices open to the program administrator, and finally, it involves stability considerations establishment and maintenance of means for the peaceful accommodation of adversary interests among parties affected by the administration of the program.

Some development administration scholars have argued that the major instruments of governance are: accountability and transparency of public leaders, electoral legitimacy, rule of law, development oriented leadership, freedom of expression and association (Collins 2000; Dia 1993; Migdal 1988; Wunsch and Olowu 1990). These scholars contend that a nation would achieve sustainable when it applies the necessary development administration tools that would propel its public management towards shared governance.

For sustainable development to take place in any African nation, such a country would depend on physical conditions and material resources as well as on the quality of human resources, educational facilities, good leadership, electoral legitimacy, rule of law, a good judicial system, good transportation network, good communication system, health care, social institutions and so on. Indeed, development in one area depends on the progress in many other areas. For example, the establishment of a new agricultural project can hardly succeed without transportation facilities, organization for supply and marketing. It might also require some minimal housing provision of educational and health services and so on. In order to achieve sustainable development in many African nations it would require a concerted effort in various interrelated areas leading towards higher forms of social and economic life. If a nation chose to develop a particular area at the expense of others, that effort might create an unbalanced development. The aftermath of such effort is that few other areas might not correspond to the overall development trend. Thus, the proportion of resources invested in each area and the sequence of projects in the development program must correspond to the general goals of sustainable development.

Furthermore, the resources at the disposal of an African nation might be smaller than the needs for development in all the sectors or areas. Governments of African nations where a market economy hardly exists should take the initiatives to formulate plans, and create enterprises otherwise there would be little development. In such a case, the public sectors of most African nations would have to represent them as a powerful economic factor that can be used to regulate or stimulate the market.

Based on the foregoing premises, some common themes to be discussed in this part of the chapter include building administrative capacity; equity; responsiveness, transparency and accountability; citizen participation (or empowerment); decentralization, public sector reorientation, rule of law, freedom of expression and electoral legitimacy. According to David Fashole Luke, these themes or persistent trends constitute a continuing challenge to the efficacy of countries caught in the management of the development process (Luke 1986: 75).

Building Administrative Capacity:

Capacity in government is the process of identifying and developing the management skills necessary to address policy problems; attracting, absorbing and managing financial, human and information resources; and operating programs effectively, including evaluating program outcomes to guide future activities (Collins 2000; Oluwo 1999; Rondinelli 1983; van Klinken 2003; White 1987). In African nations, as in the industrial nations, this process requires the assessment of an organization's capabilities at three levels: managing intra-organizational relations; or internal bureaucratic affairs; managing inter-organizational relationships, or affairs in the agency's organizational environment; and managing the broader political, economic and social relationships within which the agency operates. The specific skills necessary to accomplish these varied management tasks are neither easily identified nor routinely implemented. In effect, it is important to look not only at the particular agency, but also to look more broadly at the system within which the agency functions. In many African nations the traditional and transitional political, economic and social institutions add layers of complexity to the tasks of public management.

It should be noted that the identification of management skills depends upon the specific functions required of the managers; that is, the skills depend upon the job at hand. Managerial roles tend to have internal and external dimensions, such as meeting standard operating responsibilities as well as developing implementing strategies. Although the internal dimension is often the topic of interest (i.e., how are management decisions made?), the external dimension often raises the most difficult managerial questions. This can easily be seen in questions of concern to development administrators (practitioners) and scholars, such as how will development plans are put into practice? How are communities to be mobilized? In fact, how is development to be implemented? According to Bryant and White (1982), the presence or absence of needed skills at appropriate levels, the question of capacity often explains the non-implementability of that elusive phenomenon, development (Umeh and Andranovich, 1992: 58).

Citizen Participation:

Development as a process of increasing peoples' capacity to determine their future means that people need to be included in the process, that is, they need to participate. It is an attitude of openness to the perceptions and feelings of others; it is a concern for what difference a project makes to people's lives; it is an awareness of the contributions that others can bring to an activity (Oluwo 1999; Bryant and White 1982). Popular participation is an important dimension in the administration of public services. Within the context of development administration, participation, (that is, participation by the poor and deprived, not with lobbying or manipulation by well-organized and influential interests), involves the relationship of career administrators and the public interest. Participation in the more active sense involves exerting influence on administrative behavior and on the outputs of official action. That is, greater participation by the poor and deprived would mean their greater influence on decisions and programs relating to their welfare. Hence, there is a need to distinguish genuine participation, which implies real influence, from symbolic, manipulated, or controlled participation, which is intended to ratify rather than influence official behavior (van Klinken 2003; Montgomery and Esman 1971: 359; Olowu and Sako 2003).

A resounding theme that keeps arising in the literature is the dissociation from the 1960s models in the administration of public service. These models presumed bureaucratic hierarchies that delivered prepackaged goods and services to the publics according to classical hierarchical bureaucratic models and the prevailing center-periphery notions. Subsequent and more contemporary research and reflection suggests that, for development activities, responsive behavior from the affected publics is required if services are to be accepted and if they are to produce the intended behavioral changes, including investments of time and resources (Collins 2000; Dia 1993; Montgomery 1974).

Decentralization:

Decentralization of political and administrative authority is often thought of as a necessary institutional arrangement for the maximization of public welfare, including the actual empowerment of local government to create and undertake programs for community betterment (van klinken 2003; Michie 1989). A more widely accepted definition of decentralization is provided by Dennis Rondinelli, John Nellis, and Shabir Cheema (1984): Decentralization can be defined as the transfer of responsibility for planning, management and resource raising and allocation from the central government and its agencies to (a) field units of central government ministries or agencies, (b) subordinate units or levels of government; (c) semi-autonomous public authorities or corporations; (d) area-wide, regional or functional authorities, or (e) non-governmental private or voluntary organizations (Adamolekum 1999; Collins 2000; Rondinelli, Nellis, and Cheema 1984).

Decentralization is a multi-dimensional concept, and it is conventional in public administration to distinguish between the following aspects of it:

1. decentralization or the redistribution of administrative responsibilities within the central government from headquarters to field/or local administration;

2. delegation of decision making and management authority for specific functions to semi-independent agencies such as public enterprises, regional planning and area development authorities, multi-purpose and single-purpose functional authorities, and special project implementation units;

3. devolution to independent levels or units of government through the derogation of responsibilities over specific functions; and de-bureaucratization or the facilitation of decision-making through political processes that involve large numbers of political interests rather than having decisions made exclusively or primarily by government through legislation, executive decree, or administrative regulation (Rondinelli, Nellis, and Cheema 1983: 18-25).

Overall, decentralization can be seen as a way of increasing the effectiveness of development activities by making them more relevant and responsive to local needs and conditions, allowing greater flexibility in their implementation and providing a means of coordinating the various agencies involved at the regional or local levels (Balogun and Mutahaba 1999).

The size of most African nations is too big to manage by weak, inefficient leaders and inadequately trained public administrators. As a result, the division of certain African nations into smaller, more decentralized political system is but one of the possible solutions of ethnic and religious conflict in the continent (Collins 2000; Huxitable 1998). Nigeria, Sudan, Ethiopia and Democratic Republic of Congo are good candidates. We belief that such smaller and more locally oriented polities would produce pragmatic, efficient, effective, shared governance and improved lives for the citizenry. It is paramount that all African nations look for better and efficient ways to deliver goods and services to their citizens.

The more decentralized local government are in several African nations, and the more regional governments can make their own policies as well as develop their growth strategies, the more relevant they can become in helping NGOs to meet their objectives (Acharya 2000; van Klinken 2003). Decentralization in the governance process in the African continent could make NGOs and local governments to develop a stronger partnership as wells as see each other as major stakeholders in the sustainable development process.

Social Transformation:

The sustainable development process of several African nations must take into consideration local understanding of the workings of culture, society, and nature. These factors are important because there is an inseparable relation between the material and the spiritual worlds of local people. The sustainable development process of any African nation must be informed by local understanding of complex linkages between natural, spiritual, social, cultural, political, and economic forces of society.

Further, the emotional and spiritual well-being of the individual and the social group forms the solid rock of any development process. Social transformation is only possible if it proceeds from a development of the inner self and spiritual values of the citizens of a nation. Therefore, there is the need for the sustainable development movement in the African continent to address diverse political, ethical and spiritual concerns of the society. There is also the need to redefine both the individual and corporate responsibilities to families, communities, state or regional governments, nation-state and global citizenry.

Sustainable development could be described as a process that emanates from the socialization of knowledge. Therefore, the concept of sustainable development must be promoted in the name of the common good. An appropriate approach to sustainable development must reassess the existing definitions of property and individual ownership or rights to social goods and services.

Another important argument is that social development should be associated with individual rights of group membership with corresponding social responsibilities. This implies that the allocation and use of political power in communities must promote sustainable forms of local representation, accountability, transparency and good governance.

The practice diverting resources for the benefit of public servants and their political patrons while taxing the public and undermining respect for government should be discourage. On one hand, diverting resources of government to purchase foreign properties and holding big parties constitutes a waste of resources. On the hand wasting public funds to purchase several cars and unnecessary properties that are of no use to the economy and people should constitute a crime to humanity. Most African people should be educated on how to demand transparency of government transactions, especially in the financial realm. Empowered by self-organizations, public opinion can help to hold public servants to acceptable standards of behavior (Dibie and Gadzekpo 2003). Thus, the control of bureaucratic abuses that are endemic in several African notions requires combined pressures and sanctions from above and from below. Efforts to control such abuses can be strengthened by journalism, which is free enough and courageous enough to expose and attack instances of corruption and waste of public resources (Esman 1991).

Mutual interdependence is another vital linkage that should promote indigenousness as well as attest to the importance of community responsibility. This factor is also very important in the promotion of state, national and international responsibilities.

Responsiveness, Transparency and Accountability:

Another major problem confronting African states is the lack of accountability and transparency. Transparency is the process of decision-making that is open to the public view and can be perceived as being free of interference from special interests groups or individuals at the apex of government. Lack of accountability and transparency breeds corruption, in the sense of abuse of public office for private or personal gain. The literature on development administration suggests that to the extent that the public can affect organizational dynamics, they can either be allies or offer votes. That is, they can facilitate decisions by offering useful information, or they can slow down the process. Accountability is used in this chapter to refer to the process of guarding against the poor management or misappropriation of funds, but also politically to ensure that agreed policies and programs are effectively implemented.

Public Administrators in several African nations are confronted by several challenges and dilemmas as they try to be responsive to the needs of the public. For example, which groups or members of the public should be included in decisions (access); to whom should administrators be responsive, to the organized public or the unorganized and less visible public? (Responsiveness); what is the best way to evaluate citizen preferences when they contradict professional training and judgment? (professionalism); and what can an administrator do if organized publics either veto or dilute a project so that little is done (effectiveness) (Adamolekum 1999; van Klinken 2003; Subramanian 1990).

While the above questions tend to assume that administrators want to be responsive to the public, this assumption is not always accurate. Citizens may easily be manipulated by administrators who feel primarily accountable to their own agencies or supervisors. As a result, the public's problem is to hold administrators accountable and to find some ways to influence them. Correspondingly, accountability is particularly important precisely where political institutions are weakest (Bryant and White 1982: 212).

Overall, a top-down/bottom-up flow of communication and initiative seems to be recognized as the main ingredient in responsive and accountable administrative capacity. The tendency for policy making to be highly centralized in national administrative structure is further acknowledged as a major constraint on attempts to nurture responsive and accountable administrative capacity (Ademolekun 1999; Olowu and Sako 2003; World Bank 2000).

African nations' governments should make efforts to control bureaucratic abuses that are endemic in their respective countries. Efforts to eradicate these pervasive bureaucratic abuse is serious and continuously challenging to development administration because such unethical practices entail the demoralization of public services, the failure of discipline, the waste of resources, and the consequent alienation of the public (Esman 1991; Yukl 2006). It should be noted that cultural and social behaviors that tend to influence or effect professional practices should not be used as a medium for encouraging unethical behavior. The fact that these unethical behaviors are inhere in the culture of most African nations only confirm that nations in the continent are perpetually corrupt and cannot contribute to economic and social development. Robert Dibie and Leonard Gadzekpo (2003) contend that a conscious and principled public management with a pragmatic role of law system can limit these abuses, but only if is prepared to confront them directly.

Some of the strategies available to enforcing accountability include:

1. The public should have access to government information

2. The press, radio, and television should play a critical role of watchdog on the conduct of government business. One positive result should be the seriousness with which the privately owned media perform the role of public watchdog, serving as citizens allies in holding governments accountable.

3. The media should try to achieve accountability through investigative journalism.

4. There is the need for public officials to treat citizens with fairness and impartiality.

5. Respect for the rule of law and an independent judiciary constitute key mechanisms for enforcing accountability.

6. Elected assemblies such as the legislatures or parliaments should play a major role in both the enactment and enforcement of anti-corruption policies.

Equity:

Development includes distributional issues. To the extent that only a small segment of the population benefits from the outcome of development, development has not occurred. On a broader scale, development is a normative concept implying that ensuring more equity in access and benefits is a value in itself (Bryant and White 1982: 16). A normative dimension of development administration focuses on social justice demands, especially in a context of severe scarcity. It demands that resources and efforts must be concentrated on improving the life-chances of those groups in society not particularly well-placed to help everybody in the nation. Accordingly, the Brandt Commission echoed Peter Guy (1988) in contending that development is more than the passage from poor to rich, from a traditional rural economy to a sophisticated urban one. It carries with it not only the idea of economic betterment, but also of greater human dignity, security, justice, and equity (Adamolekun 1999; Brandt 1980: 49; Dia 1992; Huxitable 1998; Guy 1988).

Improved Performance in Public Management:

One of the major development predicaments facing most African nations is poor performance of the public sector. The management of the public sector is characterized by over-extended responsibilities. Several African nations inherited the idea of the national and regional governments as the engine of growth from their former colonial rulers. Under these arrangement or public management styles the domination of the economy by the national government became necessary.

A modern approach for correcting this colonial system of state domination of the economy is called "new public management." The measures are drawn largely from an international public sector modernization movement called the "new public management" (NPM). The NPM seeks to apply market principles to governmental administration, with an emphasis on competition, contracting, and customer orientation. It also emphasizes merit-based recruitment, promotion and increased autonomy for managers (Adamolekum 1999; Collins 2000). This approach also emphasizes performance measurements, with particular attention to the delivery of goods and services to the public. The implementation of this new responsibility of the national and regional governments and the consequences for public management is paramount to the achievement of broad-based sustainable development in several African countries.

Gary Yukl (2006) argued that the talents required to manage a developing economic are not equally distributed among all managers, but the can be encouraged and rewarded in several African nations. Therefore public management education should be required by all public servants to help sensitize those who middle and senior positions in government to this dimension of their professional responsibilities as well as help them to cultivate the requisite political and managerial skills. Lack of appropriate professional and managerial capacity as well as greed is variables that have galvanized inefficiency in the public sector in several African nations. Therefore in the twenty-first century African nations' government promote an environment in the public sector whereby managerial leadership would emerge from persons of above average talents. Such public skills could be shaped by education and experience, their devotion to duty and professional ethos into which they have been socialized. The role of African governments like their NGOs counterpart is to continuously reinforce such positive and ethical behavior with appropriate incentives and rewards in order to stimulate its continuity. Thus, development administration roles for economic sustainable growth should be designed to challenge and reward persons who display these ethical and managerial leadership qualities. Such managerial qualities are like to be available for competitive recruitment and career development. According to Milton Esman (1991) and Robert Dibie (2003) development administration is a social enterprise that benefits from excellent leadership in the public sector; however, this must be matched by efforts that evoke similar leadership in NGOs dispersed throughout African nations.

Public Sector Reorientation:

The dynamics between weak accountability and corruption among public leaders appears to be very strong in several African nations. Corrupt practice in the public sector, in turn, has severe consequences for the entire government administration system, as well as the structures, functions, and processes of public management.

In order for African nations' to achieve sustainable development corruption needs to be eradicated in the public sector (Adamolekum 1999; Olowu 1999; Olowu and Sako 2003; Huxitable 1998). Government reforms or reorientation in the future should consider the following measures:

1. A reduction in the role of the state in national economic management;

2. An enhanced role for sub-national governments; African states should enact and implement policies that seek to transfer functions and resources to sub-national and local governments.

3. A new public-private balance in respect to the production and provision of goods and services;

4. Promoting private and public saving.

5. Efforts aimed at achieving improved performance in public management.

6. Providing adequate infrastructure (water, electricity, transportation, health care system, education and communication) for public and private agencies.

7. Providing the necessary skills through general education and specialized training.

8. Reduce monopolies and oligopolies as well as maintain and expand social and economic infrastructure.

9. Managing new technology as well as investigate the development of potentials techniques through scientific and market research.

10. Seek out and assist entrepreneurs.

Professional public administrator's cadres within African governments can, however be stimulated and be assisted by NGOs in the development and diffusion of ethical attitudes, skills, and institutions that are conducive to effective managerial behavior. African public administrators must be exposed to the impact of globalization and what it means to be servant leaderships. Servant leaders must listen to subordinates, learn about their needs and aspiration, and be willing to share in their pains and frustration. Servant leaders must stand for what is good and right, even when it is not in the financial interest of their government (Yukl 2006). An ethical public servant must be willing to empower his or her subordinates instead of using power to dominate them. When this happens and more trust is developed such subordinate might inspire to become an ethical and servant leader themselves in the future. The outcome will be more public administrators in several African nations who serve as moral agent in the society and government.

Rule of Law:

The predictability of the judiciary is not yet a reality in many African states (Olowu 1999; Huxitable 1998). For example, the military governments and one-party states in several Africa nations do not respect judiciary decisions (especially in Nigeria, Democratic Republic of Congo and Sudan). In several other African nations, political executives still undermine the independence of the judicial through patronage appointments. The judicial and court system are characterized by weak enforcement capacity due to a shortage of professional staff, poor physical infrastructure, and inadequate funds (Balogun and Mutahaba et al. 1999; Collins 2000).

Several scholars contend that the rule of law should be underpinned by an independent court system and a predictable legal framework that helps to ensure settlement of conflicts between the state and individuals on the one hand and among individual or groups on the other (Adamolekum 1999; Balogun and Mutahaba et al. 1999; Collins 2000; Kiggundu 1989). The effective implementation of rule of law would help to ensure respect for property rights and contracts. African nations should be developed into becoming law-based nations where the government and individuals cannot be above the law. The law should not respect persons and strengthening judicial institutions should be a priority task if African nations want to strive for sustainable development in the twenty-first century.

Economic Development Strategy:

In the twenty-first century African nations need to establish clear economic development strategy. Strategies in this respect are groups of actions that will contribute to attaining the sustainable development goals the national and regional governments sets based on the options and resources available. According to Edward Blakely (1989) and Reider Dale (2003) strategic dimensions and issues that are crucial in attaining sustainable development in several African countries must include the following:

1. *Build quality jobs for the current populations*: The major idea in economic and employment strategy is to build employment for and with the current population in both the rural and urban communities.

2. *Achieve local economic stability*: Sustainable development will only be successful in African nations if the towns and communities have a specific approach to meet all the needs of business (i.e., land, finance, labor, infrastructure, and technical assistance in addition to labor).

3. *Build a diverse economic and employment base*: Regardless of whether the nation is high or low tech oriented, it must develop a broad base to provide continuing employment opportunities for residents.

Freedom of Expression and Association:

Freedom of expression requires independence for the press and other new media so that the people's right to participate in shared governance is backed up by the right to know. The constitutions of several African nations at independence often had a provision for freedom of expression and association. In practice, however, most African nations do not respect their citizens' freedom of expression The frequency of ethnic and religious conflict, authoritarian one-party systems as well as military rule which characterized most of African nations makes it difficult for public policies to be obeyed by political leaders. As a result, freedom of the press has been severely curtailed, with government as sole proprietors of both the print and electronic media. In some African nations where private ownership of the media has been allowed, journalists are often harassed and publishing houses shut down from time to time (Adamolekum 1999; van Klinken 2003).

In order to achieve sustainable development, there is the need for the media, NGOs and civil society organizations to play active role in the social, political and economic sphere of African nations. NGOs, community based organizations, the private sector and civil society organizations should become invaluable partners of government in the provision of goods, social services, the development and maintenance of local infrastructure and the mobilization of macro-credit for financing development projects.

Development-Oriented Leadership:

The underdevelopment crisis and the frequent ethnic and political conflict phenomenon of several African nations are due in large part to poor leadership

(Collins 2000; Gould 1980). African nations have a lot of leaders who are not committed to the development of their societies and who lack honesty and a commitment to democracy. Many scholars contend that the development crisis in Nigeria, Rwanda, Somalia and The Democratic Republic of Congo since independence for example, is a result of poor leadership style. (Adamolekum 1999; van Klinken 2003; Subramanian 1990; Huxitable 1998). Rather than serving their people most African leaders are served by their subjects. Future leadership should not be based on a one-way social contract. An ideal and democratic leader is that which serves its people and verse versa and could be removed from office or punished if he or she does not perform up to expectation.

In the twenty-first century, African nations need development-oriented leaders. These leaders should be committed to the development of the entire society over which they rule. Development oriented leaders should be prepared to serve the people and ensure the formulation and implementation of policies aimed at enhancing the quality of life of all citizens.

A good example of high-quality leadership and management of public resources is the avoidance of the "Dutch disease" in the management of the windfall from a nation's major natural resources. Dutch disease is the phenomenon whereby a nation' economy is dependent on one export product. African leaders need to diversify their economy and public practices to the extent that the citizens would benefit from such ventures.

Electoral Legitimacy:

The frequency of ethnic and political conflicts is a major reason for the collapsing of African countries such as Angola, Burundi, Democratic Republic of Congo, Liberia, Sierra Leone, Nigeria, Rwanda, Somalia, Cote d' Ivore, Sudan and so on. The frequency of conflicts is also a critical factor in the underdevelopment of the African continent. One of the solutions to civil war, civil strife, ethnic conflict and religious unrest in most African nations is electoral legitimacy.

In several African countries, electoral legitimacy can be derived from periodic open, competitive, free, and fair elections that provide to the elected political executive a mandate to govern (Adamolekum 1999; Balogun et al. 1998; Olowu and Sako 2003). Peace, in addition to the credibility of policies of governments should be based on electoral legitimacy. This could help African leaders to ensue that political executives are able to pay serious attention to tackling the problem of under development, including the nurturing of development administration capacity as an instrument for achieving sustainable development in the continent.

Environmental Awareness:

In several African nations, managing the environment and local resources is not a matter of solving technical problems; it is a way of looking for sustainable solutions. There are many technical solutions. The main impediments in several African countries are political and motivational will of both the government and the people. In fact, much of what happens in several African nations will depend on the choices and activities of thousands of farming households and women in the rural communities.

How can the regional and rural communities respond to sustainable development and environmental policies and how will household and communities manage ecological changes? First, the government must strengthen informal networks among NGOs, Civil societies and the private sector. The informal networks should be based on reciprocal exchange of goods, services and information. Targeting members of civil society and organizations and associations of women and farmers may offer a means to deal formally with the political system because they have an explicit structure, sustained and visible membership for political leverage, and a clear purpose and mandate. Networks have become key elements of the culture in most African nations for individual and household survival, accumulation, and mobility. For example, in many rural communities poor women are particularly dependent on access to the commons for fuel-wood and other forest products.

In several African nations environmental resources constitute the major means of the rural people's food production problems and ultimately need to be managed by local, small-scale collaborative efforts that are linked to large-scale planning and regulatory functions. If the government of several African nations wants to achieve their sustainable development goals, there must be a fit between their ecological objectives with regional and rural civil societies' concern of how to manage their household.

The government and people of several African nations must realize that in the twenty-first century environmental concerns constitutes a social construct through which all human beings organize their work, rights, responsibilities and relationships. Its meaning is derived from specific historical and material conditions. Understanding ecological issues will enable several African nations' government to find more effective and equitable ways of managing its natural resources for building productive rural livelihood system and sustainable development. African nations' government must work with NGOs who are interested in the protection of the environment to effectively put pressure on the international community to treat their forests and natural resources with respect and dignity. Several African nations' government and NGOs, could bargain for environmentally-friendly international trade policies as well as setting enforceable monitoring and punitive measures for violators of biodiversity and environmental protection laws for the landscape, wildlife and atmosphere in the continent.

Conclusion

The chapter has examined the pervasive ambience of present day public administration and underdevelopment in the African continent. It argued that post independence public administration in the African continent has been characterized as being one of corruption, malpractices, dishonesty, lack of integrity, absence of moral values and ethical conduct. Part of the panacea for all these public administrative problems is moral education and the effective enforcement of the rule of law. It further contends that a nation's public administration environment that is characterized by strong social values, belief, accountability practices and processes in formal organizations is likely to be heavily influenced by values and beliefs that would lead to sustainable development.

Government policies that promote broad-based sustainable development are also recommended for several African nations. These policies should transform and enhance good and equitable living standard for all citizens, promote equitable growth for women, poor, minority groups and immigrants. The policies should also promote respect for human rights, good governance and a healthy civil society of NGOs. African nations should also introduce policies that would prevent the destruction of their environment. The environment needs to be preserved so that the next generation of Africans could enjoy the same or a higher living standard and civilization.

Sustainable development in the African continent will be greatly affected by the choices elites make today as they attempt to deal with current political and economic problems. There is no doubt that African nations lacked development-oriented leaders. Bad leadership has led to several decades of under-development, ineffective policies and inadequate infrastructure. Most African nations depend too much on the agricultural sector. Unfortunately, the agricultural sector has not been able to spill over benefits to the rural and urban sector of the economy. Indeed, agriculture has not been able to generate the employment, technology, investment capability and leadership needed for sustainable development.

In order to elevate the majority of their citizens from poverty, African nations need to diversify, modernize, and expand their urban and rural economies. Due to lack of indigenous capital, it is paramount for African nations to form partnership with their private sector and to assume responsibility for economic investment. Unfortunately, that role is beginning to fall on transnational corporation and international NGOs, and could galvanize another set of problems.

The breaking of some African nations into smaller nations might be desirable solutions to most of their sectional problems, and a path toward sustainable development in the twenty-first century. Under such smaller nation-states, locally oriented politics would produce better governance and improve lives for the citizenry.

Although the civil service reform policies of various African countries have called for a professionalized and better performed public administration system, fiscal constraint has made it difficult for the respective government to achieve their goal. The civil service reform efforts in some African countries were not pursued with adequate vigor and common sense, taking into account organizational and situational contingencies. Future civil service reform in

Africa should emphasize a merit system, and accountability to elected leaders and the general public.

The mechanism of development administration is, however, the major instrument for achieving sustainable development in Africa in the twenty-first century. The concept of development administration also explores the principles of competition, contracting to the private sector, customer orientation, merit based recruitment and promotion as well as increased autonomy for managers. Development administration principles also call for the establishment of genuine partnership between government, NGOs, civil society organizations and the private sector in the process of policy formulation and implementation as well as in the delivery of goods and services.

Today, many activities conducted by various African governments, business organizations, and academic institutions are global in scope; involving interactions, and sometimes collaborations among multiple countries and international organizations, yet the public administration system in place is ill-equipped to fulfill the national objectives and the aspirations of the common people. Furthermore, NGOs projects to alleviate poverty in African countries have continued to be inclusive and involve the participation of civil society organizations, small private entities and volunteer organizations (Eade 2002; Korten 1990). Overall, national and local governments, multinational corporations, nongovernmental organizations, and international organizations, including educational institutions should all contribute to defining and solving civil society problems and underdevelopment issues.

The goals of development administration that can support the objectives of sustainable development, good governance, and shared governance are clear. African nations need a development administration system that is responsive, transparent, efficient, and inclusive. African governments must realize that its people are the owners of their government, as such public leaders should not lord over the citizens. Rather public leaders should respond to their concerns and needs with dispatch and dedication. African nations' government leaders should be compassionate, accountable and transparent. Honesty and the ability of public leaders to decide between the right and wrong actions are qualities that would promote a professional and competent development administration. African nations' government should be willing to form partnership with NGOs to efficiently and effectively deliver goods and services to its citizens.

Finally, since several African nations are full of people who are victims of poverty and neglect, it is very important that governments operating under such political environment adopt a development administration system that has a heart that feels for the poor and a mind that cares for their needs. The distinctive role of NGOs and civil society organizations provides the transformation that African nations' government need in the twenty-first century and perhaps offers development administration as a new framework for intervening in national sustainable development policies.

References

Adamolekun, L. *Public Administration in Africa.* Boulder, CO: Westview Press, 1999.

Adamolekun, L., and L. Rowlands, eds. *The New Local Government System in Nigeria: Problems and Prospects for Implementation*. Ibadan: Heinman, 1979.

Adamolekun, Oladipo. "Governance Context and Reorientation of Government." In *Public Administration in Africa*, edited by Adamolekun Ladipo. Boulder, CO: Westview Press, 1999.

Acharya, Binoy. "Networking and Collaboration among Voluntary Organizations, Local bodies and Government Functionaries in India: Experiences in Strengthening Local Self Governance." In *Applying Public Administration in Development: Guidepost to the Future*, edited by Paul Collins. Chicester: John Wiley, 2002.

Balogun, Jide, and Gelase Mutahaba. "Redynamizing the African Civil Service for the Twenty-first Century: Prospects for a Non-Bureaucratic Structure." In *Bureaucracy and the Alternatives in World Perspective*, edited by Keith Henderson and P. Dwivedi. New York: St. Martin Press, 1999.

Barbier, Edward. "The Concept of Sustainable Economic Development." *Environmental Conservation* 14, no. 2 (Summer 1987): 101-110.

Blakely, Edward. *Planning Local Economic Development: Theory and Practice*. London, England: Sage, 1989.

Brandt, W. *North-South: A Program for Survival: The Report of the Independent Commission on International Development Issues*. London: Pengiun 1990.

Bryant, Coralie, and Louise White. *Managing Development in the Third World*. Boulder CO: Westview Press 1982.

Collier, Ruth, and David Collier. *Shaping the Political Arena: Critical Junctions, The Labor Movement, and Regime Dynamics in Latin America*. Princeton, NJ: Princeton University Press, 1991.

Collins, Paul, ed. *Applying Public Administration in Development: Guidepost to the Future*. Chicester: John Wiley, 2000.

Dale, Reidar. "The Logical Framework: An Easy Escape, a straitjacket, or a useful Planning Tool." *Journal of Development in Practice* 13, no. 1 (2003): 57-70.

Dia, M. "A Governance Approach to Civil Service Reform in Sub-Saharan Africa." Technical Paper no. 225. Washington, DC: World Bank, 1993.

Dibie, Robert. "Implication of Globalization in the Teaching of Public Administration in Africa: The Case of Nigeria." *International Journal of Public Administration* 27, no. 3 and 4 (2004): 151-169.

Dibie, Robert, and Lenard Gadzekpo. "Managing Public Sector Ethics in Ghana and Nigeria." *Politics, Administration and Change* 39 (2003): 1-24.

Eade, Deborah, ed. *Development, NGOs and Civil Society*. Bloomfield, CT: Kumarian Press, 2000.

Eade, Deborah, ed. *Development and Culture*. Bloomfield, CT: Kumarian Press, 2002.

Esman, Milton. "Administrative Doctrine and Developmental Needs." In *Administration of Change in Africa*, edited by Philip Morgan. New York: Dunellen, 1974, 3-26.

Esman, Milton J. "The Maturing of Development Administration." *Public Administration and Development* 8 (1988): 125-134.

Esman, Milton. *Management Dimensions of Development*. Bloomfield, CT: Kumarian Press, 1991.

Gould, D. J. *Bureaucratic Corruption and Underdevelopment in the Third World: The Case of Zaire*. New York: Pergamon, 1980.

Holmberg, Johan, Bass Stephen, and Timberlake Lloyd. *Defending the Future: A Guide to Sustainable Development*. London: Earthscan, 1991.

Huxitable, Phillip. "The African State towards the 21st Century: Legacies of the Critical Juncture." In *The African State at a Critical Juncture*, edited by Leonardo Villalon and Phillip Huxtable. Boulder, CO: Lynne Rienner Press, 1998.

Kiggundu, Moses. *Managing Organizations in Developing Countries: An Operational and Strategic Approach.* West Hartford, CT.: Kumarian Press, 1989.

Korten, D.C. *Getting to the 21st Century: Voluntary Action and the Global Agenda.* West Hartford, CT: Kumarian, 1990.

Landau, Martin. "Development Administration and Decision Theory." In *Development Administration in Asia*, edited by Edward Weidner. Durham, NC: Duke University Press, 1970, 73-103.

Leather, A., and D. Eade, ed. *Development NGOs and Trade Unions.* Bloomfield, CT: Kumarian Press, 2005.

Luke, David F. "Trends in Development Administration: The Continuing Challenge to the Efficacy of the Post-Colonial State." In *The Third World, Public Administration and Development* 6, no. 1 (1986): 73-85.

Michie, Aruna M. "Decentralization and Public Welfare in Rural India." Paper Prepared for the Annual Western Social Science Association Meeting, Albuquerque, April 26-29, 1989.

Migdal, I. *Strong Societies and Weak States: States-Society Relations and State Capabilities in the Third World.* Princeton, NJ: Princeton University Press, 1988.

Montgomery, John. *Technology and Civic Life.* Cambridge, MA: MIT Press, 1974.

Montgomery, John, and Milton Esman. "Popular Participation in Development Administration." *Journal of Comparative Administration* (November 1971): 359-383.

Olowu, Dale, and Soumana Sako. *Better Governance and Public Policy: Capacity Building for Development in Africa.* Bloomfield, CT: Kumarian Press, 2003.

Oluwo, Dele. "Accountability and Transparency." In *Public Administration in Africa,* edited by L. Adamolekun. Boulder, CO: Westview Press, 1999.

Peace, David, Anil Markandya, and Edward Barbier. *Blueprint for a Green Economy.* London: Earthscan, 1989.

Peters, Guy B. *Public Bureaucracy in Comparative Perspective.* Tuskegee: University of Alabama Press, 1988.

Rondinelli, Dennis A. *Development Projects as Policy Experiments.* New York: Methuen, 1983.

Rondinelli, Dennis, J. Nellis, and S. Cheema. "Decentralization in Developing Countries." *World Bank Staff Working Paper* no. 58. Washington, DC: World Bank 1984.

Subramanian, V., ed. *Public Administration in the Third World: An International Handbook.* New York: Greenwood Press, 1990.

Thin, Neil. *Social Progress and Sustainable Development.* Bloomfield, CT: Kumarian Press, 2002.

Umeh, O. J. "Determinants of Administrative Development in Seven African Countries." *Indian Journal of Public Administration* 37, no. 1 (1991): 47-61.

Umeh, O. J., and Greg Andranovich. "Capacity Building and Development Administration in Southern African Countries." *International Review of Administrative Sciences* 58, no. 1 (1992): 57-70.

Ven, Klinken. "Operationalizing Local Governance in Kilimajaro." *Journal of Development in Practice* 13, no. 1 (2003): 71-82.

Weaver, James, M. Rock, and K. Kusterer. *Achieving Broad-Based Sustainable Development.* Bloomfield, CT: Kumarian Press, 1996.

WCED, *Our Common Future.* Brundtland Report. Oxford: Oxford University Press, 1987.

White, Louise G. *Creating Opportunities for Change.* Boulder, CO: Lynne Reinner, 1987.

World Bank. *World Development Report. The State in a Changing World.* New York: Oxford University Press, 1997.

World Bank. *Can Africa Claim the 21st Century*? New York: Oxford University Press, 2000.

Wunsch, J., and D. Olowu, eds. *The Failure of the Centralized State: Institutions and Self-Governance in Africa.* Boulder, CO: Westview Press, 1990.

Yukl, Gary. *Leadership in Organizations.* Upper Saddle River, NJ: Prentice Hall Press, 2006.

Index

AAWORD, 69
abuse, 5, 37, 238, 241
accessibility, 204
accountability, 1, 2, 35, 31, 34, 35, 38, 41, 50, 182, 257, 263, 263, 269
achievement, 35, 179, 257
Adamolekun, Ladikpo, 10, 35, 253, 262
admonishment, 30
advocate, 51
Africa, 1, 2, 27, 32, 35, 39, 58, 160, 176, 190, 204, 234, 257, 269
agriculture, 35, 52, 56, 121, 143, 195, 257
alleviation of poverty, 7, 48
American Enterprise institute, 3
American Evangelical church, 2
Amnesty International, 2, 56, 177–78
Anglophone, 65, 68, 74
appropriate, 5, 6, 36, 60, 68, 114, 223, 231
attitude, 47
authority, 189
Ayittey, Gorge, 49, 51

Balogun and Mutahaba, 27, 40, 253, 260, 268
basic needs, 180
BBC, 68, 69, 175
Belgium, 52, 173, 175
BONGO, 206
Botswana, 4, 5, 8, 49, 51, 85, 86, 87, 92
Britain, 48
buffer, 4
bureaucracy, 1, 33, 35, 38, 47, 48, 49, 92, 179, 233, 234, 259
Burundi, 9

CADEC, 158, 168
Cameroon, 49, 76, 141, 146,152
Canada, 4
capacity, 27, 34, 60, 221, 222, 233, 258
capitalized, 38
Catholic, 51, 52, 108, 121, 159, 166, 186, 1988, 193, 212
CBO, 49, 53, 57, 58, 67, 82, 169, 178, 179, 180, 239
CEDAW, 229
Chad, 56
charitable, 205
children, 61, 186, 192, 205, 230
China, 52
Christianity, 3, 159, 185
church, 158, 168, 185, 186, 188, 189, 212
CIDA, 40
CIG, 143
citizen, 28, 37, 55, 57, 58, 59, 67, 111, 122, 169, 184, 232, 240, 244, 259, 263
civic engagement, 122, 135
civil disobedience, 182
civil group, 3, 198
civilization, 175
civil liberty, 204
civil right, 200
civil servant, 47, 253
civil service, 28, 197

civil society, 1, 7, 11, 12, 28, 41, 42, 47, 52, 66, 141, 160, 169, 184, 269, 270, 271
co-evolution, 99
colonial era, 6, 11, 33, 159, 174, 185
colonialism, 34, 48
collaboration, 29, 41, 48, 52, 61, 99, 112, 117, 240
Coltan, 177
commitment, 38
community development, 205
conflict, 53, 122
Congo, 5, 9, 49, 173, 174, 176, 178
consortium, 58
continent, 29, 41, 47, 50, 54, 55, 261
contribution, 37
cooperation, 49, 209
corruption, 4, 38, 41, 47, 48, 55, 57, 68, 109, 157, 162, 189, 263, 270
COWAN, 121
CSO, 49
culture, 34, 35, 38, 51, 95, 173, 220, 240

DAWN, 69
debilitating crisis, 203, 204
debt crisis, 28, 49, 50
decentralization, 48, 260
democratization, 3, 65, 173, 178
dependency theory, 32, 34
depletion, 88
devastating condition, 1, 2
developing nations, 5
development administration, 27, 28, 29, 39, 40
development policy, 42, 179
dialogue, 190
Dibie, Robert, 8, 38, 67, 87, 92, 99, 122, 253, 263
disaster relief, 48, 80, 122
discrimination, 232, 238
disease, 1, 37, 173, 230
distribution, 28
diversity, 233, 238, 241, 242
donor, 199
drought, 85

Eade, Deborah, 4, 5, 29, 48
economic development, 56, 58, 86, 180, 256
economic policy, 47
economic reform, 180
ecosystem, 87
Edoho, Felix, 68, 203, 221
education, 5, 38, 40, 47, 50, 51, 54, 149, 195, 205, 238, 240, 257
EEC, 94
efficiency, 38, 223
Egypt, 182
election, 39, 181, 263, 268, 271
elite, 33, 122
empowerment, 8, 38, 53, 229, 237, 257
endangered species, 88
enforcement, 248
entrepreneurial, 35
environment 4, 20, 36, 38, 39, 42, 49, 59, 61, 81, 96, 99, 149, 205, 209, 211, 269, 271
Episcopal Church, 186, 193
equal employment opportunity, 238, 240, 248
equality, 7, 232, 238, 240, 248
equitable, 7, 52, 269
equity, 37, 165
Eritrea, 93
estrangement, 203
ethical 37, 253
Ethiopia, 4, 8, 49, 50, 51, 56, 59, 85, 91, 260
ethnic conflict, 10, 38, 51, 173, 182, 268
Europe, 48
European, 33, 48, 51, 52
exploitation, 88

facilities, 6, 40
fairness, 37, 238
family planning, 230
famine, 85, 86, 93, 204
federation, 197
fertility, 7
FONGO 206
Ford Foundation, 56, 121
foreign NGOs, 38
France, 4, 48
functionalist, 34, 165

galvanized, 48, 89, 229
Gambia, 77
gender, 7, 53, 210, 229, 232, 234, 236, 238, 240
GEF, 8, 51
geopolitics, 182
GERDESS, 8

Ghana, 4, 50, 122, 128
global, 41
globalization, 3, 7, 66, 189
GONGO, 206
good governance, 41, 115
goods and services, 47, 41, 264, 271
government, 4, 5, 7, 10, 11, 27, 31, 37, 41, 42, 47, 162, 169, 180, 197, 269
GRO, 7, 53
GSO, 100

harassment, 165, 232, 235, 238
hardship, 49
Heady, Ferrel, 32
health, 3, 49, 51, 56, 67, 70, 148, 180, 196, 239, 257, 265
heterogeneous, 39
HIV/AID, 56, 68, 149, 151, 239
honest, 37, 40, 271
hostility, 108
Hulme and Edwards, 3, 8, 52, 139, 208
human development 47, 180, 263
humanitarian, 49, 50, 51, 61, 68, 121, 147
human resources, 36, 123, 233
human rights, 8, 48, 52, 148, 157, 162, 185, 200, 209, 229
hunger, 1, 75
Huxtable, Phillip, 2, 5, 9

IFI, 5
ignorance, 37
IITA, 122
IMF, 3, 28, 48, 61
immoral, 38
impediment, 10, 27, 112
imperialism 88
implication 32
independence, 28, 48
indigenous, 11, 86, 87, 92, 99, 169, 190, 270
individualism, 33
industrial nations, 1, 48, 181, 258
infrastructure, 5, 7, 61, 114, 190, 265
INGO, 1, 2, 4, 5, 8, 47, 49, 51, 54, 56, 178
innovation, 7
instability, 2, 37, 47, 48, 49, 50
integration, 1
integrity, 47, 240, 253
international ideology, 3
international organizations, 30, 40
INTRAC, 204, 206
IRED, 8
irrigation, 39
Islam, 2, 189

Japan, 48, 161
judicial system, 11, 266
justice, 37, 38, 48, 52, 257, 264

KANCO, 58
Kabila, Joseph, 174, 184, 185
Kabila, Laurent, 174, 176, 185
Kalu, Kelechi, 4, 48
Kasavubu, Joseph, 187
Kenya, 50, 65
Kenyantta, Jomo, 65
Kinshasa, 174, 183, 200
kinship, 49, 53

law, 27, 124, 143, 199, 238, 263
labor Unions, 198
Latin America, 204
leader, 37, 113
leadership, 4, 38, 50, 59, 60
legitimacy, 169, 204, 268
Lesotho, 65
liberal democratic, 28
liberalism, 3
liberalization, 18
Liberia, 65, 70, 173, 2681
literacy, 196, 241
London, 177
London Club, 61
Lumumba, Patrice, 187

maladministration, 10
Malawi, 9
Mali, 85
malnutrition, 173, 230
management, 31, 36, 37, 38, 86, 96, 124
marginalization, 236, 237, 238
market, 27, 29, 34, 36
Mauritius, 65
mechanism, 41, 231
mediation, 28, 207
medicine, 205
micromanage, 5
military, 34
minority, 29, 33

mismanage, 4, 10, 47, 50
mismatch, 28, 29
missionary, 49
Mobutu, Joseph, 9, 174, 175, 185, 189, 191
modernization theory, 7, 33, 255
mobilize, 38
monopolize, 39
moral, 33
motivation, 121, 123, 135
Mozambique, 9
Mugabe, Robert, 58, 65, 160
multinational corporation, 29, 34, 41, 110, 190
Muslim, 248
Muslim Brotherhood, 3

NANGO, 158
Namibia, 65, 173
national government, 1, 11, 39, 160, 174, 197, 269
national security, 48
natural resources, 47, 52, 86, 88
natural disaster, 204
Netherlands, 52
neglect, 41
negligence, 37
Ndegwa, Stephen, 4, 52, 65, 123
NFGO, 206
NGO, 1, 2, 28, 30, 37, 38, 40, 50, 129, 143
Nigeria, 4, 8, 50, 109, 121, 128, 135, 182, 268
NORAD, 51
NPM, 264

OAU, 159
oceanography, 87
ODA, 51
Olowu, Dele, 253, 254, 255, 259, 263
Onimode, Bade, 3, 13, 51

Paris Club, 61
participation, 60, 86, 132, 144, 169
partnership, 37, 39, 41, 49, 50, 53, 57, 58, 67, 89
patronage, 11
peace keeping, 176
peasant, 53, 208
pessimistic, 211
pluralism, 3, 37
policy, 8
PONGO, 206
population, 27, 183, 230, 234, 253
post-independence, 1, 11, 107, 203, 269
poverty, 1, 4, 7, 37, 41, 48, 50, 148, 151, 159, 210, 229, 270
power sharing, 39
pragmatic 87, 238, 248, 263
predicament, 118, 231
preoccupation, 32
prism, 36
prismatic society, 36
private sector, 4, 7, 41, 50, 53, 60
privatization, 8, 229
productivity, 2
proliferation, 108, 141, 142, 192, 209
progressive economic, 4
proportional, 234
public administration, 27, 29, 36, 253, 260, 262, 269
public good, 205
public service 208, 229, 231, 234, 257

QUANGO, 206
questionnaire, 54, 110

ramification, 48, 210
recruitment, 41
Red Cross, 9
refugees, 51, 61, 158, 205, 210, 213
regulation, 96
rejuvenation, 60, 95, 98
religion, 1, 38, 50, 121, 122, 129
religious Conflict, 47
representation, 8
resource management, 223
Rostow, 35
rule of law, 47
rural communities, 20, 28, 49, 98
rural governance, 53
rural population, 122
Rwanda, 8, 9, 52, 174, 268

sanitation, 39, 196
satisfaction, 38
scientific knowledge, 32
sector investment program, 9
self-determination, 11, 53
Senegal, 77, 211
sexual, 232, 236, 238
SIDA, 51
Sierra Leone, 65, 173

skepticism, 210
social-cultural 37
social movement, 209
social reform, 180
society, 35
Somalia 51, 56, 213, 268
South Africa, 4, 9, 50, 56, 65, 182
specialization, 30
spillover, 165
stage theory, 35
stakeholder, 50, 169
stereotype, 53
strategic management, 204, 207, 223, 221
struggle, 5
sub-Sahara, 37, 48, 49, 51, 107, 204
Sudan, 51, 56, 65, 260
sustainable development, 2, 5, 6, 10, 27, 35, 37, 39, 47, 51, 86, 95, 107, 223, 242, 255, 257, 269, 270

TANGO, 58
Tanzania, 9, 49, 211
technology, 35, 52, 239
television, 175
Third World, 142, 148
tradition, 29, 33, 35
training, 37, 38, 40
transformation, 6, 28, 33, 37, 42, 256
transition government, 197, 199
transnational, 7

Uganda, 49, 65, 174, 211
underdevelopment, 3, 34, 41, 48
UNEP, 8, 51, 85
unethical, 29
UNICEF, 56, 148
United Kingdom, 52, 77
United Nations, 3, 5, 51, 53, 77, 175, 181, 229, 232
United States, 48, 51, 52, 110
university, 194
USAID, 40, 51, 52, 53, 122

victim, 41, 51, 85
victimize, 37
violence, 232, 233, 239
voluntary organizations, 6, 9, 28, 58, 121, 184, 254, 271
volunteer, 41, 121, 122, 125, 129, 134

war, 177
welfare, 1, 107, 141
West Africa, 8, 65, 210
WFP, 8, 51
WHO, 147
women, 7, 9, 29, 50, 51, 53, 121, 145, 157, 161, 229, 236, 240, 269
World Bank, 3, 10, 47, 48, 52, 61, 210
World Social Forum, 3

YMCA, 177
Yukl, Gary, 38, 263, 264

Zaire, 174
Zambia, 4, 9, 50, 211
ZCBC, 166
Zimbabwe, 4, 9, 49, 58, 59, 160, 173, 211

About the Contributors

Akpovire Oduaran, PhD, is professor and chair of the Department of Adult Education at University of Botswana, Gabarone. His is the formal chair of the Department of Adult Education at the University of Benin, Benin City, Nigeria. Professor Oduaran has authored and edited several books on adult education and education leadership in Africa.

Felix Edoho, PhD, is professor and dean of the School of Business Administration at Lincoln University Jefferson City, Missouri. Dr. Edoho is the author of *Management Challenges for Africa in the Twenty-first Century*. His articles have appeared in *Journal of Sustainable Development in Africa, Journal of African Business, and Journal of African Policy Studies.*

Francois Muyumba, PhD, is associate professor of African and African American studies at Indian State University in Terre Haute, Indiana. This is Professor Muyumba's last research work before his sudden death in February 2006. Before his departure from this earth and the academic world Dr. Muyumba presented at various professional conferences, and his publications have appeared in books and several peer-reviewed journals, including *Journal of African Policy Studies*. He was the founder and coordinator of the Pan African Conference at Indiana State University for several years.

Ogwo Jombo Umeh, PhD, is professor and chair of the Department of Public Affairs and Administration at California State University, East Bay, California. Professor Umeh is the author of *Culture Development and Public Administration in Africa by Kumarian Press.* His research is in comparative and development public administration, and focuses on sub-Saharan Africa, democratic governance, organizational management, and public policy.

Robert A. Dibie, PhD, is professor of public affairs and campus dean at the School of Public and Environmental Affairs (SPEA), Indiana University, Kokomo. He has authored several books including *Public Management and Sustainable Development in Nigeria by Ashgate Press, Politics and Policies in Sub-Saharan Africa*. Professor Dibie has also published extensively in peer-refereed journals in the area of public policy, public administration, sustainable development and ethics. He has presented research papers in over a hundred national and international conferences as well as served as keynote speaker in many international forums, including the United States, Jamaica, and Nigeria. He has also consulted for several universities and NGOs in the United States, the Caribbean Islands, and Africa.

Saliwe Kawewe, PhD, is professor of social work at Southern Illinois University at Carbondale, Illinois. She is the formal director of graduate studies in social work. Her published articles have appeared in the *Journal of African Policy Studies, Journal of Sociology and Social Welfare, Journal of International and Comparative Social Work, Journal of Social Development Issues, and Journal of Social Justice; Scandinavian Journal of Development Alternatives and Area Studies*. She has also coordinated several HIV/AIDS research projects in the United States and Africa.

Wilfred Gabsa, PhD, is assistant professor of political science at Palm Beach Community College Florida. He received his PhD from Georgia State University in Atlanta. He has several years experience working in both the public sector as well as NGOs in Cameroon in West Africa. His research interests are in governance and political institutions in Africa.

Josephine Dibie, MA, MBA, MPA, is a lecturer at the School of Business Indiana University, Kokomo. She has a diverse professional and academic background having worked as assistant manager in various banks and financial institution in both the United States and Nigeria. She has also worked as the budget analyst for the city of Fresno, California. She is heavily involved in professional organizations, and has presented papers and extensively reviewed city government budgets. Professor Dibie coordinated several NGOs projects while in Nigeria. She is well known for applying innovative teaching techniques and economics principles for development as well as the management of nonprofit organizations.

Johnston Akuma-Kalu Njoku, PhD, is associate professor of folk studies and anthropology at Western Kentucky University Bowling Green. He received his PhD from Indiana University Bloomington in folk studies and musicology. His research interests are the impact of Atlantic Slave Trade route to Africans in Diaspora and Cultural Diversity. His peer-refereed articles have appeared in the *Journal of African and Asian Studies and the International Review of Politics and Development.*